Archaeology Underwater

The NAS Guide to Principles and Practice

Archaeology Underwater

The NAS Guide to Principles and Practice

Edited by: Martin Dean, Ben Ferrari,
Ian Oxley, Mark Redknap and Kit Watson

Drawings by Ben Ferrari except where otherwise credited

Nautical Archaeology Society

Published by the Nautical Archaeology Society and Archetype Publications Ltd. The first edition was published with assistance from the Institute of Archaeology, University College, London and the Commission of European Communities.

ISBN 1-873132-25-5

First edition 1992
Reprinted with corrections 1995
Reprinted 1996

Archetype Publications Ltd
31-34 Gordon Square, London WC1H0PY Tel. 44 (171) 387 9651 Fax 44 (171) 388 0283

Nautical Archaeology Society
c/o 19 College Road, HM Naval Base, Portsmouth PO1 3LJ UK   Tel. 01 705 818419

Printed in Great Britain by Henry Ling Ltd., at the Dorset Press, Dorchester, Dorset

Cover design by Mic Claridge.
Photograph sources:
Cover, Christopher Dobbs; page 3, Ian Oxley; page 7, Isle of Wight Cultural Services; page 13, Kit Watson; page 29, Colin Martin; page 59, Ben Ferrari; page 89, Isle of Wight Cultural Services; page 109, ADU; page 129, Isle of Wight Cultural Services; page 149, ADU; page 199, Borough of Poole Museums Service; page 217, ADU; page 237, Isle of Wight Cultural Services; page 277, Isle of Wight Cultural Services.

Contents

List of Contributors

Contributing Editors

Martin Dean BSc MIFA
Archaeological Diving Unit

Ben Ferrari BA PhD
Royal Commission on Historical Monuments
of England

Ian Oxley BSc AIFA
Archaeological Diving Unit

Mark Redknap BA PhD MIFA FSA
National Museum of Wales

Kit Watson BA AIFA
Wessex Archaeology

Contributors

Jonathan Adams BA MIFA

Barrie Andrian BA MIFA

Adrian Barak

Robin Denson PhD PIFA

Chris Dobbs MA

Sarah Draper BA

Robert Finegold MPhil

Antony Firth BA MSc

Ian Friel BA PhD

Debby Fox Dip.AD PGCE MAAIS

Alison Gale BA

Cathy Giangrande BSc

David Gibbins BA PhD

Damian Goodburn BA AIFA

Alexandra Hildred BA MIFA

Richard Larn.

Thijs Maarleveld MA

Nick Rule MA

Paul Simpson BA AIFA

Preface to the 1995 edition

'In a simple direct sense, archaeology is a science that must be lived, must be seasoned with humanity. Dead archaeology is the driest dust that blows.'

Sir Mortimer Wheeler, *Archaeology from the Earth*

I was lucky enough to meet Sir Mortimer Wheeler shortly before his death in 1976. He had been invited by the BBC to a preview of Ray Sutcliffe's film on the investigation of the Armada shipwreck *La Trinidad Valencera* off Donegal, with which I was involved as a diving archaeologist. As images of divers stretching tapes, recording in grids and eventually raising such diverse objects as bronze siege cannons and carefully packaged wooden bowls flitted across the screen the Great Man grew increasingly restless and fidgety. I trembled with apprehension. Were our puny efforts to apply modern archaeological techniques underwater to be given the thumbs down by their greatest living exponent? Not a bit of it. 'Stick to it my boy,' the old man growled when I met him briefly afterwards, 'that's where the future lies'. He looked wistful, and then smiled. 'I only wish I was 50 years younger!'

In some respects the past twenty years have confirmed his prediction. Across the world numerous archaeological sites have been discovered underwater, representing between them an extraordinary breadth of humankind's endeavour through the ages. But not all have been treated in ways of which Sir Mortimer would have approved. Some, far too many, have been looted by casual scavengers or organised treasure hunters. Others have been injudiciously excavated by teams with good intentions but more enthusiasm than resources and skill. Only a minority has been approached with archaeological sensitivity, and properly respected as fragile and irreplaceable elements of non-renewable cultural resource. Happily, that minority is growing fast.

That it is doing so is due in no small measure to the work of the Nautical Archaeology Society, founded in 1981. As an international grouping of like-minded individuals and institutions the Society strives to further research in all aspects of nautical archaeology and, through the International Journal of Nautical Archaeology, provides an important forum for the publication of results. It has acted as an effective pressure group which, in various ways, has raised both the profile and standards of nautical archaeology, and helped to shape legislation aimed at protecting the underwater cultural resource. But legislation is only effective when it goes hand in hand with education, and the Society's most significant achievement is the structured training scheme of which this Guide is the essential complement.

As far the book's content goes I can only say that I wish that it had been available when I entered the field almost thirty years ago. I had to learn most of what it contains the hard way, by trial and error. No one need now suffer the frustrations and mistakes that involved. What the reader has here is access to the distilled know-how and good sense of an experienced group of practising diving archaeologists who are familiar with the realities of working underwater. For anyone with serious aspirations to enter this challenging field, whether as a part-time enthusiast or a full-time professional, this is a solid and dependable starting-point. I recommend it most warmly.

But the skills described in this book, and given practical form through the modular stages of the training scheme, are in themselves no more than tools. Archaeology, above or below the water, is much more than a set of prescribed techniques. Underpinning it must be insatiable human curiosity, an all-consuming drive to know what really happened in the past. This curiosity, in the disciplined mind of the archaeologist, crystallises itself into questions, and these questions demand evidence with which to answer them. It is the acquisition of this evidence, and the correct interpretation of it, that lies at the root of archaeology. In reality, of course, things are rarely so straightforward: the evidence itself may turn out to be of an unexpected nature, posing new questions, and it is the business of the archaeologist to attempt to sort out the chaos and impose some kind of intellectual order on it. There is, in the last analysis, no definitive answer to any archaeological question.

The challenge, nonetheless is to strive for solutions. On one level the quest is apparently straightforward. Objective observation and the accurate recording of evidence is an obvious first step to assessing and understanding it. But do we see things objectively? Our minds are conditioned by what we expect to encounter, and clouded by preconception. How do we see through these potentially misleading filters? And what do we mean by 'accurate' recording? To the nearest metre? Or millimetre? Depending on the situation, either might be appropriate. And how do we determine what particular features or attributes are to be singled out as 'evidence' to be recorded? Value judgements of this kind have to be made continuously by the archaeologist, who has to balance intuition and common-sense with the systematic rigour such work demands.

Another great figure from the past, O.G.S. Crawford, described archaeology as 'an art which employs a scientific technique'. There is much truth in this. Science is all-important to archaeological enquiry, and nowhere more than on sites which lie underwater. They may be discovered and assessed by non-intrusive geophysical prospection; they may be surveyed with ultrasonics, photogrammetry, or computer techniques; they may be dated by dendrochronology or radiocarbon assay; and their contemporary environments reconstructed by sampling and analysis. Science plays an important role in artefact studies by analysing the composition and origins of materials, and in stabilising or even reversing chemical and biological decay. But science alone cannot provide all the answers. It must integrate with humanistic studies and the social sciences to address the analysis of structures, and how they relate to wider traditions and technologies; to study artefacts and determine where and how they were made and used; and ultimately to attempt the reconstruction, however tentative and incomplete, of the societies—groups of real people like you and me—who created, lived in and perhaps died among the sites we now investigate.

It is the ability to recognise the capacity of evidence to speak, and to identify and integrate all the techniques which will permit it to be heard and correctly understood, that underpins the strategy of a successful archaeological investigation. There is, as Sir Mortimer Wheeler wisely observed, no single right way of going about archaeology, but many wrong ones. This handbook will keep the practitioner well clear of the latter and provide a firm foundation upon which to build good standards of archaeology underwater.

Colin Martin
President
Nautical Archaeology Society

1. The Nautical Archaeology Society Guide

1.1. The NAS Guide – Why it was written

1.2. The NAS Guide – How to use it

1.1. The NAS Guide – Why it was written

The Nautical Archaeology Society is committed to the care and appreciation of our maritime heritage, including archaeological remains that survive underwater. While encouraging members to become actively involved in the study of these remains, the NAS also realises that there has been a shortage of information on how to approach and undertake archaeological work underwater while maintaining acceptable standards. It is for this reason that this NAS Guide to principles and practice was commissioned.

As well as explaining fundamental archaeological principles, this guide provides a general introduction to archaeology and an account of the place of underwater investigations in the subject as a whole. It also describes techniques which can be used in archaeology underwater. This guide cannot tell you everything you need to know to become an archaeologist. A single book could never achieve that, just as reading a medical textbook does not make someone a doctor.

As a source of practical information, this guide is not intended as a complete reference work providing details of every technique which can be used in archaeological investigations. Such a book would be enormous and out of date almost as soon as it was published. New techniques are being developed every day – finding solutions to new problems is one of the exciting challenges of archaeology. What this guide does do is present some basic methods of overcoming

many of the difficulties involved in achieving an acceptable standard of archaeological work in what can be a difficult environment.

This book does describe methods of archaeological excavation underwater, but this is only one of many techniques which can be used to gather information. As will be shown, in many cases it is possible to get as much information as is required to answer specific questions without destruction of the evidence – an inevitable result of excavation. Such intrusive methods of investigation are a fundamental part of archaeology and are described, but they should only be used as a final option when other methods are inadequate or when specific circumstances demand their application.

This guide emphasises that archaeology is not just a set of techniques – it is shaped by basic principles. These are explained with the aim of helping you to plan and undertake projects, judge work that you might be asked to help with or simply to get more from displays and books about underwater sites. We also hope that it will help you to appreciate the responsibilities that go with any form of fieldwork.

Perhaps you have already read or heard about some of the projects which have taken place around the world. Some large-scale investigations can certainly be impressive, but remember, the success of any world famous project is based on the painstaking application of the same basic principles and techniques that you can use in your work.

1.2.   The NAS Guide – How to use it

The layout of this guide will be apparent from the contents list. We have tried to present the information in an order which is logical for those reading about the subject for the first time. We hope even the more experienced reader will start at the beginning before using the guide as a reference book, turning to appropriate sections to answer specific queries they might have.

The contributors' and editors' experiences are biased towards work in the United Kingdom, and it is inevitable that this is reflected in some of the terms used and examples drawn upon.   However, the principles and practices outlined in this guide are applicable wherever you may work.

Not every topic is covered in the same detail. Less attention has been paid to areas which are covered by readily available publications, such as archaeological photography on land. If a particular subject is not discussed in sufficient depth for your needs, suggestions for further reading can be found at the end of each section; there are also references within the text which indicate sources of information about specific points or sites. *Archaeology*, by Renfrew and Bahn (1991) is a useful companion to this guide. It provides a clear and wide–ranging introduction to the techniques and ideas that archaeologists use to answer questions about people in the past. Additional useful information, not suited for inclusion in the main text of this publication, appears at the back of the guide in appendices.   This includes a section summarising the identification of guns, a common but very significant class of object on wreck sites, and one for which there is a shortage of useful and accessible published information.

Whatever your present or future involvement in archaeology underwater, we hope it is rewarding and that you find this guide useful. If you have any comments please let the Nautical Archaeology Society know. In that way we can make a second edition even more useful to a wider range of people.

2. Involvement in Underwater Archaeology

2.1. Level of Commitment

2.2. The Nautical Archaeology Society

2.3. Part-time Involvement

2.4. Full-time Involvement

Whatever your level of interest you will find something to test your skills in the study of the physical remains of the past underwater. Ingenuity, technical skills, patience, diplomacy, flexibility, scholarship, presentation, team-work, management, administration and an open mind are some of the talents needed to face the challenge. The range and diversity of problems that arise are so wide that, inevitably, your particular experience will be of benefit to the discipline whether you are working independently or as part of a team.

2.1. Level of Commitment

Active involvement in underwater archaeology can range from occasional unpaid voluntary help by amateurs at weekends through to a full-time professional commitment. The distinction between the various types of involvement can be very blurred. For example, many professionals may also work in a voluntary capacity at weekends, and virtually all professional diving archaeologists started out as amateur volunteers.

In many countries, there is a long tradition of amateur involvement in archaeology at all levels of responsibility. It is common for underwater projects to be a combination of both paid and unpaid workers. The financial rewards in archaeology are such that most of those involved are ultimately doing it for the love of it.

One of the most useful steps anyone can take on the road to involvement in archaeology underwater, whether it is an active role or as a passive observer, is to join the Nautical Archaeology Society.

2.2. The Nautical Archaeology Society

This guide was written by members of the Nautical Archaeology Society. The NAS was formed in 1981 and, although based in the United Kingdom, it has a significant proportion of members (ca. 33%) from other countries. The membership is made up of a wide range of people who wish to be kept informed about developments in the subject. The Society is most anxious to include anyone with an interest in any of the many forms of archaeology underwater or related land-sites, whether involved on a part-time or full-time basis, whether diver or non-diver.

The Society's *Newsletter* is circulated to all members and contains reports on conferences, notices of meetings, expeditions and research news, requests for assistance and general information on all aspects of archaeology underwater. Members also have the option of receiving the *International*

Journal of Nautical Archaeology (IJNA). IJNA is published by Academic Press for the NAS. It is recognised internationally as one of the most important vehicles for the publication of papers and articles on all aspects relating to the study of archaeology underwater.

The stated aims of the NAS are: to advance education in nautical archaeology at all levels, to improve standards of conservation, recording and publication and to encourage participation by members of the public at all stages. The Society is committed to promoting the care of the underwater cultural heritage throughout the world, and to increasing the public appreciation of it.

In addition to bringing all those with a similar interest together, one of the main objectives of the NAS is to develop an effective training scheme. It concentrates on the skills which are sometimes difficult to acquire, but those most needed for any archaeological investigation – accurate underwater surveying and recording. These courses are available to non-divers or those who are not members of the Society. Enquiries about involvement are welcome from individuals and organisations. In addition to giving a chance to learn more about underwater techniques the courses also provide meeting places for those interested in being active in archaeology underwater (Appendix II).

2.3. Part-time Involvement

2.3.1. Involvement as a diver

If you wish to participate in underwater archaeology as a diver you should be trained to a basic standard. The qualification will vary from country to country. In the UK, for example, CMAS 2 star or equivalent (BSAC Sport Diver) might be the minimum requirement. You may find that many projects, due to the conditions on site, will ask for more experience than the minimum, so it is wise to aim for a higher level and log more dives than those required for the very basic qualification.

If you are not already a diver, but wish to learn, details of local diver training may be in the telephone directory or available through national diving organisations.

2.3.2. Gaining experience

Many underwater projects will accept inexperienced volunteers and will provide some tuition, but an excellent way to learn about the practice of archaeology is to participate in a land-based project. The theory and many of the techniques are the same as used underwater, and work on land has the distinct advantage for the archaeologically inexperienced that questions and problems can be dealt with immediately. The underwater environment makes direct and constant supervision difficult, and most questions and problems may only be resolved after the dive by discussion on the surface.

Many sites underwater are too deep to allow individuals to spend many hours in one day actually practicing and applying techniques. On land it is often possible to spend the full working day developing archaeological skills. This means that it is much quicker to learn practical archaeological techniques on land than underwater.

There are many organisations who can put you in touch with projects requiring volunteers in the UK. The Council for British Archaeology (Appendix V) publishes *British Archaeological News* which contains a calendar of excavations, and projects seeking workers often advertise in national newspapers. *Archaeology Abroad* publishes lists of projects outside of the UK. Whichever country you are in you should be able to ask at your local museum or library about the nearest archaeological unit or archaeological society. Failing this, approach your national museum or government agency responsible for the care of ancient monuments.

2.3.3. Involvement through discovery of a site

Many divers first become actively interested and involved in archaeology when they find an artefact or discover a historic wreck. Problems arise if they then begin to investigate the site without any knowledge of the basic skills required.

If you think you have found a site of potential archaeological interest and you want to take a responsible attitude, but are not sure what to do next, *ask for advice*. Most countries will have an organisation or museum that will be able to offer some help, and in some countries it will be a legal obligation to report the site to a relevant authority. In the United Kingdom contact the Archaeology Section of the National Maritime Museum or the Archaeological Diving Unit (Appendix V) and they should be able to point you in the right direction.

2.3.4. Involvement as a non-diver

For every minute spent underwater in archaeological work there are probably two or more hours of work on the surface or ashore. This will range from tending equipment, log-keeping, recording and drawing finds, preliminary conservation, packaging of objects and samples, through to full pre- and post-excavation research. Archaeology has always benefited from the participation of people keen to apply their experience in other fields to an archaeological problem.

Archaeological operations underwater differ from many of those on land in that they often require more technical support. Compressors have to be kept running, boat engines need to be maintained and a thousand other minor repair and construction jobs have to be done. Successful projects require people to deal with such logistical problems. They need not be divers.

Although the time a diver spends working underwater on a site may be limited by depth or other conditions, this does not mean that once logbooks and dive records are filled in there is nothing else to do. It is on the surface that both divers and non-divers can work together to contribute to the overall aims of the project. One thing that can be guaranteed is that there is always more work than team members can cope with – except when the conditions are so bad that underwater work is held up for an extended period. On long-term projects the participants sometimes pray for bad weather so they can have a rest!

2.4. Full-time Involvement

At present there are limited opportunities for those interested in underwater archaeology as a career, but the determined may be successful if they acquire the relevant qualifications and experience. Archaeology underwater is still very much at a formative stage and, for that reason, it is an exciting time for those who are active participants. It is a challenging and rewarding occupation which offers the possibility of involvement at a variety of levels.

2.4.1. How to become a full-time archaeologist

Apart from gaining experience as a volunteer on archaeological sites, the most important qualification needed to take up a career in archaeology is a degree in the subject.

There are currently no undergraduate degrees in the United Kingdom in archaeology underwater – this is probably a good thing as many people feel that it is best studied as part of the wider discipline of archaeology rather than as a separate subject. After all, the only difference between archaeology on land and underwater is the environment in which the work is carried out. Unfortunately, few general archaeology degrees for undergraduates have a substantial component of archaeology underwater.

However, a first degree in archaeology is still a vital starting point in providing a thorough grounding in general archaeological theory and practice. Post-graduate courses in archaeology underwater and related topics are available.

The gaining of general archaeological experience is as important to would-be full-timers as to part-timers, and remember that experience on land is probably a quicker and more efficient way to learn.

The Institute of Field Archaeologists is the profession's governing body in the UK. Various levels of entry to the IFA are available and members work their way up through the grades as they gain more experience. Some idea of 'what makes an underwater archaeologist' can be gained from the Institute's guidelines on membership categories. Academic training and a wide range of practical archaeological experience on land and underwater is given more emphasis than diving skills. A strong publication record is also an important requirement for full membership (see Appendix V).

2.4.2. Diving qualifications

Possessing a particular diving qualification does not necessarily add to or subtract from your worth as an archaeologist, but it must be borne in mind that working effectively and safely underwater requires a very disciplined approach.

Any person diving in the United Kingdom *as part of their work* must comply with the Diving Operations at Work Regulations 1981 (amended in 1990). At present archaeological work is exempt from some of the requirements of the legislation. The legal demands on archaeological operations are less severe than for conventional commercial diving, but all archaeologists diving at work in British waters must have an annual commercial diver's medical examination, an approved certificate in diving first aid and an up to date log book. In addition, the diving equipment must be in good working order

and divers must be trained in the use of diving and other equipment used underwater. An important consideration is that the exemption certificate in force for archaeological work could be revoked at any time. The minimum diving qualification under the Diving at Work Regulations is the Health and Safety Executive's Schedule 4 part IV (known as HSE Part IV). Under the archaeological exemption it merely states that "every diver must be competent...", but it would seem sensible to train at least to HSE Part IV if contemplating archaeology underwater as a career.

Diving may simply be the means used to get to the work site, but the more thoroughly trained you are and the more comfortable you are underwater in a working environment, the more effectively you can apply your archaeological expertise. High standards are the aim in both archaeology and diving; expertise in one does little to compensate for a casual approach in the other.

3.   Archaeology Underwater

3.1. What is Archaeology?

3.2. What is Archaeology Underwater?

3.3. What is Not Archaeology Underwater?

3.4   Suggested Reading

3.1.   What is Archaeology?

Archaeology is concerned with the identification and interpretation of physical traces left by past ways of life. Archaeology is not just description, its aim is explanation. The process of archaeological investigation is similar to the detective work of police and forensic scientists. All traces, no matter how unexciting they may at first appear, have the potential for providing the vital clue to understanding what happened before the detective or archaeologist arrives.

3.1.1.   The evolution of archaeology

What we now know as archaeology has its roots in a curiosity about old things - the stories and legends about past events passed down over generations whether fact or fiction, and surviving objects which were associated with past events. This curiosity is common to many cultures and such an interest is not recent. Medieval peasants are known to have collected stone hand-axes thinking they were of supernatural origin. Gradually, some of those interested in 'relics' began to try to explain what they were collecting and began to see that some of the material might have relevance to wider issues. For example, some people tried to prove that early man was barbaric, whilst others tried to bend the available evidence to show that some races could be shown to be innately superior to others.

Fortunately others were more enlightened and attempted to be more objective about what the material might suggest. This really marks the beginning of the development of archaeology as a discipline separate from the gentlemanly pursuit of curio collection (Antiquarianism) or the study of individual objects against a historical background (Art History). Workers began to borrow techniques from other, longer established disciplines such as geology, and started to look beyond the actual objects themselves to their surroundings for more evidence.

This was the beginning of the realisation that archaeological contexts are important in interpreting the past. Indeed, beginning with analytical techniques borrowed directly from geology, a great deal of attention came to be paid to the development of the study of context and archaeological sequences. This has lead to an awareness of the factors which differentiate archaeological from geological deposits and has thus allowed more refined study of the subject (Harris 1989).

The focus of attention moved on from examining objects from individual sites, and archaeological research began to address questions such as the migration of populations, the development of agriculture and the structure of past societies. Over the

last two hundred years the discipline has accumulated increasingly sophisticated methods and a more refined theoretical base; each generation improving on the amount of evidence that could be collected from the physical remains of societies and cultures no longer in existence. Following an initial concern with the classification and description of objects, archaeology developed into a discipline concerned with using material evidence to make inferences about people and behaviour.

The last 60 or so years have seen a great deal of attention focused on the theoretical side of the subject. This has meant that as the body of scientifically collected evidence grows, fundamental questions about the past can now be addressed more effectively, and conclusions tested more rigorously.

Work conducted in the early years of the discipline produced far less evidence about the past than we could today. This is because our predecessors unwittingly destroyed information we could have used while leaving us only tantalising glimpses of the potential of the sites they investigated (Figure 1). While it is too late to do very much about that loss of evidence, it does at least make us aware that future generations could view our work in the same way. Both professional and amateur archaeologists should feel a responsibility to hand on as much of the evidence as possible so that our successors can make sense of the clues we cannot comprehend.

The understanding of the complexity and potential of archaeological sites (rather than just the objects) has taken a long time to develop, and is not complete. A lot of experience has been painfully accumulated, and there is no reason why someone curious about the past starting out today should make the same mistakes as those 100 or 200 years ago – but it does happen. Some practitioners of underwater archaeology make contact with archaeological remains, through accidentally finding them, yet have limited archaeological experience. Just as we are learning from the study of mankind's

past, we are also learning from archaeology's past. Underwater archaeology is a comparatively new area of study which still has to prove its value to some 'traditional' archaeologists. However, as it develops, it can call upon all the experience of archaeology in general to establish priorities and principles.

3.1.2. Archaeological detective work

Archaeologists treat a site like the scene of a crime and carefully collect all the available evidence (Figure 2). The murder weapon, the evidence of the break in, the position of the body, the traces of poison, the ballistic report, the systematic search, fingerprints and the fibres matched to the criminals clothes all have their parallels in archaeology. Indeed the methods and aims are so similar that the two disciplines borrow techniques from each other and sometimes work together.

If archaeology is the collection of evidence at the scene of the crime, its sister discipline, history, is the taking of statements and the interviewing of witnesses. They are different sources of information, using different techniques but together they make up the evidence for 'the case'. It is important to be aware of the potential of historical research and to use it where appropriate. It is equally important not to be confused when the physical evidence you record appears to differ from the recorded views of the witnesses. Each has its own problems and limitations and the good detective will understand this and reach conclusions based on the stringent analysis of all the available information.

3.1.3. Preserving evidence of the past for the future

Looking around us it is plain to see how little physical evidence of the past has survived. Activities such as housing developments, road building and mineral extraction continue to eat away at the store of evidence

Figure 1. A 19th century underwater investigation in a Swiss lake (drawn by Dr Adolphe von Morlot.) (3.1.1.)

that is left. If we want to have warm homes, drive cars or have building materials this is the price we have to pay. With careful planning, however, the loss of information can be reduced. This can be done either by avoiding damage to the remains of the past or, if destruction is unavoidable, recording the sites scientifically (archaeologically) so that at least the evidence contained within them can be rescued in order to be used now and passed on to future generations.

The adaptation of building schemes to avoid damage to archaeological material and the funding of recording to rescue information is often done voluntarily by the companies profiting from the new development, although occasionally a little encouragement from legislation is required. In the UK there is very little archaeological fieldwork on land which is not 'rescue related'. In these circumstances the archaeologist must think very hard before undertaking any excavation (which is itself a destructive process) which is not rescuing information ahead of unscientific destruction.

As we have said before, future generations will be able to infer more from sites than we can. At some point in the future they may not have to excavate to extract the required information as remote sensing equipment grows in sophistication. Fieldwork has not always been shaped by such considerations, and excavations have taken place in the past which might be difficult to justify now. That does not imply criticism of past workers - it simply means that fieldworkers with very limited funds are trying to make sure that every penny spent on archaeology today is money well spent, and part of a co-ordinated and directed effort to make the most of our past.

Figure 2. Scene of the crime: 'Don't touch anything until the lab people get through.' (3.1.2.)

3.1.4. A register of sites and monuments – taking stock

There is more than enough non-destructive archaeological work available now to keep all those interested in the past busy for years. One of the most pressing requirements is for the location and recording of new sites. Whichever strategy for the conservation, or management, of the remains and evidence of the past is applied, there is one thing that is vital: forewarning of potential problems. Seabed users, legislators and archaeologists need to know what significant remains are in any one area before commercial development, or any other potentially destructive process begins.

One of the areas of expansion within archaeology over recent years has been the compilation of inventories listing sites region by region. The information contained in such Sites and Monuments Records (often referred to as SMRs) is essential for the proper management of our past. It is also important in presenting the archaeological heritage as a resource for community enjoyment, and this is achieved by contributing to local and national development plans aimed at enhancing the landscape by having suitably preserved and publicly presented sites. Creating registers of underwater sites will ultimately lead to our submerged heritage receiving similar care and management, including the development of such things as underwater heritage parks.

Systematic 'stock-taking' is beginning to take place underwater, and this is where we can all help. It has been estimated recently that well over a million sport-dives are made annually in British waters alone; clearly amateur divers have a vital role to play in finding out just what is on the seabed world-wide.

Many important sites have been discovered accidentally by divers and fishermen, and others have been found during dedicated search and survey by amateur diver-archaeologists (Figure 3). The amount of time divers, beach walkers, etc. spend on or around the seabed can never be equalled by full-time archaeologists. Consequently the amount of information about archaeological material on the seabed or foreshore held by such people is immense, and it is a database that could be put to very effective and constructive use. Local projects have already begun in some areas of the UK with significant results.

Effective use of this information is important because:

a. Local registers will develop rapidly and important new sites may be identified before their destruction.

b. Rapid development of local registers will hasten the formation of a national inventory as a tool for realistic management of the heritage.

c. The high level of public involvement will help ensure improved public presentation of archaeological work through publications, museum displays, appropriate media coverage, and increased training in underwater archaeology.

Examples of archaeological projects that have concentrated on survey and the production of registers are the wreck inspection programme conducted by the Western Australia Museums Service since 1974 (McCarthy 1982); the Yorktown shipwreck project recording sites in the York River, Viriginia, U.S.A. (Broadwater 1980); work by the Underwater Research Centre in Gdansk in compiling a register of maritime losses in Polish territorial waters (Litwin 1980); and catalogues of archaeological sites in Swedish waters (Westerdahl 1985).

Registers of sites serve two main functions:

1. To provide a listing of the location and description of sites in an area in a form that is convenient for researchers to consult and easy to manipulate. Computerised data-base applications are widely used to achieve this. A researcher, for example, should be able to

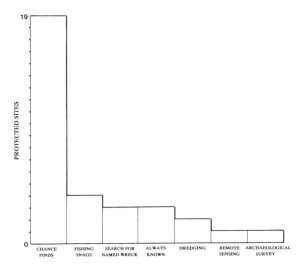

Figure 3. The way sites are discovered: method of discovery of the designated Historic Wreck Sites in the United Kingdom. (3.1.4)

find basic information on all the known medieval sites in a specific area or, in a more refined use of the system, be able to obtain information on medieval sites but only those which contained specific types of material. Such a register is a powerful tool for research as well as management of archaeological resources.

2. To provide the background information which allows an assessment of whether particular sites are in immediate danger, or likely to be damaged by new developments. If a company wishes to take gravel from an area of seabed, a comprehensive register of sites will allow a very rapid and informed judgement to be made on whether the extraction should go ahead in the intended location.

For the sites and monuments record to fulfil these functions, there is clearly a minimum amount of information required about each site:

a) An accurate position fix,

b) An assessment of the age of the site,

c) An assessment of the state of preservation of the site,

d) Factors which threaten the site in the short or long term,

17

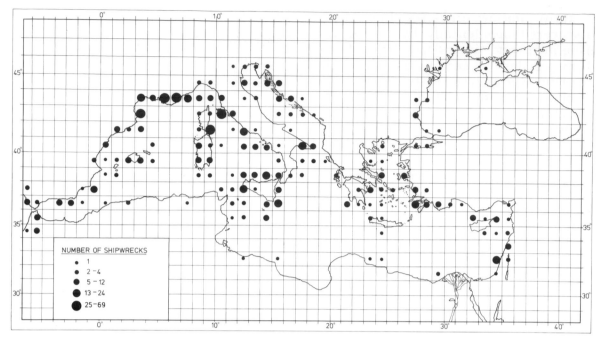

Figure 4. A diagram showing the known shipwrecks before AD 1500 in the Mediterranean. How can these sites be preserved for the future? Do the blank squares mean nothing is there, or that something is just waiting to be found? (Courtesy of Dr A. J. Parker.)

e) Any known historical associations or aspects of the site which make it particularly significant.

We cannot know everything about all sites and it may not be possible to get full information about each of these categories within the available resources. Sites can generally be regarded as falling into three main groups:

1. 'Evaluated' – those which have been inspected,

2. 'Known' – accurately located but awaiting inspection,

3. 'Suspected' – usually based on documentary references and having no accurate location.

The number of sites which fall into the category of 'evaluated sites' will depend on the effort put into this work, and the rigour with which the definition is applied. One of the problems involved in attempting to register a large number of sites is deciding how much time and money is put into investigating each one (Watson and Gale 1990). Logistics and common-sense dictate

that as much as possible should be done as cheaply as possible. Moreover, many sites may be wholly or partly buried. To excavate them simply in order to assess them would defeat the object of saving them for the future! Systematic registration of sites in coastal waters would reveal more than enough sites under threat from immediate erosion or other destructive process requiring investigation and recording, to keep archaeologists busy for many years. Finding and investigating these sites must be the priority if we are to save the evidence they contain.

3.1.5. The archaeological archive

The complete collection of all the records and finds from the site is called the archive. An archaeological archive of a site in a publicly accessible place is a valuable tool for researchers as it allows them to re-assess the evidence with any new techniques that become available, or in the light of new

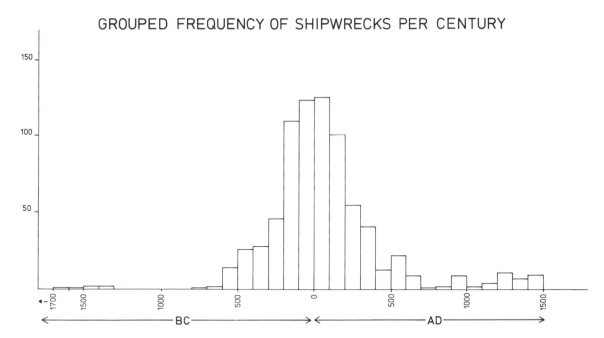

GROUPED FREQUENCY OF SHIPWRECKS PER CENTURY

Figure 5. The dates of known shipwrecks in the Mediterranean up to AD 1500. Does this tell us about levels of maritime activity in the past or just the discovery of shipwrecks in the present? (Courtesy of Dr A. J. Parker.)

information gained from other sites. The fuller the archive, the more effective any reassessment will be.

It is not good archaeological practice to exclude material from the archive because it is considered unimportant. It is impossible to guess what questions or analytical techniques will be applied to it in the future. Therefore, as far as is possible, everything should be available for assessment. While a 'complete' record of all the silver coins from a wreck might be seen to be an adequate collection of the available evidence, dispersal of the coins will prevent re-analysis by future researchers. It would be arrogant to think that all present day archaeological and forensic techniques will be acceptable in 200 years' time. If we do decide to disturb a site for either rescue or research reasons, and consequently deny future generations the chance to study that evidence *in situ*, we must at least leave posterity the full results of the excavation.

3.1.6. Publication

Publishing the results of an investigation to allow maximum access is a basic requirement. The publication usually includes a summary and interpretation of the collected information in the site's archaeological archive. When a site or project is published, the writer will probably have looked for similar evidence from other publications or archaeological archives. These parallels often cut out the need for the writer to research every item's origin. If archaeologists were required to trace the development of the clay pipe on each site producing one, a lot of effort would be wasted. This is why reference is made to previous publications where these have already been discussed and interpreted. Sometimes fresh evidence requires a reinterpretation of accepted developments and dates. Consequently, publications (important and useful when first published) may become out of date as more information becomes available. It is at this point that the original archaeological archive becomes particularly important to researchers.

3.2. What is Archaeology Underwater?

The study of the past is a massive subject. Archaeologists often specialise in one or more aspects, such as the study of cultures found in a geographic location, or a specific period in time. Some archaeologists develop expertise in a class of archaeological material, such as pottery or even ships. Less often do they develop skills for working in a particular environment, such as the sea, and those that do would normally have specialist skills in another aspect of archaeology. The archaeology of ships and boats is a natural area of expertise for the archaeologist who dives, but many archaeologists will be more interested in submerged settlement sites or some other area of study appropriate to the underwater environment.

Archaeologists who work underwater should have the same attitude to the available evidence as those who work on land and should have a familiarity with other areas of archaeological research. Since archaeology underwater is not fundamentally different from archaeology on land, the scientific standards applied should be no less stringent.

3.3. What is Not Archaeology Underwater?

3.3.1. Salvage*

Whereas archaeology is the collection of information, salvage is the collection of particular types of material for their monetary value. The salvor's role of returning lost material to trade is a valid activity but it can conflict with archaeology when that material represents the surviving clues about the past. Archaeological material is rarely of sufficient economic value for commercial

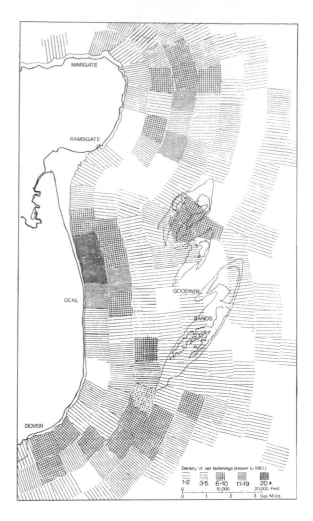

Figure 6. Another source of discoveries: the density of net fastenings in an area off the south-east coast of the United Kingdom. To make effective use of this information, each net fastening would need to be re-located and assessed. (Courtesy of Marine Archaeological Surveys.)

operations and the conflict of interests between science and reputable commerce is less common than might be expected. Unfortunately there are occasions when sites have been damaged just to keep recovery crews busy in slack periods.

*Not to be confused with the term 'salvage archaeology,' a North American term which equates with the British Expression 'rescue archaeology' (see 5.2.1.a)

3.3.2. Treasure hunting and souvenir collecting

On the fringe of salvage is treasure hunting. While financial gain is normally the ultimate motive, the allure of romance and glory also plays a part. It is surprising how many people invest in promises of easy pickings of treasure fleet bullion or can be persuaded to support 'antique mining' expeditions on the flimsiest of evidence (Throckmorton 1990). Compared to legitimate salvage, the activities of treasure hunters tend to be less well directed, less financially stable and less accountable. This means that such activity is much more threatening to archaeological remains which are often inappropriately surrounded by the mystique of treasure. By the time yet another treasure hunting expedition proves to be 'over-hyped' with unfounded promises, another part of the heritage has been destroyed.

Another activity on the fringes of salvage is the collecting of artefacts as souvenirs. Many sites have been disturbed and partly or wholly destroyed, simply because the finder has a 'general interest' in old things and wants a few souvenirs to display at home (or in a small private 'museum'). The motive may be undirected curiosity, rather than any destructive intent, but the end result is nonetheless unscientific and evidence is lost forever (Figure 9). To make matters worse, not having realised the potential value of the evidence they have recovered in this haphazard way, these individuals often disperse some of the material by selling it to help offset the cost of collecting.

Although it would be wrong to equate cynical commercial greed with what is often a deep interest in the past, from an archaeological point of view there are few significant differences in the end results of treasure hunting or souvenir collecting. Projects which set out to make a financial profit, those which concentrate on the collection of souvenirs or personal trophies,

or those which subsidise a basically recreational operation by selling material *all* destroy important archaeological evidence.

To some people the notion of a commercial recovery operation conducted to 'archaeological standards' appears achievable. The two approaches are, however, irreconcilable for three basic reasons:

a. Destruction without effective recording

The major difference between archaeological investigation and salvage/treasure hunting is that the principle aim of archaeology is the acquisition of new information which can be used now and is available for the benefit of others in the future. Archaeological work on a site is directed to this end and the end result is a complete site archive and academic publication rather than a saleroom catalogue. Any unnecessary activity (treasure hunting/ antique mining/curio-hunting/incompetent archaeology) which results in the unscientific destruction of some of the few surviving clues about the past has to be viewed with profound dismay. Without preservation in the form of adequate, detailed records that information about the past, which had survived for so long, is destroyed forever.

b. Object recovery

As will become clear later in this guide, clues about the past can come from a wide variety of sources apart from recognisable objects. Archaeology is not simply artefact retrieval. When a project is being funded by the sale of artefacts attention is focused on material perceived to have a commercial value. Other sources of evidence which archaeologists would consider vital to the study of the site, such as organic remains and even hull structure, are ignored and very often destroyed. Once the material reaches the surface, the commercial artefact filter continues to operate. Conservation (stabilising and preserving treatment) can be expensive and objects unlikely to reach a good price at auction are not worth the investment to the artefact hunter. They are discarded. The end result is a group of isolated objects, selected on the basis of commercial value, rather than a carefully recorded sample of the contents of a site which can be studied as an assemblage of interrelated clues.

c. Dispersal of artefacts – lost for the future

As we have seen, the results of the archaeologist's work which is handed on to the future (the site archive) is expected to include the finds as well as the records from the site. Forensic science teams do not sell off the evidence from unsolved cases. It is retained for reassessment in the light of new evidence. Due to their enigmatic nature the file has to remain open on all archaeological sites. No one interpretation of a site is likely to be totally correct and new methods and ideas must be tested against a complete set of the original clues if fresh, valid conclusions are to be drawn (Bass 1990).

Dispersal of material makes this form of study virtually impossible. Sites cannot be studied in isolation, but must be compared with and linked to others, and when the archive is severely compromised the usefulness of the site for comparison with others is greatly reduced. The evidence is not admissible because it is incomplete.

The damage caused by the selling of finds goes further than compromising the record of a single site. It has already been mentioned that it is a self-sustaining system of "hype" which seems to fuel many of the most threatening treasure hunting operations. The plush sales catalogues and publicity surrounding the sales of artefacts can only promote the treasure hunting myth that the past is worth money.

3.3.3. Archaeologists living with treasure hunting

As treasure hunting continues, sometimes officially condoned, those interested in archaeology are faced with a difficult choice. Not to get involved and so allow sites to be destroyed, or to try and improve the scientific standards of the treasure hunting project and risk being 'sucked in' and exploited. There is no easy answer. The treasure hunter will want:

a) respectability, which will help convince others to let their work continue.

b) the archaeologist to be the focus of criticism about the project, rather than themselves.

c) validated historical background and provenance – to increase the monetary value of objects.

In return for this, the archaeologist will often receive good pay and the chance of rescuing a small amount of the information before it is destroyed during the recovery process. All these factors will vary from project to project. Many archaeologists do not feel that the working practices and imperatives of treasure hunters can be modified sufficiently to make it possible to work alongside them, but it is important for the archaeologist to retain an open mind. The problem must be confronted rather than ignored.

Any archaeologist considering working on a commercially motivated artefact recovery project should consider the following:

a.   Does an archaeologist have to be recruited before the project is allowed to go ahead? The archaeological community may be able to prevent the destruction simply by refusing to become involved.

b.   Archaeologists will need to be well qualified and have sufficient experience to make informed scientific judgements 'under pressure'. They will also require a strong character to deal effectively with any forceful personalities encountered. Operators will often approach inexperienced, under-qualified or non-diving archaeologists who may be more easily pressurised or misled.

c. The archaeologist should not work for any form of financial reward based upon the quantity or monetary value of the materials or objects recovered from a site. The archaeologist should not work under the control of the manager of the recovery operation, and should have the ability to halt the whole operation if adequate standards are not maintained.

d. The archaeologist should not describe the recovery operation as 'archaeological' unless it is all under their control and they are directly responsible for the standard of the investigation. They should also retain the right to publish an objective and full report on the standards and results achieved and not contribute to the sanitising of a treasure hunting expedition by producing a glossy, popular volume masquerading as an academic publication.

e. An archaeologist should not give up the right to campaign against treasure hunting or actively oppose the dispersal of material.

3.3.4. Museums living with treasure hunting

If the archaeologist faces a series of difficult choices in living with treasure hunting so must conscientious museum curators. They face a similar choice between saving a small part of the information for us all, and so perhaps encourage the treasure hunter, or losing the little they could have saved in an attempt to reduce further destructive activity. By buying or even accepting gifts of objects the museum is giving both respectability and, in the case of purchase, money which will help the treasure hunter to continue destroying sites.

Less well informed or less scrupulous museums can sometimes become involved more directly. A narrow-minded view is to stock the walls and cabinets of an establishment without worrying about the effect on archaeological sites. Fortunately this attitude has no place in a modern museum and many institutions and international organisations have worked hard to develop codes of conduct which govern the acquisition of new material. Specific guidelines have been formulated by the International Commission on Maritime Museums (ICMM) regarding the acquisition of objects from archaeological sites underwater. Recommendations include:

– that ICMM member museums should follow section 3.2 of the ICMM Code of Professional Ethics as it relates to the acquisition of illicit material, and that in particular "...museum(s) should not acquire by purchase objects...where...their recovery involved the recent unscientific or intentional destruction or damage of... archaeological sites...".

– that ICMM member museums should follow Council of American Maritime Museums' policy and "...not knowingly acquire or exhibit artefacts which have been stolen, illegally exported from their country of origin, illegally salvaged or removed from commercially exploited archaeological or historical sites in recent times...".

–that ICMM members "should recognise that artefacts from underwater sites are integral parts of an archaeological finds complex which should stay together for research and display...".

3.4. Suggested Reading

a. What is archaeology?

Aston, M.
1985   *Interpreting the Landscape: landscape archaeology in local studies.* London. ISBN 0-7134-3649-2.

Fagan, B.M.
1978   *In the Beginning: An Introduction to Archaeology.* Boston.

Greene, K.
1995   *Archaeology: An Introduction.* 3rd edn London.

Renfrew, C., and Bahn, P.
1991   *Archaeology: Theories, methods, and practice.* Thames and Hudson, London. ISBN 0-500-27605-6.

23

24

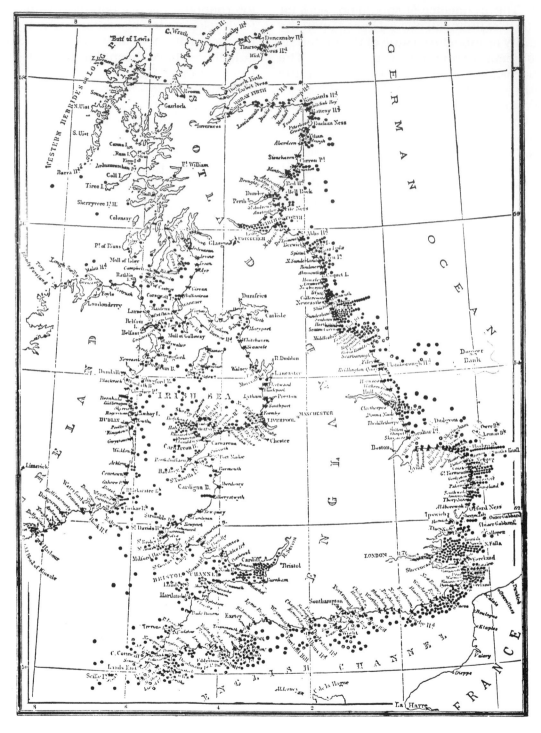

Figure 7. A wreck chart for 1876-1877 published by the Royal National Lifeboat Institution. The losses in that period give an indication of the large numbers of wrecks that may have occurred in British waters. Compare their distribution with Figure 8.

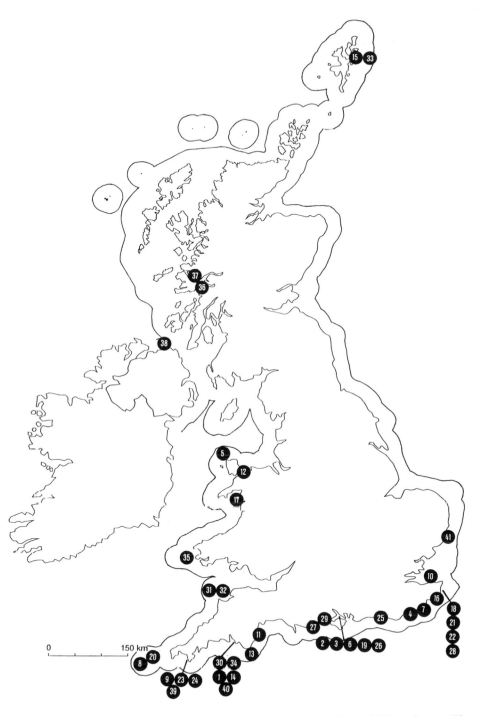

Figure 8. The location of protected historic wrecks in the United Kingdom. Their biased distribution towards the south probably reflects levels of seabed activity (sport diving, fishing, dredging, etc.) rather than actual levels of preservation of shipwreck heritage. (Courtesy of the Archaeological Diving Unit.)

b. The evolution of archaeology

Daniel, G.
1975   *A Hundred and Fifty Years of Archaeology.* London. ISBN 0-7156-1069-4.

Trigger, B.G.
1989   *A History of Archaeological Thought.* Cambridge. ISBN 0-521-33818-2.

c. A register of sites and monuments – taking stock

Brouwer, N.J.
1985   *International Register of Historic Ships.* Oswestry. ISBN 0-904614-11-5.

Cederlund, C-O.
1980   Systematic registration of older sinkings and wrecks in Swedish waters, *IJNA*, 9.2: 95-103.

Cleere, H.
1989   *Archaeological Heritage Management In The Modern World.* London. ISBN 0-04-445028-1.

Lenihan, D.J. (ed)
1987   *Submerged cultural resources study, Isle Royal National Park.* Southwest Cultural Resources Center Professional Paper No.8, New Mexico.

Redknap, M., and Flemming, M.
1985   The Goodwins Archaeological Survey: Towards a Regional Marine Site Register in Britain. *World Archaeology*16.3: 312-328.

d. What is archaeology underwater?

Dean, M.
1988   *Guidelines on Acceptable Standards in Underwater Archaeology.* St Andrews. ISBN 1-871170-00-1.

Gibbins, D.
1990   Analytical approaches in maritime archaeology: a Mediterranean perspective *Antiquity* 64 : 376-89.

Lockery, A.
1985   *Marine Archaeology and the Diver.* Ontario, Canada. ISBN 0-9692081-0-3.

Figure 9. The undisciplined recovery of material destroys evidence: this diver is only interested in the two metal objects. Many other clues have been destroyed along with much of the archaeological value of the finds themselves.

Muckelroy, K.
1978   *Maritime Archaeology.* Cambridge. ISBN 0-521-22079-3.

e. What is not archaeology underwater?

Bass, G.F.
1990   After the Diving is Over. In Carrell, T.L. (ed) *Underwater Archaeology,* Proceedings from the Society for Historical Archaeology Conference, Tucson, Arizona 1990.

Throckmorton, P.
1990   The World's Worst Investment: The Economics of Treasure Hunting with Real Life Comparisons. In Carrell, T.L. (ed), *Underwater Archaeology,* Proceedings from the Society for Historical Archaeology Conference, Tucson, Arizona 1990.

26

4. Basic Principles – Making the Most of the Clues

4.1. What is a Site?

4.2. Site Types

4.3. The Range of Evidence on an Archaeological Site

4.4. Using the Evidence

4.5. The Importance of Site Environment and the Processes of Site Formation

4.6. Suggested Reading

4.1. What is a Site?

We often talk about archaeological sites, but what do we mean by the word 'site' and how do we study them?

On land it is easy enough to imagine the remains of a castle as an archaeological site. What does a castle represent? We can picture it with its walls still intact, alive with the bustle of its occupants. It is the way of living that we want to understand and reconstruct. So perhaps we can say that a site is a concentration of the material remains of the way people lived. However the castle does not operate in isolation; without taxes the walls would not get mended; without food the residents would not get fed; without labour from the surrounding countryside the castle would have no soldiers, no servants and indeed no lord.

If we look at some of the material which is now part of the archaeological site which was once a thriving castle, we will perhaps find some pottery fragments from jugs made in a local workshop (also now an archaeological site). Some of the output from this workshop went to supply the castle, but some would have been sold in local villages and perhaps in more distant markets. Without these other markets the potters may have decided that the castle alone would be too small a market, or perhaps too unreliable a payer (invoices have been ignored since the beginning of time) to maintain a viable operation. So not only does our site (the castle) need the pottery workshop site to get jugs but also, it indirectly needs all the other sites which buy jugs from the same source.

We can therefore see that although archaeological sites are concentrations of evidence about past ways of life in one specific place, they have a relationship with other archaeological sites of similar date (Figure 10). These other sites may be half way round the world if maritime trade is involved in the distribution of artefactual material. We often study 'sites' (concentrations of evidence about past activities) because they contain more clues per square metre than the ground or seabed in-between.

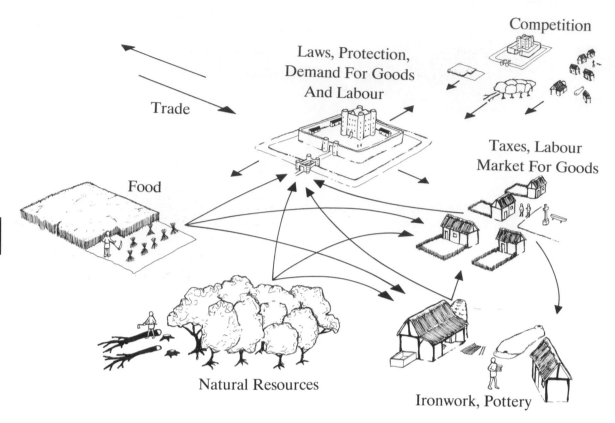

Competition

Laws, Protection,
Demand For Goods
And Labour

Trade

Taxes, Labour
Market For Goods

Food

Natural Resources

Ironwork, Pottery

Figure 10. Sites have a place in the settlement pattern of their time. Ships, for example, though very mobile, are still just part of a world-wide system. (4.1.)

A wreck site on the seabed also contains a concentration of evidence about past activities. Even though the site represents the remains of a ship that was once a self-contained mobile 'settlement' (a warship is a bit like a floating castle), it is still linked to other archaeological sites. These can be both on land or underwater, and provide evidence about such things as its ports of call, the homes of the crew, the origins of the objects on board, the forests where its timbers grew, and the ship yard where it was made. In aiming to study each site we must also explore their relationships and interdependence.

4.1.1. The importance of underwater sites

With so much work needing to be done on land, archaeologists working in the sea or rivers are often asked to justify why they make studying the clues about the past even more difficult by going underwater. This becomes a serious question when fieldworkers try to get support, financial or otherwise, for their project.

Sites underwater are important for two basic reasons:

a. They are available nowhere else

There are some sites which are rarely available on land. For example:

i. Evidence lost or deposited while using the water. Shipwrecks are perhaps the most obvious example.

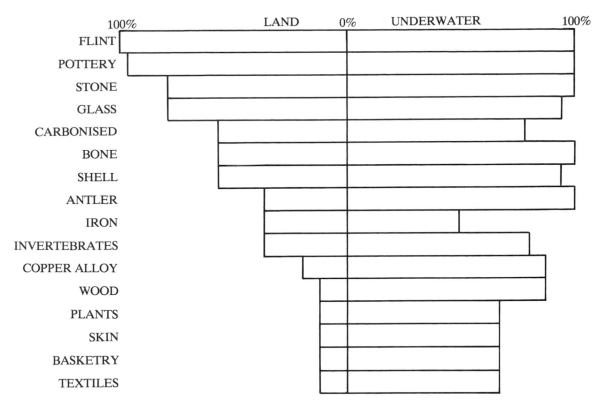

Figure 11. Survival of clues on underwater sites relative to dry sites. Information is often better preserved and protected underwater. (4.1.1.b.) (After Coles.)

ii. Sites built in or over water are rarely completely accessible to investigations based solely on dry land methods e.g. crannogs and pile dwellings.

iii. Sites which were established on land but are now submerged e.g. the prehistoric sites in the Eastern Gulf of Mexico or the prehistoric sites which were submerged when the English Channel flooded.

iv. Sites which have continued to develop during a rise in water level. Since the site will progressively retreat away from its original location earlier elements of its development will now only be available underwater.

b.   The preservation of the clues

The second reason for underwater sites being important is that the clues about the past are often much better preserved than on land (Figure 11). Individual objects are often well protected from natural decay by the underwater environment. Individual objects are also to some extent better protected from recovery or disturbance by the barrier of water above them.

The most exciting example of potential preservation on underwater sites is a feature sometimes referred to as the 'time capsule effect'. The clues usually available to us on land sites, which are often inhabited for long periods, do not necessarily give us an accurate picture of what was happening at any specific moment, instead they reflect changes and processes over time. It can therefore be difficult to see how a site functioned at any particular stage. An ideal situation would involve the site being frozen at the height of its success. Not only would individual objects be preserved from decay or reuse but they would also be trapped in the positions and associations which reflect the way they were used.

Figure 12. Levels of preservation: a model showing the surviving structure of the wreck of the Anna Marie in the sheltered Baltic waters with their low salinity and temperature. (4.2.) (Courtesy of B-M. Petersen.)

In reality, such 'time capsules' seldom occur, especially on the scale of a whole site. Very rapid burial, however, does create some of the characteristics of a time capsule. While changes to the evidence do take place during and after burial, the number of clues trapped in a relatively undistorted way can still be significant. Only a very few land sites have been buried quickly enough for the 'time capsule' effect to be a major factor, although more sites will have small-scale pockets of rapid burial (an event such as a fire can lead to the loss of a lot of material very quickly).

On the other hand rapid burial by water, *i.e.* sinking, has been a virtually daily occurrence for a very long time. While this happens most frequently to ships, on occasions even towns have been trapped in this way. It would, however, be simplistic to assume that every site underwater contains nothing but groups of closely associated material. We have to demonstrate the nature of each site by careful investigation. The possibilities are very exciting, especially in terms of the information such groups of material can provide about similar objects (Section 4.4.2) found in highly disturbed sites elsewhere.

The answer to the question, 'why make archaeology even more difficult by trying to do it underwater?' is that water hides, preserves, protects and traps clues which are often not available elsewhere. Using our ingenuity to find these clues seems a small price to pay.

4.2. Site Types

It is important to be aware of the great diversity and range of archaeological clues to be found underwater. When sites on the foreshore are included, the list grows even longer and more varied: everything from wrecks and harbour works to prehistoric footprints preserved in inter-tidal mud. Some sites (*e.g.* shipwrecks) represent high levels of technical achievement; others, such as middens or simple fish traps, although apparently unexciting, provide important information on day to day life. Indeed, the range of submerged material is such that there are few aspects of archaeological research on land that cannot be complemented or supported by information from underwater contexts.

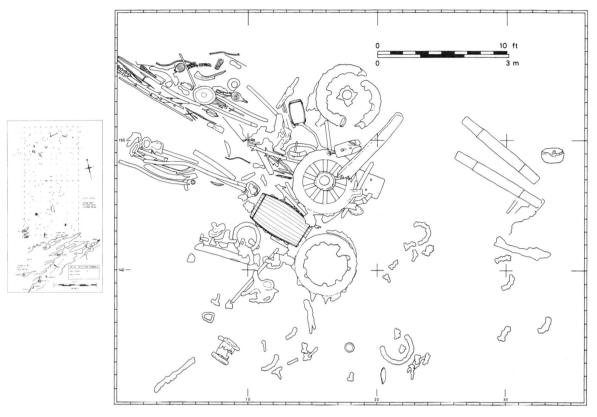

Figure 13. Levels of preservation: A plan and a detail of the northern grid sector of the Trinidad Valencera wreck-site. Most of the remains survive in isolated groupings in shallow depressions created before the natural stability of the sea-bed had reasserted itself. (4.2.)(Courtesy of C. Martin.)

An account of all the classes of material to be found submerged by inland or coastal waters is beyond the scope of this introductory manual. For the fieldworker, however, the difference between the site types lies in the scale and complexity of the subject, not the thoroughness of the investigation and recording that should be applied. Some classes of site, such as submerged landscapes, may require higher levels of specialist knowledge for successful recognition and analysis, but all will benefit from a careful and systematic approach.

4.2.1. Classifying underwater sites

If wrecks are taken as an example of one type of archaeological site underwater, it quickly becomes clear that even within this one category there is at least as much variety as there are boat and ship types. In discussing such material and comparing one example with another, it is therefore helpful to have some method of clarifying the situation through a system of classification. Such sites can be sub-divided according to age, constructional details or state of preservation,

Figure 14. Types of site: A 12m long log boat found at Hasholme. (4.1). (Courtesy of M. Millett)

Figure 15. Types of site: A Neolithic fishtrap discovered 8m below mean sea level in Bergschenhoek, Netherlands. Traps were discovered in clay beds below sea level as a result of polder reclamation and drainage schemes. (4.2). (Courtesy of National Museum of Antiquities, Leiden, Netherlands.)

as well as simply in terms of what is known about them (*e.g.* exact location and full survey, or estimated date and area of loss).

The factors affecting the formation and preservation of sites are varied, complex and differ from wreck to wreck. As more work is done in this area, it becomes harder to generalise. Sites that appear to be in a similar state on the seabed, and therefore fit easily into the same category in terms of state of preservation, may have arrived at that condition through very different processes. It is important to keep an open mind and to make careful notes on any

Figure 16. Types of site: a crannog, an occupation site on an artificial island, in Loch Voil, Perthshire. (Courtesy of the Scottish Trust for Underwater Archaeology).

mechanisms or processes acting on archaeological material in order to improve on any classification of site types. No site can be fitted neatly into a precisely defined category. To try to do this is to over simplify the nature of archaeological material. But as long as they are used sensibly, classification systems have much to offer in terms formalising vague ideas and theories within a framework (Gibbins 1990).

It has also been shown that careful search and systematic survey can produce results which allow an interpretation of sites which apparently lack any pattern and are heavily contaminated by modern material (Parker 1981). This means that although sites may be classified in terms of degree of survival, it does not necessarily imply that scattered sites deserve less attention or can be treated less sensitively. Information may be more

difficult to extract from such sites but their potential has been amply demonstrated (Muckelroy 1978). It may be suggested that the more scattered a site, the more careful the collection of the clues needs to be, because understanding the processes which scattered the site (and continue to modify it) becomes vital to its eventual interpretation.

4.3. The Range of Evidence on an Archaeological Site

A site is a concentration of clues left for us by the hustle and bustle of life in the past. These clues exist in, and have been modified by, their surroundings or environment. The following section is a brief review of what makes up a site and the sort of information we can get from the various clues. The evidence, in simple terms, comes in three

Material Type	Information Available
Human bone	Diet, disease, injuries, height, sex, lifestyles
Large mammal bone	Diet, husbandry, butchery, provisioning, disease
Small mammal bone	Natural fauna, ecology
Bird bone	Diet, natural fauna
Fish bone, scale	Species inhabiting the site or the remains of fishing activities, diet
Large molluscs (shellfish)	Diet, subsistence, trade, development of the site, shellfish farming
Small molluscs (shellfish)	Past vegetation, soil type and depositional history
Insect remains	Climate, vegetation, local environmental conditions
Parasite eggs	Intestinal parasitic diseases, sanitation, identification of cesspits
Wood (charcoal)	Date (dendrochronology), climate, building materials and technology, fuel
Other plant remains, charred and uncharred (seeds, mosses, leaves, grain)	Vegetation, diet, plant materials used in building, crafts, technology, fuel, processing of crops
Pollen	Vegetation, land use, chronologies, container contents identification
Phytoliths	As above
Diatoms	Salinity and levels of water pollution
Sediment/soil	Information on how deposits were formed, development of the site

Figure 17. Table of types of ecofactual material that may be expected from archaeological sites and what may be learned from them. (4.3.3.b.) (After Spence.)

groups: structure, sediments and contents. Sites come in many different forms but these basic components are the same.

4.3.1. Structures

What is the single most striking feature of a castle, or a workshop or a merchant's ship? Very probably it is the structure – whether made from stone, brick or wood. The clues it provides are no less impressive. We can learn about levels of technology and methods of construction. What types of raw materials were used and where did they come from? What does this imply about the supply routes and transport system available to carry these materials? We can learn about the reasons for a particular construction method by studying the design; was it for defence or prestige? What does this suggest about the political situation at the time of its construction – a time of war or prosperity?

When examining a ship the structural elements have much to tell us about the functional characteristics and performance of the vessel, vital to an understanding of its significance within the culture which produced it (for example, speed, carrying capacity, manoeuvrability, and whether it could be beached easily or even carried overland). Looking for faults or repairs in structures can also reveal much about the age, status and life-history of a building or vessel. In the case of a ship, perhaps we can even establish why it sank. Just as buildings collapse through poor design today, not every design was successful in the past, so it pays to look critically at the evidence.

4.3.2. Sediments

The arrival of the structure of a vessel on the seabed is only one in a series of steps which turn the vessel that was lost into the archaeological site we find. Fortunately the clues which can help us study and begin to understand these changes on the site can be found in any sediments which cover it. Clues in the nature and layering of sediments on the site can provide information on the break up of the vessel, movement of material within the site, later disturbance of the remains and the stability of the site today. It may even be possible to use the nature of the sediments recorded during a survey to help predict likely levels of preservation in different areas of the site.

4.3.3. Contents

Within the structures and sediments are objects such as timbers, coins, pottery and bones. They are important for the study of the past because they reflect how people lived.

a. Artefacts

Objects can show us the people of the time cooking, working, playing, worshipping, keeping warm, entertaining and decorating themselves. The shape, composition, method of manufacture, evidence of use etc. of such items are all important. In addition, because objects interact with other objects and with

their surroundings, their positions on the site and in relation to other material form important clues.

The range of man-made objects is very large and readers will be familiar with the idea of dividing them into major groupings such as jugs made of clay, guns made of iron, shoes made of leather etc. There is a vast amount of information about such classifications as well as about individual artefact types in the archaeological literature, and it is unnecessary to repeat all that information here.

b. Ecofacts

A less obvious source of information among the contents of the structure and sediments are the non-artefactual remains, which are often referred to by archaeologists as ecofacts. Animal and plant remains associated with archaeological sites have become a rich source of clues about the past. Insects, seeds, pollen, microscopic plants and animals, animal and human bones all provide evidence about the environment of the people living on the site. After all, the quality of the food, cleanliness and sanitation, pests and parasites, the accidents and diseases we have today affect our lives. The people in the past were no different.

It is important to be aware that there may be evidence which is not always immediately visible. For example, insect fragments found on archaeological sites are usually of the size range of between 0.5 and 1.0mm and so are unlikely to be recognised during the excavation itself. Test samples of likely deposits should be taken and assessed without delay. It is important that possible environmental and scientific evidence is not overlooked, and that samples of potentially valuable deposits (*e.g.* container and bilge contents) are taken (Figure 17).

Far less has been written about non-artefactual remains than about objects and so readers may not be familiar with the range of material involved. For that reason the main groups are outlined below.

i. Animal remains

Animal remains appear on sites in a wide variety of forms. Ecofacts like bones are common and can provide much information on diet and if examined for marks, on butchery practice and even organised supply systems. Animal hair is also a common component of weather– and water–proofing materials found on shipwreck sites (*e.g.* caulking). Fish bones found on an underwater site may be the remains of species which inhabited the site and as such they may be useful indicators of the characteristics of past environments. On the other hand they may be the remains of stored food, refuse, or relate to fishing activities if they are found in quantity on a shipwreck site. As is the case with mammal bones, fish bones can yield a great deal of information about diet and provisioning.

ii. Human remains

If human remains are found on site, it is a legal requirement in many countries that the relevant government department is informed. The study of human bones by specialist palaeopathologists can yield such information as physique, sex, height and diet together with the identification of occupational diseases and injuries. Human bones may occur as burial groups on a flooded land site or as the remains of the crew on a shipwreck site. On well preserved sites material other than bone may survive (*c.g.* hair, tissue remains). Biological material that may be expected to be associated with human remains includes stomach contents and coprolites (containing such things as seeds, cereal fragments and parasite eggs).

iii. Invertebrate remains

The study of insects, molluscs and parasites falls within the realm of 'invertebrate zooarchaeology'.

The analysis of molluscs can provide information on past climates and environments, diet and their use as artefacts or tools. Molluscs have specific habitat requirements which reflect the contemporary environment and can be from land, rivers or the sea. Molluscs of economic importance are usually found as food waste (*e.g.* oyster, whelk and mussel) although some may be collected for use in building materials or pottery. 'Single event' dumps can be analysed to determine the season of collection and information on the population being exploited (or even farmed).

The analysis of internal (endo-) and external (ecto-) parasites found within archaeological deposits can yield information on:
– the range and antiquity of various pests and diseases in both animals and human
– the conditions under which people were living
– the effect of these conditions and the parasites on people's health
– determining the function of certain features *e.g.* cess pits, bilges
– examining methods of sewage disposal.

Internal parasites normally survive in anaerobic deposits (*e.g.* cess pits) or preserved in fossilised faeces (coprolites) in the form of *ova* (eggs). They consist of species that infect both humans and animals (*e.g.* tapeworm, whipworm). Examples of external parasites (*e.g.* fleas) have been recovered from wreck sites.

Other insect species can provide information on past changes in local and regional climate, the infestation of food stores and an indication of the contemporary conditions (*e.g.* wet or dry).

iv. Botanic material

Plant remains can be found on archaeological sites in a wide variety of contexts. Locational information and individual measurements, together with the species identification, can provide evidence of agricultural practices, pests/blights, provisioning, stowage and diet, nature and origin of cargo. A wide range of different plant components can be preserved including wood and bark, seeds (including fruit stones and grain), fungi and mosses. Ships' timbers can potentially reveal a great

39

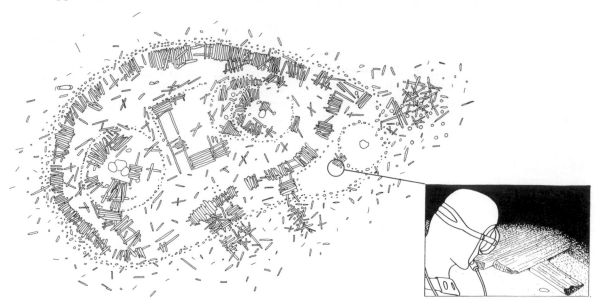

Figure 18. Position – a complicated collection of clues starts to make sense when each clue's position is noted. This is doubly important underwater where visibility may mean that the fieldworker will never see the whole site at one time. (4.4.1.). (Drawing by K. Watson.)

deal about past environments, timber resources and woodworking practices. Pollen analysis (palynology) is the study of pollen grains and spores which survive because they have particularly resilient walls. Palynology can provide information about past environments and ecology, the dating of deposits, the impact of man on the environment and in certain cases the identification of residues within containers.

Phytoliths are microscopic particles of silica which occur within the cells of certain species of plants (especially the grasses) and as such they are useful aids to identification. They are particularly useful to the archaeologist as they survive when all other traces of the plant have disappeared and are also instrumental in imposing wear patterns on the cutting edges of tools such as scythes.

Information about botanical material has survived in some surprising ways. Imprints of grain and leaves are sometimes visible on ceramic objects, and occasionally these impressions are so clear that the type of plant can be easily identified.

v. Micro-organisms

Micro-organisms, or microbes, include the bacteria and algae of the Plant Kingdom, the protozoa and viruses of the Animal Kingdom, and others which have some characteristics of both Kingdoms (*e.g.* fungi). With the exception of viruses and a few other examples, micro-organisms, like plants and animals, consist of cells (unicellular and multi-cellular). Micro-organisms can survive in the archaeological record in a number of ways which are dependent on the nature of the construction of the organism (some produce a resilient hard shell) and the nature of the burial deposit.

Diatoms are microscopic unicellular or colonial algae with a silicaceous cell wall. They occur profusely in all moist and aquatic habitats in freshwater, brackish and marine environments. The study of diatoms in archaeology can yield information such as the nature of the environment of formation of different deposits and differing levels of salinity through time (Battarbee 1988). Foraminifera are unicellular animals which secrete a test or skeleton. They are mainly

Figure 19. Association – for example using a gun requires a complex collection of personnel and equipment. The activities of a gun crew cannot be understood unless the material is recognised as belonging together (i.e. that it is associated). (4.4.1.) (Drawing by K. Watson.)

marine benthonic or planktonic forms, in which there is a considerable morphological variation, from a single, flask-shape to complex chambered examples. Foraminifera are important zone fossils that can survive in a range of sediment types providing information about changes of environment over time (*e.g.* variations in salinity in rivers and estuaries).

4.3.4. Links between categories of evidence

Although a convenient way of thinking about the elements of a site, the categories of evidence do in fact merge one with another. A ship's hull is an object which combines artefactual and ecofactual information. Sediments can form part of the contents of the hull (for example ballast or bilge deposits). Sediments can also provide the evidence of structure which has long since decayed or been dug out for re-use. The contents and the structure of the site can, like the sediments, show changes in the formation of the site over time. For example, the evidence of differential erosion of timber can often reveal past sequences of exposure and burial.

The types of evidence mentioned above will not all be present in every case. What should be remembered is that any

investigation should involve the study and recording of all the surviving strands of evidence on an archaeological site. In the past too much attention has been paid to the easily recognisable man-made objects at the expense of the often less glamorous, but equally important clues which often need a greater level of expertise to collect.

4.4. Using the Evidence

As we study the clues that have been recorded we find ourselves asking 'can we make sense of it all?'. The answer is that we can if we are systematic and disciplined and adapt ways of extracting information from other scientists. This introductory guide cannot list all the techniques ever used in archaeology but by introducing some of the main techniques of 'getting answers' it can at least demonstrate how broadly based a discipline archaeology is. The methods conveniently split into *Where* (position and association), *What* (recognition, description and typology), *How* (context) and *When* (dating).

4.4.1. Position and association

Since we are studying complicated elements which were used together we need to know where they were (*i.e.* their POSITION) and

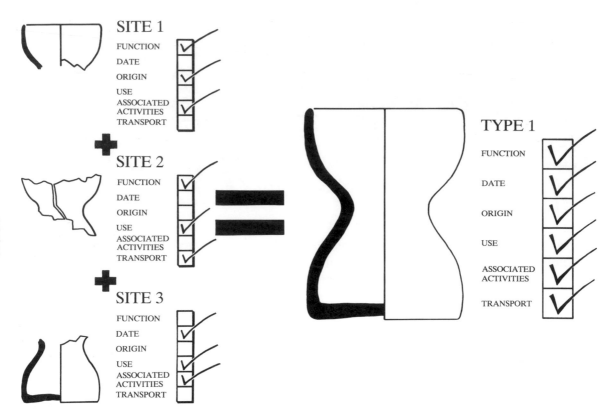

Figure 20. Typology – knowledge about the appearance and character of a type of object is accumulated from a number of sites which each contribute different elements. (4.4.2.) (Drawing by K. Watson.)

what they were with (*i.e.* their ASSOCIATIONS). You can imagine how difficult it would be to make sense of complex structures without an accurate plan and a description of the position and association of the various elements (Figure 18, Figure 19).

In looking for clues about the past we have to make do with where things ended up; where they slid, fell, were carried or washed. However if we do not note the position and associations of the clue in its resting place we have no hope of tracing it back to where it started from.

4.4.2. Recognition, description and typology

How do we know what we have found? Some of the evidence we will see because it is obvious. Some of the evidence we will begin

to understand because it is within our own experience (*e.g.* 'I recognise that object as a sword').

Some clues we will not identify because they are not immediately visible or because the particular analytical technique being employed is not suited to revealing them. In other situations clues are not exploited simply because we do not realise that they are clues. RECOGNITION has to be a co-operative process in which good communication, by publication as well as personal contact, is vital.

The physical remains of the past are so complex that no one person has sufficient knowledge and experience to deal with every type of clue that is available. In fact all the necessary specialist knowledge and techniques may not even be present in a team of researchers, but they are available

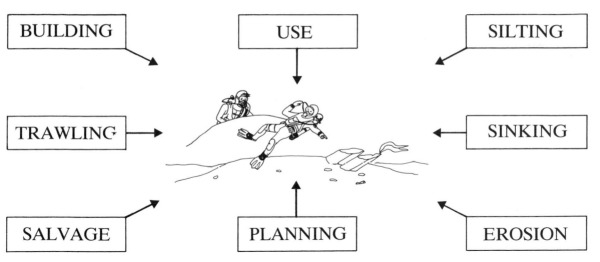

BUILDING	USE	SILTING
TRAWLING		SINKING
SALVAGE	PLANNING	EROSION

Figure 21. Many processes will have shaped the site that you discover. (4.4.3.). (Drawing by K. Watson.)

somewhere and it is up to us all to be aware of where research relevant to our own investigations is being conducted. We may not always have the ability and experience to take full advantage of every clue that is presented to us, but we can all be aware of the potential range of clues which might exist and ask for help when problems arise, rather than blundering on in ignorance. A simple maxim is 'everything that happened on this site has left a trace – it just needs to be recognised'.

A massive number of clues are found not just on our site but on hundreds of others all over the world. How do we tell others about our evidence? Indeed, how do we remind ourselves in ten years' time? Of course we have to record a DESCRIPTION of the clues from the structure, sediments and contents so that we and others can understand and use our findings. If we describe them reliably and consistently we can start to divide our clues not just into structure, sediments and contents but into *types of* structure or sediment or contents. A sword is called a sword because it has certain characteristics which it shares with a group of edged weapons. That group can be called the sword group providing us with a convenient and informative way of referring to all weapons which share those characteristics. The sword group can be split into smaller groups in the same way (*e.g.* rapiers, sabres), based on common features shared by a particular group of objects within the general group.

This process of using descriptions to define types of clue is called TYPOLOGY. The value of typology is that if your unknown piece of structure, or object has characteristics which associate it with a previously described type you can make use of and contribute to all the research that has ever been done on that type of clue. This can include use, development, construction, date, origin, etc. Your mystery find is transformed from a headache to a source of information because you took the time to record its description properly (Figure 20).

Of course it would be optimistic to assume that every typological series is totally correct. Such groups are usually built up using evidence from a wide range of sites. The more sites which produce evidence which agrees with the suggested typology, the more secure it is. Some typologies will be based on very few finds and faulty assumptions. If your evidence does not fit the accepted scheme do not ignore it or bend the facts to make it fit.

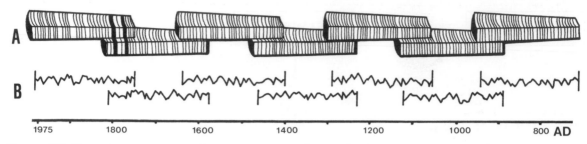

Figure 22. Tree-ring sequence. By using years of growth shown in the rings of individual trees from the same area a year by year sequence can be constructed back into the past. (4.4.4.a.i). (After Eckstein et al., 1984.)

44

It may be that the information you have recovered will be important in improving the typology.

4.4.3.   Context

When we have carefully noted the position in which a particular clue was found we can ask ourselves a very important question. How did it get there and how has it been modified since it arrived on the site we are studying? The answers we get to these questions will have a great affect on the information we can retrieve from the clues. If the clue was already there before our site was established it may point to other sites or events in the area. If it arrived when our site was in use it could tell us about life on the site, and if it arrived afterwards it may tell us about the stages our site went through to become the archaeological evidence we discover.

To understand how our clues arrived we look for evidence of what arrived with them. We try to interpret these arrivals as steps in the 'life' of the site. A step is a clue's 'context' *i.e.* how it fits into the life of the site (Figure 21). As you can imagine, a site is full of evidence of contexts. A context might be a layer of sediment washed in just after the sinking, or a layer of shingle dumped on the site 400 years later, or even a barrel rolled in on the day of the launch. Clearly it is important to record what was found in what.

Studying and understanding the context of a clue can also help in the investigation of how that clue has been modified. Ideally, every clue would survive with no modification at all and could be used with confidence. Very few do. To make things more complicated still, some changes can be the result of the way an object was used in a past society and can therefore provide us with useful information about both the object and the society which used it. Studying and recording the context of a find can be vital in separating out modifications of this sort from those caused by natural processes – they can be surprisingly easy to confuse if all the evidence is not considered together.

4.4.4.   Dating

Since we are studying the past and the passage of time, one of the main things we want to extract from our clues is the point in time to which they relate. Chronologies or time-scales give us the ability to relate events or features throughout antiquity and across the world. Widely separated cultures such as the South American civilizations and those in the Old World can be compared if we have dates for each which can be directly related. Dating techniques can be grouped into two main categories, absolute and relative dating, which reflect the ways in which the particular methods can be related to the present day.

a.   Absolute dating

Methods of absolute dating can be related to calendar years and therefore the results of these techniques can be directly linked to

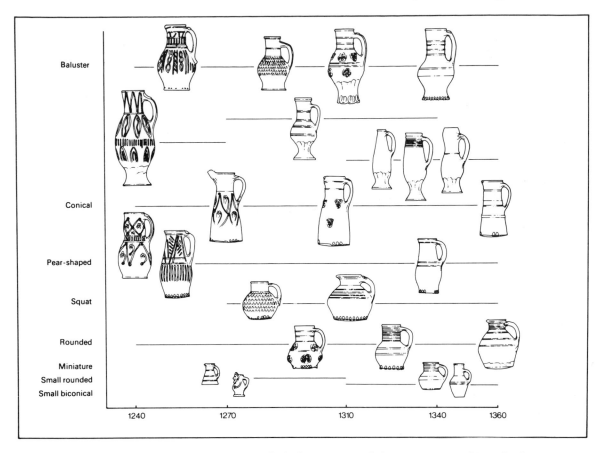

Figure 23. Dating using typology. (4.4.4.b.i). (Courtesy of the Museum of London)

the present day. To say that an event happened 900 years ago is to give it an absolute date.

We will introduce three methods of absolute dating in this section to show some of the associated problems.

i. Dendrochronology (tree-ring dating)

Many wet sites will produce large quantities of wood and this can sometimes be helpful in providing a date. As trees grow they produce annual rings of varying width according to the local conditions. This pattern is similar amongst trees of the same type in the same area. This means that the same years can be recognised in individual trees. The sequence of years can be extended by overlapping the tree-rings of trees of slightly different date. This has been done for oak until the sequence extends from the present to, in some areas,

9000 years ago. Tree-ring dating is based on matching the pattern of growth rings found on a wood sample from a site with its place in the established local sequence of variation in growth ring size (Figure 22).

Tree-ring dating can give very precise results in optimum circumstances, perhaps even to a season in a single year. Once the sample has been matched with a point in the sequence, however, you need to know what the resulting date actually means. Does the sample come from a context where a date would be useful to the understanding of the site? The wood could have been introduced onto site any time between the site being formed and your discovery of it. Similarly, wood is often re-used. Ships timbers are frequently found forming part of waterfront structures and other buildings, so care must be taken in how dating information gained

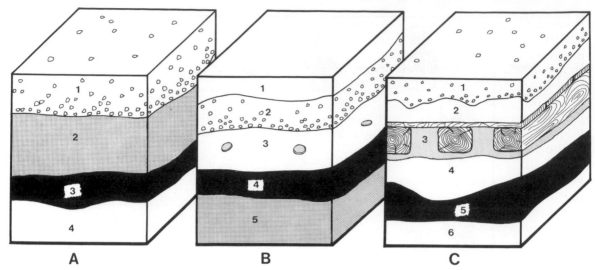

Figure 24. Stratigraphy - A). Context 1 is later than Context 2. Absolute dates can be placed in the relative dating sequence. B). A coin dated 79 AD in Context 3 says that 3, 2, and 1 arrived after 79 AD. C). A floor constructed in 1322 AD says that the contexts below it must have accumulated before then. (4.4.4.b.i.)

from such elements is used. Ships and wooden structures in general require frequent repairs. A wood sample taken from a repaired area might be significantly later in date than the rest of the structure. The sample may have been found in a ship in UK waters, but the wood may have come from elsewhere. It is also very important to remember that the date provided by dendrochronology relates to the growing period of the tree (*i.e.* the period in which the rings were formed) and not its arrival on site. Timber can be stored for long periods before it is used to allow for seasoning.

Despite these problems dendrochronology is sufficiently accurate to be used to check, or calibrate, other methods such as radiocarbon dating. Recommended procedures for dendrochronological sampling are given in Section 10.2.3.

ii. Radiocarbon dating

Radiocarbon dating is based on the known rate of decay of a radioactive isotope (carbon-14, radiocarbon) which occurs in very small quantities in all living things. For the dating process all that is needed is a sample of carbon that can be directly related to the evidence that requires a date.

During their lives all living things absorb the naturally occurring carbon-14 isotope. The amount of isotope which is absorbed depends on its level of concentration in the organism's surroundings. When the organism dies the carbon-14 level starts to reduce as the isotope decays. Since we know the rate at which this particular isotope decays we can make an accurate assessment of how long ago the organism died by measuring the remaining amount, assuming that the levels of the isotope in the organism's surroundings have remained constant.

The method is generally less precise than dendrochronology but can be used to date much earlier material. Radiocarbon measurement is normally effective back to 30,000-40,000 BP (before present, *i.e.* before 1950) and up to 60,000 BP is possible. However, as with dendrochronology, radiocarbon dating relates to the living period of the organism, not to its arrival or use on site so the same degree of care has to be used in the way in which such dates are interpreted.

One of the basic assumptions has been that the amount of radiocarbon in the atmosphere has remained constant throughout time. Calibration work using techniques such as dendrochronology suggests that the level has fluctuated and that calibration of all radiocarbon dates is now necessary to give an approximate date in calendar years.

Radiocarbon dating results include information which identifies uncertainties in the date given:

1. Radiocarbon dates are normally quoted giving an error margin. For example a date may be quoted as 1764 ± 100 years ago. This is a statement of statistical confidence of one standard deviation, meaning that there is a 68% chance of the actual date lying within the range 1664 - 1864 years ago. Higher levels, *e.g.* two standard deviations meaning a 95% chance, or three standard deviations meaning a 99% chance, mean doubling and tripling the limits respectively, so the example above would be ± 200 or ± 300 years. Therefore you can have a better chance of being within the limits, but the limits become wider.

2. Radiocarbon dates can be quoted as either before present (present being taken as 1950) *i.e.* 'BP' or in calendar years *i.e.* 'BC' or 'AD'.

3. If the radiocarbon date has been calibrated (re-assessed in relation to another dating system such as dendrochronology) then this is often indicated by adding 'cal' *i.e.* 'cal BP'.

4. Methods of measuring and calibrating dates also vary between different laboratories. The name of the laboratory and the methods should ideally appear with published dates.

It is important that factors such as the meaning of the $\pm$ statistical confidence, the method of calibration, the actual radiocarbon technique used, are all taken into account and fully understood when using radiocarbon dates. Recommended procedures for radiocarbon sampling are given in Section 10.2.3.

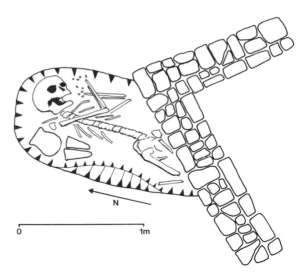

Figure 25. Stratigraphy from above: from the overlap we can suggest that the grave is earlier than the wall.

iii. Historical association

We have looked at two relatively complicated methods of gaining an absolute date. We should not overlook what is perhaps the simplest: written records, which allow HISTORICAL ASSOCIATION to provide archaeological clues with absolute dates.

While historical dates seem very attractive they do have their problems. Reliable written documents only go back a relatively short time into our past. Where they do exist it is sometimes possible to misuse them or look to them for easy solutions. For example written records tell us about the Spanish Armada but the fact that the event occurred and is recorded does not mean that every 16th century vessel found in UK waters was associated with it. In addition, historical documents are the record of witnesses, some of whom may be biased or simply ignorant. Their accuracy should not be taken for granted. In the present day, reading a selection of daily newspapers can reveal conflicting interpretations of the same event, and the same can be true of other historical documents. Archaeological dates should not be ignored simply because they conflict with documentary evidence.

In addition, as with all dates, direct historical associations relate to one point in the development of the site – in the case of a shipwreck, the arrival of the material on the seabed. Subsequent events on the site must be dated independently.

A problem can also arise with objects such as coins or cannon which appear, because of the inscriptions on them, to give a clear date and historical association . A coin may be found on a site which commemorates a particular ruler, the period of whose reign we know from historical sources. This may well give us a good absolute date for the minting of the coin, but it gives us little secure information about the date of the coin's loss or burial. Clearly it cannot have been lost before it was minted, but it could be lost a long time afterwards.

Sources of additional information on these and other absolute dating methods (such as thermoluminescence) are given in the suggested reading list for this section.

b. Relative dating

Relative dating can only tell us whether one process occurred before or after another one. It cannot indicate the length of time between the two events nor can it provide a date in years which places the event in a conventional time scale. However it is very useful for determining whether the information was deposited early or late in the development of the site, and for providing a framework into which absolute dates can be placed.

i. Typological dating

The value of typology as an aid to research has been noted above, but it also has a role to play as a form of relative dating. The form of objects designed to perform the same function often changes over time. If earlier and later characteristics can be recognised it is possible to reconstruct the sequence of development and give each object a relative position within it (Figure 23). There is a real danger of such sequences being unsound because they are based on assumptions of early and late characteristics, so as much supporting evidence as possible should be introduced to support any conclusions drawn.

ii. Stratigraphic dating

We have already seen how we can use contexts to identify the steps in the history of a site. It is a simple process to start to recognise and study the order in which they occurred. This gives us a sequence of the steps and a relative dating technique.

The ordering of contexts is known as a site's stratigraphic record. The study of this record or sequence is known as stratigraphy. The most basic principle of stratigraphy which was adapted from the study of geological strata can be summarised by the concept that a context which physically overlays another context is normally the later (Figure 24 and Figure 25).

On a particular site, the principles of stratigraphy are used to establish a sequence of above-below relationships, thereby placing all the contexts (and therefore events) into the order in which they occurred. Stratification can be studied at different scales using the same basic theory. Examining the layering of contexts in a scour pit may reveal many clues about large-scale changes to a deposit. Applying the same approach to the sediments between individual timbers can be just as revealing about equally fundamental processes in the formation of the site.

The principles of stratigraphy provide a framework within which archaeological investigations are conducted. They do not impose rigid boundaries on the way in which stratification is investigated. Applying them effectively requires a willingness to combine such principles with a good understanding of the nature of the contexts under investigation. For example, the nature of stratificaton in mobile sediments is likely to be very different to that in stable contexts. The application of stratigraphy to a site on a rocky seabed will not be exactly the same as

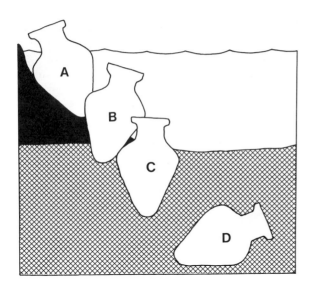

Figure 26. Some of the variations possible in the local environment of an archaeological object underwater. Each environment will affect the object differently. A) partly submerged, B) totally submerged, C) partly buried, D) totally buried. (4.5.1.c). (After Pearson.)

its application to a deep urban deposit on land. But the value of the exercise, its aims and fundamental principles, will be precisely the same.

4.5. The Importance of Site Environment and the Processes of Site Formation

This guide has so far introduced both the sources of evidence and some of the methods used to extract information from those clues. In this section we look at the site from a different angle. Before we use the evidence to build up a picture of the past we need to understand the processes which shaped the clues we find.

We must ask ourselves:

i. What are the fundamental factors which shape the past that we are studying?

ii. What affects the way in which an object becomes part of the site?

iii. How does the evidence survive until the site is investigated?

iv. What are the biases and imbalances that such processes introduce into the evidence?

v. Are these processes detectable and so understandable?

All these questions have to be addressed in order to use archaeological evidence to investigate complex aspects of past societies such as behaviour and social organisation. These processes are not muddling factors to be screened out in the final report. Their study is fundamental to archaeological research, not merely an interesting diversion from the main lines of inquiry.

4.5.1. The effects of the site environment

Environment is important for two reasons:

a. It shapes the way people live

A knowledge of the environment is more than just a pretty backdrop to events. Many of man's activities are centred on solving problems set by their surroundings. Therefore much of the past we are intending to study is a reaction to the environment. Climate, vegetation, wild animals, crops, water are all vital components which have to be studied before man's activities can be explained

While a site was active or occupied, its environment would have influenced many aspects of life *e.g.* the form of structures, the clothes that were worn, the available sources of food. The environment of an area can change dramatically over time and reconstructing past landscapes is fundamental to interpreting the remains of past societies. For example, temporary camp sites linked to Ice-Age migrations have been found in what are now temperate regions. Clearly they are not understandable by reference to their current environment. Boat finds have been made on dry land. Studies of changes in the local environment have often shown that the area was previously

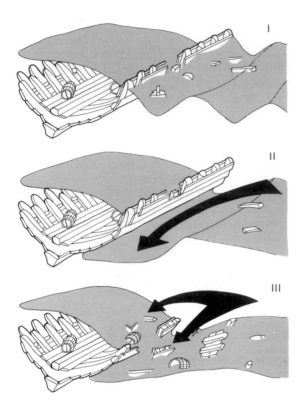

Figure 27. Scouring and silting - just two of the natural processes which must be understood by the fieldworker. They have an obvious effect on the type of information which survives.

Figure 28. The more dynamic the environment the less well material may survive - the outline of a partially sectioned iron cannon embedded in concretion on the Gran Grifon site (4.5.1.c.). (Courtesy of C. Martin.)

closer to the sea or an inland waterway allowing the find to be put in its proper context.

Archaeology underwater, in the same way as archaeology on land, is likely to be concerned with the study of reactions to environmental factors. The sea and inland waterways and lakes can be seen to have had considerable influence on man. The sea and rivers offered a plentiful supply of food, but to obtain this food reliably, certain problems had to be solved: the construction of boats, fishing equipment and fish processing and storage techniques. Water offers the opportunity for travel and communication or trade, but again to take advantage of the potential opportunities, man had to develop methods of surviving in that environment.

b.   It shapes the clues we find

Having shaped activities in the past, the environment then shapes how evidence of the past survives. This can vary in scale from chemical changes in soil to erosion by sea or river action.

The environment can often be a major initial influence in terms of deposition. The ways in which material moves from occupied sites into the archaeological record differ considerably between stable, temperate zones and areas prone to flooding, earthquake or volcanic eruption.

The aquatic environment's influence on deposition can be very significant. The most obvious and dramatic example is that of a shipwreck. The sinking of a vessel results in a group of associated material arriving on the seabed in one event, although of course it may be scattered to varying degrees. This factor can be very useful for archaeologists as has been discussed above. Water can also cause deposition by abandonment. Rising sea levels can force occupation sites to be abandoned. However, this process of deposition will take place over a period of time as opposed to the short lived but intense process of shipwreck. This may mean that less material is eventually deposited, as the occupants will have every opportunity to remove what they want. However, the process of innundation is likely to be far gentler than the process of shipwreck so more material may survive very near to where it was actually used, and in association with related objects rather than being scattered.

As soon as objects or structures have fallen out of use or are lost to become part of the archaeological record, the environment remains important as it helps to determine what evidence survives, in what form and what position. Certain specific conditions will promote the survival of particular material types. In general the more robust materials (such as stone and pottery) survive better than others (such as wood, textile or leather). The more aggressive the environment the less well material may survive. Studying the nature and impact of the environment of a site is vital to understanding the evidence that we eventually recover.

c. The marine environment

Even within one broad environmental category, such as underwater sites, there are variations which might be significant in terms of which materials survive and which do not. Waterlogged conditions and burial in oxygen starved conditions such as those found in soft silts underwater can promote the preservation of a wide range of organic

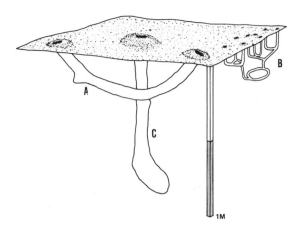

Figure 29. 'Burrow forms of a) Nephrops norvegicus; densities of three to five burrows per square metre are not uncommon; b) Calocaris macandreae. c). Cepola rubescens; densities of five burrows in four square metres have been recorded. (Ferrari and Adams 1990; 140). (4.5.1.c.)

51

and inorganic material. All underwater environments do not promote survival in this way. On some sites, the preservation of artefactual material can be poor due to turbulence from heavy swell or tidal conditions, particularly in shallow water and around abrasive or rocky seabeds. Generalisation is always problematic, and from early suggestions that well preserved material was only to be found in deep water and soft sediment, appreciation is growing of the way in which micro-environments within a site can create pockets of preservative conditions atypical of the general area.

The degradation of organic and inorganic materials on an underwater site is dependent on chemical, physical, and biological factors (Figures 26, 27, 28). These include environmental conditions such as temperature, pH (level of acidity or alkalinity), salinity, and water movement. Other important factors are the length of immersion or burial and the nature of the object/ material itself (its size, composition, robustness). It is not always clear how these factors interact to cause the various types of decay and there is a need for further research

Figure 30. Accessible material re-used. The break-up of a shipwreck by commercial salvaging and local people on the foreshore in the early 20th century. (4.5.2.b.) (Courtesy of the University of St Andrews.)

in this area. Often one set of conditions will favour the survival of certain types of objects whilst being detrimental to others.

Many organisms chemically and physically alter artefacts or materials deposited underwater, particularly in the sea. Wood-boring molluscs (such as the shipworms *(Teredinidae)* and piddocks, *Pholodaceae*), together with the main genus of wood-boring crustacea, the 'gribble worm' *(Limnoria)* make holes through the surface of wood making it more susceptible to degradation by other processes. Various other marine organisms burrow into rock. Larger animals such as crabs and lobsters either burrow or enlarge existing crevices and so disturb archaeological remains and stratigraphy (Ferrari and Adams 1990; Figure 29).

Micro-organisms are everywhere in the sea. As soon as an object enters the sea it becomes covered with a thin film of diatoms or bacteria and a cycle of bio-deterioration begins. In oxygen-free, or anaerobic, environments (*e.g.* in sediments) organisms such as sulphate-reducing bacteria are dominant. Their activities can accelerate the corrosion of copper alloys, and iron sulphide stains can be seen as dark patches on pottery glazes, wood and glass.

A full characterisation of the physical, chemical and biological environment of a site, as it was when it was occupied or active as well as through the later stages which brought it to the condition in which it was found, should be considered an integral part of any investigation.

4.5.2. Cultural aspects of site formation

We can use the same general headings when discussing the effects of culture as we used for environmental factors:

a. It shapes the way people lived

It would be far too simplistic to suggest that if we understand the environment we understand mankind. The one is not the only factor determining the behaviour of the other. It could be said that people do not react to the environment but rather they react to their view of the environment. Levels of technology will shape the response to environmental challenges. Factors like religion will shape attitudes (*e.g.* to issues like the eating of meat or birth control). If you think of all the motives and actions which go together to make up 'human nature' it becomes clear just how complex the problem of understanding cultural influences on the archaeological record can be.

b. It shapes the clues we find

i. Sources of clues

How does an object go from being used to being recorded as part of an archaeological site? We are all familiar with the idea of throwing out rubbish or trash. Archaeologists are familiar with the idea of painstakingly investigating the equivalent of ancient dustbins. A great deal of archaeological material was buried through being discarded, thrown into pits or left in abandoned buildings which collapsed around them.

We have all accidentally lost things – coins, wallets, car-keys. Sometimes they are found while on other occasions they may lie where they fell for many years. The same has been true since before people first had holes in their pockets. Isolated, accidental losses, sometimes traumatic such as during a fire or battle, are therefore responsible for much material entering the archaeological record.

Deliberate burial of groups of associated material is much rarer. There are examples of material buried for posterity like the 'time capsules' buried by school children. Graves may seem a more common example of burial for posterity but in many circumstances you could say this is another example of rubbish disposal. Hoards of coins or other valuables are deliberately buried to be kept safe. However, it could also be said that the ones we find are examples of 'accident' since the owner was not able to reclaim them.

There is considerable evidence of ritual activity around lakes and rivers (Bradley 1990). The superstitious nature of fishermen and sailors is also well attested and is often considered to be a cultural response to the uncertainties of the environment in which they operate. The carrying of talismans for good luck or the deliberate deposition of an ornament or weapon into a river or the sea to appease the spirits may both be represented in the evidence we recover, but will we understand what these objects mean when we find them? Moreover, there is some debate as to which objects were deliberately placed in the water and which have eroded out of riverbanks or lakesides. The evidence is unlikely to allow any simple or easy interpretation.

53

ii. Changes to the clues

We have touched upon the effect of the environment on man but another major source of evidence is the traces left by mankind's effect on the environment. The changes we can study range in scale from the disturbance of the ground to build houses or dig pits, to large scale deforestation. Much of this evidence is again created 'accidentally' by man's activities and so is one step removed from the actual activities we want to study. This evidence may not seem immediately relevant until its causes are traced back. Of course, to appreciate the impact of man on the environment we also need to understand the character of the environment before it was changed.

Occupation sites are often inhabited for long periods and the activities carried out on the site will vary over time leaving behind very complex sets of clues. These clues provide a record of the changes. It can be very valuable to study long periods of occupation in this way, precisely because changes and continuities in the society concerned should be detectable in the evidence. Yet in this situation the surviving clues do not represent a total picture of the site at any one moment.

Clues left by earlier occupation might be altered or destroyed by later activities on the same site such as pit digging or the preparation of deep foundations for modern buildings.

The recycling of material is also an important factor in modifying the evidence we eventually study (Figure 30). There is a conscious selection of what is taken away and what is left behind, which will depend on many factors. The occupants might only remove what they consider valuable (which will not necessarily be the same things that we would consider valuable today). The material removed may depend on what could have been carried with the available means of transport. Perhaps objects were selected on the basis of sentimental or ritual value.

It is very difficult to define all the processes which might result in material being removed from the site, but it is important to consider as wide a range of potential disturbances as possible. Underwater sites are no different from land sites. On submerged settlement sites after innundation, it may be more difficult for material to be recycled or disturbed by later activity but they will have been modified by long periods of habitation before they are innundated. Shipwrecks may result in a group of closely associated materials being deposited together. However, as surviving documentary records make clear, many vessels have been partially or wholly salvaged, involving selective removal of material from the site (Figure 30). Use of the seabed for fishing, anchorage or dredging will remove and add material. Finally, sites are known where a shipwreck lies on top of prehistoric remains producing the effect of later activity on a site blurring the clues left by earlier occupation (Murphy 1990).

The influence of environment and the influence of cultural factors are interlinked. It would, for example, be difficult to interpret an umbrella successfully without reference to the environment (in this case shelter from the rain or sun). However, a detailed study of the environment will not reveal why the umbrella was coloured red, green and yellow or had a certain design on the handle – these factors may simply be dictated by preference.

The fact remains that most of the material found buried on archaeological sites represents the rubbish and chance losses which have survived being picked over by later occupants of the site and the various natural processes which cause objects to deteriorate. Any investigation which tries to use archaeological evidence by assuming that a site, even a submerged one, has been free of the processes and mechanisms which modify the way that clues appear is adopting a very simplistic approach. The more complex the questions we ask of the evidence, the more rigorously we must attempt to evaluate any biases within the evidence. To achieve this we must carefully document the nature of the processes which interact to form the archaeological record.

4.6. Suggested Reading

a. site types

Coles, J.M., and Lawson, A.J. (eds)
1987 *European Wetlands in Prehistory.* Oxford, ISBN 0-19-813406-1.
Flemming, N.C.
1971 *Cities in the Sea.* London.
Milne, G.
1985 *The Port of Roman London.* London, ISBN 0-7134-4365-0.
Muckelroy, K. (ed.)
1980 *Archaeology Underwater: An Atlas of the World's Submerged Sites.* London, ISBN 0-07-043951-6.
Musées du Chateau des Ducs de Bretagne
1985 *Archéologie Sous-Marine.* Musées du Chateau des Ducs des Bretagne, Nantes.
Thomas, C.
1985 *Explorations of a drowned landscape; archaeology and history of the Isles of Scilly.* London, ISBN 0-7134-4852-0.

Throckmorton, P. (ed.)
1987 *History From The Sea: Shipwrecks and Archaeology.* London ISBN 0-85533-614-5.

b. The range of evidence on an archaeological site

i. structures

Goodwin, P.
1987 *The Construction and Fitting of the Sailing Man of War 1650 –1850.* London, ISBN 0-85177-326-5.
Greenhill, B.
1988 *The Evolution of the Wooden Ship.* London, ISBN 0-7134-3344-2.
Morrison, I.
1985 *Landscape with Lake Dwellings: The Crannogs of Scotland.* Edinburgh, ISBN 0-85224-472-X.

ii. artefacts

Adkins, L. and R.A.
1983 *The Handbook of British Archaeology.* London, ISBN 0-333-34843-5.
Stone, D.L.
1993 *Sailing Ship artifacts of the 19th Century.* Underwater Archaeology Society of British Columbia, Vancouver. ISBN 0-9695010-1-3.
Hodges, H.
1971 *Artefacts: an introduction to early materials and technology.* London, ISBN 0-212-35918-5.
Upham, N.E.
1983 *Anchors.* Aylesbury, ISBN 0-85263-636-9.

iii. ecofacts

Brothwell, D.
1981 *Digging up Bones.* Oxford ISBN 0198585101.
Chaplin, R.E.
1971 *The Study of Animal Bones from Archaeological Sites.* Seminar Press.
Dimbleby, G.
1967 *Plants and Archaeology.* London.

Evans, J.G.
1978 *An Introduction to Environmental Archaeology.* St Albans, ISBN 0246115955.
Kenchington, T.J. *et al.*
1989 The indispensability of non-artefactual data in underwater archaeology. In Barto Arnold III, J. (ed), *The Underwater Archaeological Proceedings from the Society for Historical Archaeology Conference, Baltimore.*
Magendans, J.F.C.
1987 The identification of vegetable material: tobacco from the 'Amsterdam'. In J.H.G. Gawronski (ed.) *Annual Report of the VOC-Schip "AMSTERDAM" Foundation, 1986.* ISBN 90-71690-02-4.
Osborne, P.J.
1973 Insects in Archaeological Deposits. *Science & Archaeology* 10, 4-6.
Renfrew, J., Monk, M., and Murphy, P.
1976 *First Aid for Seeds.* Rescue Publication No. 6, Hertford.
Wheeler, A. and Jones, A. K. G.
1989 *Fishes.* Cambridge Manual In Archaeology, Cambridge.

c. dating

Aitken, M.J.
1990 *Science-Based Dating in Archaeology.* London, ISBN 0582-05498-2.
Clark, A.
1987 *Scientific Dating Techniques.* Institute of Field Archaeologists, Technical Paper No.5, Birmingham, ISBN 0948393041.
Eckstein, D.
1984 *Dendrochronological Dating.* Handbooks for Archaeologists No.2, European Science Foundation, Strasbourg, ISBN 2903148392.
Fletcher, J.
1978 *Dendrochronology in Europe. Principles, interpretations and applications to archaeology and history.* British Archaeological Reports IS 51, Oxford.

55

Gillespie, R.
  1984   *Radiocarbon User's Handbook.*
  Oxford University Committee for
  Archaeology, Monograph no.3, Oxford,
  ISBN 0-947816-03-8.
Harris, E.C.
  1989   *Principles Of Archaeological
  Stratigraphy.* 2nd edition, London, ISBN
  0-12-326651-3.
Mook, W.G., and Waterbolk, H.T.
  1985   *Radiocarbon Dating.* Handbooks
  for Archaeologists No.3, European Science
  Foundation, Strasbourg, ISBN 2-903148-
  44-9.

d. The importance of site environment and site formation processes

Clarke, D. L.
  1978   *Analytical Archaeology.* Bristol,
  ISBN 0-416-85460-5.
Ferrari, B. J. and Adams, J. A.
  1990   Biogenic modifications of marine
  sediments and their influence on
  archaeological material. *IJNA* 19.2: 139-
  151.
Muckelroy, K.
  1977   Historic wreck sites in Britain
  and their environments. *IJNA* 6.1: 47-57.
Murphy, L. E.
  1990   *8SL 17: Natural site formation
  processes of a multiple-component
  underwater site in Florida, Submerged
  Cultural Resources Special Report.*
  Southwest Cultural Resources Centre,
  Sante Fe, New Mexico.
Parker, A. J.
  1981   Stratification and contamination
  in Ancient Mediterranean shipwrecks.
  IJNA, 10.4: 309-335.
Rodgers, B.A.
  1989   The case for biologically induced
  corrosion at the Yorktown shipwreck
  archaeological site, *IJNA,* 18.4: 335-340.
Schiffer, M. B.
  1987   *Formation Processes of the
  Archaeological Record.* Albuquerque.
  ISBN 0-8263-0963-1.

56

5. Project Planning

5.1. The Importance of Planning

5.2. Research Designs and Fieldwork Strategies in Archaeology Underwater

5.3. Planning the Work

5.4. Strategies for Investigation: Putting the Plans into Action

5.5. Safety on Archaeological Sites Underwater

5.6. Legislation: Playing by the Rules

5.7. Suggested Reading

5.1. The Importance of Planning

There is no replacement for thorough planning where fieldwork is concerned. Planning revolves around answering the following questions: Why is the work being done? How is the work going to be achieved safely and to a high archaeological standard? How are the results of the work going to be processed, stored and made available to other researchers? Anyone considering archaeological fieldwork underwater needs to aim at achieving three things before actually commencing the work:

i) A clear (written down) idea of WHY the work is being undertaken.

ii) Suitable experience, expertise and facilities to achieve an acceptable standard of archaeological work.

iii) Suitable experience, expertise and facilities to achieve an acceptable standard of archaeological work underwater.

Archaeological sites underwater vary in character. Two sites which may be similar in terms of age and type can present very different problems in terms of their investigation. The key word in planning archaeological work is flexibility.

Most practical difficulties underwater can be overcome with time and patience combined with thorough planning and disciplined methods. Archaeological experience and background knowledge are of great importance in maintaining a high standard and in dealing with complex and unusual archaeological deposits. The value of gaining a broad range of experience, including working on archaeological sites on land, has already been noted. Similarly, reading reports produced by others doing similar work will certainly help to develop an appreciation of the difficulties which are likely to arise. Discussing your intended project with workers who are already familiar with the techniques you plan to employ can be very

valuable. Make contact with other researchers. It furthers the spread of information and it is often a good opportunity to learn from other peoples' mistakes.

5.2. Research Designs and Fieldwork Strategies in Archaeology Underwater

It is now common practice to formalise fieldwork plans into a written document called a 'research design'. Previously, planning was mostly in the minds of the people involved, with only limited points committed to paper. In the majority of cases however, fieldwork can be improved if details of the plans are written down and circulated to team members for constructive comment prior to beginning work. The research design also provides a framework for checking progress during the project, just as in business projections of profit and production are used to check on a company's performance.

5.2.1. Research designs

A research design will normally be much more than a statement of intent. It should also set out reasons for the proposed activity, and how the aims are to be achieved (the fieldwork strategy). A good research design for an archaeological project will refer to all stages of the investigation, from the initial ideas to the arrangements for publication.

Although there are no definitive rules setting out what should be included in a research design, the following elements are suggested (*cf.* Dean 1988):

    i. Reasons for undertaking the project,
    ii. Key aims and questions,
    iii. Fieldwork strategy,
    iv. Projected timetable,
    v. Availability of personnel/equipment/money,
    vi. Recording system,
    vii. Fieldwork methods,
    viii. Conservation arrangements,
    ix. Post-fieldwork research,

    x. Eventual destination of records and material,
    xi. Publication plans,
    xii. Publicity.

One advantage of a rigorous and comprehensive research design is that it encourages full discussion of the less attractive aspects of the proposed project. The action of writing down precise details of funding, team organisation, responsibilities, conservation needs and so on ensures that these areas are properly considered and catered for before any work takes place.

A good research design is the best way to show people that the project is worthwhile, and that you and your team are fully prepared to do a thoroughly competent job. This is of particular assistance if you are seeking money or support from outside organisations.

One aspect of research designs which is often neglected is that they will demonstrate to people in the future not just what you were thinking but how you were thinking. Archaeology underwater is still developing as a subject, and there is much that we do not know. When people look back on the work we have done, they may be amazed at the decisions we have made. It will be more understandable if we can make clear our point of view, our general understanding of the situation, and the constraints acting upon us.

No one can predict all the circumstances which will eventually affect a project. Research designs are not a magic solution. Although they may help you to avoid some of the more common problems, unexpected developments may require alterations to fieldwork strategies. It is a poor fieldworker who sticks to one course of action when other, more effective options become available to achieve the aims of the research.

a. Reasons for undertaking fieldwork

Archaeological fieldwork can be roughly divided into two main categories: "Research" and "Rescue".

Research archaeology implies that a gap in our knowledge has been identified. The fieldworker believes that the gap can be filled effectively by consulting the material record (in other words physically investigating a site). Due to the limited resources available to archaeology in general, most research archaeology (certainly in the UK) is search and survey work for sites and monuments records rather than excavation.

Research archaeology is aimed at answering specific questions about aspects of past human activity. These questions may have developed through the researcher's study of the existing body of information in publications or site archives. While research excavations on a stable and un-threatened site might fill those gaps, it is often possible to identify a site which is actively under threat and which might provide answers to the same questions during a rescue excavation.

Although problem-orientated investigations are important, it is totally unacceptable to focus on one type of material or one stage in a site's development to the point where other classes of information are treated less sensitively. No class of evidence exists in total isolation. For example, on a project seeking to study a ship's structure, sediments and contents should not be less well studied.

Once the decision has been made to investigate a site because it is likely to answer the researcher's specific questions, it might be argued that the only valid approach to the work on that site is to recover as much of the available information as is possible from the area under consideration. When the investigation is over, the relevant information for answering the specific questions can be extracted. Future researchers who might have different questions to ask will then have access to a full record of the site, not just a set of clues biased towards one specific problem.

Rescue archaeology (or salvage archaeology, as it is sometimes known) is carried out because a site is about to be destroyed or damaged by some action or process that is difficult to prevent. Underwater, there can be numerous threats to the archaeological remains *e.g.* aggregate extraction, civil engineering construction and natural erosion. The only way to save any of the information will be to record the threatened remains in as much detail as possible in the time allowed. The resulting documentation and site archive will help ensure that at least some of the information contained within the site will survive for the benefit of future generations (referred to by many archaeologists as 'preservation by record').

Most rescue work will be 'against the clock' so there will not be enough time to record everything which is threatened in absolute detail. This problem of targetting recording applies to both sites and the elements of chosen sites. The fieldworkers must focus their efforts on what they believe to be the most important evidence. This allocation of priorities must be developed in the same way as research questions.

There are many different degrees of research and rescue. Even so "Rescue Archaeology" and "Research Archaeology" can, in some cases, be identified as distinct branches of the subject. At the present time it is not desirable to encourage too much "Research Archaeology" because:

i. so many sites require rescue

ii. the conservation ethic demands that we do not damage sites if there is any alternative. In many cases we can use sites which are being damaged to research specific questions.

b. Fieldwork strategies

The fieldworker needs to put together a package of techniques which will be effective in answering the key questions and achieving stated aims. The package is known as a fieldwork strategy. The aims and research questions of a project will focus on particular sets of information; different techniques supply different sorts of information, so the research design will determine which techniques are necessary, *e.g.* questions relating to non-artefactual remains will require sampling. Some techniques will require the support of further techniques. For example, excavation should be accompanied by all forms of recording.

In many cases the fieldworker will have several options which will meet the *aims*, and *capabilities* become the main issue. On a site threatened by erosion, for example, the fieldworkers could excavate and record the whole site to pre-empt further loss of information, or they could continually re-survey the site as it reveals itself. The decision will depend on the time, personnel, equipment, and money available.

The options will also result in differing degrees of impact on the site being investigated. The mere presence of divers can disturb the equilibrium that has preserved a site. Some techniques have far greater impact than others. Excavation, for example, destroys its subject. Even so, the use of excavation presents many options itself -– it may be possible to achieve the aims of the project by partial, rather than total, excavation. Careful consideration might indicate that a combined survey and sampling programme will produce similar results, leaving the site largely intact. Field surveys have the advantage of being 'heritage friendly' because archaeological evidence is not destroyed during its study. Even the most careful and systematic dismantling of a deposit as part of a research programme must be clearly justified.

Time is an important factor in determining a fieldwork strategy, both in absolute terms and in the way in which it is organised. Provided that it is remembered that environmental conditions influence archaeological work underwater much more than on land, it might be possible to estimate accurately how much time it would take to achieve a project aim. It will require thought to decide the optimum strategy for applying that time – *i.e.* should 90 days' work be done in one season, or over the summer weekends of three years? All the factors mentioned in the research design could depend on this vital question.

5.3. Planning the Work

Whichever method or style of investigation is proposed there are some general considerations and organisational factors which must be taken into account.

5.3.1. General considerations

In preparation for any work, it is important to establish what other studies have been carried out in the area (hydrographic, geological and biological, as well as any historical or archaeological research). Although some organisations which commission research may see the results as a commercial asset not for free distribution, many others will make their results available to *bona fide* scientific projects. It is worth trying to collect as much of this sort of first hand information as possible as it can influence the selection of the search or investigation procedures. Before deciding on the most suitable approach, it is well worth visiting the intended work area. Important information about the area may not have been brought to your notice and second hand information can often be unsatisfactory.

The more detail there is in the research design formulated for work in the field (and after), the more effective planning can be. When doing this it is important to remember that practical issues can have more influence on work underwater than they do on land, and these must be given consideration when planning for both remote sensing and diving operations. These factors will include the following:

  i. The objective of the work
  ii. The size of the area under investigation
  iii. The size and characteristics of expected discoveries
  iv. The condition of site(s)
  v. The local environment

vi. The restraints on boat use and diving operations

vii. The time and resources available

viii. The personnel available.

5.3.2. Logistics and equipment

Anyone who has been on a diving trip is well aware of the amount of equipment required to get just one person safely into the water. If that is multiplied by the number of participants in a project and added to the equipment required for survey or excavation work, the pile of equipment builds up very rapidly. Few projects supply all the necessary equipment, and if project members are expected to bring their own diving or other equipment then that should be made absolutely clear to them.

Specific requirements for surveying equipment, compressors to run excavation equipment and the excavation tools themselves are dealt with elsewhere. Attention should be paid to safe transport and storage of equipment during project work and returning borrowed equipment promptly and in good working order. This makes it easier to borrow next time. Ensuring that everything is where it should be when it is wanted and in working order is no small feat of organisation, and appointing an individual with the right experience to supervise this aspect of project planning can pay considerable dividends.

5.3.3. Working platforms

What is going to be used as the base for the work? Various types of boat will often be appropriate, but it is worth giving some thought to potential alternatives at the planning stage. Smaller open boats such as inflatables can often be more than adequate for survey work provided the equipment used is relatively compact, robust, and splash proof. Similarly, if survey work is going to be carried out among or near to rocks, then a highly mobile small inflatable might be more suitable than a larger hard-boat when it comes to deploying and picking up divers.

Some survey work relies on more vulnerable equipment. Deploying remote sensing equipment can sometimes require covered cabin space. Make sure that you find out just how waterproof the equipment you intend to use really is, especially if the equipment is be linked to a computer to record the information directly onto disk. If in any doubt keep it in the cabin. In addition, check that the boat you intend to use is able to supply the appropriately rated power supply for the equipment. An independent generator may have to be used which will need extra space. Ear protectors should be available for anyone working near such noisy machinery.

If excavation is considered, the requirements tend to be even more specific. Space can become a problem as diving equipment competes with pumps, tools and finds-processing areas, not to mention the need to keep areas dry and clear for record keeping. A somewhat larger boat may be needed for this phase of the project than for survey. The need for pumps or compressors will also affect the choice of work platform. Not only is space required, but, as with generators, such equipment can be very noisy and even harmful to hearing over long periods. An ability to operate pumps below decks or even from a smaller boat moored away from the main vessel is an advantage and can dramatically reduce stress levels. Safe storage areas for finds and records should be given priority. Covered space kept dry and clear of diving equipment is at a premium.

Boats are not the only option. Projects have been conducted very successfully from more permanent structures, such as coffer-dams, when the site is close to the shore (Figure 33). These structures have advantages in terms of deployment of equipment and access to the site but they can be very expensive to construct, maintain and remove. There is also the danger of driving piles through parts of the site which were not detected in pre-construction survey work. Other alternatives include unpowered

Figure 31. Working platforms – On a shallow site a scaffolding platform can carry equipment, help support divers above delicate areas of the site and give protection from other water users. (5.3.3.) (Courtesy of National Museum of Wales.)

barges or pontoons moored over the site. Both can provide a great deal of working space but will obviously have to be backed up by boat transport to the shore. Establishing sufficiently secure moorings to leave such platforms anchored on site for long periods can be problematic and emergency plans for bringing them to safety in the event of bad weather should be established. Lockable storage on a platform left on site can make preparing for work and packing up at the end of a session much easier as equipment can be left in place.

Cost will often be the main factor in determining what sort of work platform is used, but be broad-minded - space and stability are at a premium, however they are achieved.

5.3.4. Planning and preservation conditions

The need to study the physical, chemical and biological characteristics of an archaeological site has already been noted (Section 4.5). Knowledge gained from an appreciation of the influence of environmental factors on the preservation of different types of material can be useful in the planning stage of a project, particularly if excavation is considered.

It may be useful to try and predict the types of objects and materials which might be encountered given the prevailing conditions on site. For example, a site covered by deep silt is more likely to produce substantial elements of wooden structure than one characterised by a rocky seabed

Figure 32. A well organised, tidy deck is essential if confusion and hazards are to be avoided. A: finds processing:– putting finds into boxes, labelling and bagging up finds; B: diver writing up logs; C: diver in the process of being briefed before entering the water; D: support being provided to diver by finds assistant; E: wet storage area; F: diver returning to surface with boxed finds recovered from the site; G: adequate supply of packing and labelling materials; H: kit and cylinders well stored.

with little sediment. Plans for recording and conservation can be made accordingly, although any preparations should be flexible enough to cater for the unexpected.

It may also be useful to try and predict the presence of contexts which are going to be suitable for sampling (*e.g.* for botanical remains: middens and cess pits on flooded land sites, deck and bilge deposits on shipwreck sites). Specialist analysis and facilities can then be arranged. Environmental evidence is often destroyed or missed because it is not looked for. Explicitly considering the potential for the survival for these types of material at the planning stage makes this less likely.

5.3.5. Planning for photography

Photography is so useful a technique for survey and recording that any project is likely to be able to make use of it. But planning is still required. At a basic level the requirement to have a camera available at all times should be considered at an early stage. Different conditions will require different equipment (*e.g.* flash, a variety of lenses). Discussing the type of photographs likely to be required and the conditions they are likely to be taken in with an experienced photographer should enable a basic list of specific requirements to be made.

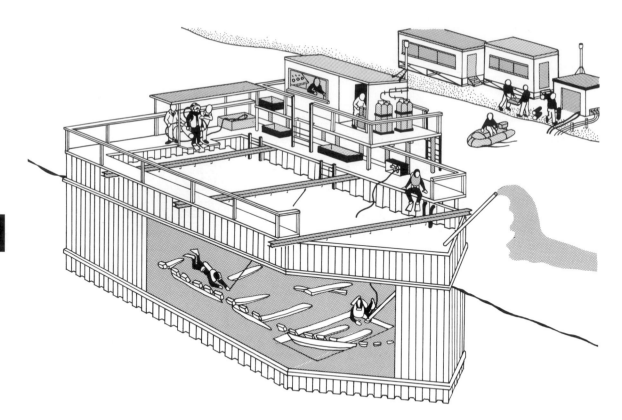

Figure 33. Working platforms – an example of the use of a coffer-dam. (5.3.3.) (After the Yorktown Shipwreck Archaeology Project.)

If you intend to develop film in the field then facilities must be arranged. If you intend to process the film at a later date then a safe way of storing the film should be arranged, especially in a hot or dusty climate.

5.3.6. Planning for conservation

Facilities for conservation should be organised well in advance of disturbance to a site. Expert advice should be sought at an early stage and, if resources allow, a trained conservator is the obvious choice for undertaking this task. It is never possible to predict every type of material that will appear, but experience from other sites will allow some judgement of the type of facilities required. Many projects, even quite large ones, are unlikely to be able to deal easily with every problem.

The treatment of large iron objects by hydrogen reduction or the freeze-drying of waterlogged timber will require specialised facilities. If objects of this type are likely to require treatment of that nature, then the planning stage should include making contact with operators of the relevant equipment. You should ensure that they are able to cope with the material and that you are aware of any special conditions or requirements.

Many objects, especially particularly large or complex ones, may not be conserved immediately. Secure space for storage in stable conditions must be arranged along with the tanks or containers in which they will be kept. Particularly large objects may require mechanical lifting devices for handling.

PLANS

PHOTOGRAPHS

FINDS

FINDS

DIVE LOGS

FINDS

DIARY

SECTIONS

Figure 34. When planning work in the field consider the work afterwards too. Failure to do this may cause a crisis in space and resources. (5.3.8.)

5.3.7. Planning for processing and publishing

The most expertly organised and executed fieldwork is worth little if the information gained is not thoroughly analysed and made available to other researchers. Of course, the precise nature of information retrieved from a project cannot be predicted at the outset; the amount of time and resources that will have to be committed to processing information and producing a report may only become clear as the work progresses or nears completion. However, that is not to say that such considerations can be left until the work is completed before they are addressed. If material appears that is likely to require a specialist report as part of the publication, arrangements should be made promptly – do not assume that the relevant specialist will be ready to drop everything to produce a report to fit in with your schedule or that they will be willing to work for free.

One of the most important aspects of this area of planning is time allocation. Post-fieldwork processing and publication is a very time consuming business. A day in the field can produce results which will take a week or more to process (often much more). Another consideration is equally simple but vital – space. Make sure that there is somewhere available and suitable to do the work – dry, clean and warm! Easy access to standard office equipment, including word-processing facilities, will be an enormous help (as will someone who can type). Many projects will not be able to assemble all of the required equipment in one place but making use of favours from a number of sources can achieve the same end, although co-ordinating the work is slightly harder if it is spread around various locations.

It should be borne in mind that 'post-fieldwork processing' such as drawing and photography should begin immediately after an object has been raised, so that details which might not survive through the conservation stage can be recorded. This means that people and facilities ought to be available for processing even while the fieldwork is continuing.

5.3.8. Planning for archive storage

The assembled records and archaeological material from a project must be stored somewhere accessible to future researchers. The archive of a project will be complex and demanding both on the size and quality of storage (Figure 34). Before work is undertaken plans must be made for a suitable store. If it is expected that a museum will take the archive they must be consulted!

5.3.9. Team organisation

It has already been noted that no one individual has all the skills (or stamina) required to manage and undertake every aspect of an archaeological project. Recruiting project members with the appropriate range of expertise and the ability to work together is an important part of the planning stage of an investigation.

There are many ways in which teams can be organised. A single person taking overall responsibility for archaeological and management decisions being only one. Projects have been organised on a committee basis with varying degrees of success just as dominant single personalities are not always appropriate. In some larger projects it is useful to separate management of the personnel on a day to day basis from the archaeological direction of the work, although an aloof and dictatorial figure issuing directives on how the work is to be carried out without regular contact with the team is unlikely to win the affection of colleagues.

Many projects find that a strong archaeological direction linked to the effective use of supervisors to implement the detail of the work is effective as long as good communication is maintained across the whole of the team organisation. People want

to know why they are doing something and they deserve to be told. The project leader should be able to co-operate with other institutions and people at planning, 'field' and post-excavation stages of any operation. Appointment of a deputy can be helpful in sharing administrative obligations.

The management of any project involves the matching of appropriate personnel to the tasks generated by the work. This could involve the delegation of work to an existing team, or importing specific expertise to match the requirements of the operation. Clearly, effective management of the personnel is crucial to the success of a project. Making the most of the expertise and enthusiasm available, and applying the right amount of pressure to each team member, is a solid foundation on which to build a good working environment. This requires an open mind, the ability to discuss developments freely and the willingness to give encouragement when it is needed. Team members are likely to respond well if they feel that they are valued and making a significant contribution. Achieving this often relies on carefully matching experience and aptitude to the available tasks, as well as giving team members the chance to gain new skills without feeling frustrated by what they perceive as a lack of ability.

In many projects the lack of resources will prevent access to a full range of expertise. For instance, scientific analysis can be very expensive if a commercial rate has to be paid. It is sometimes possible for members of a team to learn some basic skills, but project organisers must realise that if they do not have sufficient resources to conduct a research excavation properly it is better to concentrate on non-destructive activities, such as survey.

If individual talents of members of a team are to be used to advantage, flexibility in the team structure will be necessary. However, it is important for the project leader to ensure that responsibilities are defined and compatible with the overall aims, and that the operation is kept under control and to an accepted time schedule. It is also important to build enough flexibility into the schedule to allow team members to spend time learning and practising new skills.

Planning, including the devising of a detailed research design, will identify the work-force requirement necessary at various stages during the project. It is better to identify the specific tasks likely to arise during all stages of the project, and then allocate them to team members and external consultants if necessary. It is poor management to build up a team and then hope that they will be able to cope with the task successfully.

a. Specific responsibilities

On any project it may be necesary for specific responsibilities to be allcated to individuals (further information on roles can be gained from relevant sections of this guide). Responsibilities may include:

    i. Logistics (Section 5.3.2)

    ii. Diving organisation and safety (Section 5.5)

    iii. Boat-handling and maintenance

    iv. Domestic organisation

    v. Finds handling (Section 11.2)

    vi. Recording (Section 6.0)

    vii. Environmental and scientific archaeology (Section 10.2)

    viii. Photography (Section 9.5)

b. Specialists

In archaeological investigations, a number of specialists may have to be consulted. The best solution would be to have them all permanently on-site. If this is not possible then means of obtaining guidance should be established and one person given specific responsibility for maintaining the link. Specialists, either on-site or available for consultation, might include:

    i. an archaeological scientist

    ii. a finds specialist

    iii. an archaeological conservator

    iv. an archaeological illustrator

Locating such people is not always easy and the person with the greatest knowledge of a particular type of find may not necessarily be found in a major institution. The background research that you carried out to formulate your research design will have indicated the individuals or organisations with interests in the relevant areas.

It is important to realise that the best specialist is not necessarily the one who tells you what you want to hear.

Specialists will make contributions throughout the duration of the project. For example, someone who is particularly knowledgeable about ships' structure may require to dive on the site as well as examine survey drawings. So do not wait for any particular stage before seeking expert help and advice.

c. Volunteers

Much of the work on many projects is undertaken by volunteers and this source of labour is likely to remain essential. These people can range from complete novices looking for a new interest to vastly experienced fieldworkers with high levels of expertise. They are a valuable resource and it is a foolish project director who ignores their potential. A diver may not be a full-time archaeologist but may possess photographic skills at a professional level – so make use of their abilities. However, projects are undertaken with a serious aim and the requirements of a volunteer looking for recreation are not always compatible with the demands of project work, especially when time is running short or conditions are difficult. Good communication can make participation in a project enjoyable and instructive without compromising the work. Sometimes you just have to take pleasure in the end result.

Many projects reserve the right to ask a team member not to dive if their equipment does not satisfy the diving officer in terms of being fit to use, particular attention being paid to test dates for breathing air cylinders. If some equipment is to be provided, then it is worth informing everyone which sort of adaptors or hose fittings are attached to project equipment so that everyone can try to ensure that their suits, demand valves etc. are compatible.

You should be insured when taking part in any diving or archaeological activities. The question of insurance is a particular problem on part-time projects where much relies on goodwill. Whatever arrangements any project claims to have made, take out personal insurance. Make sure it covers you for the country you will be in, the activities you will be undertaking and the work practices you will be following. If the project's practices do not fulfil the conditions of your insurance it is foolish to take part.

5.3.10. Costs

The cost of the projected work must be given full and thorough consideration. Are sufficient funds available to undertake the work effectively and safely? Clearly many survey-based projects are likely to be far cheaper than those involving excavation. Moreover, once the fieldwork is over, are there sufficient funds to finance the post-excavation processing and storage of material? If funding is not available for this phase of the project, then it is irresponsible to undertake the fieldwork without very good reason. This is especially true if any disturbance to a site is being considered.

The variety of costs incurred can be surprising *e.g.* fuel, photocopying, chemicals, spare parts, insurance, accommodation (for workers, finds, records, equipment), travel, postage, specialists' expenses, telephone bills. Even part-time projects have to consider such expenditure.

The potential cost of conservation requires particular attention. Conservation work cannot be undertaken cheaply and treatments are expensive in time, expertise and materials. Even after conservation, objects must be stored or displayed under secure and environmentally controlled conditions. Large projects which have produced many finds can require large budgets and full-time staff members to deal with the conservation. It is not acceptable to be selective and only deal with the material which appears to be attractive or immediately informative. Raising material involves a commitment to its care and study. Raising an object and then searching round for someone who will conserve it for free is not good practice, but it often happens, much to the annoyance of overworked professional conservators who are accused of being unhelpful when they explain repeatedly that they do not have the time or resources to take on additional unpaid work.

5.4. Strategies for Investigation: Putting the Plans into Action

While drawing up the plans which will allow some effective fieldwork to take place, working methods should also be planned. Careful consideration should be given to the way in which information is to be retrieved whether the project is a survey or an excavation.

5.4.1. Searching for specific sites

What is the object of the search? Whether the aim is to locate a specific site or to search an area to gain information on the nature and amount of archaeological material present, explicit strategies should be formulated so that all involved are clear about the objectives of the exercise.

Strategies employed in the search for a single site can be made more effective by using existing information. Historical sources, local tradition or reports from fishermen can all be useful. Information about location will help define the search area. Search techniques will be influenced by the possible characteristics of the site. The more reliable and precise this information, the simpler the search strategy.

Unfortunately, few people who have attempted to locate such sites have been able to do so without difficulty, even when records of the vessel's loss included references to prominent features still visible today. Strategies for searches of this nature are likely to include tracing place-names that may no longer be used, and calculations of the influence of prevailing conditions and the movement of surviving material way from where the loss was recorded as having taken place. It is also worth remembering that because no official records of salvage exist, it does not mean that unofficial and unreported looting has not occurred.

5.4.2. Survey strategies for investigating an area

Given that pin-point locations will rarely be available for sites, searches intended to be site specific will often include elements of area survey. Area or regional survey requires a quite different approach as the aim is to investigate the range and extent of archaeological material in a given part of the seabed. This means that search strategies will have to be developed which have the ability to detect the full range of potential materials present. In the search for a specific site which is known to have a large number of iron guns aboard, a magnetometer (Section 8.1.3) is a very useful piece of equipment. Running the magnetometer over an area is likely to give an accurate indication of whether or not the target site is there. However, what it will not pick up is other archaeological material which does not cause a magnetic anomaly. Therefore in a search to assess an area it is clearly not suitable as the only method of detection.

Other methods of search and survey are described in Sections 7.0 and 8.0. Whichever methods are used in such a search, it is unlikely that every item of archaeological significance in an area will be detected. The most we can hope for is to deploy a sufficient range of techniques to give us the best chance of detecting the widest range of material, and this will include diver searches as well as remote sensing methods. It is important to be fully aware of classes of material that will not be detected by the available techniques and to make such deficiencies clear in any report.

In an ideal world, a regional search would involve covering every part of the targeted area. This is rarely possible due to time and logistical constraints. If the whole area cannot be covered then a strategy for collecting useful information from only parts of it must be formulated.

The strategy for choosing areas to be searched can be random or targeted to different degrees. Statistically random searches attempt to remove subjective influences, permitting critical assessment of site distribution. Established procedures for achieving random samples are available (Mueller 1975). Targeted searches address an area which, because of perceived characteristics of preservation, is considered likely to hold remains. Targeted searches may also be aimed at areas where a threat is known to exist.

Random and targeted searches can be combined. You may wish to target a series of areas where ship losses, for example, are likely to have occurred. You may then select a search area from this series at random. Alternatively, the region may be sub-divided into seabed types and a random sample of each category surveyed in detail. It is essential that the process used to make the choice is made explicit in the research design and any reports generated.

5.4.3. On-site survey strategies

Once a site has been found a survey of some form can be carried out. The strategy adopted for surveying a site is usually straightforward – to achieve as accurate and complete a record of the site as is possible without disturbing it. As is made clear in Section 9.0 this can involve a wide range of techniques.

STUDLAND BAY WRECK SB1   **DIVER REGISTRATION FORM**

NAME	H.A.M.S.A.C. MEMBER	YES	NO

ADDRESS	IF A MEMBER OF ANY OTHER S.A.C. STATE CLUB

ORGANISATION REPRESENTED:

TEL No.

MALE	FEMALE

MEDICAL   ADDRESS

DIVING QUALIFICATIONS

OTHER RELEVANT SKILLS

TEL. No.

WHEN AVAILABLE

OFFICE USE ONLY
LOG BOOK CHECKED

ALL DIVERS MUST BE LICENSED BEFORE DIVING, ONE WEEK'S NOTICE NEEDED.
MEMBERSHIP OF S.A.A. AND B.S.A.C. OR EQUIVALENT IS ESSENTIAL.

Figure 35. Example of a diver registration form. Diving operations should be carried out within the competence of team members. Where volunteers are new to a project it is sensible to get their diving and other relevant qualifications in writing. (Courtesy of the Studland Bay Wreck Project.)

Some decisions do have to be made. For example, if a number of sites are discovered during an area survey in advance of gravel extraction, how much time can be spent on each site? Time and money might be running short, and perhaps only a few sites perceived to be the most important can have substantial resources committed to them. It may be necessary to narrow down the immediate priorities of the survey work and to decide that an assessment of the extent, date and cohesion of each site is more important in these circumstances than a complete measured survey. A considered, informed decision on which sites should receive further attention could then be taken.

Where a single, non-threatened site is discovered, there is no need whatsoever to compromise in this way. Survey strategies will still be dictated to some extent by available resources and equipment, but this should only affect the mechanics and schedule of the work (not the end result) as effective survey projects do not necessarily require substantial resources.

The methods involved in the collection of this evidence are covered more fully in Section 9.0, but commonly used procedures include:

a. Establishing the extent of the site by extending systematic searches well away from any readily apparent concentrations of material detected visually or through the application of remote sensing equipment.

b. Setting up fixed reference points in appropriate places and labelling them (Section 9.2.7).

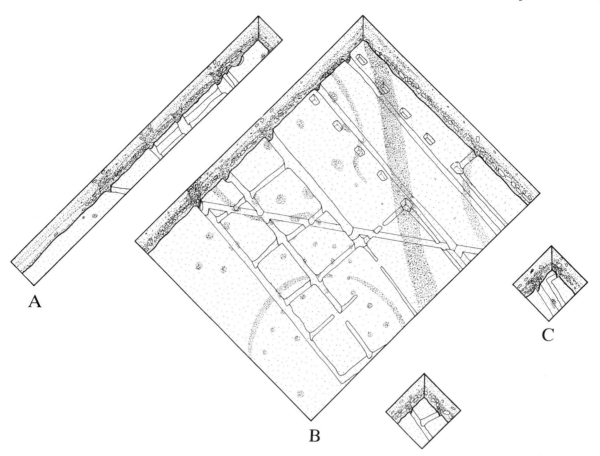

A

C

B

Figure 36. Excavation strategies: an example of the way different strategies will provide varying levels of information: A, trench; B, area; C, test pit. The more comprehensive coverage of the area excavation must be balanced against the extra resources needed and the greater destruction to the archaeological resource. (5.4.4.) (Drawing by K.Watson.)

c. Drawing the distribution of archaeological material that has been detected (Section 9.3), together with any other useful information, *e.g.* topography (Section 9.4.6).

d. Carrying out metal detector and other remote sensing surveys. These can, among other things, identify concentrations of ferrous material without disturbance to the site. Such exercises are only valid when carried out systematically, and in a manner which allows the location of anomalies to be accurately recorded.

e. Recording as much information with video and stills photography as possible, to support information collected in other ways (Section 9.5).

5.4.4. Excavation strategies

When excavation is justified, various strategies can be employed, and each must be evaluated in terms of the balance between information retrieval and impact on the surviving remains. The most destructive option, total excavation, might not be necessary. Many excavation strategies involve some form of sampling, using test pits, trenches or larger, more open areas (Figure 36).

a. How large a sample to excavate?

i. Sampling

The aim of sampling by excavation is the recovery of information which will allow reliable inferences to be drawn about the site with the minimum of damage to the total available evidence. The practical benefits include a smaller scale commitment (in terms of time, resources, conservation and storage responsibilities etc.) compared to total excavation.

The location and size of the sample units will require careful consideration. Relevant factors might include: the particular aims of the sampling strategy, the extent of evidence as revealed by previous work, the resources available and on-site conditions.

Sampling by excavation is particularly useful in answering specific questions. It has been used to determine whether a structure represents the bow or stern of a vessel, to demonstrate a stratigraphic relationship between two contexts and to investigate whether there is an archaeological deposit below the surface sediment.

Sampling by excavation must be accompanied by an evaluation of how representative the sample is of the whole. In an ideal sample, all elements of the site would be represented in the same proportions as they exist in the whole. The sample achieved must be judged against this ideal. The results of this process will affect the confidence with which conclusions can be drawn from the evidence recovered. In general terms, reliability will increase with the coverage and relative size of the sample.

It is worth emphasising that sampling by excavation is only of value as part of a strategy based on a clear set of aims and questions relating to the site.

ii. Total excavation

Total excavation is a 100% sample, but anyone contemplating this strategy should ask themselves whether their aims could not be achieved with a smaller scale disturbance of the remains. An honest appraisal of the various factors involved might suggest that continuing the work after a certain point will simply duplicate information already retrieved. Can this be justified bearing in mind the additional costs involved in processing and conserving the material? It is certainly true that a larger excavation may produce a more complete picture of the site. However, this must be carefully balanced against the potential loss of evidence to other researchers and the diminishing returns of new information to the current investigator.

There are occasions when full scale excavation is more clearly justifiable, *e.g.*, in advance of the complete destruction of the site by gravel extraction. Even in these situations, a decision must be taken as to whether sufficient resources will be available to see the project through the potentially expensive phase of post-excavation work (Section 12.0).

b. Test pits, trenches and area excavation

There are various approaches to sampling by excavation and total excavation. Sampling often takes the form of several discrete excavations. Even total excavation is rarely practical in one operation. Excavations vary in size from small test pits to large areas. The size of the excavation is defined by various factors including the risks of exposing large areas of vulnerable material, the physical characteristics of the site, the concentration of the evidence and operational considerations such as access and safety. The overriding concern will be whether resources are available to support the amount of work proposed.

The more limited areas of excavation such as test pits and small trenches sometimes provide insufficient evidence to answer the research questions involved while still being destructive. Key relationships can be destroyed without a significant gain in information. The possibility of significant damage being done to a site without a

Figure 37. Surface support vessels on an archaeological expedition should be well organised, and equipped with standard safety equipment: a: first-aid kit, fire extinguisher, safety procedures (including lists of local coastguard addresses, local decompression chamber, telephone numbers and call signs) and exposure blanket; b: radio and flares in watertight container inside cabin; c: rigid 'A' flag; d: float for throwing; e: shot line; f: stand-by diver; g: rescue boat (manned); h: deck space kept as clear as possible to avoid accidents. Each team member, from log-keeper to look-out, should have clearly defined responsibilities (5.5.)

concomitant gain in information must be appreciated; they should therefore be used with great care.

Any strategy adopted should be the result of a careful consideration of all the factors and an attempt to address specific questions or achieve identified aims. Speculative trenching, or 'start at one end', aimless, total excavation is very unlikely to yield satisfactory results.

5.5. Safety on Archaeological Sites Underwater

The importance of safety during archaeological work underwater is paramount, Just as land excavations operate codes of safe practice, it is recommended that a 'code of diving practice' is adopted for each project. The recording of diving operations must be given as much emphasis as any other part of the project. Personal dive logs should be maintained, as well as a project log of dive times and conditions.

5.5.1. Codes of practice

The wide variety of conditions and working methods on different sites makes the universal adoption of any existing code difficult. Most archaeologists have in the past tended to work to the most suitable code available, and developed supplementary sets of rules particular to their project. Large projects in particular have found it necessary to write their own codes. As new techniques and procedures are adopted and developed, codes of practice will require updating. In addition, the regulations of governments with regard to the health and safety of those employed on diving operations will vary from country to country. Codes of practice for archaeological sites underwater would normally be drafted with reference to numerous sources (*e.g.* commercial, scientific and sport diving manuals), or they may use

a standard scientific diving code such as the *Code of Practice for Scientific Diving* produced by the Underwater Association (Gamble *et al.* 1989).

Some codes will be more suitable than others and in unusual circumstances more than one code will be in use on the same site. This can happen when two separate professional diving organisations are involved in one project and responsible for two different aspects of the work on site. It is far less complicated to have one specified code of practice and this is to be preferred but, whatever code is in use, it is important that everyone involved is familiar with its application.

5.5.2. Control of diving operations

The appointment of a controller of diving operations who has no direct responsibility for archaeological work, is a sensible arrangement on larger projects. This person, often referred to as the Diving Officer, has to organise, regulate and record the diving operations in a way that creates as safe a working environment on-site as is possible (Figure 38). It is a job, however, that requires tact as well as experience; ensuring safe diving without seeming overbearing or patronising takes considerable skill. Each individual diving operation may be controlled by a suitably qualified and experienced Diving Supervisor other than the Diving Officer.

The Diving Officer should be accessible to divers with queries or complaints about diving practice on-site and it is often useful to have full and open discussions about any incidents which occur, no matter how minor. Some people need prompting to voice anxieties, especially if they feel overawed or intimidated by other, more confident, but not necessarily competent, individuals. Don't wait for a serious incident before making an honest appraisal of how safe people feel with working arrangements.

STUDLAND BAY WRECK SB2 **DIVING OFFICERS LOG**

ARCHAEOLOGIST		DIVE LOG No.
DIVE MARSHALL	SKIPPER	DATE
SAFETY OFFICER		WEATHER FORECAST
SAFETY BOAT IN ATTENDANCE (FOR EVENTS SEE REVERSE) TIME IN	YES NO TIME OUT	SURFACE CONDITIONS
		TIDES
STATE OF SEA	SURFACE VIS.	UNDERWATER VIS.

DIVER	1st DIVE		2nd DIVE		3rd DIVE		TOTAL HOURS
	IN	OUT	IN	OUT	IN	OUT	
	AREA		AREA		AREA		

CONTINUATION SHEET USED   TICK

Figure 38. Example of a Diving Officer's Log. The DO's responsibilities for the smooth and safe running of the diving mean that keeping control of activities is vital. Good structured recording is the first step. (5.5.2.) (Courtesy of the Studland Bay Wreck Project.)

5.5.3. Potential diving problems and solutions

The individual diver is ultimately responsible for the standard of archaeological work achieved on-site. Any factor affecting the diver's efficiency will also affect the work and these should be minimised as far as possible. Factors to consider include:

a.   Physical problems

Physical problems include nitrogen narcosis, decompression, cold and exhaustion, visibility, equipment malfunction, poor communication, loss of dexterity, bad weather, water movement and current.

Cold is a common problem in archaeological work which requires the diver to be stationary for long periods. More insulation than would be used for a normal dive might therefore be required or, alternatively, shorter shifts can be worked in very cold water. The extent to which efficiency suffers as the diver becomes chilled, and the safety problems associated with cold, are well known. Clearly, there is nothing at all to be gained from allowing divers to become colder than is absolutely necessary.

b.   Psychological problems

Psychological problems include Impaired assimilation, recall and judgement, anxiety, over-enthusiasm leading to disregard for personal safety.

All the above can lead to poor standards of work as can lack of basic diving skills such as the ability to maintain neutral buoyancy. However, nothing is more important than the safety of the people involved.   Strict adherence to the spirit as well as the letter of any safety regulations combined with common sense is vital.

c.   Diving techniques

Sport diver training should be adequate for allowing a diver to operate safely within most projects, but there are some aspects of work underwater which are not covered in such training.   Some of these may even run contrary to some of the practices taught to sport divers.

The advantages of neutral buoyancy are rightly emphasised in terms of sport diving and good buoyancy control is at a premium when engaged in photography or the investigation of a delicate deposit. However, to be effective, some tasks and environments require the diver to be negatively buoyant

whilst actually working.   On occasions, provided it is within the Code of Practice in use on the site and prevailing environmental conditions allow it, divers may also find it easier to remove their fins when working. This can help to avoid accidental damage to archaeological material and increase the comfort of the diver when supported by a grid or rock. Similarly, diving with a partner is a mainstay of safe sport diving, but this is not always possible or practical in a working situation and alternative safety procedures will need to be implemented.   It is possible to draw a distinction between diving alone and working alone with other divers in the vicinity. Lone divers must have an effective means of communicating with the surface, and there should also be a standby diver ready to give assistance if necessary.   The most effective communication systems are by rope signals or hard-wire telephone between the diver and the surface.   Through-water communications, though less restrictive than an umbilical, are less effective, particularly if the diver is in the shadow of rocks or similar upstanding features.   On some sites it may be possible to allow divers to work alone provided there are adequate safeguards. If a number of divers are within a restricted area, and if each one is charged with periodic visual checks of the others, it may be possible to create a reasonably safe working environment. This can only be done where the visibility and other environmental factors make it feasible, and the divers are suitably experienced. Divers new to working alone sometimes tend to concentrate too much on their task and not pay sufficient attention to others around them.   In some circumstances it is possible to have safety divers touring the site to check on individuals.

The solution adopted will depend on the conditions on-site and the experience of the work-force, but it is important to ensure that no diver is pressured into adopting a practice they are not comfortable with. Alternatively divers should not feel worried about refusing to adopt procedures which they consider unsatisfactory. Some very experienced diving archaeologists prefer not to work alone unless connected directly with the surface, while others are happy to consider it if there are other divers on-site. It is also vital to remember that any diving procedure adopted conforms to the Code of Practice in use on the project, and that the procedure also complies with any local or national legislation that might apply.

5.5.4. Safety during excavation

If the work of the project involves excavation, there are additional safety factors which must be considered. An excavation, with pipes, hoses and lines in abundance, can be a daunting and unfamiliar place for the inexperienced worker who may spend more time worrying about safety than the job in hand. Likewise, the process of excavation can concentrate a diver's mind to the point where contents gauge and dive timer are not given due attention. Complacency is just as problematic as anxiety and neither contributes to a high standard of work. It makes sense, then, to introduce less experienced team members to such situations in a progressive way rather than simply hoping that they will cope. A lot should also be done in terms of rationalising the way that lines and hoses are placed on the site to avoid snags or confusion. Every one is a potential hazard and must be removed unless entirely necessary. As with many working situations, it is very useful to establish a shot line which is used for all ascents and descents. By establishing a fixed route to the site divers can get to work with minimum fuss.

During excavation care must be taken to ensure that no items of equipment or large objects capable of causing blockages are sucked into the mouth of an airlift or dredge. When the lower end of an airlift becomes blocked it rapidly becomes buoyant and will suddenly rush to the surface if not tethered. Less experienced divers should be carefully coached in safety procedures. A means of shutting off the airlift instantaneously must be within easy reach of the diver operating the equipment. For safety many divers have an octopus rig as a second supply of air, but these can be dangerous when used with an airlift. If the spare second stage gets sucked into the airlift, the air in the cylinder to which the valve is attached will be rapidly used up. Incidents of this nature have lead to fatalities.

There is no archaeological investigation in the world that is worth the health or lives of those involved in it. Those responsible for a project must avoid generating an atmosphere where people become willing to take risks and push their luck 'for the sake of the project'. Get the job done, but do it safely and effectively, even if that means taking a little longer.

5.6. Legislation: Playing by the Rules

It is important for the investigators of archaeological evidence underwater to be aware of the interest of public authorities in their activities. Most countries have laws relating to archaeological sites, and affecting work on those sites. The next five sections will consider the characteristics of legislation worldwide as applied to archaeology underwater.

5.6.1. Where the laws apply

The application of legislation to sites underwater depends on their position relative to land. The ability to make and enforce laws, or jurisdiction, is derived from the sovereignty of states. The sovereignty of a state is mainly focused on its land territory, but it also extends to a belt of sea adjacent to the coast.

The change from land to sea is very important because the laws are usually different on each side of the boundary. Unfortunately the natural boundary is not constant; tides move up and down the beach. The legal boundary is generally fixed at one state of the tide – high or low water. High and low water are not constant either, so you should check whether the reference is to the mean, spring mean or astronomical tide. Different definitions are used in different situations. The boundary can vary between countries, and between national and local rules within a single country. The definition may also vary according to purpose – high water for some rules and low water for others. It is particularly important that archaeologists on the foreshore know which definitions apply to their activities.

The notional lines on the beach have effects further out to sea, as they are used as the baselines for maritime zones such as the Territorial Sea. The baseline is usually the low water line as marked on large scale charts. In special circumstances baselines can be drawn off-shore, across estuaries and harbour works for example. Sand banks which only appear at low tide can also act as baselines. 'Straight baselines' can be drawn along coasts with many inlets or fringing islands.

Baselines out at sea are important because the sea on their landward side, referred to as Internal Waters, may be subject to specific laws. They will also extend the outer limit of the Territorial Sea so that it is more than the usual 12 nautical miles off-shore.

Archaeology underwater in lakes and rivers will normally be subject to terrestrial legislation, which may rely on completely different principles to maritime legislation. It is also possible that a different range of government or non-government authorities will be involved.

Looking to the sea the most important distinction concerns the limits of the Territorial Sea. The Coastal State has sovereignty in the Territorial Sea, so it can make laws and enforce them. There are a few limitations concerning the navigational rights of foreign ships; it may be difficult, for example, to declare a protected or exclusive area for archaeological purposes within a traditional shipping area.

It is probable that the coastal state will have exclusive control over activities such as archaeology in the Territorial Sea. This means that you should consult the relevant laws of that state. It is possible that some other state might claim a degree of control in the case of foreign shipwrecks. In Australia, for example, the continued interest of the Netherlands government in old Dutch shipwrecks was recognised in a formal meeting between the two states. In addition to laws governing the conduct of archaeology, there may be distinct provisions regarding ownership. We will consider ownership below, but at this stage it is important to note that the rules affecting ownership will largely depend on the law of the coastal state.

The outer limits of the Territorial Sea are usually twelve nautical miles from the baseline. Some states do not exercise any jurisdiction over archaeology underwater beyond the Territorial Sea. However, twelve nautical miles is not very far given the capabilities of modern boats, and there is plenty of activity beyond the Territorial Sea which can affect archaeology. Archaeology certainly does not respect the twelve nautical mile boundary. The types of control considered below may seem irrelevant when considering their furthest extent (200 nautical miles or more from the shore) but they are important where a site thirteen nautical miles off-shore would be otherwise unprotected.

The grounds which can be used to exercise control over archaeology beyond twelve nautical miles vary. One concept which is used by several countries is the Contiguous Zone (CZ). This is a belt of sea which extends no more than twenty-four nautical miles from the baseline in which the coastal state has certain rights. The United Nations Convention on the Law of the Sea (LOSC) specifically provides that states can consider archaeological remains in the CZ in the same way as remains in the Territorial Sea. The Council of Europe tried very hard to get many countries in Europe to apply this provision. Some countries have done so while others disagree with the interpretation of the LOSC, and some, such as the UK, recognize the principles but choose not to have a CZ.

The two other grounds on which coastal states can try to apply their laws to archaeology underwater are the existence of Continental Shelves (CS) and Exclusive Economic Zones (EEZ). Both the CS and the EEZ extend hundreds of miles off-shore. Coastal states have sovereign rights for certain purposes over the sea and seabed delimited under these principles. The rights are usually limited to extractive industries such as hydrocarbon and mineral exploration and fishing. Control can also be exercised over pollution in the EEZ.

The use of CS rights to control archaeology has been limited by an opinion of the International Law Commission in 1956 declaring that the rights certainly did not apply to shipwrecks. The validity of this statement could be questioned in that it pre-dates the first scientific archaeological investigations beneath the sea. The concept of the Continental Shelf has been used in the interests of archaeology as a by-product of established CS rights. Norwegian, US and Irish legislation, for example, require that off-shore activities, notably hydro-carbon exploration, take steps to avoid impacting archaeological sites.

The EEZ concept is relatively new and some countries, including the UK, do not accept the need for it. It is possible to use the concept indirectly to provide for archaeology beyond the TS in the same way as the CS: *i.e.* the activities in the EEZ should be conducted in a way which limits adverse effects on sites. EEZs could be used more creatively, given the growing identification of archaeology with the rest of the environment. Coastal states have rights in the EEZ for protecting and preserving the marine environment: this is a clear mandate for them to extend their control over archaeology within 200 nautical miles of the coast. Morocco has a law regulating excavation by foreign states or individuals within its EEZ.

Before moving on it is important to note that legislation is not always limited by distance. Jurisdiction can be extended on various grounds which can affect the conduct of archaeology.

In some legal traditions, nationals remain subject to the laws of their states wherever they are in the world. That is to say that a tourist might be prosecuted when they return home if they have broken their own state's laws in another country, even if it is not a crime in the country being visited. Ships also have nationality, so the flag state's laws apply to the activities of boats wherever they are, which could involve legislation relating to archaeology. The UK's Merchant Shipping Act provides an example of Port State jurisdiction. The Act is applied to material brought ashore in the UK, even if it was found outside the territorial sea.

5.6.2. Protection

The most direct laws affecting archaeology underwater are usually centred on protection and control. The law will state what you are allowed to do, what activities are prohibited, and what conditions must be satisfied in carrying out investigations. Such laws will frequently state their application, giving a legal definition of archaeology. This may not correspond to the definition of archaeology preferred by archaeologists. The law will also state which sea areas it applies to. There are very large variations between states within this general pattern.

There are several types of protection which might apply, all with different consequences for the archaeologist.

In some cases protection is limited to shipwrecks. Although most people are aware that archaeology underwater involves far more than wrecked vessels, many laws indicate a more restricted view. This may be inevitable when a discipline is still evolving, where there are specific needs for protection, and where there are constraints on official responsibilities.

Definition of the scope of a law is sometimes achieved by considering age. Laws often apply to sites older than a certain date (*e.g.* 1900, 1850), or they use an elapsed time (100 years, 5 years). The period might refer to the date of construction, or the date of submergence. Some laws do not rely on time, and apply to material considered to be of archaeological or historical importance, which requires a degree of discretion and selection. Ambiguity can be avoided by applying the law to 'embedded' material as in the US Abandoned Shipwreck Act 1987.

The application of protection to a site can vary. Some laws provide for the protection of an area while others just relate to the remains themselves. Treatment of remains may vary too. Norwegian law, for example, used to apply to all elements of a wrecked vessel except the cargo. Laws which apply to remains, rather than to an area, are most suitable for widely dispersed sites.

Some legislatures favour a form of 'blanket protection' whereas others serve to protect specific sites. Blanket protection is useful in that there is little ambiguity – if it is old it is protected. Such laws can be difficult to enforce. The major drawback with laws that require specific designation is that the authorities need to know about the site, and it may take some time to enact the designation order. The effect is to encourage secrecy and hurried activity by those who wish their operations to remain unrestricted by the law.

Secrecy is often countered with reporting obligations. In many cases you could end up in court if you do not tell the authorities what you have found. This can be difficult to police, but possession of unreported material will be fair evidence of a criminal act.

Blanket protection permits protection without location, but this can also be achieved using other formulas. The advantage of being able to protect a site by name or by description is that it discourages 'treasure hunts' and the destructive practices associated with staking a claim.

It is widely recognised today that the best way to protect archaeological remains underwater is to keep them there. Many laws prohibit the removal of material from the seabed, even when there is a reward for finding material. In France for example, you could be paid for reporting an artefact but fined if you brought it along with you!

Laws protecting archaeology underwater can involve all sorts of prohibitions, including the use of equipment which would be used while investigating. In some countries even the least intensive sorts of investigation could require a permit or a licence. Licensing schemes are frequently used to control activities on sites, so it is essential to establish what conditions and requirements apply to particular intentions.

5.6.3. Ownership and reward

These two topics are linked because ownership is sometimes offered as a reward, or the process which resolves ownership generates the reward. There are many different systems which apply, but six general cases are widespread. The law relating to ownership may well be separate from that concerning protection – each aspect of the law can stand by itself, but they should be considered together to see how investigations might be affected.

a. Finders keepers

This is perhaps the most widely held attitude when considering remains at sea, but in many cases it has no basis in law. The principle has been supported in United States' courts, but in the UK, for example, the practice has only arisen because the law is ignored. It is not really suitable as a building block for careful investigation or sensible management of the heritage because material goes directly into private collections. Some regulations try to harness self-interest in order to record material by giving the remains to the people that report them.

b. Original owner

Many legislative schemes have to make provision for the rights of the original owner. This is because ownership does not end with loss but often requires a legal act of abandonment. It can be difficult to prove abandonment, so laws often allow owners to reclaim material that has been found. The time period for claims is usually limited so that the issue of ownership can be resolved within a relatively short time. Some states get around the problem by declaring that abandonment has taken place if there has been no claim within a limited period following inundation. The rights of original owners may remain relevant, despite the passing of many generations, because material is often owned by governments or companies which maintain their rights for centuries.

c. State ownership of unclaimed material

Systems which provide for ownership claims need a procedure for deciding who gets the material if an owner does not come forward. The state is the most common beneficiary, except where there is a proper 'finders keepers' rule. Crown ownership in the UK fits into this category.

d. State ownership of material of archaeological importance

This is not the same as the situation above because the motive for the state taking ownership is different. Many countries recognise that archaeological remains are of interest to the entire population and are part of their inheritance, to be passed on to future generations. States give effect to this principle by acquiring the rights to archaeological, historical and artistic material. This may be selective, applying to particularly fine examples, or general, applying to all examples.

e. Salvage reward

Salvage is a marine activity which the authorities have tried to encourage through the ages. Salvage law serves to reward those who take risks while trying to save things which would otherwise be lost. Salvage law continues to apply in some countries and there are specific procedures which must be carried out. Most commentators agree that salvage law is not acceptable for dealing with archaeological remains.

f. Reporter's reward

Rewards for reporters of finds are different from rewards for salvors as they provide an incentive for reporting rather than recovery. Reporters' rewards can be non-monetary but they frequently rely on cash payments. Cash rewards may re-introduce commercial pressures, so care must be taken over the amounts offered and their relationship to market value. Cash reward systems must be backed up with adequate funding or officials may be tempted to hand the material back in place of the reward. This is another way in which 'finders keepers' can develop without the legislation actually intending it.

5.6.4. Miscellaneous laws

There may be other laws which have an effect on the investigation of cultural material in addition to rules referring directly to ownership and protection.

Many countries have some sort of control over the export of cultural material, in order to hold on to items of national significance. Any investigation which involves the crossing of frontiers must take account of such regulations. This might be the case where archaeologists are visiting a country, or where material has to be sent abroad for identification or dating. Travelling displays and lecture series which include artefacts may also invoke export laws.

Archaeological investigations may fall under rules relating to working conditions, minimum qualifications and insurance. It is

83

essential to check this out before work starts, especially given the potentially hazardous nature of work underwater. It may be necessary to seek clarification of the regulations applying to archaeologists who are paid, and those who are not paid, especially when they are working together. Similarly, boats and other equipment (air cylinders, compressors) used in archaeological operations should comply with the relevant regulations.

It is also worth watching for anomalous legislation which may have an effect. It is possible that laws are so worded that material coming ashore counts as imported goods, so there could be duty payable. In the UK, for example, wines and spirits which emerge from excavations can be taxed. In some situations the equipment used on archaeological projects will be affected by customs regulations and local laws (for example, when shipping it into a foreign country).

Some states apply special rules to limited areas. Areas may be designated for environmental, military and safety purposes and may involve restrictions on a wide range of marine activities. The restrictions might be quite detailed and can vary through the year.

Local rules might affect the conduct of operations. Harbour and beach access might be restricted or require permission. Local support could be essential to the smooth running of a project, so it is advisable to fit in with the local way of doing things.

5.6.5. Responsibility

Archaeological investigations will proceed more smoothly if they run within the law, rather than against it. An apparently minor offence could cause serious delays and inconvenience.

Unfortunately, legislation is not always easy to read. In addition the interpretation and enforcement of the rules may be somewhat different from that written down. In all cases it is recommended that you should approach the relevant authority for advice before you start. Ignorance is no protection in law – the responsibility lies with you.

This means that not only do you have to know about the law, you also have to know which office or department runs it. This may be even more complicated, ambiguous and contradictory than the law itself. Still, you should persevere. In some states there will be pamphlets available which may be of assistance. Elsewhere you may have to rely on whatever advice is available from other archaeologists, divers, curators and so on. The Nautical Archaeology Society provides a good point of contact on legislation affecting archaeology underwater in the UK Some suggested reading appears below, but on occasion there is no real alternative to reading the legislation itself.

5.6.6. A case study: legislation in the UK

The following paragraphs serve to illustrate the points above, and inform archaeologists working in the UK.

i. The two most influential pieces of legislation affecting archaeology underwater in the UK are the Protection of Wrecks Act 1973 (PWA), and the Merchant Shipping Act, 1894 (MSA). In effect, the law providing protection is separate from the law affecting ownership.

ii. The PWA applies to the United Kingdom waters and the seabed submerged at high water of ordinary spring tides. UK waters are defined as any part of the sea (including estuaries, "arms of the sea" and any part of a river within the ebb and flow of ordinary spring tides) within the seaward limit of territorial waters. The MSA applies to any tidal water within the limits of the UK. The archaeology of lakes and rivers is covered by land legislation. The Ancient Monuments and Archaeological Areas Act 1979 can apply to monuments within the seaward limits of UK territorial waters.

iii. The breadth of territorial waters is 12 nautical miles, set by the Territorial Sea Act 1987.

iv. The UK does not currently claim a Contiguous Zone, or an EEZ. It claimed rights to a Continental Shelf in the Continental Shelf Act 1964. The limits of the Continental Shelf have been established in the North Sea and in the Channel, but delimitation is still disputed in the Atlantic. Although the UK makes extensive use of its mineral and hydrocarbon rights on the Continental Shelf, off-shore operators are not required to take account of archaeology which might be affected. The UK claims an Exclusive Fisheries Zone of 200 nautical miles, but this is regulated through the Common Fisheries Policy of the European Communities.

v. Both the Merchant Shipping Act, 1894, and the Protection of Military Remains Act 1986 (PMRA), have application beyond the Territorial Sea. The MSA uses port state jurisdiction to apply to all material landed within the UK, wherever it was found, and the PMRA can apply in international waters if the offence is carried out from a British controlled ship or by a British citizen.

vi. The PWA can only apply to shipwrecks. Its scope is defined in terms of archaeological, historical and artistic importance, rather than a time period or date. The PWA is used to protect an area within which certain activities are prohibited. The designated area is often a circle with a radius of between 50 and 300 metres. The PWA can only apply to specific sites within a known position because it relies on the definition of an area. The MSA is, in contrast, a blanket law applying to all material wherever it was found. The PMRA can be used to protect remains without their position being known.

vii. The MSA includes an obligation to report material, while the PWA prohibits the unauthorised removal of material, thus protecting it *in situ* and the only exception is where a person has been given an excavation licence, which usually requires conservation facilities and an acceptable future home to be available. The PWA prohibits the use of "equipment constructed or adapted for any purpose of diving or salvage operations" in a designated area, unless such use is permitted in a licence.

viii. The MSA recognises the rights of original owners, but provides for Crown entitlement to unclaimed wreck, except where rights have been granted to any other person. A period of one year is allowed for claims of ownership.

ix. To encourage reporting of historical material, salvors have been allowed to keep unclaimed finds in lieu of a salvage award. In such cases the finder is required to pay expenses, and 25% of the value of historic coins (no longer collected if they go to an acceptable museum). Otherwise unclaimed wreck has been sold at market value with the charges and salvage paid from the proceeds. Once finds have passed to the salvor, they are free to dispose of them as they wish. However, museums are able to acquire finds by negotiation with the finder and it is Government policy to encourage salvors to offer finds to museums; many have done so without paymnet.

x. Miscellaneous rules to watch out for include the Diving Operations at Work Regulations 1981, updated in 1990 and presently under review. These apply to all operations where the divers are paid for their work in British waters.

xi. As mentioned above, wines and spirits found as "wreck" will be treated as imported goods due to the MSA, so duty may be payable.

xii. Certain areas of sea may be restricted through the Wildlife and Countryside Act 1981, which provides for Marine Nature Reserves. There are only two of these at present. Areas restricted for military use (such as firing ranges) are clearly marked on Admiralty Charts.

5.7. Suggested Reading

a. strategies

Adams, J.
1985 Excavation strategies and techniques. In Gawronski, J. (ed.) *Amsterdam Project. Annual report of the VOC-Ship 'Amsterdam' Foundation 1985.* Amsterdam, ISBN 90-71690-01-6.

Dean, M.
1988 *Guidelines on Acceptable Standards in Underwater Archaeology.* St Andrews, ISBN 1-871170-00-1.

Hunter, J. and I Ralston, (eds.)
1993 *Archaeological Resource Management in the UK: An Introduction.* Institute of Field Archaeologists/Alan Sutton, Stroud. ISBN 0-7509-0275-2.

Mueller, J.W. (ed.)
1975 *Sampling in Archaeology.* Tucson, Arizona, ISBN 0-8165-0482-2.

Watson, K. and Gale, A.
1990 Site evaluation for marine sites and monuments records: Yarmouth Roads Wreck investigation. *IJNA.* 19.3: 183-192.

b. planning

English Heritage
1989 *The Management of Archaeology Projects.* London, ISBN 1-85074-246-4.

Palmer, R.
1986 *Underwater Expeditions.* Royal Geographical Society, London.

c. safety

British Sub-Aqua Club
1987 *Safety and Rescue for Divers.* London, ISBN 0-09-163831-3.

Flemming, N.C. and Max, M.D.
1988 *Code of Practice for Scientific Diving: principles for the safe practice of scientific diving in different environments.* Unesco, Technical Papers in Marine Science No.53, Paris.

Gamble, J.C., Clark, P.F. , Pagett, R.M. (eds.)
1989 *Underwater Association Code of Practice for Scientific Diving.* 4th Ed., Underwater Association for Scientific Research Ltd., NERC, London.

Health and Safety Executive
1991 *Diving Operations at Work, Guidance on Regulations* . Her Majesty's Stationery Office, London. ISBN 0-11-885599-9.

d. legislation

Altes, A.K.
1976 Submarine Antiquities: A Legal Labyrinth. *Syracuse Journal of International Law and Commerce,* 4,1.

Council of Europe
1978 *The Underwater Cultural Heritage.* Doc. 4200 (Rapporteur J.Roper), Strasbourg.

Cycon, D.E.
1985 Legal and Regulatory Issues in Marine Archaeology. *Oceanus* 28, 1: 78-84.

Dromgoole, S.
1989 Protection of Historic Wreck: The UK Approach Part I: The Present Legal Framework. *International Journal of Estuarine and Coastal Law* 4, 1: 26-51.

Dromgoole, S.
1989 Protection of Historic Wreck: The UK Approach Part II: Towards Reform. *International Journal of Estuarine and Coastal Law* 4, 2.

Joint Nautical Archaeology Policy Committee
1989 *Heritage at Sea: Proposals for the better protection of archaeological sites underwater.* National Maritime Museum, ISBN 0-948065-07-9.

O'Keefe, P.J.
1984 The Law and Nautical Archaeology: An International Survey. In Langley, S.B.M., and Unger, R.W. (eds), *Nautical Archaeology: Progress and Public Responsibility.* British Archaeological Reports, International Series No.220, Oxford, ISBN 0-86054-284-X.

O'Keefe, P.J., and Prott, L.V.
1984 *Law and the cultural heritage Vol. 1: Discovery and Excavation.* London, ISBN 0-862-05065-0.

e. UK Statutes:

Protection of Wrecks Act 1973 c. 33.

Merchant Shipping Act, 1894 part IX.

Ancient Monuments and Archaeological Areas Act 1979 c.46.

Protection of Military Remains Act 1986 c.35.

Wildlife and Countryside Act 1981 c.69 ss. 36-7.

6. Recording

6.1. The Need For Recording

6.2. Planning the Recording: What to Record

6.3. Constructing the Recording System

6.4. Suggested Reading

6.1. The Need For Recording

If we and our successors are going to use the information retrieved from a site then it needs to be readily available in an organised form. There is no one alive today who could remember all the relevant details about everything that came from even a small site. There is a clear necessity to document and illustrate our findings as we make them. This will allow us to have all the details available to work on even months or years later in a convenient way. Ideally, fieldworkers or their successors should be able to 'reconstruct' the site from the store, or archive, of records of a site. This is essential if the site has been destroyed and cannot be studied again, but it is good discipline even for non-destructive survey. It is in your own interests. How are you going to convince people of the value of your conclusions if you cannot show them the results of the investigation on which they are based?

The aim of recording is to note what is there as accurately and completely as we can, giving each piece of information equal weight and without letting the possible interpretation of the information affect the way it is recorded. Recording should be an objective process. Of course it is also important to know what people thought about the site as they recorded it – it would

be a pity to lose those flashes of inspiration which explain objects and relationships. However, such comments and ideas are kept clearly separate from the objective record of the site. The way we interpret information is likely to be affected by our own backgrounds and culture which give us a set of ideas and experience against which we judge things. This may lead us to make very different assumptions about something from those of the society which used or created it in the past. Therefore we must attempt to record things in a way which avoids such problems as far as possible, so that any prejudices or influences that slip into the interpretation of a site are not based on another set of prejudices and influences which appear in the recording.

6.1.1. Recording systems

The development of a documentation system should begin when project is planned. It must be capable of recording information relating to aspects as diverse as the location, identification and interpretation of all the evidence from a site. To make sure a recording system fulfils its objectives it has to be constructed so that it stores and manages the recorded clues in a manner that is simple to understand. The system should make it easy for the user to cross-reference

A

IWMSMR: EXCAVATION ARCHIVE | CONTEXT SHEET

CO-ORDINATES | PRN | CONTEXT NO.

SITE NAME | TRENCH | SIMPLE NAME

LENGTH | WIDTH | DIAMETER | DEPTH

SEDIMENT
- COLOUR
- TEXTURE
- CONSISTENCE

STRUCTURE
- COARSE COMMENTS
- CONSTITUENTS
- BONDING AGENTS

DIVISION OF | DIVIDED INTO

EARLIER THAN
- BELOW
- FILLED BY
- CUT BY
- BUTTED BY

CONTEMPORARY
- WITHIN
- CONTAINS
- BONDED WITH
- SAME AS

LATER THAN
- ABOVE
- FILL OF
- CUTS
- BUTTS

CUT BY SAMPLE

INTERPRETATIVE COMMENTS

REFERENCES

PART OF | CONSISTS OF

B ARCHAEOLOGICAL DIVING UNIT | DIVING OPERATIONS LOG

DIVER: | SITE: | DATE:
SUPERVISOR: | STAND-BY: | TENDER:
CHAMBER: location: | tel.no.:

WEATHER:
Temperature:- air: | surface water: | bottom: | Sea state:
Surface vis.: | Cloud (%/type): | Wind (dir/str):

UNDERWATER visibility: | TIDE (direction/strength):
BOTTOM TYPE:

TABLE: | SCHEDULE: | NO STOP:
TISSUE CODE: | *LEFT SURFACE:*
SURFACE INTERVAL: | MADE BOTTOM:
| LEFT BOTTOM:
REACH FIRST STOP: | DEPTH: | LEAVE STOP:
REACH SECOND STOP: | DEPTH: | LEAVE STOP:
| *REACH SURFACE:*
SURFACING CODE: | MAX.DEPTH: | DURATION:

SCUBA: | Cyl.w.c.: | AIR:IN: | OUT: | (bar)
SDDE: | Bank change (time): | / | / | /

RECORD OF COMMUNICATIONS/WORK DONE:
TIME/DEPTH
/
/
/
/
/
/
/
/
/
/
/
/
/
/
/
/
/
/
/
/
/
/
/

SIGNED:- DIVER: | SUPERVISOR:

Figure 39. Examples of recording pro formas. A: context sheet (courtesy of the Isle of Wight Maritime Heritage Project), B: dive report form (courtesy of the Archaeological Diving Unit), C:

information which exists in a variety of forms (*e.g.* individual observations, photographs, drawings etc.).

6.1.2. Notebooks or pre-printed forms?

Traditionally the director entered the details of a site in a site notebook. This has the advantage of being easy to set up and flexible. The disadvantage is that it is difficult to note each of the many characteristics of each clue consistently and objectively. It can also be harder to extract the information when the time comes to analyse it.

It has become normal practice to use pre-printed forms (or "pro-formas") for recording much of the information. In effect the recording form asks the recorder questions, prompting a consistent level of information in return. Regardless of the number of pieces of information that have to be recorded, or how many different people do the recording, the same details should be noted. Entered in an ordered, standard, manner the information should also be easier to consult and analyse. The disadvantages of forms are that they need more preparation before use and more explanation during use. Badly filled-in forms produce information as incomplete and garbled as any site notebook. Unfortunately there is no 'off the shelf

C

TIMBER RECORDING SHEET

Grid Square(s)		Area/Section	TIMBER	Site Code	Context

1. Type
2. Setting
3. Inclination & orientation
4. Cross-section   (Draw on diagram below)
5. Condition
6. Dimensions in m/mm
7. Conversion
8. Tool marks
9. Joints & fixings
10. Intentional marks
11. Surface treatment
12. Other comments
13. Methods & conditions   PTO

Stratigraphic matrix

This context is

Your interpretation :

PTO

Reused   Yes   No   Unknown   Discussion :

PTO

Specialist recording form nos : Building ?   Boat ?   Other ?
Plan nos : P   (X)   Structure no :
Other drawings : S/E   Site book refs :
Timber drawing no :   Matrix location :
Photographs (tick when taken)   Card nos :

Levels (tick when taken)	Timber cross section	Checked interpretation :
TBM : BS : IH :	sapwood / bark	

No	FS	Reduced
1		
2		
3		
4		Bark Y N Environmental
5		Sapwood Y N Species : Initials :
6		Knotty Y N Dendro sample (tick) : Date :
7		Straight-grained Y N Other samples :

PTO

Provisinal period | Accession no < > | Group | Initials & date

MUSEUM OF LONDON

D

SEA VENTURE TRUST   FINDS   RECORD   CARD

SITE CODE: B/SV	NUMBER 86/A100/	PART 3	FILE	CARD 1 OF 2
OBJECT NAME STAVE	TYPE BARREL	CLASS STOWAGE	MATERIAL/S WOOD	
OBJECT DATE 17th C	DATING METHOD CONTEXT	IDENTIFIER CG	DATE 3/6/86	

LOCATION DESCRIPTION
DESCRIPTION OF CONTENT – LAYER DEPTH ETC. LOCATION IN RELATION TO SHIP STRUCTURE

SECTOR/AREA F14
CONTEXT 2/3
IDENTIFIER J.A.

ON SITE RECORDING
D.S.W. ✓   PHOTOGRAPHED B/W   BY   DRAWN ✓ BY J.A.
IF NOT DSW TRILATERATED TO: SHIP   COLOUR   BY C.D.   VIDEO ✓ BY J.A.
GRID   PHOTO MOSAIC   BY   CINE ✓ BY T.J.
DATUMS   OTHER:

DATUM	PA2	PA3	SA1	SA3		
DISTANCE						
CO-ORDINATES	X	Y	Z	RESIDUAL ERROR	DSW FILE	

PART OF A 96 97 98   ASSOCIATED WITH   FEATURE 10
EXCAVATOR/COLLECTOR: A.J. WINWOOD   DATE 3/6/86   REFERENCE
DIVE LOG NUMBER 1   DATE 4/6/86

DIMENSIONS IN MM.

MARKS/INSCRIPTIONS
INITIALS CRU – CARVED INTO WOOD

PHOTO

CONDITION good   COMPLETENESS   NUMBER OF FRAGMENTS/PARTS 2

STORAGE/PRE CONSERVATION   INITIATED BY CG   DATE 4/6/88
COLD STORAGE FRESH WATER.

PRE CONSERVATION RECORDING
DRAWN 10/6/86
PHOTOGRAPHED   B/W 1 ✓ 20   FILM NO.   COLOUR 1 ✓ 22
PHOTOGRAPHER C.D.

SAMPLES TAKEN INSIDE CONTENTS   TAKEN BY IO   5/6/88

NOTES

POST CONSERVATION RECORDING
DRAWN 10/6/87
PHOTOGRAPHED   B/W 1 ✓   FILM NO. 51
TRANSPARENCY   1 /
PHOTOGRAPHER
TO MUSEUM   5/5/88

timber recording sheet (courtesy of the Museum of London), D: finds record card (courtesy of the Sea Venture Trust.)

standard recording system available. Different projects and groups have all developed systems tailored to their own needs (Figure 39).

6.2. Planning the Recording: What to Record

When considering your recording system the first step is to work out what you want to record. Familiarise yourself with all the aspects or categories of information that you are likely to encounter on your site. Does the system only have to record boats, or other types of structure as well? Will the system be used in both survey and excavation? There is no point in setting up systems which conflict.

Compile a list of information that it will be necessary to record on your site. It is important to remember to record both observations (what you saw) and interpretations (what you think they mean) as fully as possible, but not to confuse them.

General factors that need to be recorded:

i. Position: site name/code, trench code, location measurements/position co-ordinates,

ii. Description: name of clue, form/shape, sediment colour, sediment texture, sediment compactness, composition, condition, dimensions, date/period,

iii. Relationships: before context(s) "x" – below, filled by, cut by, butted by, contemporary with context(s) "x" – within, contains, bonded with, same as, after context(s) "x" – above, fill of, cuts, butts,

    iv. Associations: associated with, types of object found in the context, timber jointed to, timber fastened to,

    v. Interpretation and motives: interpretive comments, reasons for taking sample, method of excavation, notes on circumstances of recording, excavation, recovery of material etc.,

    vi. Co-ordination of records: relevant plans and sections, relevant photographs/video, relevant dive logs, conservation records, storage records, scientific analysis,

    vii. Who says?: recorded by?, checked by?, expert opinion of?,

    viii. 'Explanatory doodles' – annotated sketches, sketch matrix.

The following points show how different elements of this list can be emphasised for the different categories of information.

6.2.1. Recording decisions

Recording should begin as soon as any category of evidence is found. At the earliest possible stage it should be given some form of unique identity number. The way this is done will vary with the object concerned.

Sketch plans can be made explaining which record belongs to which clue if physically attaching a label is not possible or desirable. It may be that if an object is revealed during an excavation it can be more conveniently labelled with less risk of damage once it has been removed from the sediment. The sketch plan should also include location, orientation and any important features should these be visible. Section 6.3.4 discusses the materials which might be suitable for labels.

Be flexible about how clues are measured in to the site plan. Measurements for the position of long objects will be much more informative if taken to both ends (giving angle of rest and orientation) as opposed to a single measurement to a central point. Whichever points are measured in make sure they are re-identifiable. They should be distinctive features, which are then described

with the measurement. If there are a number of associated pieces of evidence take measurements between them and describe their relative positions.

The ways in which objects can be recorded in detail once on the surface are described (see Section 12.0). However, it is not necessary to raise objects to record them properly. Guns, structural features and even pottery fragments have been effectively recorded *in situ* without damage to the site and risk of information loss which can often be caused by raising them to the surface.

A good 'in place', or *in situ*, record of an object should be good enough for specialists, or for initial publication. Specialists who demand that material be raised are not necessarily thinking of the long-term good of the object. Perhaps they are more concerned with involving themselves in the least effort and they are underestimating your ability to record material objectively. In addition, they may not understand or appreciate the important links that their particular type of artefact or evidence has with other categories on the site. These links should be recorded and studied before one class of evidence is removed from its context and associations.

Even if the material is to be raised for more detailed study, when an object appears to be particularly delicate or fragmentary it is worth spending more time on a detailed record of it *in situ*. Measured drawings and more intensive photographic and video recording (of the object and the process of lifting) might ensure that important information is saved even if disaster strikes.

The registration of large groups of similar objects represents a problem. Should they each receive a single unique number and individual documentation or be grouped together? Imagine 10,000 lead musket shot or 200 wooden bowls. There is no single correct solution. Basic principles might include the following:

    i. Be aware of the potential information - consult specialists.

    ii. Think how the information will be best recorded in your system so it can be retrieved

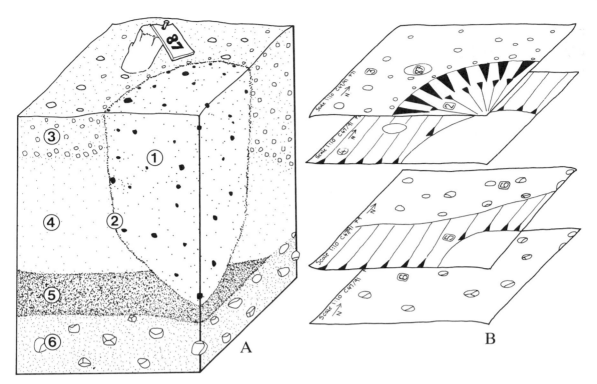

Figure 40. Planning contexts: a) a representation of some contexts on a site, b) an example of recording contexts in plan. Each plan is made after a context has been removed. (6.2.2.)

– consult the team members involved (finds supervisors, director etc).

iii. Record in more detail than seems necessary.

iv. Record an explanation of the recording strategy you adopted.

On many projects guidelines covering problems like this have been formulated to ensure consistent responses to similar situations (Spence 1990).

6.2.2. Recording contexts

What do archaeological contexts look like? Contexts can be categorised as structures, cuts (*e.g.* scour pits), fills and layers. The easiest context to recognise on a shipwreck is the vessel's hull that survives as a coherent structure and this, obviously, is an indication that the hull sank to the seabed. Collapsed parts of the hull may represent the events in the disintegrating of the ship-structure. Collections of objects (*e.g.* a pile of cannon balls or a galley-oven made up of a large

number of galley-bricks) can also be recorded as contexts if this helps their understanding. The digging of any hole by nature or by man (*e.g.* previous salvage) is obviously a very important event or process and as such they should be recorded as a context. These holes or voids may fill up and the hull will perhaps become buried (usually in distinguishable stages). Each of the layers of the infilling material should be designated as a context as each represents specific episodes in the history of the wreck.

The reason these layers are recognisable is because the material in them is slightly different to the neighbouring layers. Differences may only be slight so great care is needed to recognise them. All the variables which make up the distinctive character of a context should be recorded for all the contexts encountered on a site. For deposits, this might include parameters such as: colour, texture, consistency, particle size (for sediments), bonding agent, main constituents, sedimentary structures, shape,

93

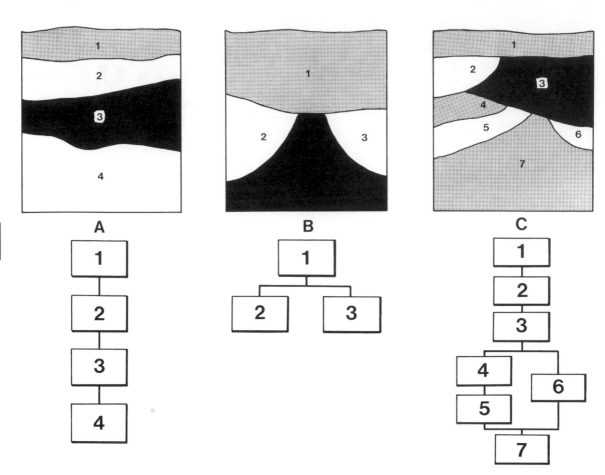

Figure 41. Stratigraphical diagrams: (e.g. Harris 'Matrix'), a) a simple sequence of direct relationships between contexts, b) relationships can be demonstrated between contexts 2 and 1, and 3 and 1, but not between 2 and 3. c) using the basic principles shown in a) and b) the direct relationships in sequence c) can be clarified in diagrammatic form. (6.2.3.)

dimensions and precise location. Further details about the nature of these parameters and their recognition can be found in the *Soil Survey Field Handbook* (Hodgson 1976).

Of course life is never as simple as we would like it to be. Once a layer has been formed over another layer various processes, such as burrowing animal activity, or even earlier salvage, can cause disturbance to this neat pattern and blur the boundaries between the two. Fortunately such processes tend to leave traces which allow their influence to be detected and allowed for.

6.2.3. Recording stratigraphy

It is very important that in recording contexts the positional relationship of each one compared to those around it should be recorded. This can be done by a written description (below, above, within etc.) supplemented by a diagrammatic representation of the sequence of individual contexts. This method of presenting an analysis of the sequence is sometimes known as a Harris matrix (Harris 1989). These diagrams are often constructed as an investigation progresses to clarify relationships between contexts within the

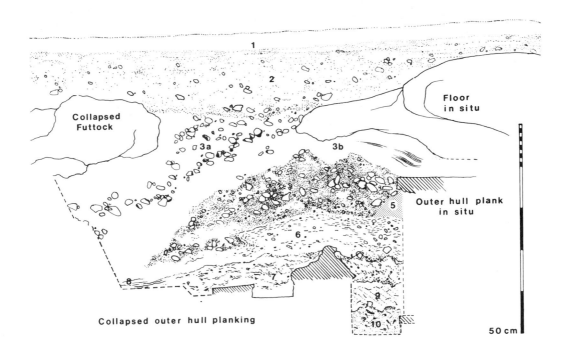

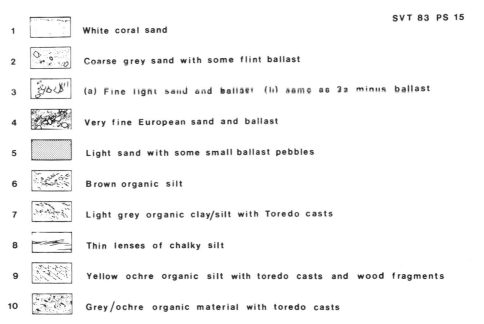

SVT 83 PS 15

1		White coral sand
2		Coarse grey sand with some flint ballast
3		(a) Fine light sand and ballast (b) same as 3a minus ballast
4		Very fine European sand and ballast
5		Light sand with some small ballast pebbles
6		Brown organic silt
7		Light grey organic clay/silt with Toredo casts
8		Thin lenses of chalky silt
9		Yellow ochre organic silt with toredo casts and wood fragments
10		Grey/ochre organic material with toredo casts

Figure 42. Contexts recorded in section: complex layers of sediment associated with the remains of a Bermudan shipwreck. (6.2.3.) (Courtesy of J. Adams and the Sea Venture Trust.)

Figure 43. Surface marks: tool marks, for example, can give information about how the timber was shaped and the tools used. (6.2.7.b.i.) (Courtesy of D.Goodburn.)

site (Figure 41). Measured drawings of the physical relationships between contexts are also fundamental to the site record and should be cross-referenced in the other documentation relating to the stratigraphy.

6.2.4. Recording environmental evidence

The way in which the environment of a site influences the survival of evidence has already been discussed (Section 4.5.1). Having identified the significance of this area of study it is important to develop effective recording strategies for it. Consulting the specialists whose work might be most directly influenced by environmental factors is very sensible. The conservator will want to know the details of an object's burial environment so that the optimum conservation treatment can be decided upon. Scientific dating methods may be influenced by factors in the site's environment and those responsible for the dating will want the relevant information in a usable form.

Space may be provided on dive sheets and survey or excavation record sheets to record details of localised environmental factors around individual objects or areas of structure. Studies of the general environmental factors affecting the site may require a specifically designed form to accommodate all the information that might be relevant.

6.2.5. Recording samples

Investigating environmental characteristics of a site might involve taking samples for subsequent analysis in controlled conditions. Non-artefactual deposits might also require sampling for study. It is very important to record what proportion the 'sample' is of the whole and to record the information carefully on the Sample Record (*e.g.* 15 litres recovered of an estimated 50 litres). Details of the sampling procedure used to recover the samples should be recorded in detail. The sampling strategy adopted in the field together with some indication of the density of the material collected over the site or the concentration within particular features should be included.

Details of the length of time and condition of storage, together with the current location of the original samples (and all sub-samples if located elsewhere) should be recorded.

6.2.6. Recording objects

It is important to keep an open mind and record all evidence with equal care. Animal bones should receive as much attention as gold coins. Do not discard or destroy materials/deposits simply because they do not appear to be of immediate value. The most unattractive or unlikely items could be ancient packing materials or the last traces of a delicate object (Figure 17). It is particularly important to record the associations; such information may be crucial to determining whether the material was the contents of a container or the packing around it. Traces relevant to such questions can be very insubstantial so record any details you observe even if you do not fully understand their significance.

6.2.7. Recording timbers

There is very little literature on timber recording compared to other classes of artefact, and so the following section offers some specific advice on how to do a thorough job of recording what is likely to be a major element of many submerged sites. The techniques for drawing timber are covered in Section 12.2.7.

a. Minimum requirements

It has been common practice in the past for archaeologists to develop their own techniques for recording structural wood, whether from platforms, docks, trackways, bridges, palisades, boats or shipwrecks. Guidelines are now being developed to provide advice on the minimum records that should be assembled from structural wood, whether it is lifted, or left *in situ* (Nayling 1989; Marsden 1991; English Heritage 1990; Spence 1990).

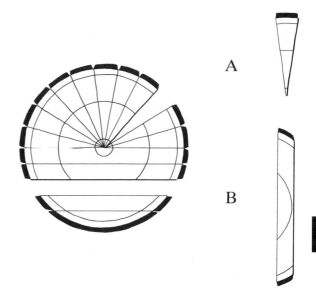

Figure 44. Surface marks: evidence of conversion. Note the different positions of the tree-rings. a) radially split plank, b.) tangentially sawn plank. (6.2.7.b.iv.)

On discovery, wood is often very fragile or soft and prone to damage from tools. It is important that any such damage, whether from tools or divers, is marked and recorded and distinguished from original markings from the outset. Care should be taken to avoid the risk of surface scoring by tools being badly handled, or the selection of inappropriate tools for the job. It may be better in some cases to leave the wood in an uncleaned condition until it reaches the laboratory or finds processing area. They should on no account be allowed to dry out before recording (see Section 11.2).

If timbers are being raised it is essential to record the precise location, orientation, angle and inclination of small detached elements, as it may be possible to assign them to their original position.

b. Suggested measurements and observations

Guidelines produced by English Heritage (Coles 1990) list the following measurements and observations as important for good archaeological recording:

i. The appearance of the wood

1. Its size and dimensions, major breakages, and number of fragments.

2. Any surface features such a tool marks, wear, bark, and surface treatment (paint, charring etc.), carpenters marks and setting out lines (Figure 43).

3. The surface condition (fresh to abraded/ weathered, on a scale from 5 (fresh) to 1 (worn); all sides and ends noted.

4. Internal condition of the timber (useful for assessment for conservation treatments) by insertion of needle and recording depth of penetration (on a scale from 5 (solid) to 1 (soft).

ii. Functional interpretation of the wood

1. Character of the original (based on size and section).

2. Purpose within a structure (*e.g.* ceiling planking, futtock, floor timber, piling).

3. Fitting details (such as joints, fixings, nails, pegs, treenails, with a sketch for easy identification).

4. Re-use of timber? Modification and use elsewhere?

iii. Natural features

1. Species identification (normally by sampling, except where a trained person can identify types on site).

2. Natural growth features (knots, growth pattern).

3. Induced growth features (such as coppiced heels, healed cut branches).

iv. Technological interpretation of the wood

1. Details of its felling (where visible), and conversion from log or branch (*i.e.* radially or tangentially split or sawn (Figure 44). The position of heartwood, sapwood, bark. Cross-sections drawn at intervals may be useful.

2. The shaping or surfaces, sides and ends.

3. Details of the finishing of the wood (carpentry and adjustments).

4. Evidence from woodworking debris (*e.g.* wood shavings in bilge deposits).

c. Wet wood

Many of the above details will be most visible while the wood is wet. Much information can be recorded on a standardised record sheet in combination with photography and line drawings. As stated above, drawings should distinguish modern and ancient damage, and whether areas are man-made or the result of natural processes. It is important to note traces of wear on surfaces, and compression caused by other structural elements. The position and character of joints, holes and nails should be recorded, as should tool marks, tool 'signatures' (the fine striations left by the sharp edges of individual blades), sapwood, heartwood and bark.

d. Observations to make on waterlogged wood

i. Raw materials should be described and sampled for identification. This should not only be tried on hull timbers, but also fastenings, waterproofing materials, paints, rope etc. The quality of the timber should also be noted (*i.e.* was the planking straight-grained with no knots? Was bark left on the frame elements, or wane or 'live edge'? If the surviving natural features of the timbers are recorded properly, the 'parent logs' from which they were cut, and possibly parent trees, can be reconstructed. This makes it possible to reconstruct aspects of ancient landscapes (Goodburn 1991).

ii. How were the raw materials worked? It is useful to think in terms of technology known for the period, to view timber in terms of how it was converted from the tree (*i.e.* radially cleft or sawn), and how they were 'dressed' to shape (*i.e.* secondary trimming).

iii. An important part of (ii) is the recording of tool marks, by description, measured sketches, casting impressions and photography. Casting can be done with plaster or synthetic rubber compound (some will set when damp). As they are flexible, it is possible to record undercuts and very fine detail, but the rubber compounds have a limited life-expectancy, and hard resin or plaster positive casts should be made from the moulds at an early date. The flexibility of the rubber can lead to a tendency in some to curl. As casting can be time consuming, it is usual only to cast the best preserved examples of each type of mark.

iv. The order of construction should be recorded. For example, was the hull planking assembled before framing (which in a clinker vessel might be shown by riveted nails covered by frames). In some apparently 'carvel' built vessels, the planking was assembled before frames, using temporary clamps which can be traced through the plugging of small nail holes near the plank seams.

v. How was the vessel planked up? Detailed recording of the shapes of the planks should allow this to be worked out. Tracings on polythene are an effective method of recording the details and should be made directly on the faces of the timber to avoid distortion. The polythene also helps to prevent the timber from drying out during the recording process.

vi. The locations and appearance of samples of fastenings should be recorded.

vii. Assembly marks, gauge marks, mouldings should be looked for, and the units of measurement estimated where possible.

viii. It is important to look out for surface treatments, paints etc. Where found their method of application and location should be recorded. Mineral deposits on timber surfaces can be confusing here, and it may be advisable to take samples.

ix. Wear and 'in use' damage and repairs should be carefully recorded, as they might mark events in the life history of the vessel. The re-use of timbers from other constructions should also be recorded. Many wreck finds are found to be partly built from timber from other ships or boats.

x. Modern breaks such as those caused by dredger or drainage machinery should be drawn with a different type of line to distinguish it from a worked edge. This will assist assembly of damaged timber on paper when the actual timbers are too large or awkward, or too fragile to repeatedly handle.

xi. Part of the recording process is the sampling of wood for species identification, and possible further scientific analysis (see section on dating). Information can be obtained from the growth patterns of the wood, leading to evidence for woodland composition and management. Environmental indicators such as attack by teredo, gribble worm, beetle or fungus, should be recorded.

xii. Stills photography should be undertaken on wood to record not only general characteristics, but also detail: wear, tool-marks, etc. This is best done on slightly wet timber, where the skilful use of lighting and reflections can show up fine detail.

e. Dismantling structures for study

A number of wreck investigations have involved careful disassembly and recording of intact structure, followed by controlled re-burial and monitored storage on site (Tuck and Grenier 1989, 32). Objects and components may be subsequently found beneath the hull, and disassembly of the hull may not only provide detailed information on construction, but also permit fuller stratigraphic analysis throughout the site, including the comparison of pre- and post-wreck material. It can aid detailed study of tool marks, construction marks, timber dimensions and cross-sections as well as examination of the (normally buried) exterior faces of structural components, the extent of marine growth and marine borer activity, the details of hull maintenance.

It is important to realise that this approach is only justifiable if:

i. destruction of the site is unavoidable,

ii. resources are available for the proper study of all the timber to maximise the information on the structure,

iii. every attempt is made to secure the future curation of the timber by qualified staff.

Pulling apart structure simply to make artefact recovery easier is totally unjustifiable.

Prior to disassembly of a particular area, a complete record of all integral timber structure is necessary. In some cases it may be necessary to do three separate surveys: firstly prior to recovering the ceiling planking, secondly prior to recovering framing elements and thirdly prior to recovery of external planking and keel. It may be essential to undertake full-scale underwater tracings on exposed and relatively flat surfaces such as the top of the ceiling planking or the inside of the hull planking. Alternatively, large casts of areas of structure can be undertaken, even underwater, using rubber compounds or other suitable substances (Murdock and Daley 1982).

Care, patience, and constant recording are essential in any disassembly operation. Dismantling may be assisted by the corrosion of iron spikes, a situation that conversely can complicate the lifting of intact structures. On the other hand treenails can sometimes be remarkably efficient at keeping the integrity of a structure and so it is important to carefully select tools and procedures that are compatible with the scientific objectives of the work to minimise damage to the timber.

6.2.8. Gun recording

Just as with any other object recording should begin as soon as a gun is recognised. In addition to information required for any artefact type (*e.g.* site code, unique artefact number, context, position and associations) the following categories should be considered when recording guns:

a. Orientation description (aspect, angle of slope, upturned etc.),

b. Material (*e.g.* cast iron, wrought iron, copper alloy),

c. Maximum length,

d. Maximum diameter (external),

e. Minimum diameter,

f. Bore diameter,

g. Presence of external features (*e.g.* trunnions, lifting dolphins, cascabel),

h. Inscriptions or markings,

i. Evidence of carriage,

Sample gun recording forms are given as Figs 144, 145, 146 and it is advisable that guns are sketched and photographed *in situ* paying particular attention to decorative features. It should be stressed that no attempt should be made to remove concretion underwater (Section 11.2.11).

6.2.9. Conservation records

Once in the conservation laboratory, or on-site base, registration of each find must take place before embarking on any treatments. Even if your conservation is being carried out by specialist laboratories, copies of your records will be needed for reference during treatment. Registration cards are shown in figure 39. Details of how the object was stored while awaiting transport to the conservation facility should be noted.

Prior to undertaking conservation treatments, or before the long-term storage of unconserved objects, it is essential that objects or assemblages of objects be photographed with a scale and label. A small contact print of the artefact should be attached to the record cards to aid identification. A full record of all the treatments applied to an object should be kept. Many objects will require further treatment in the future and this will be more effective if the conservator knows the detailed history of the item including the specific solutions, adhesives, chemicals or solvents employed.

6.2.10. Recording survey results

The results of survey need to be recorded as carefully as any other evidence. You may know what you mean on the day the survey is done, but in ten years time you probably will not, and others certainly will not. As much relevant information as possible should be committed to paper:

i. The type of measurement (distance *e.g.* slant range or horizontal, relative depth, slope, bearing, offset),

ii. The identifying names of the datum points used in the measurement,

iii. The measurement, whether metric or Imperial (together with the units used),

iv. An estimate of confidence in the measurement (see Section 9.2.3),

v. A cross-reference to other documentation where the measurement was originally recorded. This might be a dive log, a sheet from a diver's underwater slate, or the record sheet of the dive supervisor when diver communications are used,

vi A summary of information used (*e.g.* number of points surveyed, number and types of measurements taken).

6.2.11. Recording plans and sections

On the drawn-up results of the survey work, *e.g.* plans and sections, further information should be added so that they relate to their sources of measurements. In both the register and on the drawing itself the following information should be recorded:

i. code/site name,

ii. plan number,

iii. subject (plan or section of what?),

iv. recorder,

v. draughtsman,

vi. date,

vii. scale,

viii. position (*e.g.* grid coordinate for plans, square),

ix. orientation (*e.g.* north indicated on plans, and the direction sections are facing).

6.2.12. Recording photographic results

A record of all the photographs taken on any dive should be made on a log sheet or index card. This is essential, as many details of pictures will often be known only by the photographer and may easily be forgotten. Experience has shown that it is best to make brief notes about the photographs whilst still underwater, and then write up the log sheet soon after the dive. The documentation must then be finished when the film has been developed and the exact frame numbers and results are known.

An example of a photo log sheet is included here (Figure 39) which might act as a basis for your project. Naturally the most important information is the subject matter of each shot, but the angle of view and the area or object number are also needed for cross-referencing. Extra information on technical aspects can be added in other columns which are particularly useful for recording the results of test exposure made on the site. Processing details should be included and the film number should also be clearly marked on the negative sheets. Transparencies are sometimes numbered purely on a sequential system rather than a film/frame no. system but the details must still be recorded soon after the dive.

Video footage should be dealt with in a similar way but might also require a written description of what it shows if there is not a recorded commentary. One close up of a timber can look very much like any other. Any log of the video film should be compiled on a running time basis as this will also be of great value when doing any editing. If an edited version of a video survey is prepared it is worth noting which tapes the footage was taken from, and storing this information with the edited compilation. If someone sees an area of interest they can then easily trace a tape which might show more detail. Mark the video cassettes and the boxes clearly so that if they are separated the tape is still easily identifiable.

6.2.13. Dive logs

The primary record of work underwater will be the dive log (Figure 39). Dive logs are the source of first hand observations and as such will be referred to frequently in the post-fieldwork processing. They will also provide an important insight on the effectiveness of diving operations and effect of conditions on the information recorded. It is important to enforce the completion of dive logs as soon as possible after the dive. They should include information on:

i. the diver (name, equipment),
ii. the dive (time, depth, decompression),
iii. the conditions (visibility, current),
iv. the planned work (tasks, equipment),
v. the results (measurements, observations, sketches, cross-references to other records).

6.3. Constructing the Recording System

Rather than have just one form to cover all aspects of archaeological recording, it is easier to have one for each recognisable category of evidence *e.g.* context details, object details, sample details, and perhaps specialised sheets for timber or human skeleton details. Such an outline scheme would form the basis of your recording system for archaeological material.

The same approach can be used on the record administration forms like those for plans, photographs and survey information.

There is no limit to the number of boxes, often referred to as 'fields', that you choose to record. The more that the information is broken down into manageable sections the more reliable the recording is likely to be. Be aware, however, that going to extremes can make the recording process slow and intimidating. Nor is there any limit to the number of groupings you can create. If you have a large number of cannon to record then create a form dealing just with ordnance (Figures 144, 145, 146).

As long as all the forms are cross-referenced, dividing recording into blocks makes it much more manageable. It does not exclude the additional use of a notebook for unstructured recording. This can be particularly useful for noting non-archaeological but significant events during a project, *e.g.* compressor malfunctions, personnel problems or simple flashes of inspiration which might otherwise go unrecorded.

Another unstructured element of recording, explanatory sketches, should be positively encouraged. It is said that "a picture paints a thousand words". In addition to descriptions and reference to the measured plans and sections, leave space in your recording system for annotated sketches.

6.3.1. Using an existing system

When setting up a new system it is useful to examine existing examples. The various projects which devised them will have suffered the 'teething troubles' of the setting-up and planning process, and they will obviously have gained valuable experience in the use of their system. It is important, however, to remember that their system has been designed for that organisation's particular approach and recording task. They may also have designed it to be used in conjunction with a specific recording manual (*e.g.* Spence 1990). So, don't copy the system without knowing how it is meant to be used. Either you will slavishly be doing work that you will not be able to use or you will be overlooking information you may require at the analysis stage.

6.3.2. Explaining, documenting and supervising the system

i. The more sophisticated the recording system the more explanation it will take for people to be able to use it.

ii. It is very important when designing a system for recording your site that future researchers, and not just you, can understand how it works. It must therefore be effectively documented.

iii. Try to avoid ambiguous terms. With any system it is a good idea to agree to the use of terminology (particularly in relation to the naming of boat or ship's structure) – perhaps by deciding to use a certain glossary or reference book.

iv. It is important that information is recorded fully and reliably for each part of the site. Mistakes and ambiguities do happen. A checker is a good idea. On a small project this is likely to be the project leader but on a long term or large project it is more effective if a checker is appointed. This can be combined with administering the records and the allocation of unique reference numbers.

6.3.3. Consultation

It is very important when thinking about what to record to consult the organisations who will eventually have to use your system. For example, if the work involves the raising of objects, ask the museum that has agreed to take the material (and the archive) what they want recorded.

6.3.4. Referring back from records to evidence

Whatever the nature of the recording system, it is vital that any researcher has the facility of referring back to the original evidence, so it is important to have the means to attach clear and permanent labels to each part of the archive (whether object, plan, photograph or sample etc.).

a. Numbering systems

Each aspect which is recorded should be given a unique 'name' or 'label' by which all the records of it, or affecting it, can be identified. A label should refer to the site, the context and the number of the clue itself. The type of labelling is a matter of debate or personal preference. Once again, the people who will have to use the system should be consulted (e.g. museums). The label should be unique, unambiguous, and as 'idiot proof' and logical as possible in allocation.

Using an outline recording system with five basic categories as an example, a simple approach would be to divide a single run of numbers into five blocks (e.g. 0001-999 for contexts, 1001-1999 for objects, 2001-2999 skeletons, 3001-3999 timbers and 4001-4999 for samples). The numbers could be printed onto the forms to avoid any duplication. An object would then be allocated the number of the sheet that describes it, and it should be referred to by that number in all subsequent records and references. New numbers, either for more of the same sheets or new sheets, would be added on at the end (e.g. context 5001-5999 and ordnance 6001-6999).

Another common method is to give each category a run of numbers of its own with a letter (or letters) prefix. Remember to use the prefix (otherwise the number will not be unique), agree the use of the prefix and avoid the use of ambiguous prefixes. The prefix may even be a code signifying the material type e.g. 1 = stone, 2 = ceramic, etc..

Avoid the use of interpretative prefixes. These are difficult to assign reliably and uniquely (e.g. "S" could be interpreted as starboard and sample). In addition, it only takes a change in interpretation or terminology to render them illogical and misleading.

A similar use of numbers or letters should be used to make the site code e.g. "CW" (the Cattewater wreck) or "20 000" (the Yarmouth Roads Wreck). The year of work is sometimes added e.g. "CW 76".

Other labels within the archive are likely to be codes representing dive logs, plans and sections, photographs (e.g. "b/w" = black and white, "ct" = colour transparency), conservation records, scientific analysis records, datums. It is a simple and effective strategy to assign each plan or section a number prefixed with 'plan' or 'section', but again it is question of personal preference. As a general rule codes should either be part of the main system or totally contrasting (e.g. datums all letters, whereas forms exclusively numbers). Two or more similar numbering systems running in parallel are liable to cause confusion.

As an additional check on duplication and for increased ease of administration, registers of the assignment of labels can be kept noting the number, the subject, the recorder and date, and the position.

b. Tags and labelling

The labelling should be as secure as possible without causing any damage to the object. The best methods of labelling are using either spun-bonded polythene fibre labels marked with a waterproof marker pen (spirit-based) or plastic 'Dymo'-type labels, although these are affected by solvents, heat, and light. The labels can be attached to the objects by means of synthetic line, or packed into 'Netlon' plastic mesh along with fragmentary objects. In the case of large timbers the labels can be attached using dipped galvanized or copper nails, or stainless steel pins. Do not use nails that are barbed on the end, as when these are removed (for photography, for instance) the wood will be damaged.

Samples and other materials which are double-bagged, should have one label between the bags and one outside. Each label should include: the site code, the context number and its unique number. The labels themselves should be in high contrast with their markings *e.g.* white plastic 'garden tags' marked with black, spirit-based, waterproof felt-tip pen.

It is often most effective to give finds and samples labels and numbers as soon as possible to cut down the risk of loss or confusion. This can mean establishing a system for doing this on the project boat or work platform. A supply of the relevant materials will be required along with a means of noting which numbers have been used. The sooner that this information is transferred to the main site recording system the better.

It is difficult to ensure that object and number stay together, especially as during recording and analysis the object may be handled a number of times by different people. One solution is to physically mark the object with its number and site code. An example of marking pottery in this way is discussed below. Common sense should allow observations made about this class of material to be applied to others.

c. Marking pottery

This example describes one possible procedure for marking pottery. Whoever is doing the work, regular checks should be made to ensure that the marking is neat, legible, as small as possible and correct.

Problems in these areas invalidate the whole process. The following general guidelines should be borne in mind:

i. Mark the sherds so that the marking would appear on the inside or undersides of the vessel or object if it were restored.

ii. Mark on a base where possible.

iii. Use white ink on dark surfaces.

iv. Use clear varnish on the surface area to be marked. Any numbers on this varnish can subsequently be easily removed with acetone or a suitable solvent.

v. Check what has been written. 6's can look like 9's, a's like o's, 2's like 7's.

vi. Treat each sherd as a special case – if in doubt ASK.

vii. Don't mark over a glaze if it is possible to mark elsewhere.

viii. Don't mark on a fracture.

ix. Don't mark on a lip or rim.

x. Don't mark so that the writing would appear upside down if the sherd were correctly orientated.

xi. A cocktail stick dipped in ink can make a good substitute for a nib pen, and will not scratch the surface of the sherd.

Different material will require slightly different solutions. Timbers, for example, may be easier to tag securely than other materials. Remember that the point of the exercise is to make sure that the object is easily and confidently related to the written record.

6.3.5. Computers as part of the recording system

The field of computers, especially micro-computers, is very dynamic and rapidly changing. The computer or software considered powerful today is often outdated or obsolete in a very short period of time. For this reason it is not sensible to recommend specific brand names or configurations.

Many archaeological projects have designed recording systems with computer storage in mind from the outset. If you intend to purchase a computer to manage the site record you should familiarise yourself with the characteristics of the hardware and software available. There will be a bewildering choice of options, such as architecture, storage capacity, display quality, processing power, portability etc. As a general principle you get what you pay for so decide what features you really need to fit within your budget. On the other hand, if you already have a computer, it can probably be made to serve. Access to large amounts of storage capacity is probably the only necessity.

Putting all the information in one place can be very convenient, but clearly it also means that the information becomes vulnerable to total loss if a problem occurs with the machine being used. A carefully observed system of backing up should be established. 'Backing-up' is the process of making copies of the information on a separate storage device in order to minimise any loss of records resulting from a problem with the main device. The copies should then be stored in a safe place well away from the original so that no one disaster will destroy both.

a. Database programs

A database is nothing more than a collection of information but a database program in combination with a suitable computer makes the manipulation and presentation of these records much more convenient. Its use allows for comparison between evidence both from different parts of the site and different sites, the formation of bibliographic files, and the cataloguing of objects for further study. Database program use further enhances the more mundane aspects of site management: work rosters, payroll, and site reports. Properly developed and applied, the database program offers a degree of systemisation and organisation previously unavailable to the working archaeologist.

Databases can be divided into two types, physical or relational. A physical database is one that lists records one after the other. A relational database, the type most useful in archaeological work, allows access to any point in the database from any other point in

the database and, most importantly, allows for the comparison of records between separate databases.

6.3.6. Working towards the site archive

All of this effort is directed towards producing the site archive, the importance of which has already been discussed.

However you decide to record the evidence you are observing do treat it as something you will have to make sense of later. In the case of rescue or total research excavation those records will be the greater part of all that remains of that site (see Section 12.0).

The maintenance of the archive generates the considerable responsibility of storage. This should be planned before the project starts. (Section 5.3.8).

6.4. Suggested Reading

a. recording systems

Gawronski, J.H.G.
1986   *Amsterdam Project: Annual Report of the VOC-Ship "Amsterdam" Foundation 1985.* Amsterdam, ISBN 90-71690-01-6.

Schofield, J. (ed)
1980   *Site Manual, Part 1: the written record.* London.

Spence, C. (ed.)
1990   *Archaeological Site Manual.* London, ISBN 0-904818-40-3.

Stewart, J.D.
1982   Computerising archaeological records - a progress report on the work of the MDA. In *Computer Applications in Archaeology Conference Proceedings*, 4-10, University of Birmingham.

b. recording contexts

Hodgson, J.M. (ed)
1976   *Soil Survey Field Handbook.* Soil Survey Technical Monograph No.5, Harpenden. ISBN 0-904818-40-3.

Spence, C. (ed.)
   1990   *Archaeological Site Manual.* London, ISBN 0-904818-40-3.

c. recording timbers

Coles, J.M.
   1990   *Waterlogged Wood.* English Heritage, London, ISBN 1-85074-335-5.
Marsden, P.
   1991   Recording ancient ships. In Coles, J.M. and D.M. Goodburn (eds.), *Wet Site Excavation and Survey. Conf. Proc., Museum of London, October 1990.* WARP Occasional Paper No.5, ISSN 0950-8244.
Murdock, L.D. and Daley, T.
   1982   Progress report on the use of FMC polysulfide rubber compounds for recording archaeological ships' features in a marine environment. *IJNA,* 11.4: 349 -352.
Nayling, N.T.
   1989   *The Archaeological Wood Survey: a review of the potential and problems of waterlogged structural wood.* Ancient Monuments Report 62/89, Ancient Monuments Laboratory, HBMC, London.

d. computers as part of the recording system

Carter, J., Covill, J., Stevens, W. and Grenier, R.
   1987   A Feasibility Study of a Diver Operated Computer and Data Acquisition System Designed for Underwater Archaeology. In Albright, A.B. (ed.) *Underwater Archaeology Proceedings of the Society of Historical Archaeology Conference.* Savannah.
Graham, I. and Webb, E. (eds)
   1982   *Computer applications in archaeology 1981.* Institute of Archaeology, London.
Richards, J.D. and Ryan, N.S.
   1985   *Data processing in archaeology.* Cambridge Manuals In Archaeology, Cambridge, ISBN 0-521-25769-7.
Ruggles, C.L.N. and Rahtz, S.P.Q.
   1988   *Computer and quantitative methods in archaeology 1987.* British Archaeological Reports IS 393, Oxford.

7. Position Fixing

7.1. Introduction

7.2. Optical Methods of Position Fixing

7.3. Electronic Methods of Position Fixing

7.4. Suggested Reading

7.1. Introduction

Fixing the position of archaeological remains so that they can be related to other evidence is an essential part of archaeological work (Section 4.4.1). Pin-pointing the exact location of a site, or the relative position of one site to another, is generally known as position fixing. Position fixing can be difficult enough on land, when surrounded by features plotted on large-scale maps. At sea identifiable and charted features may not lie immediately adjacent to a site, so accurate position fixing can be even more problematic.

Position fixing relies on the same basic principles as surveying on an archaeological site, but on a much larger scale. Points of unknown position are measured in to those which are already known using relatively long-range techniques involving the measurement of distances or angles. The exception is the simple alignment of transits (see below) where the human eye and a suitable chart or map is all that is required. At the other end of the spectrum of sophistication are a range of electronic systems with the potential for a high level of efficiency and precision.

There is no simple answer to the question 'which method is best?' and various factors have to be considered before a decision is made. These include:

i. likely number of fixes,
ii. equipment or resources available,
iii. degree of accuracy required,
iv. expertise and experience of the personnel involved,
v. time available for investment in preparatory work.

On both maps and mariners' charts the position of an archaeological site is normally expressed as a co-ordinate in either degrees and minutes of latitude and longitude, or as a numerical co-ordinate of the national survey grid system (such as the National Grid Reference in the UK).

It should be noted that there is an important difference in the notation of the two systems. With latitude and longitude the horizontal co-ordinate (or Latitude) is given before the vertical (or Longitude) and has the appropriate suffix of (N)orth or (S)outh, depending which side of the equator the position lies. The longitude has the suffix (E)ast or (W)est, depending on which side of the zero meridian (the line joining the north and south poles and which passes through the old Royal Observatory in Greenwich) the site is located.

Map grid references in the UK are conventionally expressed the other way round with the vertical lines, or 'eastings', given before the horizontal lines, or 'northings'. There is nothing in the way the co-ordinate is written to denote which is which, and consequently confusion can arise if the

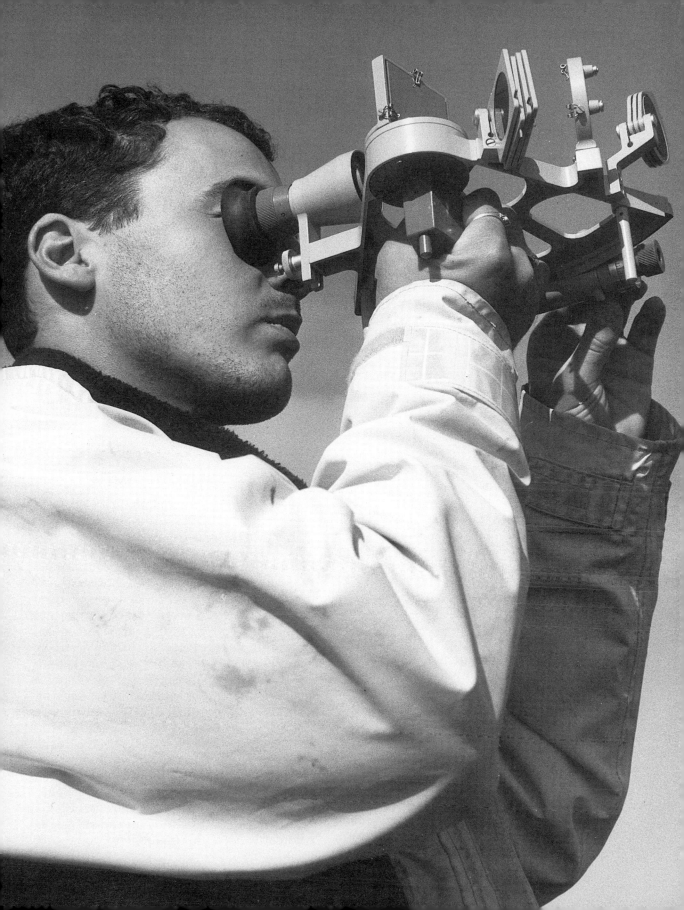

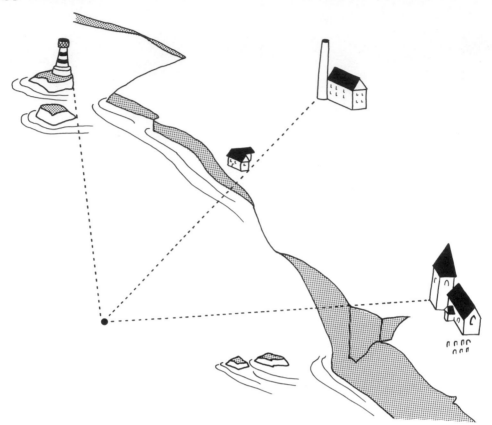

Figure 45. The use of coastal features as transit marks to establish the position of a site (after Rico).(7.2.1.a.)

convention is not remembered. It is important, however, to denote the map sheet number.

7.1.1. How many points?

Fixing the position of a single point on the seabed will rarely be of much use, unless it is to plot an isolated find such as a sherd of pottery or an anchor. When positioning a site it is better to fix two or three points which can be cross-checked against each other using survey techniques more appropriate to short-range work (Section 9.3).

Theoretically, it is possible to fix just one point on the site and to give an orientation. In practice, orientation is difficult to plot to a sufficient degree of accuracy and the lack of an inbuilt cross-check can lead to errors.

7.1.2. Degree of accuracy

Selecting an acceptable degree of accuracy in position fixing is not straightforward. A distance which is less than a fine pencil line width on the chart or map used for plotting is a useful rule of thumb as a maximum error, but more precise plotting is normally desirable. A line width of 0.5mm on a relatively large scale chart of 1:10,000 has a scale width on the ground of 5m, whereas on a small scale chart at 1:100,000 it will have a width of 50m.

One of the major obstacles that have to be overcome when fixing the position of sites on the seabed is the difficulty of deciding which point on the sea surface lies precisely above the point being fixed. A tight line between a secure datum and a buoy on the surface is commonly used, but it is difficult to be sure

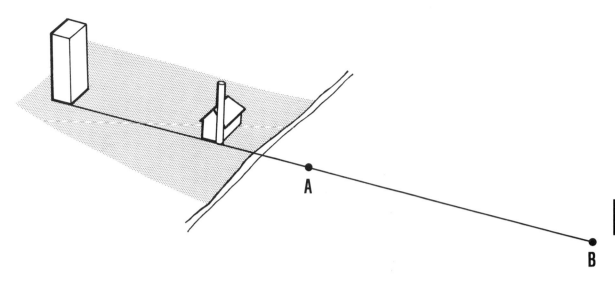

Figure 46. Accuracy of transits: A position fix at A will be more accurate than at B. (7.2.1.b.)

the buoy is exactly over the datum even in a very clear water, and particularly when the buoy is affected by tidal streams and currents.

7.2. Optical Methods of Position Fixing

Low technology methods have been the mainstay of hydrographic surveying for the last two centuries and have been used to produce results of a consistently high quality. The main drawback of optical methods is their reliance on features of known position being visible to the surveyor. Mist and haze, rain and snow, and extreme light levels can all interfere with the efficiency and accuracy of the survey. Regardless of these difficulties they have distinct advantages for those involved in archaeological surveying, not the least of which is the relative cheapness of the equipment compared to the electronic alternatives.

7.2.1. Transits

a. Principle and method

The visual alignment of two charted features establishes a line of sight which can be drawn on the chart; a second pair of aligned features, at approximately 90 degrees to the first and visible from the same position, will give an excellent intersection when plotted (Figure 45). A third transit will act as a check to see whether the observed features actually are the ones charted.

b. Accuracy

This system is simple and potentially very accurate, particularly if the distance between the two features in alignment is a large proportion of the distance between the observer and the nearest feature (Figure 46). It is also inexpensive as all that is required is an appropriate map or chart, and perhaps a camera to record the transits.

Although the technique is extremely useful, problems can arise. Archaeological sites underwater and useful charted features are rarely conveniently positioned relative to each other. A choice may exist between

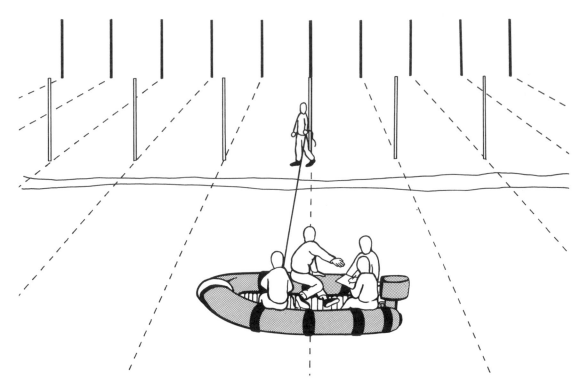

Figure 47. Temporary transits formed by setting up paired ranging rods along a shore baseline. When collecting data close inshore, or on inland waters, additional locational control can be provided by a tape measure or a distance line. (7.2.1.b.)

features which do not quite line up and give an open transit (features just apart from each other) or a closed transit (one partially or totally hidden behind the other).

Often natural features have to be used and these can be difficult to equate precisely with what is shown on a chart; for instance, the base of a cliff or the edge of an island or rock can differ as the water level changes in tidal areas. In many instances the lack of suitable charted features will dictate that uncharted features will have to be used. Sometimes artificial transits, such as pairs of surveyor's ranging poles (Figure 47), will have to be placed in appropriate positions. As with uncharted features, if these temporary alignments have to be used to plot the position of a site each will have to be separately surveyed in to the appropriate chart or map.

Establishing beforehand which features will be available for transits is not always practicable because they may not be visible due to poor horizontal surface visibility, or because they are masked by intervening landforms or vegetation.

7.2.2. Compass bearings

a. Principle and method

To plot a position a charted feature is aligned with the sights on the bearing compass and a reading taken. Bearings should be taken on at least two, but preferably three separate features and, ideally, with a difference in angle between them of approximately 60 degrees. If two bearings are plotted on a chart by either using the compass rose printed on the chart, or by physically measuring with a protractor from magnetic north, the two lines should intersect at a point coinciding with where the readings were taken. A third bearing will act as a check on accuracy and should pass through the existing intersection. Frequently a small triangle called a 'cocked hat' appears (Figure 48) and the larger this is, the bigger the error.

b. Equipment

A prismatic or hand bearing compass, or binoculars with a built-in compass may be used from boat or shore. Traditional bearing compasses employ a compass card rotating in a liquid, but hand-held electronic fluxgate compasses are now available which give a digital readout. These have a greater potential accuracy but the models so far encountered only give a bearing to within 0.5 degree.

It is easier to get consistent readings with a hand-held fluxgate compass by pressing a button at the time when the charted feature is in alignment with the compass sights, thereby automatically recording and storing the bearing. It is possible to do this a number of times for each bearing until an acceptable level of repeatability is obtained.

c. Accuracy

The simple procedure of taking a fix requires practice to achieve consistent results in a moving boat, particularly with conventional magnetic compasses, as the compass card is normally moving continuously in response to the movement of the vessel. The major drawback with all magnetic compasses is their susceptibility to magnetic interference from electronic equipment, iron and steel. Great care has to be taken to make sure the bearing compass is not deviating. Unlike a ship's compass, it is not normally fixed in one position on the vessel. This means that its relationship to potential sources of deviation often changes each time it is used, making correction factors very difficult to calculate.

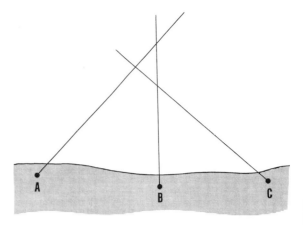

Figure 48. A large triangle of error, or 'cocked hat'. The smaller the triangle the better the fix. (7.2.2.a.)

It is important to remember that the bearings taken are relative to magnetic and not true north. The differences between the two slowly fluctuates in time and also varies with the geographical location. Charts and maps usually have the relevant information printed on them and it is normally possible to calculate the difference between true north, magnetic north, and the north alignment of the reference grid of the map or chart being used, if that does not coincide with lines of longitude running true north-south between the Earth's poles. On a moving boat within the size range normally used in archaeological work, the potential differences are academic because it is difficult to obtain consistent readings to within about 2 degrees, even in relatively calm conditions.

7.2.3.   Sextant

a.   Equipment

The sextant is one of the most useful optical position-fixing tools for coastal surveying. It is basically a protractor and telescope linked by mirrors which allow an angle between two separate features to be measured (Figure 50).

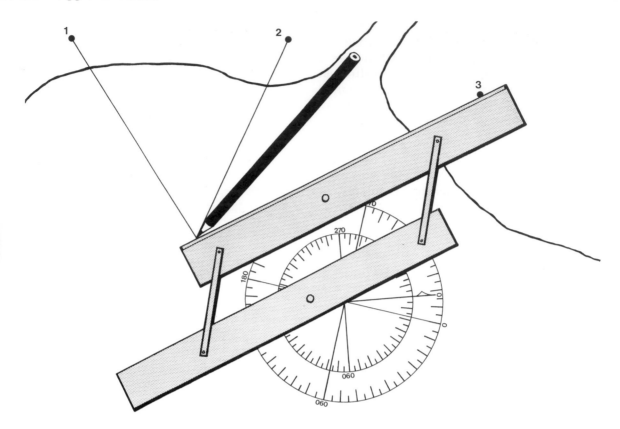

Figure 49. Transferring bearings taken on-site by magnetic compass using a parallel rule and the compass rose on a chart. (7.2.2.a.) (After Rico.)

Although superseded by electronic devices (Section 7.3) for much survey work, sextants are still used by professional hydrographic surveyors in certain circumstances because they are accurate, portable and can be deployed quickly (unlike many electronic systems), and can be relatively inexpensive.

b. Principle and method

Although it is possible to establish a global position by taking vertical angles between heavenly bodies and the horizon, for general archaeological purposes the sextant is normally used to measure horizontal angles between visible features of known position.

Angles in the region of 60 degrees give reliable results but, in extreme cases, angles as low as 30 and as great as 120 degrees might have to be used. Traditionally two angles between three charted objects are used for position fixing but, to increase the confidence in the fix, it is better to take a third angle involving a fourth charted object as this will give a check on the accuracy of the first two readings.

Once a set of angles has been taken the position can be plotted on the chart by a number of different methods. The angles can be drawn on a piece of semi-transparent draughting film and then laid over the chart and moved around until the lines pass through the appropriate features, the intersection of the lines being the plotted position (Figure 51). For increased accuracy thinner lines can be inscribed on the film rather than drawn, using the point of a draughting compass. A more common plotting method is to use a station pointer, a protractor with one fixed and two moving arms set at two of the measured angles. This

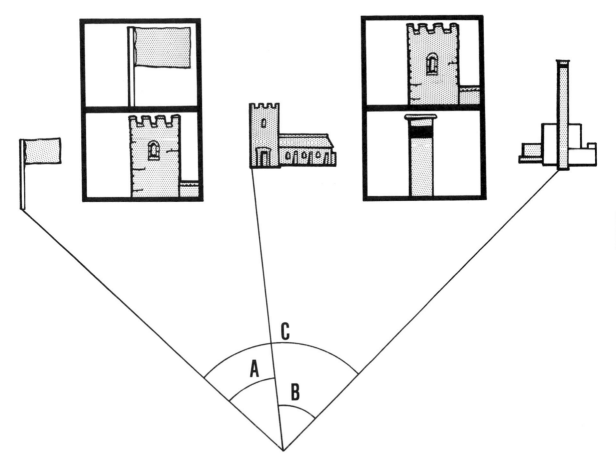

Figure 50. Taking horizontal sextant angles. Angle A is measured between left hand side of the flag-pole and the left hand side of the church tower by lining them up in the split-viewfinder. Angle B is measured between the left hand side of the church tower and the left hand side of the chimney. Angle C, measured between the flag pole and the left hand side of the chimney, should equal angle A plus angle B. (7.2.3.b.)

is also moved about the chart until the arms pass through the three features, then the centre is above the plot position.

Alternatively the plot can be constructed geometrically (Figure 52), the simplest method being to draw a baseline between the left hand pair of features and draw a line at an angle of 90 degrees, minus the measured sextant angle, out from each end. For example, in Figure 52, the sextant angle between A and B was 40°, So the lines extend from the baseline at 90° - 40° = 50°. The sextant angle between B and C was 45° so the lines extend from the baseline at 90° - 45° = 45°. The intersection of these lines is

the centre of a circle of radius equal to the distance between the features and the centre. At any point on this circle the angle between the two features will be constant. So a second circle has to be drawn constructed in the same way on a baseline drawn between another feature and one of the pair already used. The intersection of these two circles is the plotted position. It is possible to construct a whole series of circles based on different angles, and these horizontal sextant angle charts can be very useful if a lot of survey work is to be undertaken in the same area using the same charted features.

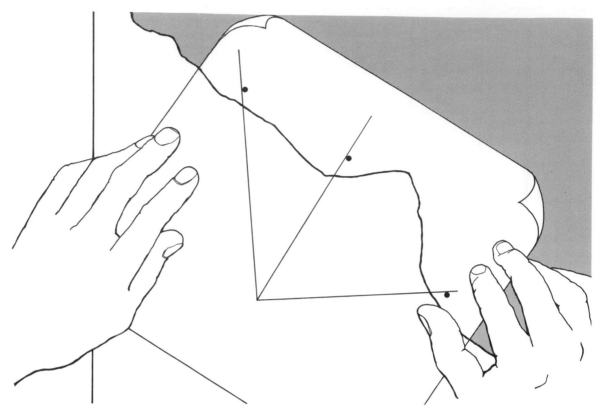

Figure 51. Sextant angles can be scribed on plastic drafting film to within about 20 minutes of arc (1/3rd of a degree.) This can be sufficiently precise to plot a position on a large scale chart. (7.2.3.b.)

c. Accuracy

Position fixing using horizontal sextant angles can be accurate to within 1m radius in ideal conditions, but it requires practice to take consistent readings in a moving boat. The relative position of the features used is important because if the angles between them are too small or too large accuracy tends to decrease.

The cheaper sextants are made of plastic and can measure angles down to 0.2 minutes of arc (equivalent to 1/300 of a degree). This is more than adequate for taking horizontal angles as the minimum accuracy plottable by drawing methods is considerably more than one complete minute of arc, although plotting trigonometrically the potential accuracy can be fully exploited.

The major drawback of the cheaper sextants is the relatively poor quality of the telescope optics which can make accurate sightings on features more than a few kilometres away difficult, especially if the conditions are misty or light levels are low. Plastic sextants may also be more susceptible to distortion in hot weather. All sextants, regardless of cost, are delicate scientific instruments and need treating as such. Adjustments and routine care varies with each model and should be covered in the manufacturer's instructions.

One of the shortcomings of the above systems is the difficulty of plotting angles on the chart with the same degree of accuracy as they were taken. Even with a large protractor definition of only about 15 minutes

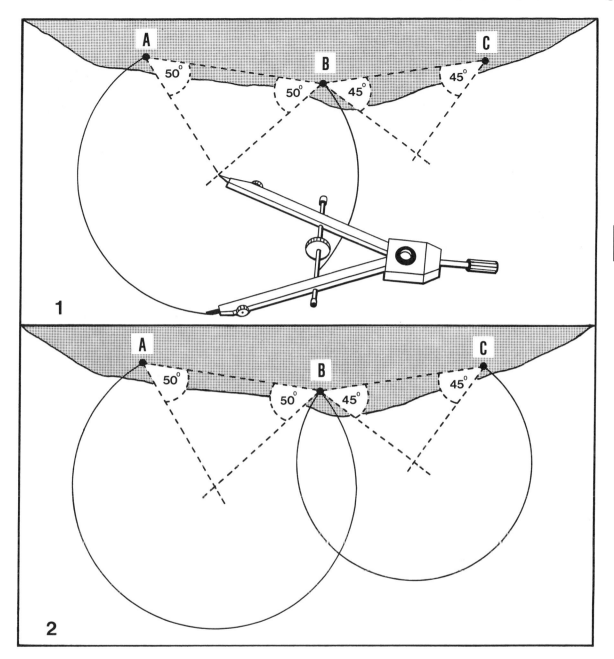

Figure 52. Sextant angles can be plotted geometrically from baselines between charted features. (7.2.3.b.)

of arc are possible at best, and sophisticated station pointers with a vernier scale are only capable of being set to within 1 minute of arc.

An advance on mechanical plotting is the use of one of the programs which can be run on programmable calculators and portable computers capable of operating in a small boat. These can calculate plotted positions trigonometrically. Typically the co-ordinates of the three principle charted features have to be entered, then a fourth, to allow a checking angle to establish the degree of

Figure 53. Using a theodolite to fix the position of a wreck at low tide when the site is exposed. (7.2.4.a.) (Courtesy of C.Dobbs and the Amsterdam Foundation.)

confidence in the measurements. The various angles are entered and from this information the plotted position is calculated to a level of accuracy which can be less than one metre. Because of the potential of a high degree of accuracy, the projection used to represent the Earth's curved surface as a two-dimensional drawing on a chart may have to be taken into account, and this information has to be entered into some computer programs.

7.2.4. Theodolite

a. Principle and equipment

The principle of using theodolites to measure angles is the same as that for the sextant. In essence a theodolite is a telescope which can

be swivelled both horizontally and vertically against fixed scales for measuring the angle. They require a stable base on which to set their supporting tripods. Consequently they are not designed to be operated from a boat, but they can be used successfully from the shore to fix the position of objects on the sea surface within visible range.

b. Method

If a series of buoys over key points on the seabed need to have their positions fixed, the position of the theodolite itself will have to be fixed by taking angles between visible charted features and plotting the results in the manner previously explained for sextant work (Section 7.2.3). From that station, angles between a charted feature and each

Figure 54. Surveying a submerged site in shallow water using a shore-based E.D.M. (7.3.3.b.) (after Morrison.)

individual buoy can be measured and the process repeated from another station located at an appropriate place.

Once the position of the two stations has been plotted, lines drawn at the angles measured from each station will intersect (ideally at about 60 degrees) to give the buoy positions. As always, a check on the plot is desirable and so readings from a third shore station should be taken.

This system of plotting from the shore can also be done with a sextant. It is often the only practicable method where charted features are not visible from the position which needs to be fixed. Sites very close to shores with featureless cliffs or high sand dunes often suffer with this problem.

When coupled with an Electronic Distance Measuring device (Section 7.3.3), a theodolite can quickly plot numerous buoy positions from a single survey station, although readings should be taken to each point from a second station as a cross-check. The theodolite/EDM combination can also conveniently track and plot the course of a vessel carrying out remote sensing or other survey work if the operator repeatedly takes readings on the moving vessel.

c. Accuracy

The potential accuracy of a good theodolite is in the order of 1 second of arc (1/3600 of a degree) much greater than a sextant. However the theodolite is also more vulnerable, complex and expensive. In addition, to achieve reliable measurements a certain level of familiarity has to be gained preferably through tuition by an experienced surveyor. However, the theodolite is by no means outside the scope of a small project as these instruments can be hired. It may even be possible to call on the assistance of an appropriate museum or archaeological organisation as they often have theodolites and EDMs (Section 7.3.3).

7.3. Electronic Methods of Position Fixing

A major development in survey technology in recent years has been the increasing success of site location and position fixing by electronic equipment. The advantage of many systems is that, when used in conjunction with remote sensing equipment (Section 8.1.3), they can be very efficient at providing large amounts of positional information in a digitised form, which can be combined with other digitised survey results and then manipulated and analysed by computers. Their main disadvantages are the relatively high cost compared to low technology methods and their complexity, making physical protection and maintenance more difficult. Learning the skills necessary for the full utilisation of such equipment is probably no more difficult than learning those required for many low-technology methods.

7.3.1. International hyperbolic navigation systems

a. Principle and equipment

These are systems based around a network of permanent radio transmission stations on shore. They require a suitable receiver on a boat which interprets the signal and calculates a position. Recent versions can update every few seconds. Two common versions of this are Decca and Loran C which operate in slightly different ways.

It is expected that eventually some International Hyperbolic Systems will be phased out as greater use is made of Global Positioning Systems (Section 7.3.4).

b. Accuracy

These systems are not accurate enough for precise survey work because the position indicated will normally only be resolved to within 0.01 of a minute of latitude or longitude. At best, this is theoretically equivalent to not less than 15m at the latitude of the British Isles. In practice, its absolute accuracy is probably ten times this distance; more than adequate for conventional ship navigation, the task for which the system was designed.

Despite this, the degree of repeatability a fixed combination of aerial and receiver on a boat can give is very useful. This means that once a position has been visited, and the co-ordinates as indicated on the instrument are recorded, it is relatively easy to use the same instrument to get within approximately 50m of the original position: a distance sufficiently large to be of limited use as a position fix for surveying purposes, but sufficiently small to make relocation of a site or object on the seabed a reasonable proposition using appropriate search techniques (Section 8.0).

7.3.2. Microwave shore stations

a. Principle

These systems take advantage of the near constant velocity of radio waves which are transmitted from shore stations and interrogated by the mobile Distance Measuring Unit (DMU) in the boat. The information collected on the boat can be passed directly to a computer which can display the heading the helmsman should steer along a planned course. Similarly a plotter can be linked to record graphically the track actually taken. This is an important feature if an area of seabed is to be covered systematically during remote sensing and other surveys.

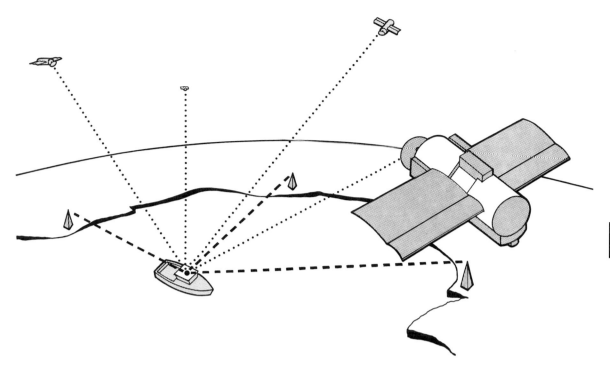

Figure 55. Satellite and hyperbolic systems. By knowing the exact position of satellites or shore stations the receiver can calculate its position. With 'differential GPS' techniques this can be sufficiently accurate for archaeological surveying. (7.3.1.b.)

b. Equipment

The drawbacks of the system are the cost of the equipment; the need to calibrate at least daily against a known distance; signal problems caused by 'range holes'; possible vandalism on unattended shore stations (it is not unknown for the 12 volt batteries powering trisponders to be stolen); the requirement to fix the position of the trisponders before starting work; and, in many countries, the need for permission to be obtained from the appropriate government agency before the trisponders can legally transmit radio signals - in the UK permission must be sought from the Department of Trade and Industry.

These commercially available systems, such as the Motorola Mini Ranger, require the user to set up at least three trisponders on temporary shore stations at appropriate places on the nearby shore or on fixed structures standing in the sea. Their position

has to be established accurately and this may entail surveying them in by conventional means if they cannot be located precisely on convenient charted features.

c. Accuracy

The DMU calculates the distance from each station and gives a position to within about 1m if conditions are good, or about 3m in typical conditions with a rolling boat.

The advantages of the system outweigh the disadvantages if surveys are going to take place within the range of the established shore stations over a prolonged period. The ability to position shore stations in places most suitable for the survey; the level of accuracy suitable for most survey purposes; the speed with which information is collected and the ability to have navigational information and survey results displayed instantaneously can make the operation much more efficient than many other

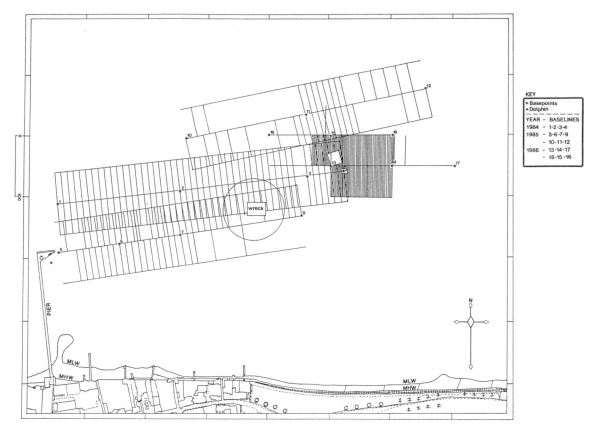

KEY

* Basepoints
▲ Dolphin

YEAR	-	BASELINES
1984	-	1-2-3-4
1985	-	5-6-7-9
	-	10-11-12
1986	-	13-14-17
	-	18-15-16

Figure 56. Search patterns employed to locate Roman material on the seabed. (Courtesy of the Isle of Wight Trust for Maritime Archaeology.)

methods. The information can also be collected in quantities and format suitable for computer manipulation.

7.3.3. Electronic distance measurement

a. Principle

Like many electronic surveying systems electronic distance measurers (EDMs) rely on the near constant speed of radiated energy close to the visible end of the electromagnetic spectrum, commonly the infra-red wavelength. The time taken for a pulse of energy to reach a target and return to the instrument is measured, and using the known velocity of the energy through air, the distance is calculated.

b. Equipment

The energy beam is reflected back to the instrument by a prism (sometimes in arrays to increase the target size). For short-range work of less than 500m simple red plastic reflectors, of the type used on the backs of some road trailers, can be substituted. These reflectors are inexpensive and far less prone to salt-water and physical damage than the more sensitive, and very costly, prismatic reflectors supplied by manufacturers.

EDMs of varying degrees of sophistication are being used more frequently for location control for coastal work. The more complex variants can be interfaced with a computer and plotter to produce drawn surveys as the work progresses. All but the basic models can be used to record the track of a survey vessel working off-shore. The major disadvantages of EDMs are the cost and the limited maximum range, particularly if the target is bobbing about on the ocean. There are important operational benefits which make them most suitable for accurate archaeological surveying close inshore (Figure 54).

EDMs are usually either coupled with a theodolite (Section 7.2.4), or built into one unit known as a 'combined' or 'total' station which has all the facilities of both instruments but without the disadvantage of possible misalignment between the optics of the theodolite and the EDM. The facility to measure angles and distances accurately means that most instruments can automatically calculate additional useful information. For instance, the angular difference between the horizontal and the inclination of the line of sight between EDM and reflector, together with the actual measured distance or 'slant range', allows both the true horizontal distance and the height differences between the survey point and the target to be computed.

The normal movement of even the most stable ship is too great to allow such equipment to be used effectively at sea. For this reason theodolite-mounted EDMs and total stations are invariably shore-based. Simpler hand-held 'guns' which just display the distance to reflector are available, and these may be more suitable for some purposes on board a boat, but they are less accurate than the tripod-mounted type. There are other systems, such as geodimeters and tellurometers, but it is outside the scope of this handbook to describe all the high-technology instruments that could theoretically be used on archaeological projects.

c. Accuracy

The accuracy of these instruments is high because a series of measurements are taken for each fix over a short period, usually between about 0.5 and 5 seconds, depending on the accuracy required. A statistical average is then converted into a distance with an accuracy in the order of about 5mm over an approximate maximum range of 4 kilometres. At sea the normal maximum operational distance is more likely to be closer to 1 kilometre because of the difficulty of keeping the beam and reflector in alignment for a sufficient time for a meaningful statistical average to be computed; this problem increases with the motion of the sea. In calm conditions with clear air the maximum working range can increase dramatically to more than 10 kilometres.

7.3.4. Satellite navigation systems

a. Principle

These systems depend on the interrogation of signals transmitted by satellites. The satellites are equivalent to datum points and measurements are computed from the information transmitted to the systems receiver, and a position calculated. Complete military networks are now in position and capable of exceptional accuracy combined with ease of use. A good explanation of satellite navigation systems has been written by Ackroyd and Lorimer (1990).

b. Equipment

Two different satellite systems have almost total world coverage. Both are termed Global Positioning Systems (GPS), the USA's Navstar GPS, and the USSR's Glonass. Both were originally conceived as aids to military activities but both are now open to civilian users, although Glonass receivers are difficult to obtain. Other systems, such as ' Satnav', were designed at the outset for commercial use but there are too few of those satellites to allow continuous updating of a position, and they have been superseded by GPS.

The cost of GPS units has fallen dramatically and the models at the lower end of the market are comparable in price to all but the cheapest Decca and Loran-C

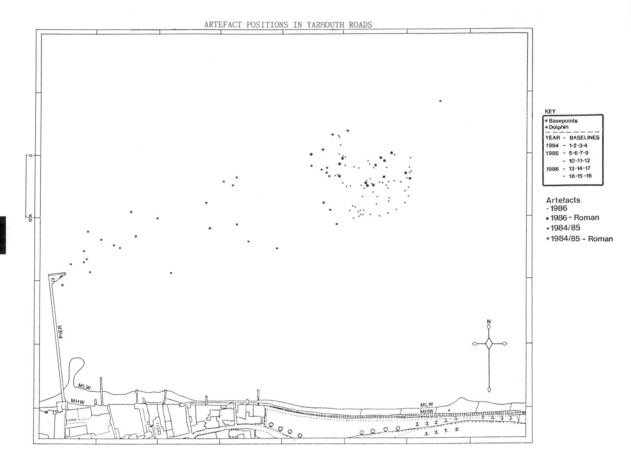

ARTEFACT POSITIONS IN YARMOUTH ROADS

KEY

■ Basepoints
▲ Dolphin

YEAR – BASELINES
1984 – 1-2-3-4
1985 – 5-6-7-9
– 10-11-12
1986 – 13-14-17
– 18-15-16

Artefacts
· 1986
● 1986 – Roman
▪ 1984/85
+ 1984/85 – Roman

Figure 57. Plot of Roman artefacts resulting from the search in Figure 56. The more intensive search pattern in the east resulted in a higher concentration of finds. (Courtesy of the Isle of Wight Trust for Maritime Archaeology.)

units. The least expensive are not necessarily the least accurate, and the most important feature to look for is a sufficient number of channels to collect data from as many satellites as possible. Receivers with five or six channels are more efficient than the simple hand-held units multiplexing on a single or dual channels, yet are not always dramatically more expensive.

c. Accuracy – (stand-alone GPS)

The theoretical accuracy of GPS is very high but, because the US Department of Defence perceives this as an asset to potential enemies, the system has been designed to be downgraded if required so that only US military approved users can fully exploit the system. Most GPS satellites transmit on two channels, one for the military (P-code) and the other for civilian access (C/A). 'Selective Availability' (S/A) is introduced into the C/A channels when the US military think it necessary and this has the effect of reducing accuracy to most of us. In practice the differences have not been as dramatic as anticipated, and a positional uncertainty in two dimensions without S/A imposed has been increased by a factor of about three with it in operation.

The actual accuracy of GPS will vary with the type of receiver (multiplex or multi-channel), the antenna, the available constellation of satellites, the imposition or otherwise of S/A, and how the figures are presented. In some manufacturers' literature you will often see two-dimensional accuracy (the most appropriate for most uses at sea) of about 15m root mean square (RMS). RMS indicates a statistical probability of one standard deviation and so, in ideal conditions, the antenna has a 68% probability of being within a circle of 15m radius, and a 95% probability of being within a 30m radius circle (2RMS). Some instruments actually display the computed two-dimensional accuracy, normally to one RMS, and this is very useful as an indication of the current state of your system. The accuracy of a standalone GPS unit can sometimes fluctuate dramatically due to such things as changes in the useable constellation of satellites.

The imposition of Selective Availability will decrease the accuracy to about 90m radius 2RMS which is far too inaccurate for fixing the position of archaeological sites, but probably close enough to allow relocation of known sites. However one of the major advantages of GPS is the ability to increase the accuracy of the system by using 'differential' techniques.

d.   Accuracy (differential GPS)

It is possible to achieve accuracies of 2m radius 2RMS by having a second GPS unit on the shore at a known position as close as possible to the mobile unit, but preferably within about 20 kilometres. The base unit needs to be positioned very accurately either on a convenient national survey station (e.g. a 'trig. point' in the UK), or at any point surveyed in to within less than 1 metre. The difference between the base unit's actual position and that given by the GPS display, can be applied to the mobile unit's reading to give a more accurate corrected position, provided the same satellites are interrogated by the two units.

This level of accuracy is sufficient for most remote sensing survey and site position fixing applications, but the efficiency of data transfer between the base and mobile units affects the ability of the system to be used for

accurate tracking and navigation during survey work.   Automatic data links are available that can correct the calculated distances between the base unit and satellites, a more useful and accurate correction than the simpler positional correction for the mobile unit. Provided the information collected at the two units is synchronised, post-survey processing can give corrected positional results for the mobile unit. This cuts out the need for expensive data links but it also reduces the efficiency of the system particularly when using it as a means of very accurate navigation.

It is possible to transmit the correction verbally using marine VHF, CB, cellphone or similar communication system, but this is usually only in the form of a geographical position correction. On some sophisticated units capable of displaying satellite to unit distances it is possible to add correction factors to these measurements. In any event it is important to match the satellites in use, although this may not always be possible if the mobile unit is operating close under a cliff or similar obstruction which masks the essential line of sight between the antenna and satellites.

It is possible to buy positional information from commercial organisations. A variety of organisations have set up base stations which transmit data for use by a mobile unit. Single units have been set up close to difficult port approaches, and chains of base stations have been positioned covering large areas of the globe.   To receive the information a suitable mobile GPS unit and appropriate receiver are required. This often incorporates an unscrambling device which decodes the transmitted information. A rental charge is normally made for the use of the service and the hire of the decoding machine, and this may put it beyond the range of most archaeological budgets. The accuracy may not always be sufficient for some archaeological purposes if the base stations are some distance away, but this will probably become less of a problem as more systems and base stations are installed.

7.3.5. Radar

a. Principle and equipment

Specifically designed to identify the position of distant objects, these instruments work by interpreting the reflections of very high frequency radio waves, commonly in the region of 1000MHz, emitted and collected by a rotating antenna scanning through 360 degrees. The speed of rotation is usually about once every two seconds in commercially available radars. The radio reflections are reproduced on a video-type screen as images which vary in brightness with the passing of a rotating highlight synchronised to the rotating antenna. These images can sometimes be difficult to interpret in bright conditions, and this is why many display units are enclosed within shades to exclude extraneous light.

b. Accuracy

Many modern instruments have an electronic cursor which, when placed over an identified reflection on the screen, will give both a range and a bearing from the position of the scanning antenna. The degree of range accuracy, in optimum conditions, is about 1% (about 20m for every nautical mile between antenna and target), and bearing accuracy within 2 degrees.

This sort of accuracy is good enough for most navigational purposes, but is not sufficient on its own to accurately pin-point archaeological sites on the seabed. Like the hyperbolic navigation systems (Section 7.3.1) it can be very useful for establishing an approximate area in which more precise search or positioning systems can be established.

7.4. Suggested Reading

Ackroyd, N., and Lorimer, R.
    1990   *Global Navigation: A GPS user's guide.* London, ISBN 1-85044-232-0.
British Sub Aqua Club
    1986   *Seamanship for Divers.* London, ISBN 0-09-166291-5.
Maloney, E.S.
    1978   *Dutton's Navigation and Piloting.* Annapolis, MD, ISBN 0-87021-164-1.
Ministry of Defence
    1978   *Manual of Map Reading.* HMSO, London, ISBN 0-11-771905-6.

8. Search Methods

8.1. Basic Principles

8.2. Historical Search

8.3. Suggested Reading

8.1. Basic Principles

Searches can be divided into two types:

i. Those deploying a diver or a submersible and relying on the human eye or hand-held equipment.

ii. Remote sensing surveys usually employing electronic equipment controlled from a boat, or other craft, on or above the surface.

The techniques used and the intensity of a survey will be affected by the factors taken into account while planning the search (Section 5.4.1). Whatever search method is used, it is vital to know where you are and where you have been. This will save time in search operations and will significantly enhance the information recorded. A search only has value if the position of the area covered, the identified targets, together with other pertinent observations, are accurately reported and recorded. Divers should complete detailed dive logs (Section 6.2.13) recording all information of potential interest for subsequent analysis. Similarly events indicated by remote sensing equipment during the survey should be logged, either electronically or manually.

8.1.1. Coverage

Unless a well thought out sampling strategy has been devised a common objective is 100% coverage of the selected area. Unfortunately '100%' is difficult to define in this context because of the varying degrees of efficiency of different techniques. For instance an intensive visual search may cover every square centimetre of the seabed but miss an object a few millimetres long, or a larger one camouflaged by a temporary dusting of light silt. Similarly magnetometer search corridors separated by 50m might be sufficient to detect the wrecks of large wooden ships armed with iron cannon, but might not detect other targets of archaeological significance such as a single cannon or submerged prehistoric settlement.

It is also important to realise that no search operation, no matter how rigourous and intense, can say with absolute certainty that there are no archaeologically significant finds or sites in the area covered. The fact that nothing has been detected does not mean that nothing is there. Technology has a long way to go before it is possible to be certain of recovering all the available evidence.

8.1.2. Diver search methods

These mostly depend on visual observations, but hand-held instruments, such as metal detectors, can also be deployed. The speed and efficiency of the search is proportional to both the size of the targets and the visibility. Small objects on a muddy seabed are a challenge to locate.

There is a large variation amongst divers in terms of ability to notice things on the seabed. This ability is related to factors such as commitment, concentration, familiarity

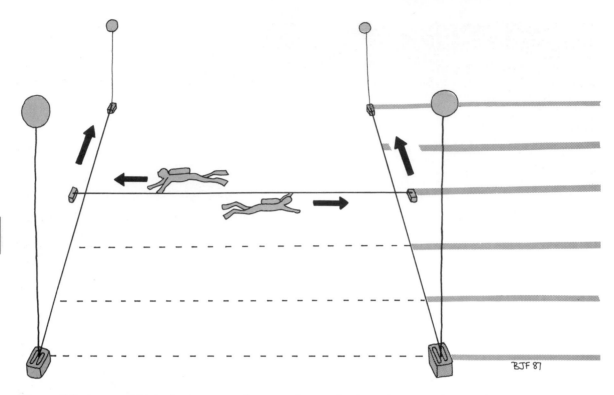

Figure 58. A possible jackstay search procedure: the baseline is advanced a pre-determined distance after each diver has completed inspection of their side of the line. The distance between baselines will depend upon factors such as visibility and obscuring plant growth. (8.1.2.c.)

with the target material, training in systematic observation, apprehension caused by diving conditions and lack of experience.

a. Towed searches

The complexity of the method ranges from the diver holding on to a weight on a line through to towed vehicles with moveable vanes capable of altering their attitude and elevation relative to the seabed. A common and inexpensive system uses a simple wing or board capable of sufficient movement to fly the diver up and down over changes in seabed topography. All these systems rely on the surface crew controlling and recording navigation, making due allowance for 'layback' between the diver and the boat.

Alternatively the diver can be pulled along by an underwater vehicle. These diver propulsion vehicles (DPVs) vary in complexity from simple electric motor driving a propeller held in front of the diver or strapped to the air cylinder, through to sophisticated wet submersibles. The major drawback, apart from cost, is the difficulty of position fixing. Surface marker buoys attached to the diver can be tracked from the surface or, alternatively, it is possible to use through-water navigation systems based on acoustic trisponders placed at known positions on the seabed.

The effectiveness of a towed search will be dependent on visibility and speed of the diver over the seabed. At 1 knot the diver is

Figure 59. A swim-line search. (Courtesy of J. Adams and Cyprus Underwater Survey.)

covering just over 30m a minute or 0.5m a second and this can be an effective way of covering relatively large areas of the seabed during one dive. In many circumstances, however, this will be too fast to allow observation to the required detail.

If the diver can control the speed and even stop the forward movement to inspect potentially interesting sightings, the efficiency of the operation is dramatically increased. While rope signals are possible, diver to surface communications maximise the benefits of the method. Telephone-style (hard wire) communications with the diver's microphone connected by wire to the surface tend to be clearer and more reliable than through-water versions but being physically attached to the tow boat with no quick release mechanism can lead to safety problems. With efficient communications it is possible for the surface team to log and plot observations made by the diver. Without communications a less satisfactory alternative is for markers to be dropped on the seabed in the vicinity of any sighting that requires further investigation. These will then have to have their positions accurately fixed to enable them to be re-located and assessed.

To reduce the inherent risks to the diver and to avoid pressure related illness, very careful control of depth is important – this is often difficult to achieve when being towed. A possible solution is to make use of the new generation of diving computers. These can record all relevant depth and time details, and also have the ability to give an audible warning if the ascent rate is too fast. It should be noted however, that some researchers in diving medicine have expressed reservations about relying too heavily on this type of equipment.

Figure 60. Plotting contact positions is made easier when conducted within a site grid: a metal detector may be used constructively during the pre-disturbance survey and assessment of a site to record the possible location of metal artefacts.

In conditions of poor visibility there should also be some capability for detecting potentially dangerous obstructions in the path of the towed diver. One solution is an echo-sounder with a clear graphic display on the tow boat.

b. Swimline (freeline) searches

Patience and perseverance are prerequisites for this method but it has been used with success on many archaeological projects in the past. The system relies on a string of divers, often between three and six, spaced along a line at intervals equivalent to less than the limit of clear visibility so that complete coverage is possible. The search is often undertaken with one groundline to guide a controller in the middle, or two groundlines at either end of the swimline. These groundlines can be as long as necessary (up to a kilometre is not unknown) and should be reasonably straight. To achieve this they are probably best laid from a moving boat. It can be difficult to lay long groundlines precisely. However, as long as the line is straight, the two ends can have their position fixed (Section 7.0) so that at least there will be a record of where the search took place.

One of the difficulties with this system is maintaining sufficient communication between the divers to allow the line to advance smoothly. This problem increases proportionally to the number of divers on the line, and it is also intensified by poor visibility. Usually, if a diver needs to stop to make an observation, or is ready to move off again, this is indicated to the others by a code of signals. With practice it is possible to communicate quite complicated messages along the connecting line using a set of bells (short tugs) and pulls (long tugs). Standard rope signals can be found in many diving manuals, but additional ones appropriate to the individual operation can be devised.

Another difficulty is the variation in dive duration between individuals at the same depth and in the same environment. Matching the size of the air cylinders to the breathing capacity of the divers will help. The problem is that if a diver withdraws prematurely from the search and there is not a standby ready to take over immediately, there can be a discontinuity in the search pattern which is awkward to correct.

A third problem with swimlines is the difficulty of plotting the position of sightings during the search. Markers can be dropped at points of interest and the position fixed later. If the number of markers needed by each diver is excessive, an alternative search method, such as the jackstay system (Section 8.1.2 c), may be more suitable.

Swimline searches are often more effective in clear shallow water, but this technique can be deployed successfully in deeper water if there is a standby replacement diver together with other divers to support the needs of the search. For instance if the actual investigation of potentially interesting sightings is undertaken by a follow-up team rather than the line divers, the overall efficiency of the search method will be increased.

With discipline, good communication and rehearsed procedures this technique can be very flexible, allowing the search line to be stopped periodically to record the nature of the seabed, or count the number of surface indicators (potsherds, for example) to compile a distribution map.

c. Jackstay (corridor) searches

This is a useful system if total coverage of an area of seabed is required during visual or metal detector searches, but it requires more pre-search organisation than the two methods outlined above.

The minimum requirement is usually two long groundlines laid parallel at a convenient distance apart, often 10m, 30m or 50m, and a further line, the jackstay, laid at 90 degrees between the two groundlines. It is more efficient to use two jackstays to define a corridor, as an area with defined edges can be more effectively searched. Once the area between the jackstays has been searched another corridor is laid, usually by leap - frogging one line over the other (Figure 58).

Fixing groundlines to the seabed can be achieved in ways similar to those suggested for datum points (Section 9.2.7). In fact the ends of groundlines are likely to be datum points. One of the problems with groundlines is keeping them straight on the seabed. In shallows, water movement may mean the line has to be weighted or pinned to the seabed to prevent unacceptable lateral displacement. Even in deeper water groundlines may have to be placed along the line of maximum prevailing current to help prevent sideways movement; even then fixing to the seabed is likely to be required if the lines are going to be used as part of a site co-ordinate system for locating observations. The more intensive the search, the more precise the location control required becomes and therefore the less that sideways movement can be allowed in any of the lines.

The jackstays themselves are less permanent features and may only be in position for as little as five or ten minutes, depending on the size and intensity of search. The method by which they are anchored must depend on the nature of the seabed, and that might be totally different from one end of the line to the other. Line fixing will probably rely on either the mass/weight of an object, such as a 50 or 25kg metal block, or on a pin or other fastening forced into bed-rock, immovable boulder, or sediment. Even heavy weights can be pulled across the seabed with surprising ease (except when you want to move them of course!), and so it is common for a weight to be pinned to the seabed for additional security.

If the groundlines and the jackstays are graduated for maximum accuracy in location control, one of the groundlines should be considered as a zero axis, and the zeros of the jackstays can then be positioned on that line. It is difficult to keep the space between groundlines constant, and therefore the other end of the graduated jackstay will not always coincide with the other groundline at the required distance. Rather than spend unnecessary time making everything perfect, and without sacrificing offset survey precision, simply concentrate on the line of the jackstay passing across the appropriate graduation of the groundline. To do this it helps if the jackstays are overlength.

While groundlines are usually made from rope/line acquired from boat chandlers or fishermen's stores (leaded line is useful), the jackstays are often tape measures or, better still, thin plastic measuring lines that are available in 50m lengths. In many circumstances it can be advantageous to extend the length of these with about 2m of elastic cord ('shock cord' or 'bungey-cord'). The advantage is that it keeps the line under permanent tension, therefore making it less of a problem should a diver accidentally apply pressure to it during the search. It also means that, provided there is sufficient elasticity, one end of the jackstay can be leap-frogged at a time with less expenditure of time and effort than if both ends have to be released before the line can be moved.

The normal range of corridor widths between jackstays is 2m to 8m, depending on the number of divers searching each corridor, the visibility, and the type and size of expected targets. For intensive work, a maximum of two divers in a narrow corridor allows short, accurate offset measurements to be taken from the jackstays to give a precise location for each observation (Section 9.2.1).

Experience has demonstrated that a 1m wide strip for each diver in a 2m wide corridor is suitable for very intensive seabed searches using a metal detector, almost regardless of visibility or nature of the seabed. In areas where the seabed is uniformly covered in fine sediment, such as sands and silts, the width of the strip to be subjected to an intensive visual search by each diver can be greater. It can be as much as 6m in certain circumstances, even wider if the expected target is relatively large (for example, a ship-sized ballast mound). Before a decision is reached as to the width of strip that can be effectively searched on a given site, all the factors outlined in Section 5.3 must be considered.

d. Grid searches

If an area needs to be searched thoroughly, and features need to be located with precision, then the grid search has much to offer. The first step is to lay a series of groundlines at 90 degrees to each other at an appropriate spacing to create a grid over the site. This distance will depend on a variety of factors but is commonly between 2m and 50m. Groundlines left on the seabed for any time tend to get damaged or disappear, but if the intersecting points or anchorage points have been adequately fixed, the grid should be reconstructable in future seasons, even if the actual lines have gone.

Once the grid has been established, the corridor search technique can be easily deployed and the location of points can be readily identified by site co-ordinates with, conventionally, a series of numbers on both the horizontal and vertical axis with the zeroes at the bottom left (southwest) corner. Sometimes one of the axes is replaced by letters to help those inexperienced in the use of co-ordinates as a way of expressing a position. By using an appropriate number of digits it is possible to define a location down to the nearest millimetre, although that would not normally be necessary (Figure 60).

e. Circular searches

This is a simple search system that is often useful in poor visibility. It does not lend itself to total seabed coverage but is useful for trying to locate a known object whose position has not been accurately recorded. It can also be of use as part of a sampling strategy to assess different areas of the seabed before intensive searching begins.

The system relies on a graduated line, often a tape measure, being attached to a fixed point on the seabed. The diver swims round in a complete rotation using either a compass (to take the bearing at the start and finish) or obvious marker on the seabed as a guide to when a circuit has been completed. A very satisfactory solution is to set out a graduated, straight groundline (running out from the centre of the search area) to act as a start/finish indicator. The distance between each circular sweep has to be related to the visibility and the type of target.

It is usual to begin in the centre and sweep at ever increasing diameters. However, starting at the maximum length of sweep can be more effective if a known object is thought to be upstanding from a flat seabed. One circuit should result in a snag if the target is in the circle. The distance line can then be followed back to the object. During normal searches such snagging is clearly not desirable.

The problem of unwanted snags can be reduced if the distance line is lightly buoyed at the mid point. Some tension is usually maintained on the line to ensure that the diver keeps to the correct track. If the line catches on an obstruction, releasing the tension should allow it to rise and hopefully release itself from the snag. In very poor visibility it is not always clear that a snag has occurred until the search pattern has been grossly distorted.

Once the position of the centre of the search area has been fixed, observations made during the search can be recorded by noting the distance from the centre and the magnetic bearing to it, using a hand compass. In this way each plot will be recorded but the level of accuracy will be as limited as surveying using the bearing circle method (Section 9.3.5).

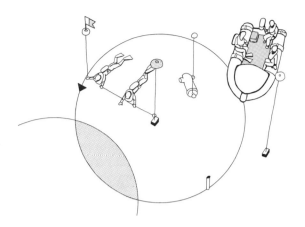

135

Figure 61. The circular search. The diver at the outer end of the sweep-line holds a surface marker buoy (SMB). Surface support also uses an SMB to position itself close to the search area so that they can minimise boat drift.

f. Metal-detector searching

Although these instruments are 'remote sensing' and some types can be towed behind a boat, it is the numerous diver-held versions which have proved to be a valuable tool to many archaeologists. Unlike magnetometers they can detect both ferrous and non-ferrous metals, and those used underwater usually work on the pulse induction principle. Pulses of energy are emitted and produce a temporary magnetic field around the search head. The rate at which this field decays is prolonged in the presence of metal. Comparison between the decay rate and the original pulses allow detection of metal objects of large mass to a maximum range of approximately 2m, and objects the size of a single coin at a distance of approximately 10cms.

Metal-detectors are used in three principal ways during archaeological work. During the pre-disturbance survey of a site, concentrations of metallic contacts and isolated responses can be mapped. The second way is to ascertain the approximate position of objects in a layer which is about to be removed. This can contribute to a very high recovery rate for metallic artefacts which might otherwise be overlooked due to size or poor visibility. The third use is to locate metal artefacts on bed-rock which are either invisible because of a light dusting of temporary silt, or because they are hidden in holes and crevasses in the rock.

Hand-held metal-detectors must be used systematically if they are to be worth using at all often. This entails total coverage employing the corridor or grid search techniques (Figure 60). It is important that the search head of the instrument covers every square centimetre of the area of seabed under investigation.

Investigating metal-detector responses by digging around an anomaly without regard to the other clues (Section 4.3) that might be disturbed is not a valid archaeological technique. Nor is any approach involving a diver with a metal-detector swimming in a random pattern over a site, looking for souvenirs.

8.1.3. Remote sensing surveys

Developments within the fields of marine geophysical surveying and deep water surveillance have made available a range of equipment which, in many circumstances, can allow more effective archaeological investigation of the seabed. It seems certain that such equipment will become increasingly important in archaeological work, particularly if developments mirror those elsewhere in the field of electronics where increased efficiency has been matched by reduced cost.

Remote sensing equipment can often be deployed in sea conditions worse than those in which divers can operate safely. Their greatest advantage, however, lies in the ability of the instrument to collect large amounts of information quickly and at some distance from the source. This allows search patterns to be much more widely spaced and at a greater 'over the ground' speed than could ever be achieved by divers. They can also operate in zero underwater visibility, and detect certain classes of information that remain buried out of sight.

Additionally remotely operated vehicles (ROVs) can perform many of the tasks of a diver, including visual searches and photography. Some underwater videos with image intensifiers are capable of showing greater detail on a surface monitor than the diver can see while underwater.

The power requirements for remote sensing equipment varies considerably. Some have power packs built in, or can be supplied from one or two automotive batteries (12 or 24 volts are typical requirements). Most ROVs and some video systems will require 110v, and this is most conveniently supplied by a portable generator. It is most important to guard against electrocution; even battery-supplied low voltages can be dangerous to divers in the water. Earth leakage trips should always be incorporated into electrical circuits if there is any risk at all.

Even the best equipment requires some experience and care on the part of the operator before its full potential can be realised. The most important source of expertise is normally the manufacturer's operating instructions, and these should always be read thoroughly, and then re-read until the operator is totally familiar with the particular version of the instrument. Careful examination of the manufacturer's information always pays dividends, especially as operating procedures can vary greatly even between models from the same source.

Practical experience, coupled with an understanding of the basic principles involved, is particularly important when utilising instruments that require some interpretation of the readout. Even something as relatively straightforward as an echo-sounder with a graphic display is not always easy to understand without some previous experience.

It is sometimes argued that geophysicists are the only people capable of interpreting the results from using remote sensing

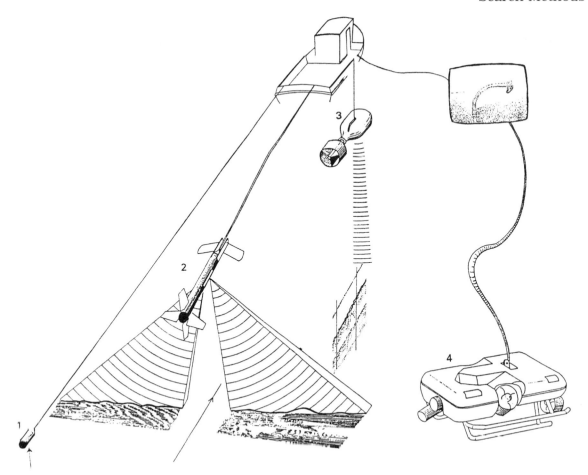

Figure 62. The triple system of magnetometer (1), side-scan sonar (2) and sub-bottom profiler (3) provides information on contacts that can be quantified and interpreted. A remotely operated vehicle mounted with video or stills camera can be useful in recording deep sites and for general site surveillance. (8.1.3.a.) (Drawing by M. Redknap.)

equipment. This need not be true. With appropriate training and sufficient experience the averagely intelligent person, including some archaeologists, can operate most instruments and interpret the readouts to a standard sufficient for most archaeological purposes.

a. Remote sensing search patterns

In good sea conditions, sidescan sonar can cover a swathe up to about 1000m wide across the seabed, whereas an echo-sounder with a narrow cone transducer might only cover a strip 1.5m wide in 10m depth of water. Such varying widths of seabed search highlight the difficulty of deciding what spacing is required between tracks to give a search pattern with 100% coverage of the seabed. Unless the potential target type is known, or at least decided upon, and the capabilities of the instruments deployed are fully understood, there could be gaps in the search area (Section 5.4.1). The experience of many archaeologists supports the formulation of a law which states that important information is invariably found in areas missed in previous searches.

138

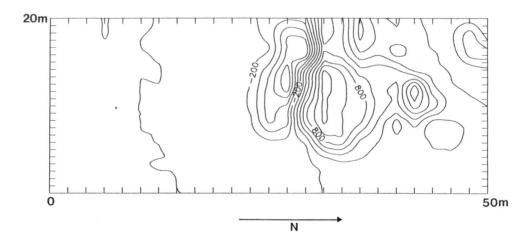

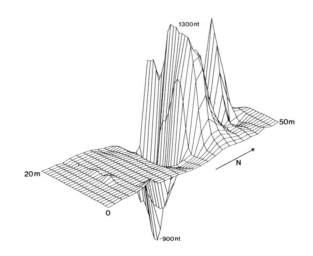

Figure 63. a) 'Close-plot' magnetometer survey of a foreshore wreck (cf. figure 30), with examples of the computer-based manipulation of the results: b) contour plot, c) 'egg-box' plot. (8.1.3.b.ii.)

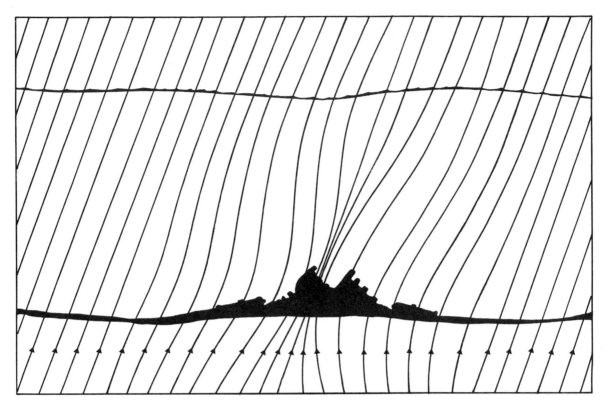

Figure 64. The changes in magnetic field direction over a wreck site. (8.1.3.b.ii.)

The search patterns appropriate to diver investigations of the seabed are also appropriate to larger scale investigations, the differences being in the scale of the operations and the method of location control. For intensive work two overlapping corridor scarch patterns at 90 degrees to each other are commonly used. The resulting grid search pattern helps reduce the chance of gaps in the coverage.

At present micro-wave shore stations (Section 7.3.2) are one of the most accurate ways of location control during remote sensing survey work, although tracking with an EDM can be effective for work closer inshore (Section 7.3.3). Probably the most convenient is GPS (Section 7.3.4), particularly in automatic differential operation with computer graphics to assist the helmsman. A less accurate method but useful where the swathe is wide, as can be the case with sidescan and magnetometer work, is to use the latitude and longitude information displayed on a hyperbolic navigation system such as Decca (Section 7.3.1). With practice it is possible to steer a course along a particular parallel to 0.01 of a minute as depicted on the display. Experienced users of radar will find it possible to achieve similar results (Section 7.3.5).

Alternatively, placing buoys on the surface of the sea to act as guides can be sufficiently precise, provided there are a sufficient number and in appropriate places. This, however, can lead to problems with towfish catching buoy mooring lines.

Sometimes integrated systems of magnetometer, sidescan sonar and sub-bottom profiler are deployed during archaeological work. The amount of data collected can be very large, and more than 20 megabytes of storage would be needed for each hour. If reprocessing is required, the standard technique is to collect the

Figure 65. Side-scan sonar images of wrecks in the Thames Estuary. (8.1.3.b.iii.) (Courtesy of Marine Archaeological Surveys.)

information on magnetic tape, but often for archaeological purposes it is collected as hard copy in the form of paper rolls. These can be assessed visually once ashore without the need for reprocessing digitised records.

The output from individual echo-sounders and magnetometers is often readily digitised and can be displayed in a variety of ways using computer graphics (Section 9.4.6). Few metal detectors have anything other than basic displayed information, but it is possible to collect this manually by noting where the readings were taken, and keying the information into a computer. Manual recording is possible with most other types of instrument and this too can be manipulated by a computer graphics package (Figure 63).

b. Equipment

i. Echo-sounders

This is one of the simplest forms of electronic search equipment, and, because many models are manufactured in large numbers, they are one of the cheapest. The instrument transmits a pulse of energy and the return signal, or echo, is collected, interpreted and displayed as a piece of information. The pulse is at the acoustic end of the electromagnetic spectrum and echo-sounders usually use a frequency somewhere between 50kHz, good for deep water penetration, through to 500kHz, which can give higher resolution images.

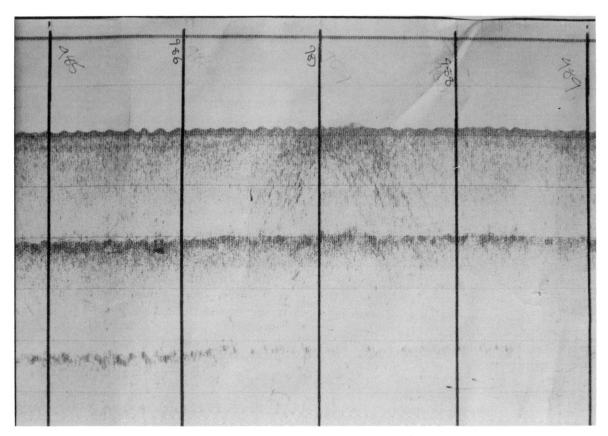

Figure 66. Sub-bottom profile of a 70-gun warship on the Goodwin Sands which sank in 1703. (8.1.3.b.iv.) (Courtesy of Marine Archaeological Surveys.)

The pulse is transmitted and received by a transducer usually mounted on a boat, although they can be mounted on remote sensing towfish, or even in submersible diver-held units. The angle of the cone of energy on most commercially available instruments can vary between 2 degrees and 45 degrees depending on the type of transponder. High resolution instruments use much finer cone angles, such as 0.2 degrees.

Apart from being an important safety feature when towing divers or when streaming a remote sensing 'fish', the echo-sounder can be used to assess the seabed quickly for depth and approximate seabed type. Another useful role is location of targets which are not buoyed but which stand proud of the seabed. Locating a site which is known but not buoyed requires a disciplined approach

to increase the chances of success. Using one of the methods available for site position fixing (Section 7.0) a buoy (or a pattern of buoys) can be dropped and a systematic search undertaken around them by a boat with an echo-sounder.

The most useful echo-sounders for archaeological purposes have some sort of graphic display, either a paper roll, a video screen, or a liquid crystal display (LCD), and the ability to transfer the results automatically to a computer so that it can be cross-referenced with other types of digitised information. In this way computer-generated graphics can be produced and manipulated to assist the interpretation of the available information. This facility is now available built in to some relatively inexpensive echo-sounders aimed at the leisure industry. The advantage of a paper roll is that it gives a permanent, easily accessible display on which it is possible to write observations.

There are many robust and completely waterproof echo-sounders with all three types of graphic display, ideal for use in small open boats. Some models are capable of expanding their vertical scale and achieving a high degree of resolution. Some paper roll models can resolve down to 2.5cms, a level which can only be beaten by high-resolution scientific instruments. LCD displays generally have a coarser image because the display is made up of 'pixels', small blocks shaded from white through grey to black, to create a monochrome image of the seabed. The smallest size that a pixel on the commonly available echo-sounders can represent is about 5cms. Similarly video displays, made up of lines of information on a screen rather than blocks, are limited in their degree of resolution. Some of these inexpensive LCD instruments have the capability to store and recall a number of images but these can normally only be recorded for posterity by drawing or photographing the screen image.

Unfortunately the interpretation of echo-sounders' readings is not made easy by the movement of the boat in which the transducers are mounted. Unless the water is calm, and the boat does not move vertically, an exactly flat seabed will be displayed as a series of peaks and troughs. The rougher the water and the more the boat moves, the larger the difference between the peaks and the troughs. Although the readout can at first seem impenetrable, with experience it is possible to understand what is happening on the seabed. A useful technique is to keep the boat stationary and note the pattern of change and use this to compare with readings during a search. In this way it is sometimes possible to identify real features on the seabed hidden among hummocks created by the movement of the transducers.

ii. Magnetometers

Magnetometers measure the strength of the earth's magnetic field and can detect variations in this field caused by the presence of ferrous material or objects. In the case of proton magnetometers this measurement is achieved by creating a strong magnetic field in a hydrocarbon fluid, such as kerosene, by passing an electric current through a surrounding coil of wire. The spinning protons in the fluid align themselves with this temporary magnetic field, and when the current is switched off they realign themselves and 'precess' back to the direction of the local (or ambient) magnetic field. As they do so a small signal is generated which is directly proportional to the strength of the earth's field. This 'gyromagnetic' ratio is a precise relationship between the signal strength and field strength, and can be used to detect very small variations in the earth's magnetic field.

The recognised international unit for measuring magnetic field intensity (or magnetic flux density) is the nanotesla (nT). Many instruments manufactured in the USA and some other countries are calibrated in other units *e.g.* Gammas (γ) but fortunately one nT = one γ.

Shape, orientation and magnetic permeability can affect the degree of influence a ferrous mass has on the earth's magnetic field and therefore the ability of a magnetometer to detect its presence. It is important to remember how influential distance is in the detection of magnetic anomalies. For instance a reading of 8nT produced by an object at a range of 20m will give a reading of 512nT at a distance of 5m.

The fish of a magnetometer weighs about 5kg, compared to about 30kg for a sidescan fish and 80kg for combined sidescan and sub-bottom profiler. It has to be towed sufficiently far away from the boat and other towfish so as not to detect them, and as close to the seabed as possible, especially when searching for items of small mass. One of the benefits of a magnetometer is its ability to detect buried magnetic material that might not be located by other means. Each model will have different ways of achieving optimum operational efficiency and so the manufacturer's recommendations should always be followed.

One of the disadvantages is the problem of relating the signal to a target at a known bearing and distance. Only by good location control and recording during a systematic search pattern, can sufficient information be collected to identify the likely location of anomalies. The 'layback' between boat and fish must be taken into account when plotting the position of anomalies.

In systematic magnetometer survey work using digital data collection methods it is possible to generate graphic representations of the magnetic anomalies (for example, contour lines joining points of similar magnetic field intensity, or isometric representations derived from readings taken at known positions in a search area (Figure 63). In this way it can be possible to determine the shape and size of anomalies.

The technique of 'close-plot' or 'micro-magnetometry' survey can involve suspending the fish very close to the seabed using a float. By pulling the float slowly by hand along set courses, the fish can be made to follow a pre-determined pattern. Very precise control of the fish as it travels over the seabed, together with the ability to co-ordinate magnetometer readings with position, will allow sufficient measurements to be collected to produce detailed information on the site. To do this requires excellent location control and this is probably best achieved by using a 'total station' (Section 7.3.3) to track a reflector mounted on the float, and good communications between the magnetometer operator and the surveyor (see Green 1990, 81).

Similarly the operation can be carried out with less expensive equipment by laying a grid system on the seabed (or dry land) and man-handling the fish between each intersection. This can be done by a diver pulling on a line on the seabed but care has to be taken not to let the diver's equipment interfere with the magnetometer readings.

Diver to surface communications are essential for the efficient operation of this technique.

iii. Sidescan sonar

This method works on exactly the same principle as the echo-sounder but instead of electromagnetic energy being pulsed downwards in a cone shape, two separate fan-shaped beams are directed either side of a towfish and selected signals are interpreted and displayed graphically. Some sidescan sonar sensors (transducer arrays) are fixed to the boat but, unless the water is very shallow, the beams are not sufficiently angled relative to the seabed to give adequate information of archaeological value.

Sector-scan sonars have beams which are moveable. These systems are mainly used to monitor the changes in the position of objects, including divers, around commercial or military installations, but they can be deployed from survey vessels.

Frequency is generally similar to echo-sounders, with 100kHz used for general purposes; 500kHz for long range. It is emitted in a thin beam approximately 0.2 to 1 degree wide, but with a typical fan angle of about 40 degrees. This can often be adjusted relative to the horizontal to allow for operation at different distances from the seabed to avoid too wide a gap between the search swathes.

The display is normally in the form of a wide paper roll marked by a stylus which indicates the topography of the seabed as a form of negative image consisting of acoustic highlights and shadows. The more dense an object, the stronger the return signal and the darker the image. With experience the different signals reflected off rocks, sandwaves, wreck features and other projections can be identified.

The advantage of sidescan is the ability to look sideways at objects projecting above the seabed. If the height of the towfish above the seabed is known it is possible to calculate the height of the darker coloured reflections by making comparisons with their white acoustic shadows. In this way some degree of assessment of archaeological material on the seabed can be made, and the information can often be improved if a number of passes are made along different sides of the target.

Like many forms of remote sensing the information collected during sidescan sonar runs may well require some interpretation and, at the end of the day, ambiguous information leading to contradictory interpretations might only be resolved by visual inspection by divers or video.

iv. Sub-bottom profilers

Along with magnetometers and metal detectors, sub-bottom profilers are capable of detecting buried archaeological material. They work on the same principle as echo-sounders but with a lower operating frequency (usually in the range between 1kHz and 7kHz) allowing penetration of sand and silt.

To reduce the amount of signal energy lost to water penetration, the trandsducer is usually mounted on a fish towed close to the seabed, often coupled to a sidescan fish. A high energy discharge from a capacitor linked to a small plate in contact with the water, produces a clean cone-shaped pulse downwards and signals are reflected back off the seabed, interfaces between strata, and objects that may be buried in the sediment, including bedrock or archaeological material.

The lower frequency 'boomers' operating at around 1kHz can be used to define objects up to 60m below the seabed and have limited archaeological applications. 3.5kHz is a useful general frequency for a 'pinger' employed in archaeological work, but on some models the frequency can be altered to suit the sediment type and degree of penetration required.

The information is usually presented graphically on a paper roll and if the instrument is coupled with a sidescan, the two sets of data can be presented on the same roll.

Apart from cost, one of the major drawbacks of these instruments is the relatively narrow path they investigate through the seabed. It would be very resource-consuming to try and achieve 100% coverage with a profiler, and so they are probably best used as either a method of sampling through the seabed during sidescan work, or as a means of homing in on a specific target identified by other means. Typically this could involve quantifying the amount of surviving structure of a wreck or inundated habitation site, only part of which may be exposed above the seabed.

v. Aerial photography

Aerial photography is a remote sensing method and has been used successfully to detect sites both underwater and in the inter-tidal zone (Morrison 1985: 85). There are obvious difficulties with the application of this technique in nautical archaeology because of the difficulty of resolving images of sites through the water.

8.2. Historical Search

There are many written records which will help in any search. These will vary from eye-witness accounts of sinkings to newspaper stories of chance finds by fishermen. The accuracy of recorded positions and the detail of accounts will vary but this is still a valuable, if time-consuming, source of information for locating or identifying underwater sites. The wreck locations given in medieval documents are rarely precise and the majority of shipwrecks in the Middle Ages are unrecorded.

8.2.1. Where to look (in the United Kingdom)

i. The Wrecks Officer (Hydrographic Department, Ministry of Defence, Taunton, Somerset TA1 2DN) maintains details of wrecks, only a proportion of which are shown on Admiralty charts. The Wrecks Officer will provide details for a fee or in exchange for new information. The Hydrographic Department holds limited information on early wrecks.

ii. National Maritime Museum, Greenwich, London SE10 9NF. Holds information on some 10,000 wrecks around the world. Many of its departments may be able to help in particular for wrecks with British connections.

iii. Public Records Office, Ruskin Avenue, Kew, Richmond, Surrey TW9 2DU. The Admiralty papers may be useful for references to ships of the Royal Navy.

iv. Lloyds, Lime St., London EC3M 7HA. A fairly comprehensive list of commercial shipping lost world-wide since 1748.

v. The India Office Library and Collections, 197 Blackfriars Road, London SE1 8NG. Material on ships of the English East India Company. Prime source for material on India and Asia. Day ticket available.

vi. The British Library, British Museum, Great Russell St., London WC1B 3DG. Holds a large collection of old books, foreign works, maps and the publications of international bodies. The national collection of manuscripts. Reader's pass required.

vii. British Library Newspaper Library, Colindale Avenue, London NW9 5HE.

viii. Trinity House, Tower Hill, London EC3.

IIx. Royal Commission on Historical Manuscripts, Quality House, Quality Court, Chancery Lane, London WC2A 1HF.

ix. Royal Armouries, Tower of London, London EC3N 4AB.

This far-from-comprehensive list of major sources in Britain should provide sufficient contacts to guide you to less familiar sources. Court records, diaries, personal letters, family papers and newspapers (*e.g. The Times* from 1788) covering the local area may provide important details on date, name, country of origin and destination of vessel. You can try the nearest large public library or reference library, or the nearest county record office where local manuscripts, court records, diaries, parish records (for deaths) may be held. Many of these documents will not have

been catalogued, and research may take considerable time. Large libraries may hold the Calendars of State Papers, many with references to shipwrecks and sufficient detail of the contents of the original documents to establish whether the originals should be consulted. In 1825 a Commission was issued in the United Kingdom for printing and publishing the documents of the State Paper Office, and since that date over 200 volumes of the Calendars of the Domestic, Foreign and Colonial Papers up to George III have been published. For shipwrecks up to c.1700, manor rolls, Vice-Admiral's Reports, Cinque Port Papers and archives of the duchies of Cornwall and Lancaster may be productive.

There are a number of additional sources of documentary evidence that should be consulted if a comprehensive interpretation of the site under investigation is to take place.

i. Reports of previous dives in the area (often in newspapers, magazines or newsletters).

ii. Early Admiralty charts.

iii. Tidal currents as reported by harbour boards or coastal pilots.

iv. Maps showing the site geology.

v. The memories of local people, dock workers, fishermen, officials etc. Oral tradition and local legend will often recall past events, and they may recall activities within living memory

vi. The Meteorological Office, for details of recent or past weather patterns.

vii. The British Sub Aqua Club has published approximately 250 records of wrecks most post AD 1914 (all in Hydrographic Department's record). Your local and national diving club will have their own records of sites.

viii. Collections of photographs (from 1840s).

ix. R.N.L.I. Journals (from 1840s).

8.3. Suggested Reading

a. diver search methods

British Sub Aqua Club
1987   *Sport Diving.* London.

Giangrande, C., Richards, D., Kennet, D., and Adams, J.
1987   Cyprus Underwater Survey, 1983-1984. A Preliminary Report. In *Report of the Department of Antiquitites Cyprus, 1987.* Nicosia, Cyprus.

Lockery, A.
1985   *Marine Archaeology and the Diver.* Ontario, Canada, ISBN 0-9692081-0-3.

Throckmorton P. *et al.*
1969   *Surveying in Underwater Archaeology.* London.

b. remote sensing surveys

Barto Arnold III, J.
1981   Remote sensing in underwater archaeology. *IJNA* 10.1: 51-62.

Breiner, S.
1975   *Marine Magnetic Search.* Geometrics Technical Report No.7, Sunnyvale, California.

Schurer, P.J., and Linden, R.H.
1984   Results of Sub-bottom Acoustic Survey in a Search for the Tonquin, *IJNA* 13.4: 303-309.

Tarlton, K.
1983   Electronic Navigation and Search Techniques. In Jeffery W. and Amess J. (eds), *Proceedings of the Second Southern Hemisphere Conference on Maritime Archaeology.*

c. aerial photography

Morrison, I.A.
1985   *Landscape with Lake Dwellings: the crannogs of Scotland.* Edinburgh, ISBN 0-85224-472-X.

Pugh, J.C.
1975   *Surveying for Field Scientists.* London, ISBN 0-416-075304.

Richards, D.G.
1980   Water penetration aerial photography. *IJNA* 9.4: 331-337.

Wilson D.R.
1982   *Air Photo Interpretation for Archaeologists.* London.

d. historical search

Westerdhal, C.
1980   On oral traditions and place names. An introduction to the first stage in the establishment of a register of ancient monuments for the maritime cultural heritage. *IJNA* 9.4: 311-329

Fisher, D.
1983   *State papers available for research in the South West.* Nautical Archaeology Society, South West Section.

9.   Surveying Underwater

9.1.   Archaeological Survey Work

9.2.   Surveying Basics

9.3.   Survey Methods

9.4.   Survey and the Third Dimension

9.5.   On-Site Photography

9.6.   Suggested Reading

9.1. Archaeological Survey Work

We have seen that fieldwork should be undertaken with clear aims and objectives in mind (Section 5.2.1). It may be that an accurate non-destructive survey answers the questions posed by the research design. An accurate survey can be the end product rather than simply the first phase of a project, and it is important to evaluate the potential of survey for gathering clues carefully and objectively in this respect.

Where further investigation, perhaps sampling or excavation, is felt to be necessary, pre-disturbance survey is the essential first step in ensuring that a complete record of a site is made. The pre-disturbance survey is, however, much more than an exercise done for form's sake. It will provide information on the original condition of the site (since any disturbance of the site has a much wider effect than just the parts under investigation) and provide a benchmark for future monitoring.

The pre-disturbance survey also provides a body of information on which a fieldwork strategy can be based. Such information allows decisions to be made concerning, for example, the positioning of trial trenches. On sites where archaeological material is scattered, it may be particularly difficult to know where to concentrate the investigation. Without an accurate record of the location of the material evidence, any excavation will be a 'hit or miss' affair, wasteful of time, resources and clues about the past.

Surveys can provide evidence not only of the depth and extent of surviving material on the site, but also of the range of the material likely to be encountered. This allows appropriate funds, conservation facilities, and expertise to be arranged well in advance of any disturbance to the site (Section 5.3).

The question 'how much information should be recorded?' is often asked in connection with survey. The short, but perhaps daunting, answer is 'as much information concerning archaeological material and its environment as can be collected employing non-destructive methods'. The basic requirement, however, is the production of an accurate three-dimensional picture of the site, usually recorded as a two-dimensional plan with supporting descriptions and measurements.

A survey will not necessarily be restricted to one season's work. A site may have to be visited regularly to assess changes in sediment depth. This is particularly true if resources are to be committed to investigation of a site under threat from erosion. Successive surveys can indicate the true nature of sediment movement, and the likely pattern of degradation of a site may be predictable through monitoring of mechanical, biological and chemical processes. Decisions regarding excavation or stabilisation and monitoring of the material can then be taken based on sound information, not guess work.

The more information that can be collected through non-destructive pre-disturbance surveys, the more effective future work on the site is likely to be, both in terms of planning further investigation and avoiding unnecessary damage to the material.

9.2. Surveying Basics

Everyone can take measurements accurately if they want to. None of the techniques described in this section is particularly complicated. Even those which do involve some mathematics are still easy to apply in terms of actually taking the measurements. Effective survey, a vital component of archaeological fieldwork, comes primarily from the careful recording of accurate observations and measurements, not from having access to expensive and sophisticated hardware. This section describes various methods of achieving satisfactory results through the systematic application of basic techniques.

The methods described below can be used in many situations; from producing a survey of an entire site to plotting find locations; from planning the local topography to recording structure, new contexts or other evidence exposed during an investigation. On most sites several methods will contribute to the production of the survey. Adaptability is both a measure of a useful technique and a sign of an effective survey team. The aim is to produce an accurate and detailed three-dimensional record of the site; the way in which this is achieved will depend on what is to be surveyed, the local environment and your ingenuity.

9.2.1. XYZ coordinates

The aim of survey is to record the position of a point, or target, in relation to known fixed points. A point exists in three dimensions which are referred to as x, y and z coordinates (Figure 67). By convention these usually correspond to Eastings, Northings and depth/height. A two-dimensional (x and y) plan view is used in many surveys. Surveying in two dimensions is usually simpler and quicker than in three dimensions, but it still records a great deal of information. The third dimension or z component can then be added where height/depth information will increase the value of the survey. Other methods exist, such as the Direct Survey Method and the SHARPS system, which calculate the x, y and z coordinates automatically (Sections 9.2.5. e. and 9.4.5).

9.2.2. Accuracy

It is almost impossible to lay down hard and fast rules for the level of accuracy that a survey should achieve, but it is something which must be considered well before the start of fieldwork. Accuracy will depend on the purpose for which the measurements are taken. For instance a preliminary survey to establish the visible extent of a site will not need to be as accurate as the detailed surveying of relationships of objects about to be lifted. Although there are often a number of different levels of accuracy required on a site, each appropriate to the task in hand, it is worth recording individual measurements to the nearest millimetre. This may seem excessively fine, but it must be remembered that accuracy will rarely be better than the original measurement. Inaccuracies can accumulate when carrying out a survey, but this problem is reduced if the original readings are as true as possible. In addition, the discipline of taking 'millimetre-precise' measurements obliges the surveyor to take greater care.

The acceptable overall error within a survey plan of a site will depend on circumstances. Research excavations often aim for less than plus or minus 10mm (one centimetre) from one end of the site to the other. In practice this is very difficult to achieve using conventional tape measurement, and plus or minus 100mm may often be the end result. If survey work is undertaken to rescue evidence before it is destroyed by non-archaeological activity, then the acceptable level of error could be larger. On very large sites, covering more than a thousand square metres, an overall error of plus or minus 500mm may be acceptable, but if it was a rescue excavation with severely limited time the error might rise to plus or minus 1 metre across the site. Anything larger than that and the 'survey' would probably be better described as a sketch plan.

Overall survey accuracy can be improved by:

i. Surveying in site datum points accurately (Section 9.2.8).

ii. Using a precise means of measuring distance (Section 9.2.4).

iii. Carefully recording the distances measured, together with where from and to (Section 6.2.10).

iv. Monitoring survey accuracy (Section 9.2.3)..

v. Making time to do the job properly.

9.2.3 Monitoring survey accuracy

This can be done in a number of ways, but probably the most useful is to measure the 'average absolute residual,' usually abbreviated to 'average residual.' This is calculated as follows. Measurements are taken and the survey is drawn up as normal, producing a plan from which the coordinates of every point can be obtained. Distances between points on the plan can be compared with the actual measurements taken

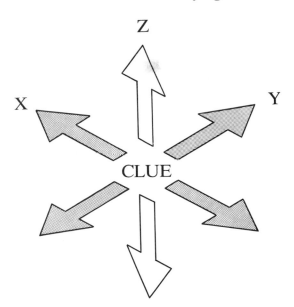

Figure 67. Every clue has a position in three dimensions which can be referred to as 'x', 'y' and 'z' co-ordinates. (9.2.1.) (Drawing by K.Watson.)

underwater. Clearly, any differences mean some kind of error, either in the original measurements, in the plan, or shared between both. The value of any difference is known as the residual, and the average value of all residuals can be calculated and used as a measure of how well the plan fits the original measurements. If average residuals are shown on both published and archived drawings it will give other researchers a quantified measure of survey accuracy. Unfortunately this practice is not yet common in all archaeological survey work.

For example, a plan is plotted at a scale of 1:10. Two points are 30.5 cm apart on the plan although the actual measurement taken by the diver was 301 cm. In this case the residual would be 30.5 x 10 – 301 = + 4 cm. Note that residuals can be negative as well as positive. The average absolute residual of three measurements with residuals +4 cm, -3 cm and -2 cm is (4 + 3 + 2)/3 = 3 cm. As can be seen, when calculating the average absolute residual, the + and - signs are ignored.

Figure 68. Sketching timbers prior to further survey work is often useful. (9.2.4.) (Courtesy of C. Dobbs.)

The average absolute residual is time consuming to calculate when hand-plotting, but can be generated automatically by several computer programmes that automate such plotting (see Section 9.4.5, Direct Survey Method).

9.2.4. Basic advice

There are some fundamental points which should be borne in mind:

a. Practise the techniques

Familiarise yourself with equipment on land before you take it underwater. This can save a lot of frustration and wasted dive time.

b. Survey from the framework to the detail

Establish a 'framework' covering the overall area of your survey and then fill in the detail. Starting with a small area in detail and working outward can lead to cumulative error and poor coverage.

c. Check measurements

Check measurements are the only way to confirm that a mistake has been made and are worth the extra time and trouble. For example, if two measurements are needed to fix a point by a particular method, make it a rule always to take three. There is no point in taking measurements if you do not know how good they are. If the original measurements were made in particularly

Figure 69. Cross-checking a survey: for example, checking the widths of timbers to see whether they are correctly represented in the survey (9.2.4.c.)

poor conditions, this should be noted. Asking a different diver to re-take problematic measurements is often effective.

d. Expect to make mistakes

Everyone makes mistakes, especially underwater. An analysis of data from over 10 sites indicated that approximately 5% of all measurements were gross errors, such as measuring to the wrong datum point, getting the tape badly snagged or mis-copying from the dive slate due to bad handwriting. Drawing-up of results as soon as possible and calculation of the 'residuals' (Section 9.2.3) will help keep things under control. In poor conditions, such as low visibility, it can be useful to have a diver available to swim along the tapes to check for snagging and other errors. Remember that errors can occur at all stages in the survey process right up to printing the final publication, so try to minimise hand-copying of data and make checks at every step.

Figure 70. A clinometer can be used to measure angles of timbers or other features. (9.2.4.g.)

e. Standardisation

To avoid confusion, all equipment used should be calibrated in the same units, and the same conventions should be used. A distance of 1m 12cm 4mm can also be written 1m 12.4cm, or 1m 124mm, or 1.124m. The vast majority of workers, above and below sea level, now use metric measurements. All workers should also agree on how measurements will be recorded and comply with the agreed method.

f. Scale

Plans should be prepared at a scale large enough for the smallest feature to be illustrated (often 1:10 or 1:20). The scale should always be clearly indicated.

g. Full recording

Survey results should be recorded in a form clear enough for a competent draughtsperson who has never visited the site to be able to draw up the results. Additional information, for example, clinometer angles (Figure 70) or compass bearings (Figure 71) should be gathered and included in the the survey records to complement the measurements from the methods outlined below.

h. Organise the information

It is often useful to draw up a table before the dive, listing points to be surveyed and providing boxes for the measurement. This helps to ensure everything gets done and that the results are legible. You might even want to get a form made up and copied to ensure standardisation of recording (most photocopiers will copy onto drafting film).

Figure 71. A compass can be used to record the alignment of timbers or features. Remember to check that the compass is not adversely affected by proximity to ferrous material. (9.2.4.g.)

Alternatively, if the diver is in communication with the surface by throughwater or hard-wired communications, results can be recorded and checked on the surface which leaves the diver free to get on with the measuring.

9.2.5. Surveying hardware

A wide variety of equipment can be used underwater but good results can be achieved with simple tools.

a. Measuring tapes

Many different varieties are available, in terms of both length and design. Fibreglass reinforced plastic tapes with few metal fittings will avoid rust and decay problems. Examples with cases that can be easily dismantled for cleaning have advantages in sandy and silty environments (sediment particles can jam the winding mechanism). Work underwater is tough on tapes. It is made even tougher if we try to tie knots in them or pull on them to release them from snags. All tapes can be stretched thus introducing inaccuracy to the survey, so try and keep a standard pull on tapes when in use. Manufacturers usually recommend a pull of about 2kg but, underwater, a pull of between 5 and 7kg is probably better as it reduces bowing of the tape caused by water movement. It is good policy to check all tapes at regular intervals against a known distance equivalent to the

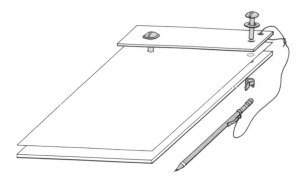

Figure 72. Recording underwater: a simple board can be constructed to A4 format. (9.2.5.d.)

tape's maximum length, and then replace those that are sub-standard. A tape may be a basic tool but it must be looked after.

b. Rigid measuring rules

These are normally up to 1m long and have advantages for short measurements because they are rigid, compact and cheap.

c. Survey chains

Usually available in lengths from 20 to 50m, chains have the great advantage of being accurate (they do not stretch as the links are rigid). They can be unwieldy underwater and they are prone to rusting unless they are made from stainless steel, which is expensive. While many land surveyors swear by them, others swear at them as they have to be carefully maintained (*e.g.* washed and greased after each immersion in seawater).

d. Materials for recording measurements

It sounds obvious, but make sure you take something on the dive with you that is suitable for recording the information you collect. An A4-size drawing board is often used for general survey (Figure 72). It should have a method of temporarily attaching drawing film, a pencil, preferably of the propelling type, anchored so that it can reach all parts of the board and be negatively buoyant. A permanent underlay of gridded drafting film is very useful when using offsets or planning frames.

e. Acoustic systems

Sophisticated acoustic systems developed for three dimensional tracking and position fixing underwater have been employed in underwater survey with variable results. Systems such as S.H.A.R.P.S. (Sonic High Accuracy Ranging and Positioning System) clearly have immense potential in terms of speed and accuracy (Waddell 1990; Kyriakopoulou 1990) but, to date, no archaeological project seems to have had total success with the system. It is probably only a matter of time before it, or similar systems, become commonplace on larger archaeological projects, although development still appears to be necessary before it will completely satisfy archaeological needs.

f. Computers

The data resulting from all the techniques described in this section can be processed manually, *i.e.*, by hand-plotting with the aid of ruler and compass. There are an increasing number of computer programmes which automate, and can refine, this painstaking process. These programmes have the advantages of reducing human error, improving fit of plans to measurements, increasing the ability to mix measurements of different types, increasing the speed of processing and often improving the ability to isolate and quantify errors (if check measurements have been used).

9.2.6. Establishing the primary survey framework

To survey from the known to the unknown requires a framework to be imposed on the site. This can take a variety of forms, from a rigid grid to a network of individual datum points, or a combination of the two. It is essential that it provides a set of points, surveyed into each other to form a web of measurements, from which further measurements can be taken to record the details of the site.

9.2.7. Site grids

"Site grid" is a confusing phrase which means something slightly different to different people. Some people use it to refer to rigid structures placed on the sea bed of which there are two basic forms:

a. Surveyed grids

These are usually carefully constructed structures, accurately surveyed and levelled, and often made of rigid tubing such as scaffold or gas pipe. Alternatively they can consist of carefully positioned rope or light line anchored to the seabed. Scaffolding is useful because it is easily fastened using readily available clips. Such grids can be used to support a network of datum points, from which actual measurements are taken and survey details recorded by the various methods described later.

Attempting to use rigid grids for survey purposes can be problematic. Distortion or movement of the grid (caused by environmental factors or divers pulling themselves along it) will create errors in any subsequent measurements. Frequent checks are therefore essential. Such structures can be very time consuming (not to mention expensive) to put in place. Very careful consideration should be given to alternatives before choosing this option for a survey framework. A network of datum points independent of a rigid grid can often be easier to establish and more flexible in use.

b. Diver guidance and support grids

These can be made of the same materials as above but require less positional accuracy. These are either just a guide to help workers locate themselves within a site by dividing it up into convenient areas or, if solidly constructed and suitably positioned, a structure on which divers can support themselves while working. This use of a rigid

Figure 73. Diver using underwater note-board to record measurements. (9.2.5.d.)

framework placed around trenches has been shown to be enormously beneficial to careful excavation.

c. Theoretical survey grid

To confuse things further, other people talk of a site grid and mean the theoretical grid which can be superimposed onto a plan to give the x, y, and z co-ordinates for the survey.

9.2.8. Datum points

A datum point is a reference point from which survey measurements are taken. To be useful in this role it must fulfil several criteria:

i. It must not move.

ii. It must be precise. "The top of the rock" is too vague. A specific pin point on the rock must be chosen and marked.

157

Figure 74. Diver supported by a site grid frame. This keeps divers and their equipment off delicate parts of the site, in this case the labelled hull timbers, while they are working.

iii. It must be conveniently placed for the intended measurements. The aim is that each datum should be in direct line of sight (for unobstructed measurement) with as many others as possible. They should also be in a position to be used in the surveying of other points yet to be fixed. This is not always easy to predict.

iv. Its position relative to every other datum point on the site must be known, and it should have a unique number or code for identification.

Datum points have been established in many different ways. Climbing pitons have been driven into rock, and bolts and hooks have been glued, cemented or fired with a bolt gun into place. Hooks can be attached to rigid grid frames as datum points. More simply, nails and hooks have been driven into timbers of the structure actually being surveyed, although this is potentially damaging to the structure. Problems can arise when establishing datum points on mobile sediments. It is surprising how much even heavy objects will move. Many solutions have been tried, including vertical scaffold poles weighted by concrete sinkers. Common to all these methods are a hook or ring to which a tape can be attached and a unique identifier such as numbered or lettered tags or floats).

A reconnaissance and sketch of a site will help in deciding upon the appropriate locations and it is worth taking some trouble with this. Additional points can easily be added later, and additional datum points at a lower level will almost certainly be necessary if an excavation proceeds to any depth. Having too few datum points can seriously compromise the accuracy and speed of a survey.

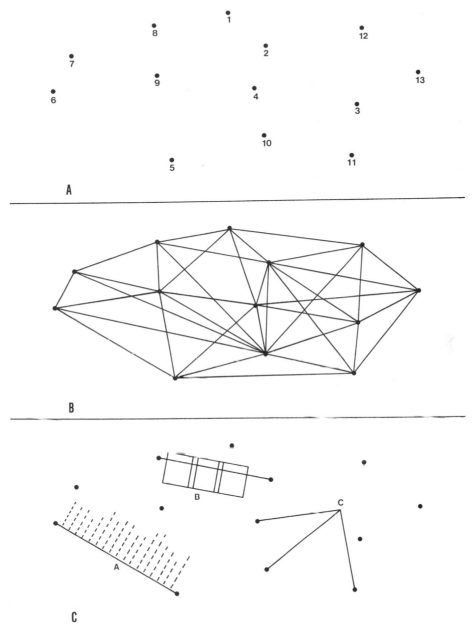

Figure 75. The web of measurements between datum points on site: a) datum points can be placed wherever they will be most useful providing their positions are known accurately, b) each datum should be surveyed in just like any other point. It is possible for a web to be free floating so that the position of the datum points are calculated relative to each other. A datum web can also be started from a fixed base line (e.g. joining points 6 and 11), c) you can use the same datum points for various types of detail surveying (e.g. a. offsets, b. planning frame, c. triangulation.) (9.2.8.)

160

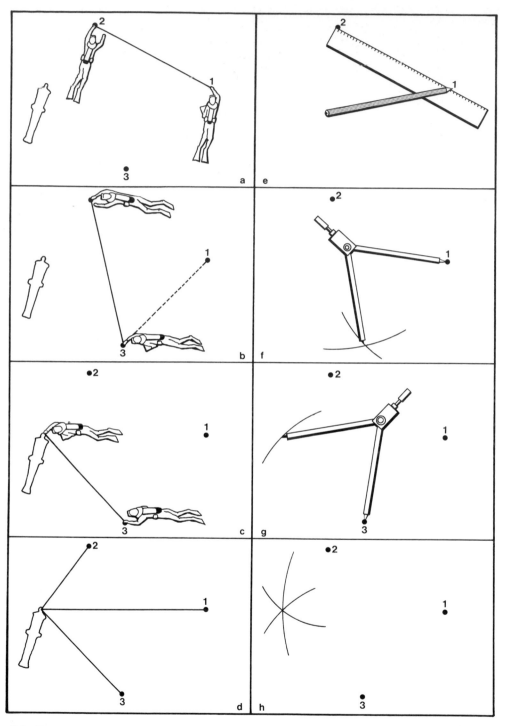

Figure 76. Triangulation: survey and drawing up results: a) establishing a baseline, b) establishing a secondary datum, c) using the secondary datum as the third 'check' measurement to an object, d) a point on an object is surveyed into three known datum points, e-f.) drawing up the survey. (9.3.1.a.)

Figure 77. Offsetting. (9.3.2.a.) (Courtesy of Cyprus Underwater Survey.)

9.2.9. Building up a survey (the 'primary site web')

Once the datum points have been established, the next step is to survey each one into all the others to establish their relative positions and produce a web of basic measurements. This will then produce a master plan onto which further detail can be plotted, moving from the 'known to the unknown'. If the web of datum points is to be used for three dimensional survey such as DSM (Section 9.4.5), each datum's relative height will usually also have to be determined. The techniques used for surveying the position of such points are the same as those used for other surveying purposes, so they are discussed together.

During the primary survey it is always worth the effort to survey datum points in as accurately as possible. Any inaccuracies at this stage will be passed on to later stages of the survey, so check measurements are essential. Calculation of the residuals (Section 9.2.3) will identify the errors, and the use of computer programs like *DSM* will also calculate the best fit for the web.

A basic first step can be to set up a baseline (imaginary or actual) around which further survey can develop. This carefully measured line between two secure datum points is often placed to cover the length of the site, but convenience, distance and topography may prompt other arrangements. It is better to have a number of straight baselines surveyed into each other rather than one crooked one which is presumed to be straight. A baseline is just a starting point around which everything else develops. It can provide the basis for offsetting (Section 9.3.2) or the three known points (the two ends and a third a known distance along the line) necessary for triangulation (Section 9.3.3). A baseline must be accurately surveyed, but it does not commit you to continuing the survey in any particular way.

9.3. Survey Methods

The following sections discuss the methods involved in applying and drawing up the results of a range of simple survey techniques.

9.3.1. Triangulation/ Trilateration

'Triangulation' is sometimes defined as surveying using the measurement of angles, and 'trilateration' as surveying using the measurement of the sides of a triangle. In common with normal usage in the archaeological profession this guide will use the term triangulation to refer to any survey method where triangles are used to plot the position of a point.

a. Method

Distance measurements are taken from two datum points whose position have already been fixed (*e.g.* two ends of a baseline) to the target to be surveyed. When plotted by hand, the intersection of these two distance lines (arcs centred on the datum points) locates the point. For precision surveying a measurement from a third known point should be taken as this will provide an immediate check. With just two measurements, if an error is made the two arcs drawn as described below will usually still intersect; with three arcs plotted they cannot intersect unless accurately measured and drawn (Figure 76).

Although all the known points may be on a single baseline better results can be achieved if the points surround the subject. Sufficient, conveniently placed datum points are required for this method and the angle of intersection for the distance lines is generally best kept between 60 and 120 degrees. The aim is to avoid extreme acute or obtuse angles. This method has the advantage that the degree of error in a set of measurements becomes clear as the results are drawn up (the greater the error the larger the triangle or 'cocked hat' formed by the intersection of the three lines). If this is unacceptably large the measurements should be retaken.

As was suggested before, if visibility is poor it is often useful to have a diver available to swim along the tapes to check for snagging. Erroneous measurements are not always easy to spot whilst underwater.

b. Drawing up the results

Equipment required to draw up the results of triangulation surveys includes a compass (a beam compass can be useful) and a scaled ruler. The drawing up process begins with the known positions of the datum points being marked. The compass is then set to correspond to the distance from one of the datum points to the point being surveyed according to the scale at which the survey is being drawn up. For example, a measurement of ten metres will be drawn up as ten centimetres if the plan is being drawn at a scale of 1:100. An arc is marked on the paper. This is repeated for the other points, the final result usually being a 'cocked hat' of intersecting arcs as described above.

c. When to use triangulation

Accurate over greater distances than offset measurements, this technique has a wide range of applications from measuring datum points in to each other to fixing the location of primary features and find locations. However, it does suffer from the fact that most sites are uneven, and so the measurements should be taken horizontally to ensure that a true distance is recorded. One answer is to use a plumb bob to position a horizontal tape over the object to be surveyed. A float can also be used (either weighted or attached to an object or feature), but without a spirit level, it is still difficult to ensure that the tape is horizontal. An alternative solution is dealt with in Direct Survey Method (Section 9.4.5).

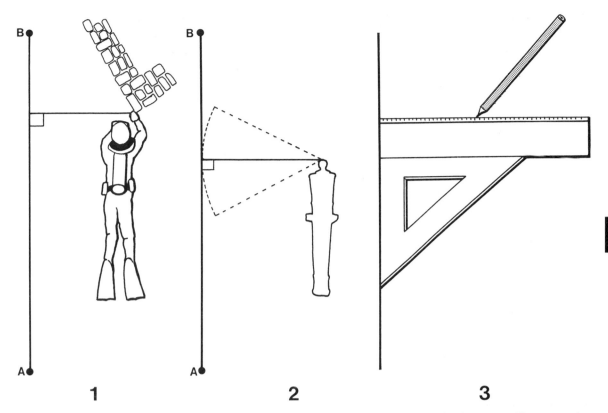

Figure 78. 1) offsetting, 2) a method of establishing a right angle, 3) plotting offset results (9.3.2.a. and b.)

9.3.2. Offset measurements

Once a baseline is established, a great deal can quickly be achieved with offset measurements (distance measurements taken at a right-angle to a datum line; Figure 78).

a. Method

A tape stretched between two datum points can provide the baseline for this method. Clearly mark on the survey record which datum formed the zero end of the baseline and which side of the baseline measurements were taken. If datum points are not in convenient positions then temporary ones can be established and surveyed into the main network with triangulation.

The accuracy of this method relies on judging right angles, difficult on land and far harder underwater. A useful technique is to place the zero end of the tape on the point to be plotted and to move the other end along the datum line until the shortest distance is noted, thus giving a line perpendicular (*i.e.*, at 90°) to the baseline. (See Figure 78, 2).

b. Drawing up the results

As with triangulation this is a very simple procedure. A straight datum line, with one end noted as zero, is marked onto graph paper. Scaled measurements up the datum line can be marked off and then the distance out from the baseline can be determined to locate the surveyed point. Alternatively, plain paper, a scaled ruler and a set square can be used.

Offset survey can often be drawn up underwater. The advantage of this is that subtle details can be added and errors spotted. The time spent taking careful measurements and drawing up while you can see the subject can also help in making sure that it is studied carefully. However it is usually only practical on shallower sites when more working time is available.

c.   When to use offsets

Grid squares can be laid out, find locations plotted and detailed features recorded. When survey work is being conducted in narrow areas, such as within deep gullies, offsets can be very useful indeed. This method of survey can be made more accurate by use of the '3:4:5' triangle, but offsets are still relatively inaccurate over distances greater than a few metres. They are not generally useful for measuring datum points in to each other. However, measurements can be taken quite quickly and once a baseline is established this method can be used to gain a rapid impression of the general extent and shape of a site, allowing more effective planning of a subsequent, more accurate survey by other methods.

9.3.3.   The 3:4:5 triangle

In addition to creating right angles for survey measurement, the '3:4:5 triangle' method can be used to construct grid squares off the initial baseline for searches or the convenient division of a site. Pythagorus's theorem states that, in a right angle triangle, the square of the hypotenuse is equal to the sum of the squares on the other two sides. Thus a triangle with sides in the ratio 3:4:5 will contain a right angle opposite the longest side (or hypotenuse). This method can be manipulated to set out all four corners of a grid and the size of the grid varied by using multiples of the '3:4:5' ratio (*e.g.* 6:8:10) (Figure 79).

  To establish a right angle using this technique mark out a line 4 metres long (this can be a section of an existing baseline). Attach a tape to the zero end. Run the tape out to 5 metres. Attach a tape at the 4 metre end and run it out to 3 metres. Stretch these two tapes out until the two marked distances meet and pull them taut. When they are

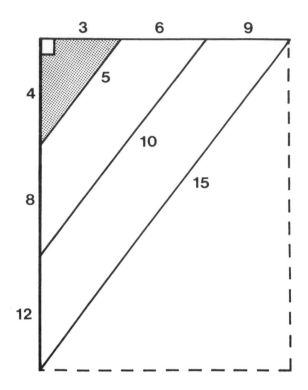

Figure 79. 3:4:5 triangles: increasing the ratios. (9.3.3.)

both tight mark the spot. A line drawn from this spot to the 4 metre mark on the baseline will be at a right angle to that baseline (Figure 80).

  Isosceles and equilateral triangles can be used to the same effect if a point half-way along the base is joined to the apex.

9.3.4.   Planning frame

The above methods can provide accurate position fixes but are not satisfactory for recording complex detail or associations, largely due to the sheer quantity of measurements that would be required. This can be more easily done using a planning frame. This consists of a frame, often one metre square (a measurement which usually refers to the INTERNAL size), normally subdivided using string or twine into smaller squares of 10 or 20cm. Size and

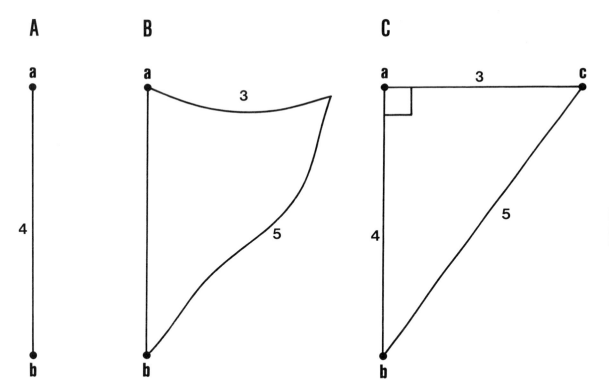

Figure 80. Steps to be taken in using 3:4:5 triangles to lay out a grid: A) establishing a base line between points a and b; B) tapes attached to a and b with appropriate distances marked at the 3:4:5 ratio, C) tapes pulled taut to fix point c at right angles to baseline. (9.3.3.)

constructional details of frames vary but whatever size is chosen the frame must not distort and the stringing must be tight.

a. Method

The diver positions himself over the frame and uses the squares to transfer detail directly onto a gridded surface, normally plastic drafting film, at a smaller scale (1:10 or 1:20 are common).

An essential feature of this system when planning is that the frame must usually be horizontal. This can be achieved by using adjustable legs and spirit levels attached to the frame. It is equally important that the diver's eyes are vertically above the point he is drawing. Double stringing the frame (Figure 81) is a very effective way of achieving this.

When both sets of strings are in line the diver knows he is in the correct position, vastly reducing parallax and perspective distortion.

The closer the frame lies to the subject, the easier and more accurate the survey will be. As with all methods, poor visibility will make this system slower to use. But it need not drastically effect the accuracy of the end result. Plumb-bobs and hand tapes are very useful in conjunction with this technique and different coloured strings to mark 10, 20 and 50 cm divisions can be very helpful in quickly relocating the subdivision being drawn.

Complete coverage of a site can be built up square by square, or specific areas of interest can be identified and drawn. With either method, certain key points must be borne in mind:

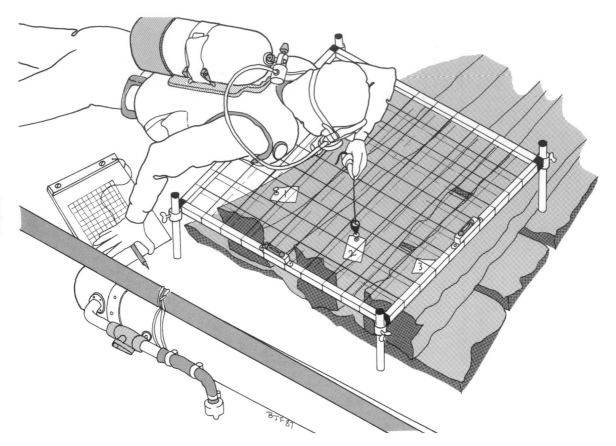

Figure 81. Using a plumb-bob and levelled drawing frame. A double-strung frame helps counteract distortion caused by not being directly above the subject. Inside each square even greater accuracy can be achieved using a plumb-bob or weight line. (9.3.4.a.)

i. Coverage

Ensuring that coverage of an area is complete is often made easier by overlapping squares. This can also help in aligning individual squares later when drawing up the survey. Before moving a frame to a new position it can be helpful to place markers to indicate the corners of the area just drawn to allow accurate repositioning and ensure total coverage.

ii. Location

It should be possible to locate each square drawn on the survey. This can be done by moving the frame along a baseline and noting each frame's position. Alternatively the corners of frames can be measured into datum points by triangulation or related to a rigid grid if one has been constructed.

iii. Orientation

Each drawn square should have magnetic north marked on it along with the site code, an individual reference number and locational information.

iv. Standardisation

Ensure that all workers represent various materials and features in the same way. Devising a simple set of standard symbols and conventions can save a great deal of trouble.

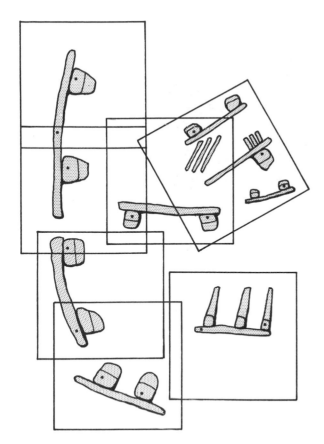

Figure 83. Using datums to position a planning frame survey. (9.3.4.a.ii.)

v. Datum points

The task of aligning and co-ordinating the results from a large number of individual drawings is made much easier if a surveyed datum point appears in each square which can be related to the master plan of datum locations. If a complex structure is being recorded in this way, it pays to have a large number of datum points, surveyed into each other which can act as check measurements when drawing up the results.

b. Drawing up the results

An extensive survey by drawing frame may result in a large number of individual squares. These have to be co-ordinated and traced off to form the completed survey. The original survey drawings should not be inked and joined to form a survey drawing. They form the primary survey record and should be carefully stored as part of the archive and a check on the finished plan.

As mentioned above, overlapping squares and datum points will greatly assist in the process of accurately aligning the individual squares. Another check is a comparison between the overall dimensions of the structure or area being surveyed and the dimensions shown on the resulting plan. This should reveal any gross errors.

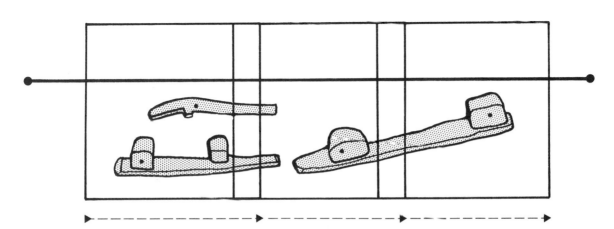

Figure 82. Using a baseline to position a planning frame survey. The line of the baseline and the distances along it should be included in the plan. (9.3.4.a.ii.)

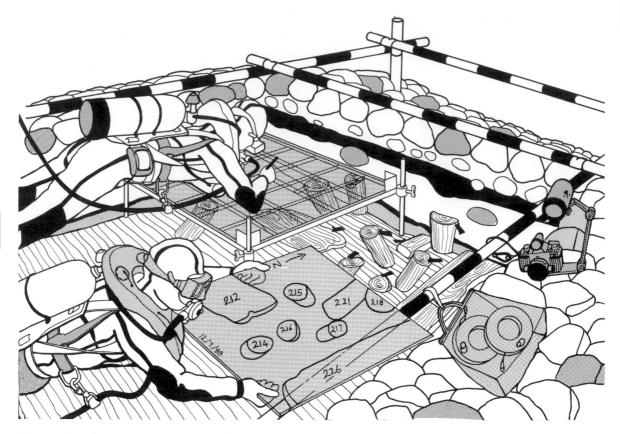

Figure 84. One metre squares of transparent, rigid plastic can be used for tracing complex associations in conjunction with a planning frame. (9.3.4.c.) (After Morrison.)

c. When to use it

The planning frame can be used very effectively in surveys of large areas of structure. Detail can be recorded accurately and relatively quickly. Finds positions and complex relationships between artefacts can also be recorded with this method as can detailed records of topography. The planning frame can also be used as an adjunct to diver searches. Very detailed coverage can be achieved by placing a frame along a baseline and searching each sub-division systematically.

This method is also flexible in terms of orientation. The planning frame can be used in the same basic way, positioned vertically to record sections and areas of standing structure. All the same considerations apply as when the frame is used horizontally.

A very successful variation of this system involves details being traced directly, onto sheets of transparent rigid acrylic or P.V.C. laid over a double-strung planning frame, using wax crayon or chinograph pencil. The completed squares are taken to the surface where they can be scaled down by drawing or photography, or simply traced off at the same scale onto draughting film. The original sheet can then be cleaned and reused.

9.3.5. Bearing circle

This method has very limited application to archaeological work beyond establishing the approximate limits of a site. A raised board is positioned on the seabed on which a 360-degree protractor is fixed. The 0/360 degree mark is aligned with magnetic North.

Figure 85. A radial method of surveying. (9.3.5. and 6.)

A tape is connected to an arm which pivots on the centre of the board/protractor. The position of a feature is recorded by reading off the bearing and distance from the position of the equipment. Small errors in reading off bearings lead to errors in plotting and these increase with distance. For example, an error of 1 degree over 10 metres produces an error in position of 17.5cm, whereas a 1 degree error over 50m will produce a positional error of 87cm. A three-dimensional version of the bearing circle called a hydrolite has also been used.

9.3.6. Plane table

This method of survey requires very good visibility and on land its use is generally restricted to exercises requiring a lower degree of precision (for example large scale topographic surveys). However, it does have advantages in that it is a very simple system and the plan forms under the eye of the surveyor. Mistakes can therefore be spotted and rectified immediately.

The equipment consists of two units. A levelled board on a tripod and a sighting device, or alidade, with a straight edge. Four conditions must be fulfilled in setting up a survey:

a. Setting up a plane table

Keep the following points in mind when setting up a plane table:

i. The table must be levelled.

ii. The plane table must be positioned over a known point on the sea bed using a plumb-bob suspended from below the tripod. This point is marked on the plan exactly over the actual point on the seabed. This station, "point A" forms one end of a baseline.

iii.   Another point is selected on the seabed, "point B", as the other end of the baseline. The distance from point A is measured and with a scale ruler point B is marked on the plan. The table is then orientated so that the baseline on the plan runs along the baseline on the seabed.

iv. Direction of magnetic north is recorded on the plan.

b. Plane table operation

A diver on the plane table sights through the alidade, which is pivoted around point A, to the point to be surveyed which is indicated by another diver with a ranging pole. A light line is drawn onto the plan along the straight edge of the alidade and numbered (or annotated to indicate what it was aligned on). The diver with the staff also records the order in which features are surveyed.

When all features have been surveyed a tape is used to measure off the distance to each feature from point A. A scale ruler can then be used to mark off these distances on the lines of sight drawn onto the plan giving the positions of the features. An alternative method is to record all the lines of sight from point A, then move the table so that point B on the plan is exactly over point B on the baseline and reorientate the table so that once more the baseline on the plan runs along the baseline on the seabed. Lines of sight to all the features are taken as from point A. This gives a series of intersecting lines of sight which represent the positions of the features.

9.3.7. Photogrammetry

Photogrammetry is essentially the taking of measurements from photographs. It is a flexible survey system but does require good visibility to make use of the full potential, and this limits its application on many underwater sites. It is often believed that photogrammetry can only be used if sophisticated and specialised equipment is available, but this is not so. At its basic level all that is needed is a standard camera and information about the relative position of a few identifiable points visible in the exposure.

The level of technology at the other end of the spectrum can be considerable with precision photogrammetric cameras and lenses taking stereoscopic pairs of photographs which require expensive plotting equipment to extract measurements. With such specialised equipment training is necessary to not only take the photographs but also to produce results to a high degree of accuracy. These can range from three-dimensional images of the topography of an archaeological site to a record of intricate detail on the surface of an artefact.

In this guide, only the basic photogrammetric technique below is outlined. A more detailed account is available in Williams (1969), and for its application to underwater sites (including the use of stereo images) see Green (1990: 101-122).

A simple photogrammetric technique is to photograph a reference object of known size, such as a 1m square planning frame with 200mm divisions, which is parallel to a more or less flat surface. This surface need not be horizontal, but it is a technique most frequently used for plotting things like the distribution of scattered objects over an area of seabed visible from the camera position. By using the divisions on the calibrated object it is possible to extend their alignment across all parts of the exposure by drawing lines on the photograph or on a transparent overlay. This creates a perspective grid over the visible area and although the squares appear slightly distorted by the perspective they are regular squares of known size. The 200mm divisions can be used to plot the scatter to a reasonable degree of accuracy because the seabed is flat and the plane of the drawing frame is close to that of the seabed. The accuracy of the plot would be reduced if the scatter was on an uneven surface or if the plane of the reference object was not parallel to the surface. The accuracy of the plot also diminishes away from the reference object.

Using the same basic principles it is possible to place a three-dimensional calibrated reference object, such as a skeletal

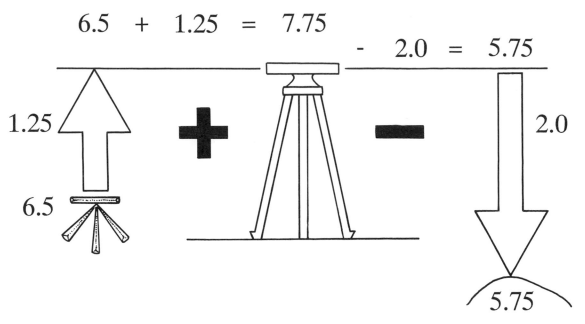

$$6.5 \quad + \quad 1.25 \quad = \quad 7.75$$
$$- \quad 2.0 \quad = \quad 5.75$$

1.25

6.5

2.0

5.75

Figure 86. The principle of levelling. (9.4.1.) (Drawing by K. Watson.)

cube, in a series of photographs and use that to determine the position of objects in any plane, and some success with this method has been achieved on archaeological sites (Morrison 1969).

9.4. Survey and the Third Dimension

We have looked at ways of measuring in two dimensions, known as the x and y co-ordinates. However, it is very rare for archaeological sites to be flat and much of the information is in the third dimension – the height/depth or z co-ordinate.

9.4.1. The principle of relative heights

Survey in the third dimension is still a matter of measuring from known points to unknown ones in order to, in this case, establish relative heights.

The problem in applying the principle of relative heights underwater lies in the taking of reliable measurements through the water. Establishing relative heights will rarely ever

be impossible but the best solution will depend upon the particular circumstances of each site. It must be remembered that a one-step transfer of heights between a known benchmark and a temporary one (often referred to as a temporary bench mark or TBM) is reasonably accurate, but multiple steps increase the chance of error.

9.4.2. Using benchmarks on land

If the site is shallow enough it may be possible to use land survey techniques of levelling using a theodolite or the simpler dumpy (engineers') level, and a measuring staff.

In the example in Figure 86 the height of the theodolite (7.75m) is the height of the datum point (6.5m) plus the reading of the measuring staff seen through the instrument's telescope (1.25m). With the theodolite remaining in position, the staff can then be placed on the point of unknown height, and the reading on the staff (2.0m) (seen through the sight of the theodolite) is

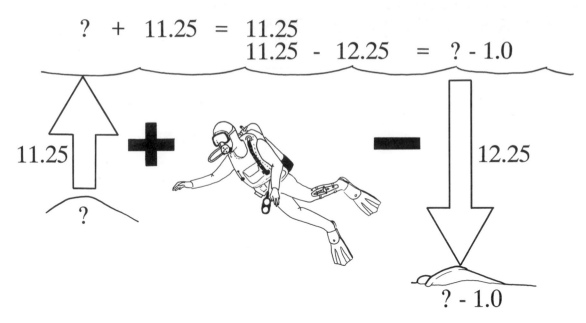

$$? \quad + \quad 11.25 \quad = \quad 11.25$$
$$11.25 \quad - \quad 12.25 \quad = \quad ? - 1.0$$

11.25

12.25

?

? - 1.0

Figure 87. Using the water surface to measure relative heights. (9.4.3.) (Drawing by K. Watson.)

subtracted from the known theodolite height (*i.e.* 7.75m). The result is the height of the unknown point (5.25m). If the water depth is greater than about 3m this method becomes very difficult with problems of an unwieldy staff length and difficulties in communication between the theodolite operator and the staff-holder.

9.4.3. Using the water surface for establishing relative heights

When working under the air-water interface this would seem an obvious benchmark to use as it is reasonably level and sometimes flat enough to be easily measured from.

A problem with all methods of measuring from the surface is that the water rarely keeps still. Both wave action and tidal fluctuations mean that the benchmark can move. Waves can have an effect but appropriate techniques reduce the need to wait for a flat-calm day. The rise and fall of the tide is also something which can be allowed for. The answer is to use the interface

like the theodolite in land levelling *i.e.* just to transfer a height from one point to another, rather than as a benchmark itself.

A permanent feature of the site is designated the site temporary benchmark (TBM). Measure from the surface to this TBM. Next, measure to four or five other points then subtract the depth of the TBM from the depth of the other points. The difference is the relative height of the other points below the TBM. In this way the whole site can be related to one central point (the chosen feature or TBM). Returning to the TBM every few measurements helps prevent tidal changes introducing inaccuracies (for added accuracy or if the time between TBM measurements is unavoidably long any difference between two TBM readings can even be averaged out over intervening measurements) (Figure 87). It then only takes one measurement of the TBM to a land benchmark to relate the whole site to a known height.

If the site is shallow, use land levelling techniques to measure the relative height of the TBM directly. On deeper and/or off-shore sites this must be calculated indirectly by measuring from the TBM to the water surface and simultaneously from the water surface to the land benchmark. This can be achieved in a number of ways. For example, a level of the surface of the water at the nearest land benchmark can be directly related to the water level over the site because the sea is for our purposes flat. It is possible to use tide gauges and tide tables to gain a measurement of the height of the water (lowest astronomical tide plus tide gauge or table reading); however tide gauges must be checked for accuracy, and predicted tidal heights are affected by atmospheric pressure and wind strength and direction.

There are various ways of measuring from the surface which are detailed below. All the methods have their advantages and yet again your choice should be the most appropriate for the circumstances given the degree of accuracy required, the time and the resources available.

a.   Depth gauge

Most divers use a depth gauge as part of the equipment to control their dive. They can be used to give depths for archaeological survey, but common analogue gauges are not designed for this level of precision: they are graduated no finer than metres or feet, their repeatability is not reliable and individual examples from the same manufacturer will vary in the reading they give. This means that even using a single depth gauge is unlikely to give a result within 1m of repeatability.

Commercially available electronic gauges and computers tend to be more accurate and give more consistent repeatability but, to date, even these have not normally given readings better than ± 100 mm. Their use should therefore be restricted to general topographic survey techniques which can accommodate individual weighting of measurements. More sophisticated depth meters have been developed specifically for archaeological underwater. Botma and Maarleveld (1987) describe a hand-held meter

which is accurate to ± 5 mm over a range of ± 5 m around a reference level. The meter can filter wave and swell fluctuations, compensate for different water densities and remain accurate in currents up to 1 knot. Unfortunately the meter has never been mass-produced and 'one off' productions can cost several thousand pounds.

The depth of tethered divers using surface supplied air is often monitored by the diving supervisor on the surface. This can be done electronically but the traditional method is to have an open-ended tube attached to the diver and connected to a sensitive pressure gauge on the surface. These pneumo-gauges are capable of measuring to ca. 150mm when fitted with a large and appropriately calibrated dial, and so may be of use for some rough survey work provided the open end can be positioned by the diver on specific points.

b.   Buoyed tape

In the right conditions, measuring down from a buoy on the surface can be an extremely accurate method. Clearly, this method is best used on a very calm day. To help overcome any minor fluctuations in height caused by waves, buoys with a tall thin shape tend to be less prone to wave-induced movement than wide shallow buoys. If the buoy is a small surface marker type it may have insufficient buoyancy to prevent its being pulled underwater inadvertently. The tape must be kept under tension and as near to vertical as possible. This will be very difficult in strong currents.

c.   Echo-sounders

Boat mounted echo-sounders have too wide a beam to allow for the measurement of precise areas on the sea bed such as datum points. They do however provide a good impression of the depth range of a site for developing fieldwork strategies.

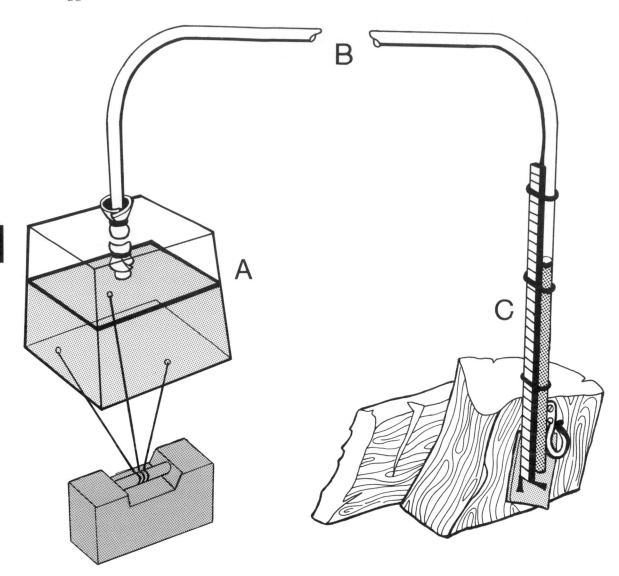

Figure 88. A simple underwater level or 'bubble tube': a) plastic container forming a reservoir of air, b) 15mm transparent, flexible, plastic tubing, c) measuring rod fixed to the open end of the tube. (9.4.4.a.)

9.4.4. Measuring relative heights within a site

a. Bubble tube

Sometimes known as an 'aqua level', the bubble tube uses the principle that an air/water interface will always try to be level. Air is introduced into a flexible transparent tube. The buoyant air arches the tube, and the ends of the bubble (the two air/water interfaces within the tube) will be at the same level. It is then possible to make height comparisons between the TBM (Section 9.4.3) and other points on the site within a radius equivalent to just under the length of the tube. Theoretically this could be any length, but in practice a tube more than 20m long becomes difficult to manage.

The technique is to fasten one end of the tube close to the TBM and measure the difference in height between the bench mark and the bubble in the tube. This will give the height of the base of the bubble at both ends of the tube. The free end of the tube can then be positioned close to any point and a vertical measurement taken between the point and the bubble. This can then be deducted from the height of the bubble to give the height of the point if it is lower, or added if the point is higher.

Care has to be taken not to let air bleed out of the system by holding the free end too high or too low. This problem can be reduced if a large volume reservoir is incorporated at the fixed end (Figure 88), sufficient to take the air in the tube should the free end be held too low. The air/water interface in the reservoir will alter very little unless a lot of air is allowed out at the free end. Although the surveyor is normally at that end, and air bubbling out is unlikely to go unnoticed, it is always worth bringing the free end back to the TBM at intervals to check for any significant air loss.

The tube is usually of about 15mm internal diameter. The larger the bore of the tube, the less problem there will be with the bubble 'sticking' through friction; unfortunately the larger the bore the bigger the problem there will be with the buoyancy of the tube.

b. Vertical offsets for sections, profiles and elevation

The offset method of measuring is often used in the vertical plane following the principles described in Section 9.3.2.

The results of offsets for sections (a cut through sediments), profiles (outlines of shapes) and elevations (faces of structures) have to be fixed in three rather than just two dimensions. The height is normally reliably fixed by making the baseline level and measuring its height (or rather depth) at both ends. The baseline itself is usually a taut string (*e.g.* whipping twine) or tensioned wire. A tape positioned close to, and parallel to, the baseline proper provides the reference for the 'along' measurement. Because a tape cannot be pulled taut enough measurements are taken to the baseline. Measuring vertically can be aided by using a plumb-bob.

9.4.5. Direct Survey Method (DSM)

DSM was developed as an alternative to triangulation for sites with a significant third dimension. The most common method of survey on sites with deep excavated trenches, or rock gullies, is to triangulate in mid-water and measure down using a calibrated plumb-bob (often a tape with a weight at one end and a float the other). This gives a plan position and a depth from the more-or-less horizontal tape whose zero is on a datum of known height. In this way it is possible to transfer datum points to lower levels in gullies and trenches, but it is difficult to work very accurately with this method. DSM was devised to overcome the problems inherent in this approach, and to avoid the midwater gymnastics required to coordinate a minimum of two tapes and a plumb-bob just to fix one point. DSM allows the diver to measure from any datum points in line of sight directly to the point to be surveyed. This type of measurement is sometimes referred to as a 'slant range'. Although the above-water processing of measurements is more complex than conventional 'drawing up', underwater it is simpler, faster and inherently more accurate.

Although it is possible to process DSM measurements by hand, a 'best fit' computer program is normally used. DSM requires a minimum of three direct measurements; if these are imagined as lengths of string attached to three datum points it can be seen that they will meet at the apex of a three-sided pyramid, which represents the point being surveyed. Three direct measurements can normally meet at two points, one above the datum points, and one below. As in all good surveying practice a check measurement is essential, so four

175

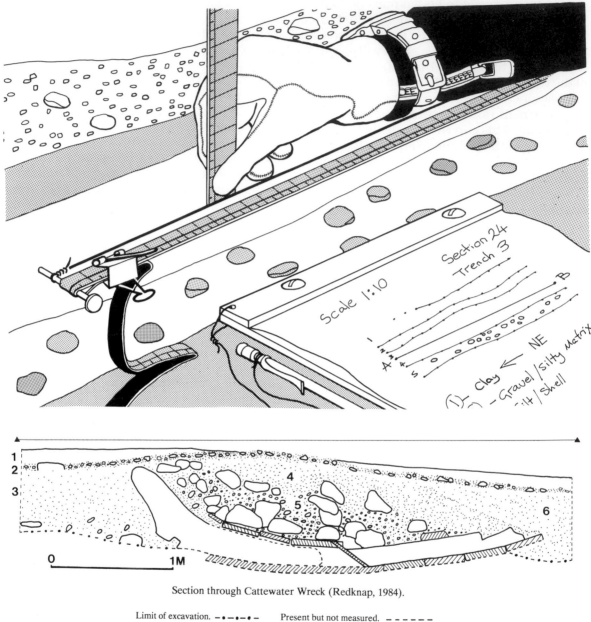

Section through Cattewater Wreck (Redknap, 1984).

Limit of excavation. — • — • — • —   Present but not measured. – – – – – –

1.   Fine grey silt.
2.   Compacted laminar grey clay with rounded (flint) pebbles 5-25 cm diameter.
3.   Fine, light grey shelly sand, with stones and shells in lower horizon.
4.   Orange-yellow sandy gravel.
5.   Grey silty sand and gravel with stones c. 2-30cm in diameter.
6.   Greyish silt, slightly sticky.

Figure 89. a) recording a section by vertical offsetting: the position of relevant points on features (such as the edges of contexts, stones and objects) are recorded in relation to the levelled base-line (A-B on the noteboard), b) an example of a section drawing through a wreck site. (9.4.4.b.) (Courtesy of M.Redknap.)

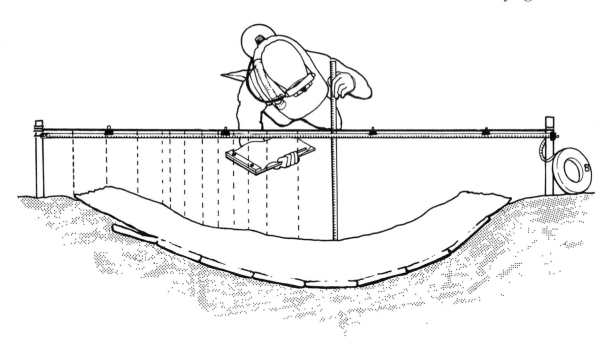

Figure 90. Surveying in three dimensions: recording the profile of a wreck using vertical offsets from a horizontal datum. (9.4.4.b.)

measurements are always used. This permits an estimate of error and helps distinguish between the two solutions.

a. The 'DSM' program

A commonly used program designed to deal with 'phantom pyramid' calculations is simply called *DSM*. It runs on a computer of the IBM PC type and, in use, the following has to be entered into the program:

i. x, y, and z coordinates of the datum points;

ii. Distance measurements from each datum point to identified points;

iii. A rough estimate of the coordinates of the point being surveyed. This is to help reduce processing time, and there are ways of automating this.

iv. A cross-reference to the project record system (*e.g.* dive logs).

The program then runs through a number of cycles, or iterations, and at each iteration a 'guess' coordinate of the point being surveyed is adjusted so as to better fit the measurements. As the guess becomes closer and closer to the 'best fit' answer, the adjustments become smaller. The program stops when either a maximum number of iterations has been exceeded, or else the adjustments at each cycle become too small to be important.

The program can then output the following:

i. The x, y and z coordinates that best fit the supplied measurements. These can be plotted by hand or computer as a two-dimensional plan, or they can be fed into a computer-aided draughting program to give a three-dimensional view of the site,

ii. The original measurements, cross-references, etc.,

iii. An estimate of confidence. This can take a number of forms but the most useful is the average residual which, as usual, show how well this answer fits these measurements (Section 9.2.3).

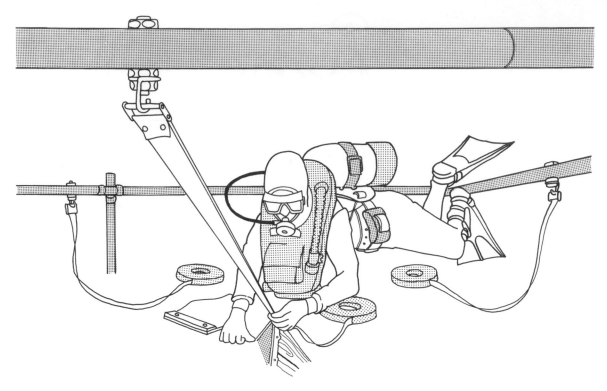

Figure 91. Direct survey measurement (9.4.5.)

b. The advantages of *DSM*

The advantages of the *DSM* program are:

i. Simplicity underwater. Bottom time is always valuable, and *DSM* is often favoured for its speed of use, while its simplicity makes it popular on difficult sites (for example in low visibility).

ii. Flexibility. The *DSM* program can also process triangulation measurements, relative depths, slopes, and bearings, thereby allowing great flexibility when surveying difficult areas.

iii. The ability to identify errors. If four measurements are taken the program can identify that an error has occurred; if more than four are taken the program will increasingly be able to identify which measurement is in error.

iv. Speed of processing. If a computer is used, the processing time is largely limited by the time taken to type in the data, which may well have to be done for the project recording system anyway.

v. The ability to communicate with other programs. The program's output can be fed directly into databases, digital ground modelling and other plotting programs.

c. Other factors to consider

Some additional factors should be considered:

i. A computer is needed. While hand plotting is technically possible, only the most dedicated would consider it a sensible option.

ii. The details of the processing are complex, and require an overview of the underlying theory in order to avoid pitfalls (such as getting the wrong apex).

iii. If the site is fairly flat, the z co-ordinate can be poorly fixed. This is in fact true for most other techniques; but because *DSM* is so rigorous you cannot ignore it.

(a)   (b)

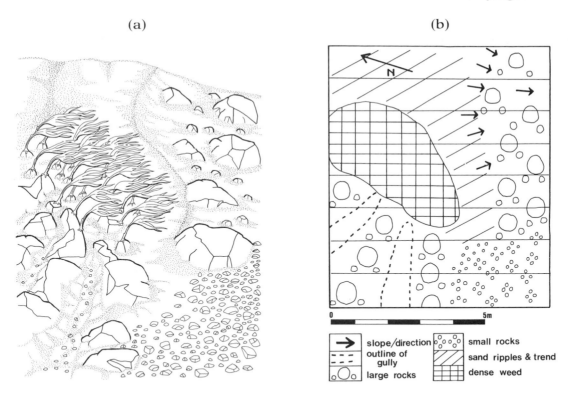

→ slope/direction	o°o°o	small rocks
--- outline of gully	⟋⟋	sand ripples & trend
○○○ large rocks	⊞	dense weed

Figure 92. Translating the visual image into written record: the seabed (a) can be depicted by the use of symbols as in (b). (9.4.6.)

9.4.6. Recording topography

Details of the surface of the sediments and bedrock lying underwater should include information about relative heights of features. To record this topography appropriate surveying methods such as triangulation (Section 9.3.1) can be used to produce a site or area plan. Major standing features such as large outcrops and boulders should be indicated, but judgement has to be used to decide to what level of detail the topographic information should be recorded. There is no set formula. More complex features may have to be recorded with a drawing frame, but this will not often be necessary unless an exceptionally detailed record of the topography is required.

If the underwater terrain is relatively flat, the only measurements that may be necessary are spot-heights at points which will indicate the slope, or lack of it, together with an indication of the sediment, bedrock or weed cover. Spot-heights can also be usefully established at the top and bottom of obvious features such as gullies, ballast mounds, and underwater cliffs.

a. Contour surveys

One of the most effective ways of representing topography is by a contour map where each line represents a string of points of the same height (or depth) in the area. The closer together parallel contour lines are, the steeper the slope. Although time consuming, contours are one of the most effective ways of illustrating underwater topography. There are a number of ways of establishing contours, but probably the most efficient method underwater requires the measurement of spot-heights at regular intervals over the site. This would normally be done on a grid pattern with a spacing of anywhere between 0.5 and 10m, depending on the nature of the topography and the degree of detail required.

Once the pattern of heights is established, and once the contour interval (height difference between each contour) has been chosen, it is possible to deduce with a reasonable degree of probability where the contour lines would intersect the grid in the gaps between each measured height (Figure 118).

It is not unknown for people to guess contours and just draw them in by eye. While this might be useful in the first stages of an investigation (for instance, to convey to other divers the impression of the seabed), such spurious contour maps should not be used in reports and publications. If, for reasons beyond the control of the investigator no other survey has been done, as might happen in a rapid emergency investigation, then it might be considered reasonable to present such evidence, but it must be indicated clearly on the drawing that it is just an impression and not a measured survey.

b. Digital Ground Modelling (DGM)

It is possible to produce contour lines automatically by inputting each spot-height into a computer running a DGM program, together with their positions. There are a number of advantages with this method:

i. The recorded positions need not be on a grid laid out in any regular pattern, although results are better if the measurements are collected from reasonably regular positions.

ii. The program will construct the contours almost instantaneously once all the information has been entered.

ii. Most DGM programs will calculate and display the information in other graphical ways, such as wire diagrams (egg-box diagrams), or profiles across the site or area in any direction. Results from magnetometers, sub-bottom profilers and

metal detectors can also be entered. This will allow overlays and comparisons of a wide variety of sources to be displayed. The only requirement is that the position of each reading is known.

9.5.   On-Site Photography

9.5.1.   Introduction

Photography has the potential of being one of the most useful recording techniques for the archaeologist on underwater sites. As well as being objective and cost-effective, it also quick. This section aims to introduce the reader to a number of techniques, disciplines and items of equipment to enable better results over the wide range of requirements a project has for underwater photography. Although some basic factors will be discussed because they are absent from other publications, any complete newcomer to underwater photography will also need to refer to specialized books and experienced underwater photographers. This section is mainly intended to illustrate the additional thought and procedures required of an archaeological photographer who has to work underwater.

Although the underwater photographs are important, particularly as a record of evidence on site, a project as a whole will require photographs for a variety of different purposes. One common fault is to take a large number of pictures without a clear idea of what each is intended for. There will usually be a distinct difference between record shots of the site and artefacts, and public relations photographs. The images required for insertion in a popular journal will be different from those required for an academic lecture, while other pictures, important as a record for the site archive, will not always be of use for public presentation. The composition needed for each purpose are often different, and it is rare for one picture to adequately cover the entire range of requirements. It is difficult to take too many photographs but, before

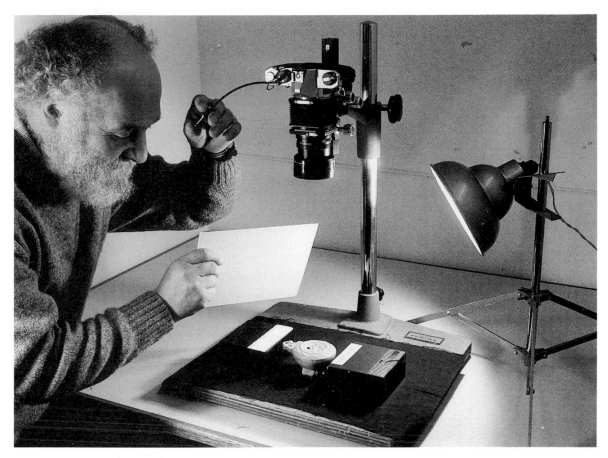

Figure 93. Photography of objects as part of the recording system. (9.5.2.) (Courtesy of C.Martin.)

pressing the shutter release, always think of why the photograph is being taken and whether the main subject is clear. By this simple act you can improve the value of the photograph and reduce the number of wasted exposures.

9.5.2. Surface photography

Photographs of the range of activities that take place above water are important for many of the reasons outlined above and are often taken successfully by people with a range of photographic experience. In archaeological projects more technical photographs are often necessary, and these will normally require some basic photographic skill. Fortunately many projects seem to have a keen photographer eager to take on tasks such as artefact photography; an essential element of recording.

A description of standard photographic techniques would take up a large proportion of this volume. Therefore readers new to photography should consult relevant, detailed publications such as *Photography in Archaeology and Conservation* (Dorrell 1989). Notes on the specific requirements of artefact record photography are included here as a guide to those familiar with basic camera and lighting technique.

Figure 94. A Bronze Age axe head 150mm long. This is an example of a photograph reproduced for publication with the scale and other information removed. (9.5.2.) (Courtesy of M. Dean.)

a. Why is the photograph being taken?

Take photographs of objects for specific purposes. Negative monochrome film will often be used for recording and display purposes, and colour reversal for lecture slides and publicity. The cost of each exposure is small compared to the resources needed to take the photographs, so do not be afraid of duplicating shots. It can save money in the long run if additional slides etc. are required to send to other people.

b. Equipment

To obtain the best quality always:
 i. Use a large format camera if possible, and fill the frame with the object.
 ii. Use an f-stop that will get everything in focus.
 iii. Use slow, fine grain film.
 iv. Use a tripod or camera stand.

c. Angle of lighting

The primary lighting should always be from the top left except in special circumstances (*e.g.* where heads on coins face right these should be illuminated from the top right). Secondary lighting may be required to allow detail in the shadows to be recorded. Particular care should be taken when using sunlight not to have the shadows (*e.g.* of the camera) falling across the object.

d. Use of scales

A scale should be used in record shots, together with artefact numbers and other relevant details. Although it is possible to handwrite details on card, plastic boards with detachable numbers and letters can be obtained in a range of appropriate sizes from shopfitting suppliers. These can look sufficiently neat to be included in publicity and lecture photographs if necessary. If carefully placed, scales and identification information can be cropped out if required when printing for publication (*e.g.* Figure 94). The caption accompanying the photograph should then give the size of the object together with other relevant information.

e. Background for subject

Always use a plain black or white textureless background. Coloured backgrounds are often intrusively grey in monochrome prints, while photographs of objects placed on grass or coloured towels look shoddy. To avoid the risk of under or over exposure caused by light or dark backgrounds and objects, it is recommended that exposure meter readings are taken on a mid-grey card placed in an appropriate place, usually immediately in front of the object to be photographed. These grey cards, made by Kodak, are inexpensive and are available from large photographic stores, but suitable alternatives can be used provided they are the right shade of grey, have a reasonably matt finish, and are of sufficient size to fill the meter's field of view.

9.5.3. Underwater photography

a. Hardware

It is an unfortunate fact that underwater photographic equipment is extremely expensive as the market is still quite small. However it is important to use the right equipment where possible, and even more important to use it correctly. One essential item that is easily overlooked and can cost very little is the photographic scale.

i. Scales

Scales should always be marked in metric divisions and be of a length appropriate to the task. To reduce flare in underwater photography the scales should have a matt finish and white should be avoided as the contrasting colour. Yellow and black are probably the best combination, but some photographers prefer yellow and red for aesthetic reasons in colour photographs.

Scientific and laboratory suppliers sell ready-made scales but it is relatively easy to make your own in a selection of sizes. 50 – 100mm long scales for use with surface artefact photography are probably best made from thin white card or plastic with 1 cm divisions inked on with a spirit-based pen. A useful general purpose underwater scale can be made from square-section plastic rulers. These are usually just over 300mm long and are available in a range of colours. The divisions can be marked on directly with black plastic tape or spirit-based marker pen, although matt black paint gives a better finish. It is a good idea to cut the ruler to give an exact metric length. For ease of use underwater it is necessary drill a hole (preferably so it is not visible) in one or both ends of the rule and plug it with a small piece of lead to make the scale negatively buoyant. Lengths of 90 degree angle section aluminium, brass, or even steel, can also

make a suitable basis for a scale. A 1m scale can conveniently be made from a plastic folding rule. Yellow versions are often available from builders' suppliers.

A scale should be carried by the photographer on all dives with a camera, and can easily be tucked inside the knife straps when not in use. You should not have to resort to your knife, watch or trowel as a scale! An additional advantage of using a scale is that if there is more than one photographer on the site, and the scales are painted slightly differently, it is easy to know who should be credited with the photographs, and who should be chased to obtain the documentation. In clearer waters, particularly when photographing structures, another useful scale is a 1m long yellow spirit level (again suitably painted) as it is easy to lay these to show the horizontal or vertical. These types of scale are adequate for most uses but if many measurements are to be taken from the photograph, a scale in the form of a square or cross, or even a skeleton cube, may be necessary.

ii. Lenses

Two major problems facing the underwater photographers in many areas of the world are poor visibility and low light levels. To obtain good crisp images, the lens should be as close as possible to the subject to reduce the problems caused by particles suspended in the water. A useful 'rule of thumb' is that this distance should be no more than one third of the visibility, and preferably one quarter for record photography. This means that wide-angle lenses have to be used in all but exceptionally clear water, as close-up lenses cover too small an area for anything other than macro photographs. A wide-angle lens or attachment should be one of the first items of expenditure for an underwater archaeological photographer or project. In conditions of less than 3m visibility, a 15mm lens or equivalent attachment is required for the best results, whilst in clearer waters, a 20mm focal length may suffice (Figure 95). The 15mm Nikonos

Make	Focal length	Lens f.no	In Air	+Flat Port	+Dome Port	U.W. Contact
Nikonos	15	2.8	-	-	-	94°
	20	2.8	-	-	-	78°
	28	3.5	-	-	-	59°
	35	2.5	62°	-	-	43°
	80	4.0	30°	-	-	22°
Sea & Sea	15	3.5	-	-	-	96°
	17	3.5	-	-	-	86°
	18	2.8	-	-	-	84°
	20	3.5	-	-	-	79°
" SWL16	*	*	-	-	-	91°
" SWL24	*	*	-	-	-	63°
SUBAWIDER	*	*	-	-	-	91°
NOVATEK 28	*	*	-	-	-	74°
20	*	*	-	-	-	95°
SLR: NIKON	20	2.8	94°	66°	94°	-
:OM-ZUIKO	21	3.5	92°	65°	92°	-
:OM-ZUIKO	24	2.8	84°	60°	84°	-
:OM-ZUIKO	28	2.8	74°	54°	74°	-
:OM-ZUIKO	35	2.8	62°	46°	62°	-
:OM-ZUIKO	50	1.8	46°	34°	46°	-
VIDEO-ZOOM	8.5mm		52°	39°	52°	-
at	10 mm		50°	37°	50°	-
	12 mm		48°	35°	48°	-
8.5mm with 0.7 x converter			74°	54°	74°	-
8.5mm with 0.48 x converter			108°	80°	108°	-
12mm with 0.48 x converter			100°	73°	100°	-

* Supplementary lenses designed to fit over the Nikonos 35mm lens.
N.B. Degrees of coverage are approximate and are generally calculated in relation to the diagonal of the image, NOT the width.

Figure 95. Table to show the angle of coverage of various lenses. (9.5.3.a.ii.)

lens is very expensive but ideal if your budget can afford it, while the excellent and less expensive 20mm Nikonos lens may be adequate for most archaeological work in all but the poorest visibility. The cheaper Subawider wide-angle attachment has often been the archaeologist's traditional ally but the newer Sea & Sea lens and their wide-angle attachments, SWL 16 & 24, may rapidly take over.

Figure 95 is useful for comparing the degree of coverage of underwater lenses with land systems that you may be more familiar with. Note the significant gain in angle made by a dome port which restores the focal length attained by the lens on hand. The 90 degree angles of 15mm lenses or wide-angle attachments enable you to photograph an entire diver from a distance of 1m. The chart shows, for instance, that the Nikonos 35mm lens gives the same angle of view underwater as a 50mm lens does in air. If buying second-hand, be aware of the lack of spares and note that the older Nikonos 15mm lens and the older Sea & Sea 17 and 18mm lenses do not allow 'through-the-lens' metering with the Nikonos IV and V. The newer 15mm Nikonos, and the Sea & Sea 15 and 17mm lenses, however, allow T.T.L metering.

iii. Cameras

One frequently asked question is "should I buy a Nikonos, or a housing for my SLR camera?". At the time of writing, a Nikonos V and 35mm lens costs a little more than an Ikelite housing with a dome port but a wide-angle converter and view-finder for the Nikonos 35mm lens costs less than a 21mm f3.5 lens for an SLR. So financial considerations are perhaps not the most important. Although the housing solution will give more accurate view-finding and focusing for close-up work, the Nikonos system will give you an extra camera and is quicker to reload and change lenses. Whilst the housing will often be better for the professional photographer going down to do nothing on their dive except take photographs, the Nikonos is much smaller

Figure 96. Lighting, composition and scale are all important considerations when making a photographic record of the site. (9.5.3.b.ii.)

and less cumbersome to dive with and hence more practical as an archaeological tool. Flexible housings and the cheaper amphibious cameras are not serious contenders for most scientific recording work underwater.

iv. Film

Although colour will be needed for P.R., lectures and some of the record photography, black and white is most acceptable for the majority of the recording. Whilst some people advocate the use of colour print film in addition to colour reversal, this is not essential as it is now possible to produce excellent colour prints directly from slides using the Cibachrome printing process. All films, regardless of whether black and white or colour, whether for prints or for slides, are a compromise between sensitivity and quality. Slow films have finer grain and so can give better definition, but require more

Film	Speed	Developer	Dilution	Temp.	Dev.
HP5	400	ID-11	1+1	20	16
HP5	800	Microphen	1+1	20	18
HP5	800	Promicrol	1+1	24	16
TRI-X	800	Microphen	1+1	20	18
TRI-X	800	Promicrol	1+1	24	14
TRI-X	400	D-76	1+1	20	12
TRI-X	800	" (not rec.)	1+1	20	18
TMX	800	Promicrol	1+1	24	14
TMX	400/800	D-76	1+1	20	13
TMX	400/800	T-MAX	Stk	24	7

Figure 97. Guide to black and white film and developer combinations for use underwater. (9.5.3.b.vii.)

light to reproduce an image effectively. They can only be used if there is sufficient natural or artificial light, or if the camera is mounted on a tripod (they can be used underwater!) to reduce camera shake.

There is not a great deal of difference between the various makes of colour slide film which are developed by the E6 process. Their use will enable quick results to be obtained either by yourself in the darkroom or with a local E6 laboratory. Whilst the slower 100 ASA is recommended for finer grain, the 200 or 400 ASA versions can give acceptable results and may be more practical where additional lighting is not employed. For the best results it may be necessary to use colour film processed exclusively by the manufacturers. Experience has shown that Kodachrome 64 can give superb results if there is sufficient light, while Kodachrome 200 is a good quality general purpose colour slide film. If the project budget can afford these higher quality, but less flexible, colour reversal films they could prove to be a good investment if photographs are needed for publicity purposes.

With black and white film, again fine grain, slower films can give better results with suitable lighting, but the 400 ASA films will be more practical and allow shorter exposures to minimise camera shake, particularly if uprated by development techniques (Section 9.5.3.b.vii below).

v. Lighting

As well as reduced visibility, another major problem underwater is low light levels. Adequate light levels are equally important for definition and contrast as well as colour, and this means that an artificial light source is often required but the timing of a photography session should not be ignored. Taking photographs in the middle of the day or exploiting bright days to the full will help make the most of any available natural light.

Usually an artificial light source will be a flash gun, or strobe, but some projects have the use of mains powered lights which are equally effective. When using these an earth trip must be used and tested before each dive, and if using colour film, be sure that it is 'tungsten rated'. The advantage of mains lights is that the desired lighting can be clearly seen whereas flash photography relies on experience and judgement. The position of any light source is perhaps the most crucial factor in underwater photography and is discussed below under techniques.

b. Underwater techniques

i. Photographer's diving technique

While an expensive wide-angle lens and flash gun may make great improvements to the clarity of photographs taken on a site, an equal improvement can often be made by thinking about diving and photographic techniques.

Poor but acceptable visibility on archaeological sites is often made unworkable by divers with their knees and fins by kicking up the silts. Perfect buoyancy and fin control by a photographer are essential skills. In certain circumstances it may be beneficial for the photographer to remove their fins but this should only be done with the approval of the diving supervisor and on sites where it does not prejudice safety.

If it is other divers that are causing the problem, it may be necessary for them to be retrained, particularly if they are accidentally disturbing archaeological sediments. If the problem is caused by archaeological activities, such as excavation, it may be impossible to maintain sufficient visibility for photography. In such circumstances it may be necessary to devote a period of the day exclusively to photography. This might be first thing in the morning before silts are stirred up or, on sites where excavation is taking place, when slack water prevents digging. Alternatively it could be at mid-day when natural light levels tend to be at their best. It is far better to have such a period set aside for all but the most urgent photography than to waste metres of film and hours of diving time creating murky pictures that are of no use either for publicity purposes or as an archaeological record.

ii. Flash

Along with acquiring a wide-angle lens or converter, correct positioning of the flashgun is the most important factor likely to lead to better photographs. On murky sites the flashgun should never be used with the bracket still attached to the camera, except for extreme close-ups. Even slight backscatter considerably affects a photograph. By holding the light source well above the subject and away from the lens, a much more even coverage is obtained and backscatter is minimised. One should hold it even further away than in Figure 96, although this may well mean buying an extension cord for the flash lead. Think of the flashgun as mimicking the sun. An added advantage of this method is that it also gives the wider coverage of light which is needed for the wide-angle lens. Remember, however, that it is the flash-to-subject distance that determines the exposure for flash photography, not the lens-to-subject distance.

There is no substitute for experience and analysing your mistakes when it comes to flash photography, but it always helps to try to imagine where the light will come from, and where the shadows will then fall.

iii. Test film

Diving conditions on every archaeological site are different and it is well worth running a film through your camera to test both the equipment and local conditions before photographing in earnest. This is particularly important if manual flash exposures are being made as the amount of suspension in the water considerably affects the guide number of the flashgun. Make detailed notes underwater of the different flash-to-subject distances or f-stops used. Putting in a blank shot between different tests may help when you inspect your films, which should be analysed as soon as possible. When you have found the best flash distances and f-stop combinations, write them on a card or on the flashgun for future dives in similar conditions. From this basis exposures can be varied according to common sense, but starting in this way by using one test film will save much film and time later.

iv. Bracketing exposures

When using colour film, and particularly for important shots, the technique of bracketing is recommended. Take the picture at the f-stop you think is the optimum and then repeat the shot, first over-exposing by a stop and then under-exposing by a stop. Although film is expensive, it is cheap when compared with many other aspects of an underwater project. It is often worthwhile using up a whole film on a dive so that the camera can be opened up and checked after the dive, and so that you don't have an annoying 'short end' on your next dive.

v. Composition

Composition is an often neglected photographic skill for underwater scientific projects but it is as important to 'record photographs' as it is to spectacular publicity shots. Care should be taken to obtain the best angle to show the subject, and oblique shots are often the most effective.

The scale should be placed close (but not too obtrusively) to the object, perhaps horizontally just in front of it or vertically next to it. The scale should not obscure important detail.

vi. Cleaning

The subject needs to be as clear as possible and if this means several minutes of work to remove light overlying sand or silts, this should be done. This is particularly important when photographing wood. Joints, treenails and grain are very easily disguised, even by a very light dusting of silt. A soft paintbrush is very useful for cleaning in this situation.

Some subjects may have to be photographed because it is felt that they are too fragile to raise whole. This raises an important problem that has to be resolved by the archaeologist and the photographer

Figure 98. A photographic tower positioned on a rigid site grid. (9.5.4.a.)

together. Further uncovering of an object such as a wicker basket, barrel hooping, or the stain of a decomposed object will make the photographic recording of it clearer. This additional exposure may risk the subject's subsequent survival. On the other hand if it is not recorded photographically and still damaged then information is lost anyway. If objects or structures are fully exposed and cleaned for photography, then even more care than usual must be taken to re-bury or otherwise protect them against renewed degradation.

vii. Developing film

If photography is being relied on as an important part of the documentation process, it is vital to check the results of any shots as soon as possible. Ideally that means that a project should have a darkroom available. Serious photographers must master their own techniques of developing. As important as the type of black and white film are the developer and darkroom techniques you use.

Your temperature control, timing and agitation methods should be standardised for consistent results and you should find a developer combination that works well for you and the particular conditions you are working under and then stick to it. On murky sites, if artificial light is not used, you may have to take your photographs 'wide open' at 1/30th and extend the film development time as necessary.

Technically better results can be obtained by using a faster film rather than by extending development, but there are times when there will be no choice (for instance, if you are already using fast film, when there is none available locally and you have run out). Developers such as Microphen and Promicrol are available which will increase film speed with minimal increase in grain size. Examples of combinations are illustrated (Figure 97) presuming a 20 ounce tank, agitation of 10 seconds per minute and a diffuser enlarger. It is important to realise that any development time is a guide and if you find you need more contrast, or the negatives for your test film are thin, then increase the development time accordingly and *vice versa*.

9.5.4. Photomosaics

Underwater visibility will seldom be good enough to photograph large objects, structures or areas in one frame with sufficient detail. Even when the visibility is good enough, the lens will not give a true plan view of the whole structure because of distortion. Photomosaics are a way of obtaining a similar end-result by taking overlapping photographs and joining the prints together. Theoretically this can be done simply by 'flying' over the site, which may help to make up a pictorial view. However, lack of either precision or of any control information will not give accurate information for the site records. For a simple '*aide-memoire*' a few oblique photographs would give a better result. For a real photomosaic it is far better to do the job properly and enable the mosaic to contribute significantly to the survey and other recording methods used on the site.

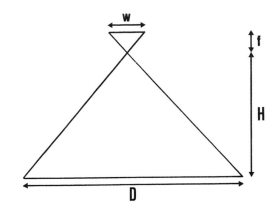

$$\frac{D}{H} = \frac{W}{f}$$

D = Distance of coverage required (in metres)
H = tower Height (in metres)
W = width of film (in mm)
f = focal length of the lens (in mm) multiplied by 1.33 for use underwater

Figure 99. Formula to calculate lens focal length and camera height necessary to give the required coverage.(9.5.4.a.) (After Green.)

a. Photomosaic techniques and equipment

There is no need to have a heavy frame or a system of rails over the site to run a photo-tower along, though there are a number of advantages in using a lightweight photographic tower which can easily be made out of 22mm plastic pipe or conduit:

i. The square frame at the base of the tower can act as a scale when printing. For instance, if the frame is one metre square and you draw lines forming a 10cm square on your enlarger easel and then line up the squares when printing, you will obtain a 1:10 image of any structure level with the frame. Tilting the base board of the enlarger at the printing stage can correct minor problems with alignment. The fixed camera to subject distance also gives consistent magnification making the printing easier,

189

inside the metre square was used. You may find that even when printed exactly to scale, the images of a ship's structure below the plane of a tower base do not quite match up, unless the structure is very flat and the base of the tower is lying flush with the surface structure. Despite the remains of the vessel being relatively flat, this effect still ocurred. The same problem can be encountered when trying to assemble a mosaic that includes a scale in each image or with scale markings running along the length of the structure: if the scale is printed at the correct size, the structural images cannot be matched, and vice-versa, printing the structure correctly results in distorted and confusing scales. For this mosaic, the image given by the enlarger was adjusted by tilting the base-board so that it corresponded to known distances on the structure such as plank widths etc. In this way the build up of compound errors was avoided. When the correct image size had been obtained, tonal adjustment of each print was made by varying the exposure. Using light grade 2 or 3 paper helped to prevent contrast variations between prints, and although the assembled mosaic at 1:10 seems rather lacking in contrast, the contrast is increased every time the image is reproduced.

The parts of each shot required for the mosaic were torn from the print rather than cut. This is because the feather-edge produced by tearing makes a smoother and less perceptible join than a cut. Like matching the tone of the prints, this is not cheating. It is merely reducing the distractions when viewing the assembled mosaic. The prints were glued together with cow-gum, a rubber solution which allows easy dismantling if necessary. A little paper glue can give extra strength once the assembly is complete. The mosaic was re-photographed on a cartographic camera with a negative size of 610 x 508mm (29" x 24").

The photomosaic was not being used as the primary means of survey. Much of the construction detail contained in the remaining timbers or any other assemblage of ship's structure would not be apparent in a mosaic. Bottom time on this site is not limited and conventional measurements were used for recording the structure as well as for the sections and profiles. This more traditional approach has the advantage that the surveyor acquires a much more detailed knowledge of the structure than is obtained from just two or three photographic dives. However, the assembled mosaic based on measurements as described above, can furnish a degree of detail that it would be futile to attempt to draw. In this way the photomosaic complemented and corroborated the drawn survey. In addition, because there was no immediate prospect of raising the timbers for conservation and display, it was felt that a detailed photographic record of the remains as they lay on the seabed would constitute an important archive record as well as a good display item. This is one reason why such attention was paid to the uniformity of tone in the individual photographs.

c. Using photomosaics

It is important to establish why you are making a photomosaic as this affects the level of accuracy and the type of control systems that are needed. Photomosaics can be used as:

i. A quick '*aide-memoire*',

ii. A display item for fund-raising and publicity,

iii. One of a number of complementary recording methods used on a site,

iv. The only recording method in a genuine rescue situation where there is insufficient time for a full archaeological record to be made. In normal circumstances it would be difficult to justify using a photomosaic as the only recording method, particularly as it cannot cope very well in the third dimension. However for a quick survey on a flat site, coupled with a number of check measurements in plan, a photomosaic may be quite adequate.

9.5.5. Video

As the price of video equipment steadily comes down, it becomes easier for underwater archaeological projects to benefit from this format. However, as with still photography, a little thought put into the reasons for its use and into basic techniques, can dramatically improve the results obtained. Its scope is as diverse as still photography and encompasses recording, publicity, fund-raising, education and training.

One particular advantage of video photography in underwater archaeology is that it can be used to record structures, or the relationships between objects or structures, which would be difficult to record on still film because of restricted visibility or access.   However, unlike photomosaics, videos can also record more complicated three-dimensional relationships.   The possibility of re-examining the sequences at a later date is of great value but full documentation must be made of the footage at the time it is shot.

a. Using video

In terms of public relations and fund-raising the advantages of having video footage of your site and the work being carried out are self-evident, although in these cases careful but ruthless editing of the film is necessary to bring all the most relevant sequences together. Long rambling shots, or constant use of the fast forward button must be kept out of any presentations. It is important to ensure that editing facilities will be available as unedited footage is extremely tedious. It is difficult to produce a video enjoyable to viewers without any editing but, if you have to do this, extra attention must be paid to the planning of the shooting so that a short succinct piece can be produced. Obtain a book on video filming that will give you extensive advice on the 'do's and don'ts', such as:

    i. Don't use too much panning,

    ii. Don't use the zoom excessively,

    iii. Don't make jump cuts,

    iv. Don't cross the 'line of action',

    v. Do ensure you obtain enough close-ups to 'cut in' with the medium and long shots.

One advantage of video is that as well as being useful for showing important sponsors and the public what the site is really like, it is also a great aid for training members of the diving team. Being able to explain features of the site and methods of work in a comfortable atmosphere on the surface where a proper two-way conversation can take place will considerably reduce, though not replace, the guidance needed underwater where time is more crucial.

b. Video equipment

The proliferation of small 'camcorders' has made the use of video on small projects much more of a possibility in recent years. Previously in the UK only large projects or those backed up by the loan of North Sea technology were able to use video on-site. Generally these were hard-wire systems with the recorder and monitor on the surface. Whilst these systems had advantages, such as live surface viewing and extra low light capabilities, the lack of a view-finder for the diver meant that communications were essential and that type of system is really designed for surface demand diving rather than SCUBA. Camcorders in housings make video filming far more workable and the bright electronic view-finders allow very easy viewing by the cameraman even in dark conditions, especially when compared to underwater TTL film cameras.   By using a dome port they can be made to operate on the principle of focusing on an apparent image, which gives the added advantage that almost no focusing will be needed whilst filming underwater. You may well want to adapt the system you obtain by bringing the view-finder closer to the rear of the housing to give you a better view, or taking off the eyepiece of the view-finder and mounting a close up lens on the inside rear face of the housing.

A number of companies now hire out videos or housings but you must try to obtain one with a wide-angle converter and a dome port. This is because a standard camcorder at its widest zoom setting of 12mm will only give a field of view of 35 degrees on the surface or about 48 degrees underwater. This is about as narrow as an SLR with a standard 50mm lens (Figure 95 and Section 9.5.3 a. ii.). This severely limits the action shots obtainable of divers in visibility of less than say 10-15m. The 0.7x 'Wide Conversion Lens' available from many manufacturers will just about restore the field of view underwater that is lost by a flat port, but if used with a dome port, it will produce an angle of around 74 degrees which is acceptable for most purposes. An alternative is to use an ultra wide-angle lens converter which needs a camcorder with a macro capability. You will often also need a close-up lens between the camera lens and the converter. These converters at least double the angle of view. Cheaper alternatives, with similar glass but different mounting, are available but some have the drawback that the front diameter of the 'hood' is 90mm rather than 74mm which will be too large for many housings. Unless you obtain a well-tried system, be prepared for some experimentation to get the best results, and try out the system in a pool first.

c. Video techniques

In terms of techniques, the same comments apply to filming as have already been outlined above when dealing with still photography. The main additional point that cannot be over stressed is that the camera must be held extremely steady. One secret to this is making the camera as neutrally buoyant as possibly by using extra weights or floats so that a very light grip can then be used for controlling it. Try to disperse these evenly so that the camera is stable laterally as well as fore-and-aft, but still not requiring too much force to tilt up or down whilst filming, even with one hand.

Although video cameras often operate in fairly low light levels, extra lighting is as important for quality as with still pictures. Keeping the lighting angle well away from the camera angle is again important and, if this involves a separate lighting assistant, good co-ordination is needed, particularly in moving shots. This is because the lighting assistant must judge the cameraman's future moves and the camera's field of view without the advantage of the cameraman's position or view-finder.

9.5.6. Photographic documentation

If photography or video is to be used as a recording technique on a site it follows that the photographs or videotape are a part of the site record or archive. This means the photographs should be backed up by full documentation and should ideally be kept with all the other site records. Notes on documentation are given in Section 6.2.12. The importance of keeping good records cannot be over emphasised. It is one of the most important duties of the photographer to keep his or her photographic records up to date.

9.5.7. Photographic checklist

Think about photography before the season starts. Agree responsibilities, and agree copyright particularly with outside photographers.

a. Try out unfamiliar equipment, particularly video cameras, in a swimming pool or similar before going out to some remote site, so that you can work through any problems.

b. Procure a wide-angle lens or attachment.

c. Brief divers thoroughly on what you are doing – especially if they are 'in shot,' but also so they do not ruin the visibility.

d. Remember to take a scale and if possible, a small notepad on the dive.

e. Just before entering the water, re-check that camera lens or housing port is secure, that flash connections are secure, and that battery compartment and other openings are sealed.

f. If necessary, tidy the area before photography to ensure clear results.

g. Before taking the first photograph check that there are no bubbles on the lens, that cord or leads are not in front of the lens, and that any wide-angle attachment is on squarely.

h. Compose thoughtfully, distinguishing between record and P.R. photographs.

i. Hold light source well away from lens to minimise backscatter (possibly 1-2m above the camera).

j. Bracket exposures for important shots.

k. Write up documentation as soon as possible after dive. Complete the record when the film is developed.

9.6. Suggested Reading

a. survey

Adams, J.
1986   Survey and Recording. In Gawronski, J.H.G. (ed.), *Annual report of the VOC-Ship Amsterdam Foundation 1985:* 19-21, Amsterdam. ISBN 90-71690-01-6.

Anderson, R. K.
1988   *Guidelines For Recording Historic Ships*. National Park Service, U.S. Department of the Interior, Washington D.C.

Atkinson, K., Duncan, A. and Green, J.
1988   The Application of a least squares adjustment program to underwater survey. *IJNA* 17.2: 119-131.

Bannister, A., and Raymond, S.
1984   *Surveying*. London, ISBN 0-582-98874-8.

Bettess, F.
1984   *Surveying For Archaeologists*. Durham, ISBN 0-900926-50-3.

Botma, H.C. and Maarleveld, T.J.
1987   Underwater heightmeter: A new handheld precision instrument for elevation measuring in underwater surveying. *IJNA* 16.2: 87-94.

Green, J.
1990   *Maritime Archaeology: A Technical Handbook*. London, ISBN 0-12-298630-X.

Hogg, A.H.A.
1980   *Surveying for Archaeologists and Other Fieldworkers*. London, ISBN 0-85664-767-5.

Kyriakopoulou, V.
1990   Underwater Surveying with the SHARPS in the 1989 excavation season at Dokos. *Enalia*, 1: 24-26.

Leach, P.
1988   *The Surveying of Archaeological Sites*. London, ISBN 0-905853-19-9.

Rule, N.
1989   Direct Survey Method and its Application Underwater . *IJNA* 18.2: 157-162.

Shomette, D.G.
1988   New Jersey project: Robots and ultrasonics in underwater archaeological survey. In Delgado, J.P. (ed), *Underwater Archaeology Proceedings of The Society For Historical Archaeology Conference,* Reno, Nevada.

Throckmorton, P.
1969   *Surveying In Archaeology Underwater*. London.

Waddell, P.J.
1990   Electronic Mapping of Underwater Sites. In Carrell, T.L. (ed.), *Underwater Archaeology Proceedings of The Society For Historical Archaeology Conference*, Tucson, Arizona, 57-62.

Watts, Jnr, G.P.
1989   The 'sinkentine': a fibreglass shipwreck model to assist in teaching three- dimensional mapping. *IJNA* 18.2: 151-156.

195

b. photogrammetry

Fryer, J.G.
  1983 A Simple System for Photogrammetric Mapping in Shallow Water. *Photogrammetric Record*, 11(62): 203-208.
Green, J.
  1990 *Maritime Archaeology: A Technical Handbook*. London, ISBN 0-12-298630-X.
Green, J. and Richards, B.
  1983 Underwater Stereophotogrammetry. In Jeffery, W., and Richards, B. (eds), *Proceedings of the 2nd Southern Hemisphere Conference on Maritime Archaeology*.
Morrison, I.A.
  1969 An inexpensive photogrammetric approach to the reduction of survey time. *Underwater Association Report*. 22-28.
Scollar, J.E.
  1975 Transformation of extreme oblique aerial photographs to maps or plans by conventional or means or by computer. In *Aerial Reconnaissance for Archaeology*. CBA Research Report, 12: 52-8.
Williams, J.C.C.
  1969 *Simple Photogrammetry*. London.

c. surface photography

Conlon, V. M.
  1973 *Camera Techniques In Archaeology*. London, ISBN 0-212-98422-5.
Dorrell, P.
  1989 *Photography in Archaeology and Conservation*. Cambridge, ISBN 0-521-32797-0.

d. underwater photography

Church, J. and Church, C.
  1986 *The Nikonos Handbook*.
Rowlands, P.
  1983 *The Underwater Photographers Handbook*. London, ISBN 0-356-09494-4.

Schulke, F.
  1978 *Underwater Photography for Everybody*. ISBN 0-13-936450-1.

e. photomosaics

Adams, J.
  1985 Sea Venture: A second interim report – part 1. *IJNA* 14.4: 275-299.
Baker, P., and Green, J.
  1976 Recording Techniques used during the excavation of the 'Batavia'. *IJNA* 5.2: 143-158.
Baker, P., and Henderson, G.
  1979 'James Matthews' excavation. A second interim report. *IJNA* 8.3: 225-244.
Green, J.
  1990 *Maritime Archaeology: A Technical Handbook*. London, ISBN 0-12-298630-X.
Rebikoff, D.
  1972 Precision underwater photomosaic techniques for archaeological mapping. *IJNA* 1 : 184 – 186.

10. Destructive Investigative Techniques

10.1. Probing

10.2. Taking Samples

10.3. Excavation

10.4. Suggested Reading

Throughout this guide stress has been laid upon the importance of survey and recording. In addition, the responsibilities which a project takes on when it disturbs a site in search of clues about the past have also been emphasised. When excavating, the level of expertise and facilities required are much higher. The work of collecting and caring for the evidence revealed during the disturbance of an archaeological site is a task which must not be taken on lightly. If it is not done to the highest standards some of the few remaining clues about the past will have been destroyed unnecessarily. There are occasions, however, when excavation or other intrusive techniques can be justified. This section briefly outlines the three basic methods which will disturb a site in search of clues: probing, sampling and excavation.

10.1. Probing

The principle of probing is fairly obvious. It is an attempt to locate sediments or structures beneath the surface layers, but in practice it is not always as simple as it might seem. Systematic probing of a site may assist the evaluation of its spread, state of preservation and depth of burial. Since its operation relies on feel, the results of probing can be very difficult to measure and interpret. It is best used to answer only very simple questions such as the depth of sediment over a buried surface, or perhaps the extent of a buried wreck structure. As with core sampling, because of the potential danger to fragile archaeological material, it should only be used after careful consideration of the consequences.

Probing will only be of lasting value if it is carried out systematically to answer particular questions. The nature of the questions will dictate the probing strategy (*e.g.* readings taken at measured intervals along a line or at the intersections of a grid).

10.1.1. Types of probe

The simplest probe is a metal rod thin enough to be pushed into sediment, and thick enough to withstand bending. A more efficient probe can be made from tubing (*e.g.* 25mm bore steel pipe) down which water is pumped. Only low water pressure is needed to penetrate all but the most compact material, and high pressure will cut through almost anything, including archaeological material. One of the drawbacks is that the water from the surface is often oxygen enriched and this may upset the anaerobic environment in which fragile archaeological material survives.

Figure 102. Probing to record sediment depths and obstructions can be an effective method of assessing the extent of some sites. (10.1.)

10.2. Taking Samples

A sample is a representative amount of material that has been collected from an archaeological or natural context. There are no sites on which sampling for environmental or scientific analysis is not relevant. Samples may be taken for a variety of reasons ranging from dating to the identification of organic remains. There is a difference between collecting a sample of a material or deposit 'to see if there is anything in it' and taking a sample to answer a specific question.

Samples should only be collected if three basic criteria can be satisfied:

i. There should be evidence that the sample will contain traces which will provide valuable information concerning the past. This is best checked by examination of a pilot sample either on-site or in the laboratory.

ii. There must be a sound reason for collecting the material. Specific questions should be asked; post-excavation analysis is made easier if objectives are clearly stated.

iii. There should be a clear prospect that the material will actually be studied. This should be established by consultation with specialists before, or at an early stage of, the archaeological investigation. However, important material should be sampled even if no scientific programme has been pre-arranged; a specialist can usually be found to work on material of significance.

These three criteria can best be satisfied if a clear strategy is agreed between the archaeologist and relevant specialists beforehand, or as soon as the problems become apparent during excavation. It is important to understand however, that even after carrying out a detailed examination a scientist may be unable to provide a simple unqualified statement. Every method of examination has its own limitations. Often one analytical method must be employed to examine one group of phenomena, and a second quite distinct method to examine other aspects of the same sample.

10.2.1. Types of 'non-artefactual' remains

It may be useful to attempt to segregate non-artefactual or environmental archaeological remains into broad categories *e.g.*:

a. 'Economic'

Environmental archaeology can make considerable contributions to our understanding of the economy of a site or period. At its simplest level this may relate to what was eaten on the site. At a more complex level the environmental information can be used to reconstruct the contemporary agricultural economy or used to illustrate differences (*e.g.* social, religious or racial) across a site or between sites.

b. 'Environmental'

This group refers to the sampling of deposits which may yield information on the general climatic, environmental or ecological conditions prevailing on or near a site.

With respect to underwater sites this may mean samples which can generate information about the formation of the site, or perhaps on the chemical and physical characteristics of the site and particular preservation conditions.

c. 'Behavioural'

The biological remains contained in certain contexts and/or their distribution across a site can relate to various aspects of human behaviour. At its most obvious the threshing and winnowing of cereal crops on submerged settlements could produce recognisable patterns among botanical assemblages. The practising of crafts or commercial activities on board ship may also reveal itself in characteristic groups of animal bone or other materials on shipwreck sites. It may also be possible to interpret the function of specific areas or determine the original contents of containers.

10.2.2. Samples for stratigraphic analysis

An important part of any archaeological investigation is a consideration of the stratigraphy of the site. Apart from visual methods of characterisation it may be necessary to take samples of the various layers present for laboratory analysis. Sedimentology, looking at particle size and composition through the depositional sequence, helps determine the changes that have taken place over time (see column sampling, Section 10.2.5. b.).

10.2.3 Samples for dating

The principles of radiocarbon and dendrochronological dating have already been introduced as have the two main techniques of absolute dating. There are many factors which critically affect how viable samples are for particular types of dating analysis. A number of very useful handbooks are available containing advice on sampling procedures and several of these arc listed under the dating section recommended reading (Section 4.6. c.).

a. Radiocarbon sampling

It is recommended that contact should be made with a radiocarbon laboratory at an early stage, if possible before any samples

Figure 103. Air or water probes can be used to explore a site but are potentially destructive. In this example measurements (distance along tape and depth of probe) are being relayed to the boat by diver-to-surface-communications. (10.1.)

201

are taken (see list in Mook and Waterbolk 1985). The following points should be taken into account:

i. Never submit a radiocarbon sample unless you clearly realise which archaeological problem you want to solve. It may have nothing to do with chronology. Dates well related to the span and significant events of site chronology should always be sought. Do not be wooed by potential samples simply because they are there. Always try and form an opinion on the chances that your sample actually dates the human activity or natural phenomenon for which you seek a date. In most cases there is no absolute certainty of association or contemporaneity.

ii. Before taking a radiocarbon sample from an archaeological deposit, section or core, study the nature of the deposit or layer and the stratigraphical conditions (geological

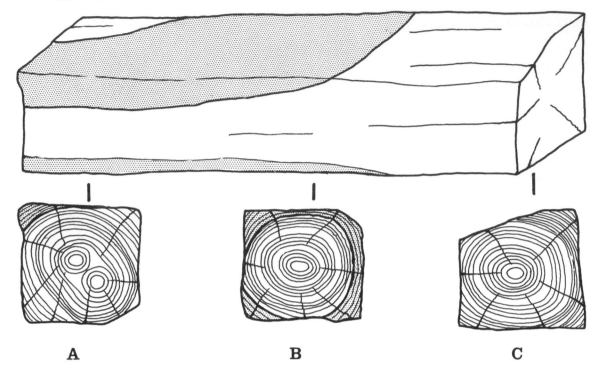

A   **B**   **C**

Figure 104. Optimum place for tree-ring sampling; a) branching is distorting the ring pattern, at c) no sapwood is present, but at b) there is undistorted ring growth and good sapwood survival. (After Nayling.)

complications, possibilities of humic contamination from higher levels, root penetration, visible animal activity from other periods, etc.).

iii. Collect more samples or a greater amount of sample than required for one dating (a later check may be required by the laboratory that has agreed to do the work). Estimate whether the amount of sample available is sufficient to provide the required precision in age. Realise that botanical, zoological or chemical identification is possible only before treatment in the radiocarbon laboratory.

iv. Pack the samples in plastic or aluminium foil or in glass bottles and immediately write the name of the site, sample number (depth and horizontal position) and the name of the collector on each packed sample. Send the sample to the laboratory (see list in Mook and Waterbolk 1985) as originally packed, together with full documentation.

v. If samples have to be stored before submission to the laboratory, keep them in a cool, dark and dry place. Don't use organic preservatives and in the case of shipwreck material don't submit samples contaminated by waterproofing agents *e.g.* tar, pitch.

b. Sampling for dendrochronology (tree-ring dating)

It is recommended that contact should be made with a dendrochronology laboratory at an early stage, if possible before any samples are taken (see list in Eckstein *et al.* 1984). The following points should be taken into account:

i. The determination of a date for a structure will require a sample or samples of wood cut from well-preserved and long-grown timbers preferably with sapwood surviving. Tree-ring sampling ideally involves selecting the widest part of the timber, free of branches and knots, and the sawing out of a 50 - 100mm thick slice. In general, ring sequences of less than 50 years will not date reliably. Size will not equate with ring width as the growth rates of the original trees might vary considerably.

ii. Long ring-pattern sequences out to, and if possible including, sapwood are ideal for dating. Such complete samples will give the dendrochronologist the opportunity to sub-select the most suitable and informative samples for dating purposes, and also offer the option of characterising the complete wood assemblage in terms of species, age and growth rate.

iii. A complete cross-section cut perpendicular to the grain is preferable, but a V-shaped piece from the back might be sufficient if the piece has been selected for conservation and display. In some cases, sections sawn from timbers can be tree-ring counted and then joined back to the main piece.

iv. Coring is also possible although it is recognised that it may cause compression and distortion of the ring sequence. An increment corer has been used successfully in dating boat finds (e.g. Tyers 1989). A careful assessment should be made in choosing the optimum coring location with reference to the extent of the ring sequence and the danger of damage to the outer (and perhaps most decayed) rings.

v. Samples should be taken to provide the longest ring sequence possible including the latest surviving ring on the timber. For the greatest precision of dates, samples that include some sapwood, preferably complete, need to be identified on-site and sampled preferentially (Figure 104).

vi. Wood that is split or cracked may require support and strapping before sawing. Great care should be taken with the outer surfaces of the wood. This area may consist of sapwood which dries at a different rate from heartwood and it tends to become detached.

vii. Package the samples to prevent either physical damage or dehydration, and label them so that each is cross-referenced to the records of the original timber.

10.2.4. How much to collect

The decision as to how much of the deposit or material to recover must be taken in the light of the answers to questions like:

i. What is the deposit made up of? What is the principal component? Is it uncontaminated? The material that it is intended to sample for must have survived, the context must be well stratified and dated, and it must be possible to take a large enough sample to yield the required minimum of identifiable material in a manner unlikely to produce a sample bias.

ii. What is its potential? What can it tell us about the archaeology of the site?

iii. What will it entail, in terms of the excavation budget and resources, to recover all or a part of the deposit?

iv. What is the opinion of the specialist who will be providing the identification and interpretation?

Speculative sampling could be employed provided that it formed part of a co-ordinated sampling programme (i.e. to provide test samples). Such samples should be processed and investigated with the minimum of delay and information about the quantity and range of evidence present can be quickly relayed to the archaeologist who has the opportunity to modify the excavation strategy regarding the original deposit. The planning stage of the excavation should include an assessment of the likely potential for scientific studies before and during the excavation itself and in post-excavation work. Account should be taken of:

i. the time needed to carry out scientific work,

ii. the cost (to include the cost of site visits and meetings as well as laboratory time),

iii. the likely importance of the analysis, both absolutely and in relation to cultural archaeological studies,

iv. the intrinsic importance for the development of the disciplines of archaeological science and archaeology underwater.

203

10.2.5. Sampling methods

a. Spot sampling

These may be small local concentrations of biological materials (excluding wood). Examples are groups of fruitstones, insect remains or small bones. Do not attempt to clean or separate the materials until they are transported safely to a specialist or more suitable processing conditions. General samples for biological analysis can be examined for the presence of many different kinds of remains (insects, fruits and seeds, parasite eggs) depending on the nature of the material and the archaeological questions posed.

The following is a basic procedure for the recovery of a sample illustrating some fundamental points:

i. Have a suitable, clean container with a close fitting lid ready.

ii. Identify the extent of the deposit from which the sample is to be taken.

iii. Record all locational details (relationships with other contexts, orientation of sample etc.) on your underwater noteboard in the form of measurements, sketches and notes.

iv. Make sure that the surface of the deposit is cleaned in the proposed sample area, to reduce the risk of contamination.

v. If you cannot recover a 'total sample' cut or gently separate a proportion of the whole deposit with a clean spatula or trowel (tools should be cleaned between samples to prevent cross-contamination).

vi. Place the sample in the container and tightly fit the lid.

vii. If you are taking a number of samples on one dive, make sure that they do not get mixed up. Use pre-labelled containers or bags if necessary.

viii. Bear in mind at all times the possibilities of contamination. Note down any doubts.

Figure 105. Taking a spot sample. (10.2.5.a.)

ix. Record the quantity of the material or deposit that was actually recovered and how that compares with the original total deposit (even if it is just an estimate *e.g.* 10kg of an estimated 100kg).

x. Raise the closed container to the surface for prompt examination by the relevant specialist.

xi. Ensure that all your notes are accurately transferred to the Sample Record Form (or equivalent documentation).

b. Coring and column (monolith) sampling

Chronologically stratified sequences, such as those found in naturally accumulated deposits (*e.g.* peats or lake sediments) should be collected in such a manner that will not disturb the sequence. Two methods are coring through sediments down from the surface and the cutting out of a monolith of sediment (usually from a section face).

Column samples and monoliths are taken by inserting a channel or tube (of stainless steel or rigid plastic etc.) into the sediment

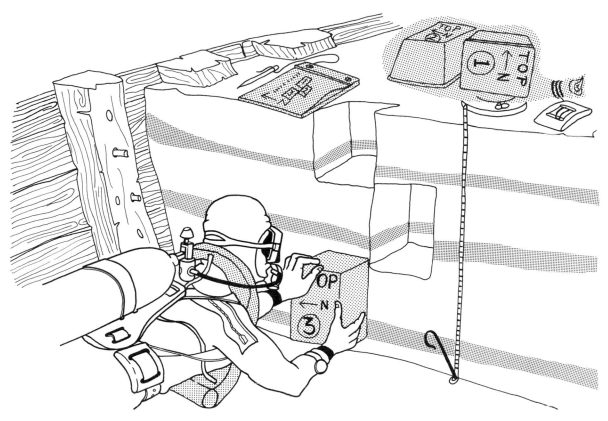

Figure 106. Column, or monolith, sampling from a section: A sketch has been made of the work (10.2.5.b.)

and then extracting it using the most convenient method to achieve an undisturbed sequence.

Monoliths, or column samples, can be made up of a sequence of separate samples (Figure 106) (*e.g.* plastic containers or metal containers placed either side of a vertical datum line). If the containers are pushed into the section it is possible to remove large blocks of undisturbed sediment. Care should be taken to avoid contamination of the contents by smearing or the introduction of extraneous matter. All the containers should be carefully labelled with orientation, sample number, and location.

Further examination can take place under more suitable conditions, where contamination can be minimised. Sub-sampling of cores or monoliths for further analysis (*e.g.* for pollen) should be carried out by specialists or under their direct supervision. X-radiography of the undisturbed column may be useful for identifying layers or structures invisible to the naked eye.

10.3. Excavation

Archaeological excavation might be defined as the disciplined dismantling of the contexts which form a site with the aim of explaining the origin of each layer and its relationship to the rest of the site.

The aim of this section is to set out various methods and processes of excavation which have been shown to produce satisfactory results. This guide cannot

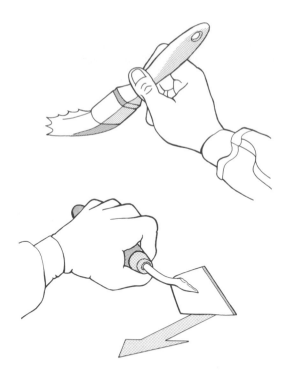

Figure 107. The trowel and the paint brush, along with the hand, are the most commonly used digging tools.

include every variation available as each problem encountered prompts a slightly different improvisation. The use of any particular piece of equipment cannot automatically lead to high standards of excavation. However, a sound understanding of the requirements of archaeological excavation, coupled with experience in the use of the equipment described below, will allow good work to be done in even the most unpromising of circumstances.

10.3.1. Defining the limits

It is important to define the area to be excavated and work to those planned limits (See Section 5.4.4.) A disciplined approach is necessary for the following reasons:

i. It increases the efficiency of the project by concentrating effort on the areas selected on the basis of their potential to answer the questions posed in your research design (Section 5.2.1).

ii. Working in distinct, regular areas allows more efficient planning of later investigations. The project will know where to continue because the precise limits of the excavation already undertaken will be recordable.

iii. Distinct boundaries of investigations help workers to be more thorough in retrieving all the elements of evidence necessary for interpreting the site. The inevitable damage caused by excavation is also then limited to distinct locations rather than spread over a larger area by wandering excavators.

iv. Disciplined work also has practical benefits such as straight vertical edges at the limits of excavation to aid recording of stratigraphy and the ability to concentrate site facilities such as airlifts and site grids.

10.3.2. Marking the limits

It should be impressed upon those carrying out the work that they must confine their attention to the defined area. This can be achieved in two ways.

i. A method of physically marking the work area will be necessary, such as rigid grids which have the advantage of protecting the excavation edges, or line which must be firmly anchored if it is to provide a permanent marker.

ii. Effective briefing on the physical limits of the investigation, and the reasons for them, for those who will be carrying out the work. Without a reasoned explanation of the need for discipline, no amount of physical markers will produce a systematic excavation.

10.3.3. Excavation by context

The need for careful investigation of the contexts making up a site has been discussed above, as has the nature of stratigraphy (Section 4.4.3). An excavator should aim to remove the layers in the reverse order of deposition (see Section 4.4.4. b. ii.). Deeper deposits should not be touched until overlying contexts have received adequate examination and recording.

Some sediments may not allow clear layers to be excavated sequentially. In this situation, control can be maintained by excavating in measured spits (for example, removing an arbitrary layer 10cm deep). The exposed surface is then cleaned, recorded and the sequence repeated until a recognisably different layer is reached. Later analysis of these apparently homogeneous spits may allow useful evidence to be extracted. Lack of apparent layering is not a justification for uncontrolled excavation technique, nor is the use of spits an excuse for ignoring context differences. Depth of excavation alone is not a reliable method of relative dating.

Where layers are difficult to distinguish, it is more important than ever to keep the work orderly and neat. Allowing excessive amounts of loose sediment to build up may mask subtle changes and also small finds.

10.3.4. Sections: permanent, temporary and cumulative

Contexts and stratigraphy should be recorded in the first instance from above as they are noted or uncovered. During survey this is all that will be available. During excavation, however, the opportunity should also be taken to record them from the side as they are cut through. This can give added information about the relationships between the various contexts. There are three ways of achieving this, all of which may be used during the same excavation.

i. Permanent sections will exist at the edge of the site where the sediments have been left unexcavated. These sections are termed permanent because they are unlikely to be removed as the excavation progresses.

ii. Temporary sections can be used to record contexts not represented fully enough in the permanent sections. During excavation parts of one or more contexts are left unexcavated while a side view is recorded. The rest can then be removed and excavation continued. Since context differences tend to be more distinct when cut through, temporary sections can be used as an aid to excavation. If a vertical face is maintained during the excavation of a context, any intrusion into underlying layers is more easily noted and stopped before it goes any further.

iii. In mobile or deep sediments where these standing walls of sediment would be impossible or unsafe cumulative sections can be recorded. This is simply the process of recording the section of each individual context before it is obscured by shoring, sandbags or a sloping excavation face. With accurate measurements along the same line, the section drawing will build up layer by layer throughout the excavation resulting in a picture of the sediments cut through at that point.

Ideally the sides of the excavation should be as vertical as possible so that a true stratigraphic sequence can be recorded in one plane at 90 degrees from the horizontal. It helps considerably with stratigraphic analysis if plans and sections are relative to the natural horizontal datum. If for some reason it is not possible to compile a cumulative section, an alternative is to record information from a sloping or stepped 'section'. This is less satisfactory because relationships may be distorted by variations in the layers either side of the line of the section. Objects and structural remains should be left in place if they are sticking out of a section. Burrowing in after the object will only weaken the section and obscure the layers. When the section has been recorded, however, it does provide an excellent source of samples of the various layers (Section 10.2.5).

The positions of sections should be marked out. In the case of temporary and cumulative sections which may not be immediately obvious, they should be clearly explained to other divers working in the area lest they unknowingly undo all your good work.

Safety is, of course, paramount in these matters and unstable excavation faces can be a serious hazard. Sandbags and shuttering should be used where necessary.

10.3.5. Excavating around objects and structures

Wherever possible the stratigraphy surrounding objects should be systematically excavated and recorded until the item is totally free of its matrix before it is removed. It is not acceptable archaeological practice to pull objects from the sediments that surround them for a number of reasons including the risk of:

i. breaking the object,

ii. damaging other items close or attached to it which have yet to be exposed,

iii. failing to record the association of nearby objects,

iv. failing to recognise which archaeological context it is associated with.

As items become more exposed they are often more susceptible to damage, either from the activities of divers or from elements of the underwater environment such as water-borne abrasives and burrowing fauna. It may be necessary to physically protect and support exposed objects during excavation. Mechanical strength can be added by splints and padding, but delicate objects will always need a skilful excavator and the cooperation of nearby divers if they are to survive in one piece. Divers' fins can cause extensive damage to both stratigraphy and other archaeological material, and so it may be necessary (safety conditions permitting) to remove fins in the area of the excavation.

Some material may not need to be recovered after it has been exposed and recorded (for example, ships' structure). Provision must be made to protect it in the long term. This may involve reburial using sand bags and sediment that has been removed during the excavation, and is commonly referred to as 'backfilling'.

10.3.6. Excavation equipment

Tools for excavation can be divided into two main types: those used in an actual digging action (*i.e.* to loosen sediment from a layer or around an object) and those used to move the loosened sediment away from the excavation face.

a. Tools for loosening sediment

i. The diver's hand remains the most sensitive, accurate, and useful tool for fanning away or scooping silt towards the airlift or dredge mouth.

ii. The 'mason's pointing' trowel is a fundamental tool on any archaeological excavation, whether on land or underwater. The small 3-4" bladed tool can be used either delicately or strongly, as circumstances dictate, scraping with the edge of the blade towards the body (Figure 107) or, less frequently, using the point. Riveted trowel blades have a tendency to break at the attachment after prolonged use and exposure to corrosion.

iii. Paint brushes of different sizes, just as hand brushes on land, are useful accessories to gently brush soft surfaces clean. They are especially useful to clean timber surfaces prior to recording (particularly for photography). Brushes can be used effectively on unconsolidated clay, silt and sand and also around organic and other fragile material. Care must be taken, however, because brushing can smear the separate layers into one homogeneous surface where differences in sediment type cannot be recognised.

iv. Any hand tool which will do a job properly may be employed: teaspoons, dental probes, spatulas, ladles, knives, hammers all have their uses. Non-metallic tools are particularly useful where it is important not to damage delicate organic surfaces. Small tools are best kept in some form of container to avoid accidental loss.

b. Tools for removing sediment

Once sediment has been carefully loosened by one of the above methods a different type of tool can be used to take it off site. Just as spoil produced by the use of a trowel on land can be removed by shovel or mechanical

Figure 108. Airlifting. (Courtesy of J. Broadwater.)

excavator, a great deal of time can be saved by selecting the right size and type of equipment to remove loosened deposits from a site underwater. The two chief concerns of directors must be the possible loss of evidence due to bulk removal of sediments, and safety on site. The two most common tools of spoil removal, the airlift and the water dredge, are discussed here.

10.3.7. The airlift and the water dredge

The airlift and the water (or induction) dredge have in the past been described as the underwater equivalent of a shovel, but their real function is to move unwanted excavated material (spoil) away from the excavation like a wheel barrow or bucket.

a. Airlift

The airlift is a simple device consisting of a rigid tube into which air is injected at its lower end, usually from a compressor on the surface. As the air rises towards the surface it lifts the tube to near vertical and creates a suction effect at the bottom. Water and any loose materials are pulled in and up. The power of the suction is dependent on the difference in depth-related pressure between the top and bottom of the tube, and the amount of air injected.

i. Air requirements

The size of the compressor required will depend on the depth of the site, and the diameter of the suction tube. It is not advisable to try and run an airlift from a high-pressure compressor of the type used to fill diving cylinders. Similarly most divers' air surface-supply compressors will not provide a sufficient volume of air to operate an efficient system, and a diving cylinder would only last for a very short time. In no circumstances should such a compressor be used to supply air to divers and airlifts at the same time.

The basic requirement is a compressor delivering air at around 7-10 bar (100-150 p.s.i.). To operate one 110mm diameter airlift at a depth of 10m a compressor capable of delivering about 2250 litres (80 cu.ft.) of air per minute would be the minimum requirement. Road compressors used to power pneumatic drills are often the best choice, provided that a sufficiently large boat or floating platform can be deployed, or the compressor can be sited on land nearby. Another limiting factor is often the cost of such units, although it is possible to borrow or hire them.

ii. Air supply hose arrangements

On small operations the hose can lead directly from the compressor to the airlift. However, it may be necessary to secure the air hose to somewhere convenient on the seabed so that there is no additional pull on the airlift once the hose fills with air and becomes buoyant.

On long-term projects where more than one airlift is in operation, it is often convenient to have one air delivery pipe from the compressor to a multiple take-off arrangement (manifold) fastened to the seabed. If this manifold is made from a long steel tube with a selection of take-off points, either manually or automatically valved, individual airlifts can be connected at convenient points by the divers. In many cases where a tidal current changes direction by 180 degrees, it may be more convenient to have a manifold both up and down stream of the site.

iii. Operation

To set up the airlift for work, start up the compressor and allow it to reach working pressure. The airlift will normally be lying

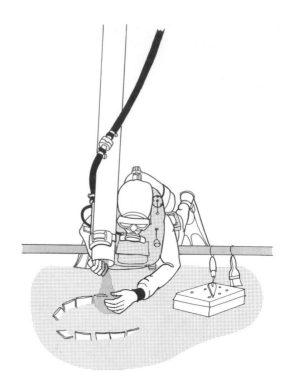

Figure 109. Airlifting: note tools secured to the scaffold frame, which also supports the diver above the archaeological deposits.

horizontally on the bottom, and when the diver opens the inlet valve air will start to bubble out of the nozzle. To make the air travel along the length of the tube it may be necessary to physically lift the pipe slightly. Air should then stop bubbling out of the nozzle and start to rise up the pipe, making it buoyant so that the airlift becomes vertical. By careful operation of the air valve, it is easy to adjust the airlift for work in a neutrally buoyant state. Slightly obstructing the intake with the hand will reduce the ratio of water to air, thus slightly increasing the buoyancy. The skilled operator can use all these devices to control buoyancy and so reduce the danger of impact by the airlift on archaeological material.

Careful positioning of the discharge is now required to ensure that removed spoil does not cascade back down on top of the previously excavated or other sensitive areas. If there is little or no current the choice may be restricted to either moving the spoil again (and again on large sites!), fixing the angle of the airlift or using a water dredge. The discharge end can be tied down to an anchorage to achieve the right angle to discharge spoil off site. Do not tie down the airlift too tightly, otherwise it will become too difficult to work. If the site has a constant tidal stream or current running across it, then the discharging spoil can be carried clear of the work area without any need for tying down.

If the discharge end of the tube projects out of the water the weight at the lower end should be adjusted. Air in the tube when in operation gives more than enough buoyancy in most conditions and it should not be necessary to bouy the discharge end. Variations of design may be required for specific circumstances: 110mm corrugated plastic hose can be used at the lower mouth end to get into awkward areas of a site, but it is essential to have the air-flow lever within easy reach of the excavator to shut off the supply of air in an emergency.

iv. Excavating with an airlift

The airlift must be used with great care. When excavating archaeological contexts, as opposed to backfill or removing loose weed accumulations, it must only be used as a means of removing spoil, normally swept gently towards its mouth using the hand or a trowel. It is best held in a comfortable position by the excavator some 20-30cm. away from the surface being excavated, possibly further if there is anything extremely delicate being exposed. The valve on the air supply allows control of the strength of suction, and so allows very fine adjustment of the rate of silt removal. If you cannot control what is entering the tube as you excavate, then you are either going too fast or have the end too close to the working surface.

A mesh on the suction end of airlift or dredge should not be required 'to prevent objects being sucked up,' nor should there be any need for devices at the top to 'catch objects that get sucked up'. Sieves may be fitted periodically at the discharge end but only as a means of monitoring the standard of excavation, and a guard over the intake may be fitted for safety reasons (Section 5.5.4).

Advantage should be taken of the unique ability of the diver to hover above the area under investigation. There are many techniques that can be tried. One advantage of a solid site grid (Section 9.2.6 b.) is that it can offer additional diver support, and a technique successfully applied on a number of sites is to clasp the horizontal bar with feet (one over, one under) to hang inclined at 45 degrees above the site. Pressure applied alternately with either foot will allow the excavator to move around the area with complete control over their height above the archaeological deposits. Height can be adjusted by control of breathing or by slightly altering the bouyancy of the airlift as described above.

b. Water dredge

This is similar to the airlift except that it operates more or less horizontally, and it is water rather than air that is pumped in at the mouth. The water dredge can have a flexible tube attached to the suction end to reach difficult places and increase mobility but, as with airlifts, the valve controlling the effectiveness of the device must be within easy reach for safety reasons.

Dredges can work as efficiently in very shallow water as in deep water. Dredges do not need to be securely fastened to the seabed, although depending upon the design there may be a tendency to push forward caused by the water discharged at the far end. The efficiency of the dredge is diminished as the length of the discharge tube increases. In practical terms this means there is a limit to the distance that spoil can be moved off the site (around 5-10m with a medium sized fire pump as the supply unit, or 10-15m if the dredge is horizontal).

211

i. Pump requirements

The amount of water delivered to the dredge head is probably the most important factor related to its efficiency. As a rule of thumb a portable fire-pump with a 75mm (3") outlet diameter will provide adequate power for two 110mm (4.5") diameter dredges. Anything more than a thousand litres per minute is sufficient. Smaller water pumps with a 50mm (2") outlet usually have insufficient delivery to provide anything more than a mild suction but, in many circumstances, this may be all that is needed. The smaller the water pump, the cheaper they are to buy or hire, and the less space they take up; the larger the pump the better the chance of having an effective dredge.

ii. Operation

The water dredge is used in exactly the same basic way as an airlift in that it should only be used to transport spoil fed to it by the excavator. It should not be used as a digging tool except when removing archaeologically unimportant material such as backfill from previously excavated areas, or collections of weed or other debris washed into the site during pauses in the investigation.

Unlike the airlift it has no inherent buoyancy and so it is necessary to adjust it to what is most comfortable in any given situation. One or two air-filled 5 litre plastic containers securely attached is usually sufficient.

One of the disadvantages of dredging is the effect created by the water leaving the discharge end at speed, and the disturbance this discharge can cause on the seabed. This jetting can be dramatic, particularly if the pump is switched on when the diver is not ready. It is also potentially damaging to archaeological remains, and so must be neutralised. This can be achieved in a number of ways. Lengthening the discharge pipe so that its weight rests on the seabed can ease the problem but it increases the risk of discharge-end damage, and makes the dredge less moveable.

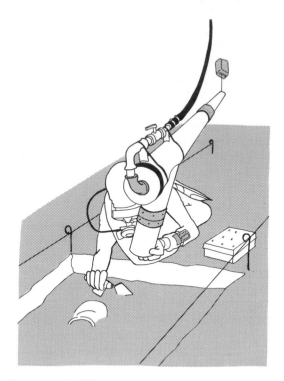

Figure 110. Water dredge operation.

Discharge pipes can be positioned above the bottom by use of weights, or other forms of anchorage, and buoys. The pipe end can then be fixed at a suitable height. Anchoring the dredge head end is also a way of reducing the effects of jetting, but it restricts manoeuvrability.

If mobility is not a problem the discharge pipe can be extended well off site (distances of over a kilometre have been achieved) provided that more water is injected into the system along its length. A simple way of achieving this is to fit the discharge end of one dredge into the suction end of the next one in the chain.

One of the simplest ways of overcoming the jetting problem is to baffle the discharge stream. This can be achieved by attaching a flat plate or board across the discharge *ca.* 0.75m from the end of the dredge. Alternative baffles can be devised. For instance, standard plastic soil pipe fittings (such as a T-piece) can be attached on the discharge end although these should be of a larger bore than the discharge pipe.

Alternatively even a slow curve (not a tight 90 degree bend), positioned to discharge upwards, can be attached and, in conjunction with appropriate buoyancy and/or anchorage. In such ways it is possible to achieve the desired effect on almost any site, without damage to the archaeological evidence. The ingenious diver and archaeologist can no doubt think of many alternative solutions to these and similar problems.

iii. Dredge construction

It is possible to purchase ready made induction dredge heads built largely to supply the numerous operators who recover golf balls from rivers and lakes in the USA. These are usually made of steel, but it is possible to make a dredge head from components readily available from hardware stores. As long as sufficient water is pumped down a tube and across the open end of a tube let into the side of the main tube, suction will develop at the other end of the side tube. The amount of suction will depend on the velocity and volume of pumped water and the overall effectiveness of the design. For instance, the water inlet pipe should point exactly down the centre of the main tube, and there should be minimal obstructions to the flow in the large diameter pipes. An example of a dredge design is detailed in Appendix IV.

10.3.8. Choosing between airlift or dredge

Generally speaking the airlift is more efficient than a dredge, but requires greater resources to operate. When choosing, however, it may be relevant to consider the different surface requirements for each type.

Both dredges and airlifts can be manufactured in a range of sizes: smaller for intricate work or, particularly in the case of airlifts, larger (e.g. 150mm - 200mm (6" - 8") diameter for tasks like the rapid removal of backfill or seaweed). To provide power for one 110mm airlift, you will need a somewhat bulkier and heavier compressor. You may be able to site it on shore and pipe the air out into the site, as has been done on several occasions.

Airlifts can be easier to handle than water dredges, but where water depth is particularly shallow, a water dredge may be the only option, particularly as it lies almost flat. However the airlift can work well in a depth of less than 2m provided a very large volume of air is pumped through it. Similarly the airlift will also work with up to a third of its length protruding above the water surface. Both tools can be controlled easily by the hand-operated valves, but can do untold damage if used in an uncontrolled fashion. As in all archaeological operations, it is in the best interests of the surviving evidence if the work is carried out in a careful and disciplined manner.

10.4. Suggested Reading

a. probing

Watts Jnr, G.P.
    1976   Hydraulic Probing: One solution to overburden and environment. *IJNA* 5.4: 76-81.

b. sampling

Buglass, J. and Rackham, J.
    1991   Environmental Sampling on Wet Sites. In Coles, J.M., and Goodburn, D.M. (eds.), *Wet Site Excavation and Survey*. WARP Occasional Paper No. 5, Exeter, ISSN 0950-8224.
Coles, J.M.
    1990   *Waterlogged Wood*. English Heritage, London, ISBN 1-85074-335-5.
Coles, J.M., Coles, B.J. and Dobson, M.J.
    1990   *Waterlogged Wood*. WARP Occasional Paper No.3, Exeter, ISSN 0950-8244.

213

Eckstein, D. *et al.*
    1984   *Dendrochronological Dating.* Handbooks for Archaeologists No.2, European Science Foundation, Strasbourg, ISBN 2-903148-39-2.

Mook, W.G., and Waterbolk, H.T.
    1985   *Radiocarbon Dating.* Handbooks for Archaeologists No.3, European Science Foundation, Strasbourg, ISBN 2-903148-44-9.

Nayling, N.
    1991   Tree-ring dating: sampling, analysis and results. In Coles, J.M., and Goodburn, D.M. (eds.), *Wet Site Excavation and Survey.* WARP Occasional Paper No. 5, Exeter, ISSN 0950-8224.

Oxley, I.
    1991   Environmental Sampling Underwater. In Coles, J.M., and Goodburn, D.M. (eds.), *Wet Site Excavation and Survey.* WARP Occasional Paper No. 5, Exeter, ISSN 0950-8224.

c. excavation

Barker, P.
    1977   *The Techniques Of Archaeological Excavation.* London. ISBN 0-7134-2739-6.

Barker, P.
    1986   *Understanding Archaeological Excavation.* London, ISBN 0-7134-3632-8.

11. Looking After the Heritage

11.1. Maintenance of Known Sites

11.2. Caring for Recovered Material

11.3. Suggested Reading

There is an immense amount of information about the past underwater, but it is a non-renewable resource. How can we look after this valuable asset? Since it belongs to all of us we are, in a sense, all stewards or curators of the remains.

Those of us who are involved in archaeological investigations must also take on extra responsibilities for the records and material we may take away from a site. These we will discuss later in this section. Those of us who enjoy visiting archaeological sites must take care not to do any unnecessary damage. Regardless of whether we study the remains of the past, or just enjoy looking at them, we all have one job in common, and that it is to make sure that archaeological material has a future as well as a past.

11.1. Maintenance of Known Sites

11.1.1. Monitoring

All sites need to be looked after. Older sites have survived because they reach a condition of near stability with their surroundings. In this state they will survive far into the future without any further help from us. However if the conditions should change, the stability will be disturbed and the site becomes vulnerable to accelerated deterioration. More recent but no less interesting sites like those from the Second World War have yet to reach stability with their environment. If we want more to survive than would naturally, we need to help the preservation process along.

If we can keep a close eye on either older or newer sites we may be able to learn enough to encourage or re-establish stability on these very vulnerable remains.

Keeping a close eye on, or monitoring the state of sites means returning again and again to see how the site has changed. A by-product of looking at a site carefully is that you learn more about it and your visits are made more enjoyable!

a. Why do sites require monitoring?

Ideally all sites everywhere should be monitored, but that is beyond any one person or organisation. We can all help, but where do we start? There are three basic reasons for monitoring a site:

i. Finding out about how sites are preserved

We know all too little about the processes which threaten or preserve the remains of the past underwater. Choosing to monitor a site not only helps to preserve that site but contributes to our wider 'management' skills. Monitoring is a way of making a very real contribution to archaeology and the future of the past. It is also perhaps the cheapest form of archaeological fieldwork.

ii. Effect of activities on site

Anybody who uses a site ought to think about the effect they are having on its future well being. On the other hand if you regularly visit a site it is an ideal opportunity to establish a project of archaeological

monitoring. The extent to which regularly dived sites suffer is still poorly understood. To monitor a local dive site would be a convenient and very useful piece of research.

iii. Effect of scientific investigation on site

Not only is it important to understand how you are affecting the site for the future, but it is also important to understand how your work is changing the evidence you want to record. Any phase of the investigation will require monitoring for its effect on the site.

b. Between survey/excavation seasons

Even while a site is being investigated, some form of monitoring can be very useful. There may be a gap between seasons of work on the site, or it may be in an area which is very exposed. It is often better to organise some form of monitoring if at all possible than to trust to luck and hope that nothing happens to the site in between full seasons of survey or excavation. This is especially true if trenches are to be left partly or fully open as such features can alter the flow of current across a site and cause erosion where you least expect/want it. Similarly, site grids are prone both to damage and to causing localised scour. Between season monitoring, in tandem with site maintenance, might allow some problems to be nipped in the bud and therefore avoid a beginning of season crisis when the state of the site is revealed.

c. After current investigations on the site have finished

When a survey or excavation has come to an end the site does not suddenly develop an ability to take care of itself! Responsibility does not end with the project. You have changed that site, perhaps making it more vulnerable. Other workers may wish to investigate the site in the future and whether or not the material survives to that date should not be left totally to chance. No one can halt the march of time or prevent large scale changes in the environment, but keeping a check on the state of a site might

allow some potentially damaging processes to be mitigated thus preserving more of the evidence contained in the remains.

11.1.2. How to monitor

So what do we look for when monitoring a site? We quite simply look for change. This is both change of the site over time, which is relatively easy to see, if not to understand or measure, and change in the rate of change which is much more difficult needing as it does a knowledge of the existing processes. Once a change has been detected it can be assessed and if it is believed to be damaging then steps can be taken to remedy the situation. Each case will be different, but we want to be in a position to predict and prevent damage to a site, not to be surprised and frustrated by it.

a. Assessing change – establishing 'baseline data'

If the basic idea of monitoring is to detect change, then it makes sense to have a clear picture of the site as it appeared when monitoring began – so called baseline or control data. Changes can then be measured against that 'baseline'. In the case of an intrusive investigation a comprehensive pre-disturbance survey should provide such baseline data (Section 9.1). If the project is restricted to monitoring then a survey should be undertaken. The more detailed the baseline survey, the more easily any future changes will be recognised.

b. Level of monitoring

General site survey methods are discussed elsewhere but it is worth making a few remarks about some methods of monitoring available to us.

i. Familiarity and keeping your eyes open

A regular swim over the site may well make it obvious that something is different. This is the least satisfactory method of monitoring since it relies on what can be remembered

Figure 111. Taking corrosion potential measurements on the engine of the SS Xantho. (11.1.3.b.) (Courtesy of Mike McCarthy, Western Australian Museums.)

about the state of the site. With no records it will not be easy to impress anyone who may be in a position to support work to preserve a potentially threatened site.

ii. Video and stills photography

This is an enormously useful way of collecting information to monitor the condition of a site over time. A photographic record can allow detailed study of specific area, and objects as well as a general impression of the condition of the site. It can often be useful to establish standard points of view for the photographic record to maximise the before and after comparison. Don't forget the scale, especially in any close-ups of particular areas of damage or erosion. Photographs and video footage often make very effective publicity material and several shots demonstrating the degradation of a structure or object over time may be just what is required to influence the trustees of that grant awarding body you've applied to.

iii. Measurements

Measured observations add immensely to the usefulness of any monitoring exercise. A complete survey and resurvey of the site may not be practical but overall dimensions of exposed material and distances from the top of objects to the seabed can be quickly taken. This can be used to give support to general observations and with a bit of thought, an overall impression of the scale of changes to a site can be achieved quite quickly.

It can be very useful to establish independent datums from which such measurements can be taken. Calibrated stakes driven into the seabed have been used on several sites to monitor changes in seabed level.

iv. Remote sensing

Large scale movements of the site or the seabed can be monitored using equipment such as side-scan sonar. The movement of sand waves over wrecks can be monitored in this way as part of an attempt to predict and mitigate any exposure of sites. The increased sophistication of coastal and oceanographic science and the instrumentation involved in the discipline means that there is a great deal of technology available that might be useful to monitor an archaeological site. Current can be measured by seabed sensors; sediment deposition can be measured by a range of sediment trapping devices. The challenge of applying techniques from one discipline to the problems of another is one that many people are keen to rise to, especially if it gets them out of the office for a day or two.

11.1.3. Some indicators of change

The ideal situation would be a comprehensive, detailed survey of the site repeated at regular intervals. When the site is to be disturbed by you this must be regarded as a minimum requirement, *i.e.* pre-disturbance survey. In other cases of monitoring, a very detailed survey may not be practical. The general survey technique, however, remains the same – establish your baseline data and fixed datum points ready for future reference and comparison. If you are only using certain features of the site as examples of what is happening all over the site make sure you have a clear idea of what process it is you are measuring.

a. Fittings and surface distributions of material

The movement, disappearance or deterioration of material on a site can be used as an indicator of many processes, *e.g.* natural scour or unnatural pilfering. It is so general purpose it is sometimes difficult to decide which of the many possible processes is causing the change. Choose indicators carefully.

At a simple level this may be a count of attached non-ferrous fittings - their loss is unlikely to be natural. Perhaps delicate features of the site which are popular with visitors should be recorded at intervals for signs of damage.

b. Corrosion potential

The analysis of the corrosion potentials of metal objects on wreck sites is a relatively new technique of non-destructive assessment. Linked to pH measurements it has been found useful in understanding the corrosion history of underwater archaeological sites (MacLeod 1989). The study of the corrosion histories of particular artefacts is also important to conservation scientists determining the optimum treatment method.

A very sophisticated industry has built up around the regular inspection of large metal structures in the off-shore oil industry. Some of the techniques employed to measure corrosion potential and the integrity of welds require a certain amount of specialised knowledge and equipment (Bayliss *et al.* 1988). However, the basis of the system is the methodical application of standardised procedures and reporting in a regularised format to allow rapid and effective comparisons between surveys. If a way can be found to check the health of something as large as an oil rig, we should be able to work out a system for dealing with a vessel's remains.

The National Parks Service in the United States has already taken the first steps in attempting to monitor the condition of large, relatively recent vessels of historic significance (Lenihan 1989). In Australia the management of shipwreck material often involves dealing with metal wrecks and many strategies have been developed (McCarthy 1986).

c. Seabed levels

Much of the seabed is very mobile and this can seriously affect archaeological sites. Change in itself is not necessarily a bad thing. If severe erosion is noted then real problems and damage can result as material is exposed and degrades or is removed. However, an equally dramatic increase in sediment level might be a very positive thing, burying the site more deeply out of harms way. Change in seabed level is surprisingly difficult to demonstrate if there are not fixed points independent of the seabed or the structure.

In addition, it is important to look beyond the site to see if what is occurring locally is part of a wider pattern of change. If the site is near to shore it may be possible to check whether general changes in beach level relate to what is occurring on the site. This may help in developing a strategy for dealing with the problem.

d. Biological survey

Changes in the condition of a site can be detected in many ways, so it is important to be broad-minded when assessing the various monitoring options. For example, it may be that a survey of the flora and fauna on a site carried out over the space of several years will show significant changes. Perhaps weed, once abundant, disappears. Maybe new varieties of fouling organisms appear . There is going to be a reason for any change and that reason may have a bearing on the long term survival of the site. Greatly increased levels of pollution may have implications for the deterioration or preservation of archaeological material as well as stunting the growth of kelp (it may also have implications for the health and safety of project members).

e. Human activities in the area

Monitoring is not just a matter of focusing on the site and the area immediately around it. As our understanding of sediment movement and erosion develops, it is becoming clear that an activity in one area may have a dramatic effect on a quite distant location. Large scale civil engineering works such as dredging for aggregates or the construction of a new marina can change the way in which sediment some miles away is deposited. Consequently, the monitoring of potential threats to a site might involve keeping an eye on who is being granted planning permission further up the coast.

11.1.4   How often should the site be visited?

The more often a site is visited, the more continuous the collection of information and the more effective the monitoring. Occasional glimpses of a site will make changes difficult to interpret and assess. Material is only observed at specific points and not in the intermediate stages which might help explain the nature and mechanics of the transformation.

Common sense and logistics indicate that the amount of time and effort that can be put into monitoring a site is often going to be limited, especially if the location is remote. The more infrequent the visits to the site are going to be, the more systematic and thorough the observation and records made have to be. Work can, perhaps, be shared by several groups with an interest in the safety and condition of the site. Remember that we are trying to detect change, which means that observations made on different occasions must be comparable and quantified. Pro-formas have been dealt with elsewhere as have the general considerations involved in recording. It is well worth creating a standard form to be used in monitoring a site as an aid to thoroughness and standardisation.

11.1.5.   Stabilisation

Once the process of monitoring has shown that a particular process is damaging to the site, a decision has to be made on how to confront the problem. It may be that a site being compromised by large scale erosion has to be excavated in advance of an unstoppable process. Smaller scale erosion may be preventable or at least moderated by sand-bagging or the re-deposition of sediment in the problem areas.

There is no easy answer but some points that ought to be considered include:

i. Sand-bags dumped in one place may actually cause localised erosion themselves, and consideration will have to be given to matters such as direction of current and flow. Similarly, some means of securing the bags together may be necessary.

ii. The difficulties involved in the preparation and placement of large numbers of sand-bags underwater should not be underestimated.

iii. Depositing large amounts of sediment on a site compromised by erosion can be both more expensive and problematic than it might initially appear.

iv. Much can be learnt from those involved in trying to control coastal and foreshore erosion. Recent research has focused on the stabilisation of sediments, and one possible solution is the use of plastic sea grasses. Planted in mats, these act as sediment traps and can reduce erosion.

v. Other strategies have involved wrapping exposed timbers in 'filter fabrics' (Section 11.2.2 c.). These materials are porous but can act to reduce fouling and erosion by current-borne abrasives. However, problems can arise in wrapping large and often awkwardly shaped areas of wooden structure.

The development of effective strategies to mitigate specific threats to a site is at an early stage, partly due to a lack of a detailed understanding of the nature of the processes affecting archaeological material underwater. Regular, methodical monitoring is a way of finding out more about these processes and using that information to help conserve archaeological material *in situ*. Hopefully this kind of work will help us to move away from the situation where discovering material often leads to it being raised, largely because there are few established alternatives. The more effective the strategies for monitoring and stabilisation become, the more attractive becomes the idea of marine parks where historic and archaeological sites can be visited and maintained 'in the wild'.

11.2. Caring for Recovered Material

Looking after archaeological evidence becomes even more important when that material has been purposefully removed from its place of relative stability for the sake of archaeological research. Finds from excavations should survive as long as any of the material still on the site, or even longer. The responsibilities of conservation and storage are serious and long term, and must be considered before any destructive investigation is planned.

To determine suitable procedures for the treatment of material removed from underwater sites it is necessary to understand the burial environment and the implications of disturbing it. These implications include:

i. the protection necessary during exposure or excavation,

ii. the planning and preparation needed for removal and transportation,

iii. the care needed in cleaning,

iv. the provision of facilities for holding treatments,

v. the costs and other implications of full conservation treatment,

vi. the responsibility for environmentally controlled storage and/or display once the object has left the laboratory.

v. a basic principle of conservation ethics is also that a treatment should normally be reversible so that an artefact can, if desired, be returned to its pre-treatment condition even after the lapse of a long period of time.

It is strongly advised that all projects have access to a trained conservator at least to advise those on-site in the safe application of pre-conservation treatments, storage and packing procedures. Post-excavation conservation treatments require the knowledge and experience of trained conservators together with the back-up of adequate resources such as a fully-equipped laboratory.

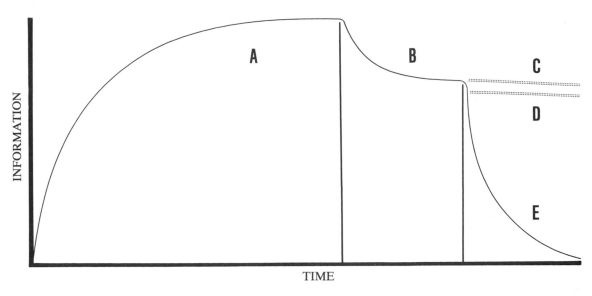

Figure 112. The relative changes in the levels of information which survive in an object: A, the gradual accumulation of information during the working life of the object; B, after burial, the object reaches a relative stability with its environment after some initial deterioration; C, information potential would remain relatively stable if the object is left buried; D, excavation with successful conservation; E, excavation without conservation (11.2.2.b.) (Drawing by K. Watson.)

11.2.1. The reasons for conservation

In this section of the manual we do not offer a series of treatments or recipes for the conservation of artefacts. Instead we consider the implications and responsibilities of raising and treating archaeological material from the underwater environment. Minimum standards for the care of the exposed site, and the safe packaging, transportation and storage of archaeological material and archaeological records are suggested. It is emphasised that stable materials and deposits are better left where they are found unless adequate conservation expertise and resources are available and that specialist conservation advice should be sought at the earliest opportunity.

11.2.2. Minimising the shock – passive conservation

A principal aim of conservation is to ensure that the evidence of the past is retained for the future, by minimising the damage caused by the change of environment during and after recovery. Using the techniques of passive conservation, this is attempted by reproducing the characteristics of the object's burial environment until it can be safely transported to a conservation laboratory.

a. Preparing for the reception of finds

It is important that all aspects of finds handling are covered in the planning stage of a project (Section 5.0) and that all concerned fully understand their responsibilities. On a large project it may be necessary to have someone on the surface delegated (e.g. finds assistants) to receive finds, assist with the lifting of heavy objects, make sure that tanks, holding solutions etc. are ready to provide

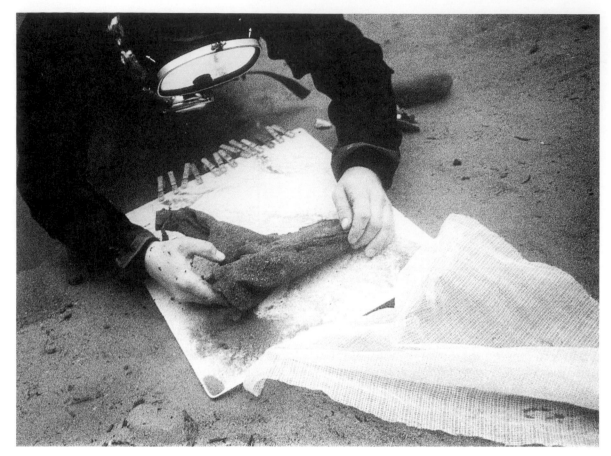

Figure 113. Fragile organic remains being transferred to a rigid supporting plate before placing a cover over them retained by clips. (11.2.2.d.) (Courtesy of C.Martin.)

appropriate storage environments for each find. Be aware that suitable precautions should be taken when handling chemicals (Clydesdale 1990).

b.   Precautions before exposing material

The material about to be excavated will have reached a state of relative equilibrium with its environment.   Exposure of it will immediately upset this relative stability and the cycle of deterioration will be given a new impetus. The material is now subjected to environmental conditions which are suddenly dramatically different. If it has been uncovered from a soft, silty seabed it will now be exposed to free-running water with an abundance of oxygen and dissolved

salts, and probably a higher temperature. If the material is then raised into air deterioration is even more likely due to the risk of uncontrolled drying. This means that if a decision has been made to disturb, expose and excavate material then it should be treated *in situ* as soon as possible, or raised and stored in a suitable environment until full conservation can begin.

c.   On-site protection

It must be appreciated that fragile deposits or objects may need some kind of temporary protection from events such as abrasion due to sediment movement or intrusive marine fauna. This may be either short-term (*e.g.* overnight) or for longer periods because factors such as Spring Tides or winter storms

Figure 114. Preparation for raising: constructing a support frame underwater for a spoked wheel. (11.2.2.d.) (Courtesy of C.Martin.)

Figure 115. The spoked wheel in Figure 114 in storage on its supporting frame. (11.2.2.d.) (Courtesy of C. Martin.)

mean that large areas of the site have to be covered or back-filled until the project can be resumed.

Temporary protection on underwater sites can be achieved by a wide variety of means. This would normally involve the laying of a form of barrier over the delicate material followed by a stabilising weight such as layers of sand-bags or back-filled excavation spoil or sediment. For the barrier layer, specialised material such as filter fabrics have been used but no long-term studies are available to assess their effectiveness. Filter fabrics (made by major industrial chemical manufacturers *e.g.* ICI's 'Terram') allow passage of water but not solids (*e.g.* particles of sediment or objects). Alternatively readily available materials such as polythene sheeting are often used, but these are possibly detrimental in the long-term because of the potentially damaging micro-environments that are formed beneath them.

d. Precautions before raising material

Full recording *in situ* must be carried out (Section 6.2) and the importance of taking record photographs, or making record drawings, of fragile finds prior to lifting or packaging cannot be over-stressed. Sometimes such photographs and drawings become the best record of an object, particularly if it has to be dismantled to carry out conservation treatments.

e. Transfer from site to surface

Pre-planning is essential in relation to the lifting of waterlogged material, which is usually fragile, difficult to move safely and expensive to conserve or process. It is often necessary to construct purpose-built apparatus prior to lifting a particularly problematical object, making sure that the materials used will not damage the object being disturbed.

Support for the material can be provided in a number of ways. Objects can be raised surrounded with their burial sediment (*i.e.*. the object or sample is raised within a block of the surrounding deposit). This not only provides physical support but can also help to minimise potentially damaging environmental changes (temperature, degree of saturation etc.). However, removing a large block of sediment may cause unacceptable damage to surrounding stratigraphy and this technique should be use with caution.

Cushioning, made from plastic boxes, water-filled polythene bags, 'bubble-pack', wet foam or a layer of sediment from the sea-bed, have all been used successfully, in conjunction with a rigid base. A section of waterlogged wood, for example, can be lifted onto a purpose-built pallet. To hold it in place, wide strips of cord or bandage that will not cut into the soft surface of the artefact are often useful. Heavy objects with soft structures need to be padded at points where the straps touch the surface of the object, to avoid producing indentations. Objects which are extremely fragile (such as rope) can be wrapped with ordinary bandage. Ensure that the bandaging does not stick to the object by placing a barrier layer such as polythene in between.

Containers uncovered on the site (*e.g.* boxes, barrels or amphorae) with their original contents *in situ* may require lifting complete. They can then be excavated under controlled conditions in a laboratory and their contents sampled and recorded in detail. Care should be taken to keep the containers

upright or to cover the opening with very fine nylon netting or polythene to prevent the loss of the contents.

f. Transfer from water into air

Never underestimate the shock that material can suffer on being transported through the water/air boundary; current and swell can easily knock objects or containers out of your hands. Be prepared for the sudden increase in weight as the load is no longer partially supported by the water, and the possibility of the weight of the water in a container causing damage.

11.2.3. Pre-treatment for short-term storage

Keep the time between recovery and full treatment as short as possible. The necessity for pre-treatment will depend upon the material type and condition. Little research has been done on assessing storage conditions and such an assessment would require quantitative studies of rates of deterioration of specific materials. This is not easy as archaeological artefacts and samples often consist of combinations of material types and complex mixtures, each of which may react differently to storage conditions and media.

11.2.4. Storage

In general, the optimum environmental conditions for short-term storage would resemble the original burial conditions. However, each object or environmental sample would have been collected from a slightly differing location. Even similar objects such as two wooden bowls found close together are likely to react differently to the same conservation treatment because of small variations in their burial environments.

Keep the level of oxygen available for deterioration processes low by using tanks or containers that closely match in size the objects contained in them. This may also be of economic benefit as the quantities of solutions can be kept to a minimum. Light may fade certain coloured materials and also promote decay processes. Therefore it is advisable to store archaeological samples and objects in the dark.

Samples or objects recovered from deep within sediments should not necessarily be immersed in water, as their original burial environment may have been only damp (not water-logged). In this situation the object or sample might be best stored, in the short term, encased in its original deposits.

It is advisable to store small objects in polythene containers or bags. If tanks for larger objects (*e.g.* ships' timbers) are not available, holes can be dug into the ground and lined with polythene to produce a temporary container. As a last resort, large objects may be wrapped in a layer of polythene sheeting, then a layer of an absorbent material (*e.g.* hessian sacking) saturated with water, followed by several layers of polythene sheeting. These wrapped pieces should be stored out of direct sunlight and be monitored regularly to ensure that the objects do not dry out.

11.2.5. Storage solutions

It is important to remember to add enough liquid to ensure that the object is completely covered and will not dry out during transportation to the laboratory. Make sure you eliminate as much air as possible from the container or packaging. Artefacts from a salt water environment can be kept in sea water until they reach the conservation laboratory.

If archaeological samples cannot be processed immediately, then it may be necessary to treat those containing quantities of organic material with a biocide solution to inhibit biological decay. This should be avoided if at all possible, as such solutions negate some methods of scientific analysis (*e.g.* radiocarbon dating and dendrochronology) and the long-term effects of immersion in biocides are not known. They may cause changes in shape or size which could affect other subsequent

identification techniques. Samples from underwater sites stored in containers with tight-fitting lids, in the dark, in an area of high relative humidity, may not require any pre-treatment prior to specialist examination. It is advisable to limit this holding treatment to as short a time as possible. Remember to treat chemicals with care, follow the manufacturer's recommendations and use gloves when handling.

11.2.6. Packing

An obvious aim is to pack materials so that they can be transported safely and securely to a suitable laboratory for processing or specialist analysis. You must provide physical protection, and aim to prevent any further damage which might be caused by changes in temperature, biological activity, salt crystallization, and oxygen levels, by providing polythene wrapping, padding and airtight boxes.

Since most of the objects will be wet, polythene buckets, boxes and bags will be the most useful. Plastic drain pipes can also be useful for delicate thin artefacts. Plastic bags filled with holding solutions can be sealed using a heat-sealer which welds a join by melting the plastic. Make sure to eliminate as much air as possible in order to reduce the amount of oxygen available to decay-producing organisms or chemical processes. More delicate objects can have custom-made envelopes of bubblepack or layers of polythene foam constructed.

The choice of container, in particular for samples, should be determined in advance with a view to their being suitable for the transport of the material through the water and into air. Rigid polythene or plastic boxes and containers (similar to those in which ice-cream is sold) are useful. They are reasonably robust and most have a relatively efficient water-tight seal. If used containers are acquired and it is intended that they are to be used for samples they MUST be cleaned thoroughly. Plastic bags can be used provided that they can be transported safely though they are not suitable for long-term storage.

Polythene sheeting or bags are not necessarily impermeable to the passage of water vapour, so even objects well-wrapped in plastic will slowly dry out over a period of time.

11.2.7. Cleaning

It is definitely not recommended that rigorous washing or cleaning of finds is carried out although it is understood that it is often important to know what something is as soon as possible. Finds should be carefully examined (preferably by an experienced conservator) for signs of any additional archaeological evidence (*e.g.* surface coatings, inscriptions, decoration) and samples taken for analysis if necessary (see Section 10.2.1).

Any cleaning or washing that does take place should be done in a careful and controlled manner under good light conditions (or even an illuminated magnifier), perhaps using a soft brush and a trickle of water. All washing, examination and sampling procedures should be noted on the relevant record for the object.

11.2.8. X-radiography

Radiography is non-destructive and it can be applied to almost all metals, organic and inorganic materials. The X-rays pass through the object differentially, according to its thickness and the density of the materials it is made of, to be recorded on a sensitive plate underneath or on a scanner screen.

The main use of X-radiography is in the determination of the types, sizes, numbers and locations of objects within concretions (Section 11.2.11). It also has usage in determining the internal construction of artefacts, and in assessing the amount of metal remaining beneath a layer of corrosion products.

It is strongly recommended that all concretions are assessed by X-radiography before any attempt is made to dismantle them. In the budgeting of any archaeological project adequate provision should be made for such methods of non-destructive assessment. X-radiography is widely used in industry and it is often possible to negotiate its use for the benefit of archaeology.

11.2.9. Desalination (salt elimination)

The removal of the soluble salts found in seawater from objects recovered from a marine environment is an important part of the conservation process for most materials but in particular ceramics, glass and stone. This process should not be attempted on badly deteriorated or exfoliating (flaking) ceramic or glass objects. These should be transported to a conservation laboratory as soon as possible.

If freshwater, or preferably de-ionised or distilled water, is available, desalination can begin, although professional conservation advice should be sought. Do not place any material directly into freshwater, as the salts will cause physical damage by the sudden creation of an osmotic pressure difference. For the first wash use a ratio of around 1:1 of seawater to fresh, as this will slow down the speed of salt removal. Over several weeks, freshwater can gradually be added to the objects until they are finally rinsed in distilled water. Final washing should take place in a conservation laboratory where there are facilities for the monitoring of chlorides to determine when an acceptable level has been achieved and washing can cease.

11.2.10. Composite artefacts

Composite objects are a conservation problem. Metals have often been used in the past in conjunction with organic materials (wood, horn, leather, bone, textile etc.) or inorganic materials (glass, stone etc.). Composite objects cannot be stored for any long periods of time in the environments recommended for individual materials, *i.e.* alkaline solution for iron and water/biocide solution for wood, as the other material would begin to deteriorate.

Each composite object should be treated on its own merits and as such a rigid policy cannot be recommended. Ideally the materials should be separated and stored in their respective, recommended environments. This should only be attempted by an experienced conservator and therefore all composites should be kept wet and transported to a conservation laboratory as soon as possible.

11.2.11. Concretions

Mineral rich concretions can form around exposed metal objects, producing a protective mini-environment, often preventing the oxygen essential for corrosion from reaching the object, thus keeping it from disintegrating completely. Such concretions may be formed physically (by the growth of organisms on the surface of the object), physio-chemically (by the solution and re-precipitation of carbonates), electrochemically, or bio-chemically (by various micro-biological activities which lower the pH).

Concretion should not be removed on site. Metals such as cast iron, bronze and silver often retain the original shape of the object in the surface corrosion layers (*i.e.* part of the concretion). If concretions are removed without using the appropriate equipment or without careful prior examination using X-radiography (Section 11.2.8) then information is likely to be lost unnecessarily. Often concretions recovered from shipwrecks consist of a mixture of fragments of metal, glass, ceramic, wood and other materials embedded in a matrix of corrosion products, marine growth and sediments. If the concretions are not treated carefully the more fragile artefacts can be easily damaged.

As the presence of chlorides in the concretions accelerates corrosion processes, the same recommendations for holding treatments for iron objects apply to concretions (Section 11.2.12 b. i.).

11.2.12. Material types

The positive identification of the raw materials of artefacts or ecofacts is an obvious first step in determining which first-aid treatment is required. The range of possible material types on an underwater site is wide, including ceramics, metals and organics. Some materials will be obvious, but others may require expert analysis before a positive identification can be made. The term 'organics' covers those materials which are made from once-living organisms such as trees or domestic animals. This is opposed to non-organics such as metals, stone and ceramics.

a. Organic materials: bone, wood, leather

Organic materials must be stored wet. Do not allow these materials to dry out even when carrying out preliminary recording (*e.g.* photography). Organics can suffer irreversible cracking, shrinking and warping after remarkably short exposure times to the atmosphere. If drying does occur, re-wetting should not be attempted. Where freshwater is not available they can be kept in seawater.

Care must be taken to ensure that items which are fragile or fragmentary are provided with sufficient support. Handling should be kept to a minimum as waterlogged organics will be very degraded. This applies in particular to large timbers which although still heavy will have lost a considerable amount of structural strength and will have soft, fragile surfaces. They must be fully supported (*e.g.* with scaffolding or planks of wood) and have all fastenings well-cushioned. Any subsequent lifting can be carried with the supporting members taking the strain.

Try to store organic materials in the dark and at a reduced temperature. Place in a refrigerator or cold store if facilities are available. The temperature should not be allowed to fall too close to freezing as the expansion of water to form ice may physically damage the delicate cell structure of organic materials. This would be of particular importance with reference to environmental samples as the identification of plant remains often depends upon the recognition of such structures.

If the material cannot be transported to a conservator immediately, storage may be necessary in freshwater with the addition of a biocide (a chemical which inhibits micro-biological decay), although if at all possible this should be avoided. A conservator should be consulted for advice or reference should be made to published texts (Section 11.3). Some biocides will negate future scientific analysis or dating techniques and ALL must be handled with extreme care and according to the manufacturer's recommendations (Clydesdale 1990).

b. Metals

i. Iron

1. Cast iron

Many of the guns, shot and anchors recovered from the sea are made of cast iron where the metal is heated until it is liquid and then poured into pre-shaped moulds. After immersion in seawater cast iron objects will disintegrate rapidly if they are not kept wet or stored in a stable environment as soon as they are raised. Cast iron corrodes by graphitisation, usually leaving behind a metal core, but with a surface crust of graphite-containing iron corrosion products. Such 'concretions' will often retain the shape of the original object (Section 11.2.11). They are, however, in a very unstable state, and if exposed to the atmosphere, fresh and rapid corrosion will occur at the graphite layer/ metal core interface, potentially forcing off the surface layers. Such a reaction is exothermic (giving off heat) which speeds up the deterioration. There are many known examples of cast iron cannon and cannon-balls heating up and even 'exploding' after recovery from the sea.

2. Wrought iron

Wrought iron has a much lower carbon content than cast iron and it does not contain any graphite. With no graphite network to hold the corrosion products together they are typically very soft and range in appearance from delicate fibres to a watery paste. The corrosion products do not normally retain the original surface markings and wrought iron will continue to corrode slowly along the slag inclusion lines (formed during the manufacturing process) unless stabilised. The slow corrosion process may continue until all metallic iron is replaced by a cavity within a hard concretion shell. In this situation various moulding and casting techniques have been used to recover the shape and form of the corroded objects.

ii. First Aid treatment for iron objects

For both wrought and cast iron the presence of chlorides accelerates the corrosion process. For this reason alkaline corrosion-inhibiting solutions are recommended for short-term storage. Specialist conservation advice should be sought and as these solutions are potentially hazardous, precautions should be taken according to the manufacturer's recommendations. Recipes for corrosion-inhibiting solutions are often quoted in conservation publications but immersion in one of the following is suggested until the objects can be transported to a laboratory:

1. 5% weight/weight (e.g. 50g/litre) sodium carbonate : freshwater.

2. 2% weight/weight (e.g. 20g/litre) sodium hydroxide : freshwater.

3. 5% weight/weight (e.g. 50g/litre) sodium sesquicarbonate : freshwater.

If freshwater is not available seawater can be used for a period not exceeding six months.

Large iron objects have been treated *in situ* on underwater sites, both to prevent further corrosion and to begin stabilising treatment. Methods of cathodic protection have been tried by attaching sacrificial anodes to the objects. Conventional conservation treatment once the object was subsequently raised was found to be more effective than on similar objects which had not been pre-treated on site (MacLeod 1989a).

iii. Copper and its alloys

Because of the toxic effect of copper on marine organisms, objects made from copper or its major alloys (bronze and brass) are rarely found heavily concreted. The corrosion products on copper alloys may retain the shape of the object. The alloys can deteriorate by mineralisation where one or more of the phases has dissolved leaving a weakened structure (*i.e.* de-zincification in brasses). This process of mineralisation may leave surface layers soft and prone to damage.

If a copper alloy artefact is raised into air from a marine environment, chlorides which have penetrated into the deteriorated object can set up a cyclic corrosion process called 'bronze disease'. The corrosion process is caused by the chlorides in the presence of the oxygen and humidity of the air. The following solution is recommended as a short-term holding treatment until the object can be transported to a conservation laboratory:

1% weight/weight (*e.g.* 10g/litre) benzotriazole (BTA) : freshwater.

It is important to remember that the manufacturer's instructions for the safe handling of BTA should be followed closely.

iv. Lead, tin and their alloys

Tin is rarely found in pure form (such as ingots). Usually it is alloyed with lead to form pewter, a common raw material for domestic utensils. Objects made out of lead alone are often found on shipwreck sites. All these metals are stable when exposed to the atmosphere in normal circumstances after rinsing in freshwater, although care must be exercised. Lead alloys are susceptible to attack from organic acid vapours (emitted by some woods, paints, adhesives, plastics and cardboard). Lead and pewter must not therefore be kept in cardboard boxes or on wooden shelves.

v. Gold and silver

Pure gold will not deteriorate in a marine environment, but gold is rarely found without some impurities, and these may corrode. Pure silver, like pure gold, can be washed in fresh water and allowed to air dry. Plated metals or alloys must be treated carefully and if corrosion products are present on the surface, these should not be removed unless expert advice has been sought from a conservator.

c. Ceramics

'Ceramic' is a term for objects made from fired clays. These materials are comparatively inert although they may be covered with hard marine organisms. The major problem with ceramics (as with glass and stone) is that dissolved salts from the seawater penetrate into the body (or fabric) of the ceramic. In certain cases the salts become concentrated just underneath the glaze of glazed-ware. Low-fired porous terracottas are the most susceptible, whereas there is less of a problem with high-fired porcelains. If ceramics that have been immersed in seawater are allowed to dry out indiscriminately there is a serious risk of physical damage due to the crystallization of the salts. The lifting off of the glaze is a particular risk.

Ceramics, therefore, must not be allowed to dry out. They may be stored in seawater until they are transported to a laboratory where controlled desalination procedures can be carried out. It is important not to place ceramics that have been saturated in seawater straight into freshwater (Section 11.2.9).

d. Glass and other vitrified materials

Glass is essentially a super-cooled liquid made by fusing acidic oxides (*e.g.* silica normally in the form of sand) with basic oxides such as sodium and potassium as modifiers to lower its melting point. The type and properties of glass produced depend on the choice and quantity of acidic and basic oxides. The earliest and simplest glass, soda-lime silica glass, is in fact still made today. Later glass sometimes has lead partially replacing the soda, to increase translucency. Metal salts (such as manganese or antimony oxides) were often added to counteract discolourations caused by iron impurities, or to colour the glass deliberately. Finished artefacts may be further decorated with enamels, staining, paint, gilding or engraving.

The process of glass deterioration in water is still not completely understood. Glass is not impervious to water and this penetration (particularly in the case of seawater) results in the formation of thin hydrated layers on the surface of the glass. The surface of the glass is degraded and begins to become opaque and breaks down into thin scales or layers. Upon exposure to the atmosphere a process of 'sweating' or 'weeping' affects glass, caused by the interaction of carbon dioxide with the corrosion products. This process also absorbs moisture from the atmosphere and the corrosion cycle will continue unless the glass is treated.

Glass from an underwater environment should not be allowed to dry out. The fragments should be stored in a wet environment perhaps in plastic bags or boxes (beware of sharp edges puncturing the bag). A suitable storage environment is seawater until the material can be transported to a laboratory for desalination (Section 11.2.9). In the case of degraded glass, conservation advice should be sought as soon as possible.

e. Stone

Stone is often found in association with shipwrecks, in the form of ballast or cargo. As with ceramics and glass the presence of dissolved salts in the body of stone artefacts due to immersion in seawater will cause problems if the object is raised and subsequently left exposed to the atmosphere, or immediately placed into freshwater. The types of rock which are most at risk would be sandstones and limestones.

Stone artefacts should be stored in seawater until a controlled system of desalination can be implemented (Section 11.2.9).

11.2.13. Research into new treatments

Conservation is not a static discipline. Research into new and more effective treatments is continuing all the time. On underwater archaeological projects conservators are often obliged to carry out research at the same time as doing the work, because of the acute shortage of resources. There is still a long way to go before it is fully understood how certain materials deteriorate underwater, and even longer still until conservation treatments can be confidently recommended that can be guaranteed to be effective for all materials from all environments. At present it is clear that techniques used on one type of object may not necessarily be effective when applied to objects made out of the same material which were recovered from a slightly different burial environment.

11.2.14. Further information and advice

A number of sources can be suggested for further information and advice. An initial move might be to contact your nearest museum or university archaeology department which may have conservation laboratories attached to them. The Conservation Unit of the Museums and

Galleries Commission is a useful place to start in the UK, and for international advice try the International Institute for Conservation of Historic and Artistic Works (IIC). Contact addresses can be found in Useful Addresses (Appendix V).

11.3. Suggested Reading

a. monitoring

Adams, J., van Holk, A.F.L., and Maarleveld, Th.J.
1990 *Dredgers and archaeology: ship finds from the Slufter.* Ministerie van Welzijn, Volksgezondheid En Cultuur, Archaeologie onder water, Rotterdam, ISBN 90-800467-1-X.

Bayliss, M., Short, D. and Bax, M.
1988 *Underwater Inspection.* Plymouth, UK, ISBN 0-419-13540-5.

Berry, A.Q. and I.W. Brown, (eds.)
1994 *Erosion on Archaeological Earthworks: Its Prevention, Control and Repair.* Clwyd County Council, Mold. ISBN 0-900121-57-2.

Brown, R, Bump, H., and Muncher, A.
1988 An *in situ* method for determining the decomposition rates of shipwrecks. *IJNA* 17.2: 143-146.

Lenihan, D.J., *et al.*
1981 *The final report of the National Reservoir Innundation Study, Volumes 1 and 2.* United States Department of the Interior, National Park Service, Southwest Cultural Resource Center, Sante Fe, New Mexico.

Lenihan, D.J. (ed)
1989 *Submerged Cultural Resources Study, USS Arizona Memorial and Pearl Harbour National Historic Landmark.* Southwest Cultural Resources Center, Professional Papers No.23, Sante Fe, New Mexico.

MacLeod, I.D.
1989c The electrochemistry and conservation of iron in seawater. *Chemistry in Australia*, July 1989: 227-229.

MacLeod, I.D., *et al.*
1986 The excavation, analysis and conservation of shipwreck sites. In ICCROM 1986, *Preventive Measures during Excavation and Site Protection.* ICCROM, Rome, ISBN 92-9077-070-8.

Wildesen, L. E.
1982 The study of impacts on archaeological sites. In Schiffer, M. B. (ed), *Advances in archaeological method and theory*, Vol 5, 51-96.

b. caring for recovered material

Buglass, J., and Rackham, J.
1991 Environmental Sampling on Wet Sites. In Coles, J.M., and Goodburn, D.M. (eds), *Wet Site Excavation and Survey.* WARP Occasional Paper No. 5, Exeter, ISSN 0950-8224.

Carpenter, J.
1983 The conservation of shipwreck artefacts in the field. In Jeffrey, W., and Amess, J. (ed), *Proc. of the Second Southern Hemisphere Conference on Maritime Archaeology.*

Clarke, R.W. and Blackshaw, S.M. (eds)
1982 *Conservation of Iron.* National Maritime Museum Monographs and Reports No 53, Greenwich, ISBN 0-905555-59-7.

Clydesdale, A.
1990 *Chemicals in Conservation, a guide to possible hazards and safe use.* 2nd Edition, SSCR.

Cronyn, J.M.
1990 *The Elements of Archaeological Conservation.* London, ISBN 0-415-01206-6.

Daley, T.W. and L.D. Murdock
1992 Excavating and raising artifacts from a marine environment. In Payton, R., (ed.), *Retrieval of Objects from Archaeological Sites.* Archetype Publications, London: 133-146. ISBN 1-873132-30-1.

MacLeod, I.D.
1987 Conservation of corroded iron artefacts - new methods for on-site

preservation and cryogenic deconcreting. *IJNA* 16.1: 49-56.

MacLeod, I.D.
1989b   *Conservation of wet wood and metal.* Proceedings of the ICOM Conservation Working group on wet organic archaeological materials and metals, Fremantle, Australia.

MacLeod, I.D.
1989a   The application of corrosion science to the management of maritime archaeological sites. *Bulletin of the Australian Institute for Maritime Archaeology,* 13 (2): 7-16.

Oxley, I.
1991   Environmental Sampling Underwater. In Coles, J.M., and Goodburn, D.M. (eds.), *Wet Site Excavation and Survey.* WARP Occasional Paper No. 5, Exeter, ISSN 0950-8224.

Payton, R.
1987   Conservation of objects from one of the world's oldest shipwrecks: the Ulu Burun, Kas shipwreck, Turkey. In Black, J. (ed), *Recent Advances in the Conservation and Analysis of Artifacts.* Summer Schools Press, Institute of Archaeology, London.

Pearson, C. (ed)
1987   *Conservation of marine archaeological objects.* London, ISBN 0-408-10688-9.

Robinson, W.S.
1981   *First Aid for Marine Finds.* Handbooks in Maritime Archaeology No.2, National Maritime Museum, Greenwich, London, ISBN 0-905555-52-X.

Rodgers, B.A. and J.O. Jensen
1990   *Conservation of Water Soaked Material Bibliography.* East Carolina University, NC.

Singley, K.
1988   *The Conservation of Archaeological Artefacts from Freshwater Environments.* Lake Michigan Maritime Museum, South Haven, Michigan.

UKIC
1983   *Packing and Storing of Freshly-Excavated Artifacts from Archaeological Sites.* Conservation Guidelines No.2, United Kingdom Institute for Conservation, Archaeology Section.

UKIC
1984   *Environmental Standards for the Permanent Storage of Excavated Material from Archaeological Sites.* Conservation Guidelines No.3, United Kingdom Institute for Conservation, Archaeology Section.

Watkinson, D. (ed.)
1987   *First Aid for Finds.* Rescue/United Kingdom Institute for Conservation, Archaeology Section, ISBN 0-903789-13-2.

12. Post-Fieldwork Recording, Analysis and Publication

12.1. Introduction to Post-Fieldwork Processing

12.2. Post-Fieldwork Processing and the Drawn Record

12.3. Specialist Analysis

12.4. Recording During the Analysis Stage

12.5. Interpretation and Gathering Supporting Evidence from Other Sources

12.6. Producing an Archaeological Archive

12.7. Writing an Archaeological Report

12.8. Suggested Reading

During fieldwork evidence will have been collected in a variety of forms and a wide range of techniques will have to be applied in order to extract the maximum information from it. Any post-excavation work is time consuming, and can be expensive. Even without excavation, the amount of evidence collected can be enormous, and it is very important to include a budget in time and resources for post-excavation work in the initial stages of planning work underwater. This stage of work may take at least three to four times the length of time taken to collect the information.

This section of the NAS Guide gives practical advice on some of the techniques that can be used, but the main emphasis will be on the purpose behind the methods – the presentation of information in forms that are accessible to all levels of interest in the past.

12.1. Introduction to Post-Fieldwork Processing

Post-fieldwork processing can be split conveniently into a number of phases:

i. Post-fieldwork processing, the drawn and photographic record (Section 12.2),

ii. Specialist analysis (Section 12.3),

iii. Recording during the analysis stage (Section 12.4),

iv. Interpretation and gathering supporting evidence from other sources (Section 12.5),

v. Producing an archaeological archive (Section 12.6),

vi. Writing an archaeological report (Section 12.7),

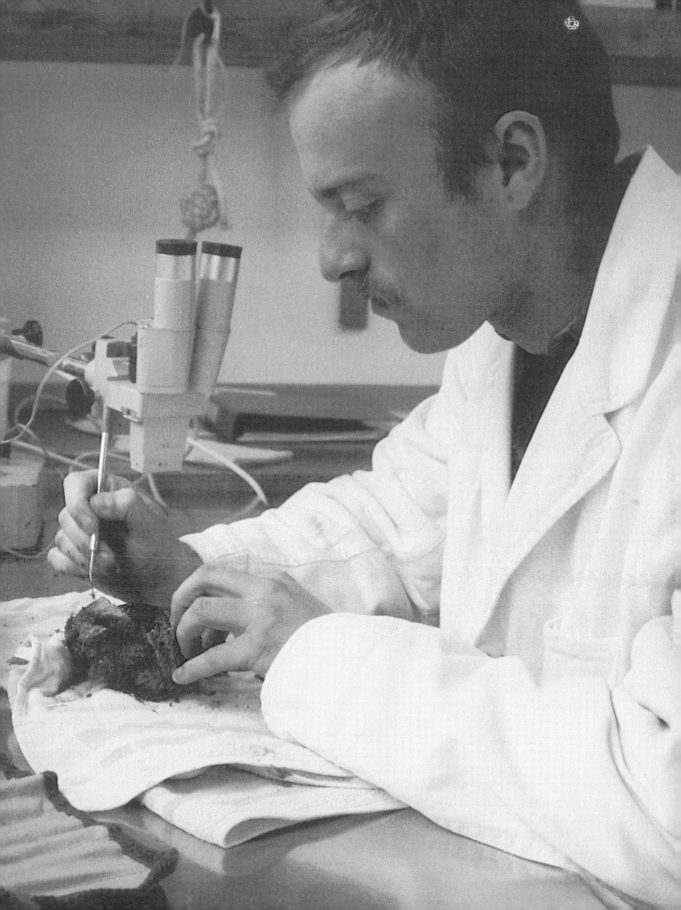

12.1.1. Basic principles

Aspects of several of the above phases will overlap and a rigid schema for such work will not be suggested. Indeed, many of the tasks listed are likely to begin while fieldwork is continuing. The main principles involved, however, are simple:

i. Post-fieldwork analysis is not a chore left for non-fieldworkers to do. It is the reason for doing the fieldwork in the first place.

ii. A high standard of fieldwork is meaningless if the information collected is not recorded, analysed thoroughly and made readily available to other workers as conveniently, promptly and fully as practicable.

iii. The collection of information continues throughout this phase as material is studied and recorded. The process can generate considerable quantities of notes and record drawings, so maintaining an efficient system of documentation is as fundamental to this part of archaeological research as it is to fieldwork.

iv. The aim of post-fieldwork processing of archaeological evidence is the establishment of the site archive. From the archive, information can be synthesised to create reports and publications.

v. Mistakes and inadequacies in the fieldwork are likely to appear as the evidence is analysed. It is important that these are not glossed over or hidden. Everyone makes mistakes and we can all learn from them. Other researchers should be given all the information they need in order to assess your conclusions objectively.

vi. The difference between analysis and interpretation is fundamental to post-fieldwork processing and should be borne in mind at every stage. Analysis might be described as making and recording measured, quantified and objective observations. Interpretation can be defined as using a set of observations to support a conclusion (they can very rarely prove a point beyond any doubt).

vii. The way you collected and analysed the evidence is of interest as well and should be recorded: the strategy you employed; the reasons for it; the success or failure of the techniques you used or invented. All of these may help other workers and will allow them to assess more effectively the validity of any conclusions.

12.1.2. Handling material and record keeping

If material is brought to the surface during a project it will already have been recorded to some extent. Its position relative to other material, its context and its position relative to site datum points will have been noted and it may well have been drawn on a site plan. Photographs may also have been taken before, during and after lifting. Once the material is on the surface there is an opportunity to record much more detail than is usually possible underwater. There can be no excuses about rescue situations or poor visibility. The information is there. It is up to us to recognise and record it.

An important word of caution. Material which has not been conserved can be unstable and fragile. Recording and analysis can involve a lot of handling and movement of an object from place to place. During any pre-conservation recording and study, try to keep handling to an absolute minimum and avoid exposing the material to dramatic changes of environment.

The importance of ensuring that any material remains securely identified by the number given to it in the initial recording process has been emphasised already (Section 6.3.4). During the post-fieldwork processing phase, objects and samples may be moved from place to place and examined by many different people, some of whom will be less careful than others in terms of putting things back where they found them. It is important to make sure that everyone handling material is aware of the need to avoid detaching or defacing labels. A specifically appointed finds assistant can be very helpful in ensuring that the material and the written record remain connected.

It may be useful, if material is likely to be moved to a number of different places, to devise a system for keeping track of changes of location (*e.g.* a set of 'object movement' forms). In this way you will be able record past locations and current whereabouts.

12.2. Post-Fieldwork Processing and the Drawn Record

The old adage that "a picture is worth a thousand words" is rarely more true than in the field of archaeological recording. Drawings and illustrations of various types provide a convenient way of conveying a great deal of information very quickly. Archaeological illustration and the production of the drawn record forms a major part of post-fieldwork processing. The need to make a photographic record has already been emphasised (9.5.2.).

12.2.1. Basic drawing equipment

There are several volumes available which deal very fully with the options in terms of drawing equipment (Green 1990 and Griffiths *et al.* 1990). Only a brief guide is offered here. A few basic items are all that is required to start with. You can add more as you go along and discover which additional items are appropriate for the kind of drawing you do. A list of initial purchases might include:

i. Pencils. A range of hardnesses is useful to allow for work on film as well as paper; from 4H to HB should cover most situations as when working on drawing film a 4H can behave more like a 2H. Accept the inevitable and buy yourself a good eraser as well.

ii. Drafting pens (also known as technical pens) are available in a range of sizes. 0.7mm is a frequently used size for many outlines, although 1.0mm may be required for larger drawings which will be heavily reduced; a

0.5mm nib may be used to outline a small drawing which will not be greatly reduced. Detail can be drawn with a 0.5mm or 0.35mm nib; a 0.25mm nib can be used for fine detail but if the drawing is going to be reduced by more than half, the finer lines are likely to be lost.

Specialised ink erasers are available; choose the type suitable for the ink and drawing surface you are using.

iii. Paper and drafting film. The smoother the drawing surface, the smoother the lines that can be drawn. Drafting film, although expensive, offers a smooth surface and mistakes can be erased by careful scraping with a no.10 (rounded) scalpel. Paper is available in a wide range of thicknesses. Choose a medium weight, smooth paper. Thin, 'bristol', board can also be used. If in any doubt the staff of a shop specialising in equipment for graphic art and technical drawing should be able to offer you plenty of advice.

CS10 paper is favoured by many illustrators. It has a very smooth surface, ideal for artwork, which can be carefully scraped to remove mistakes.

It is always worth asking about the long term stability of the drawing materials you buy (ink, paper, film, transfer lettering, etc.) and the suitability of the ink and pens for the drawing surface. Ink that fades quickly, and paper that tends to yellow and distort readily, should be avoided.

iv. Measuring equipment. Some means of taking accurate measurements is required. Callipers are very useful (and essential for drawing ceramic vessels) and should be available if at all possible. Dividers and rulers are also basic requirements and are available in a wide variety of forms.

v. A means of applying lettering and labels. Most drawings will require some form of labelling or annotation. For registration and record purposes handwritten text will often suffice. For publication this is rarely acceptable unless expertly executed.

239

Lettering stencils are widely available. They take practice to use well, but they are cheap. Dry-transfer lettering such as Letraset can produce excellent results but is expensive and frequent handling can damage the lettering. Machines are available which allow text and captions to be typed out onto clear adhesive labels which are placed onto the drawing or plan. These are expensive and rarely found outside established drawing offices. If you have access to a word processor attached to a high definition printer (such as a laser printer) lettering can be quickly and conveniently produced to an acceptable standard. Lettering and captions can be printed out as required and attached to the drawing for reproduction.

Other basic equipment which might be considered could include a scalpel, set squares, an engineers' square and graph paper.

12.2.2. Place of work

A place to work must also be organised and a few essentials borne in mind. Whatever arrangement you use you should be able to work comfortably for extended periods.

a. Working surface

Support the drawing on a suitable surface. A purpose built, adjustable drawing table is ideal but expensive. Drawing boards can be bought or made. If you are making one, it is very useful to make sure that one edge is machined straight so that a 'T-square' can be used.

It can be very useful to tape a sheet of graph paper onto the drawing surface and a thin sheet of film over that to protect it from water or ink. If drafting paper is then used the lines on the graph paper will show through and can be used to align drawings, labels and datum lines.

b. Light

You will need a lot of light. Drawing is based on observation and a strong, directable light source will help enormously in picking out detail that might other wise be missed. An angle-poise lamp can be ideal. Conventionally, objects are drawn as if lit from the top left corner so it can be useful to place the lamp on the left corner of the drawing board and also to position the board so that natural light is coming from that direction. Examine the object from a number of angles in different lighting conditions, new features might well become apparent.

As you get more experience you will find yourself adding items to this list. More pens, an adjustable drawing table or a reducing machine can all add significantly to the ease and convenience with which high quality work can be produced, but accuracy and clarity can be achieved with basic equipment of the kind listed above.

c. Storage and reference

Whether drawings are made on film or paper they should be kept in a safe, dry place. A plan chest is ideal as they can be laid flat and inspected with ease (variants in which the drawings are suspended from racks are also available). If there are to be a lot of drawings then it can help if each sheet of paper or film has its own number marked in a place that is easily visible when the sheets are in storage All artefacts drawn on that sheet would have that sheet number attached to their record cards so that the relevant drawing can be found with ease. This helps to prevent loss of information

12.2.3. Drawing up survey work

a. Maps, plans and sections

Survey work on and off site is likely to have produced a large amount of information which must be processed and prepared either for publication or the archive. The methods used for plotting survey results are covered in the survey section (9.3). This discussion focuses on ordering the records and preparing them for future use and analysis. The following types of survey drawing are typically found in an archive or report:

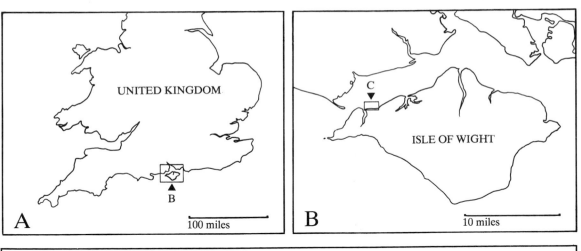

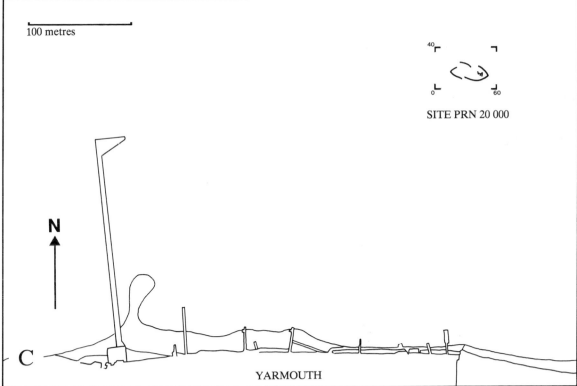

Figure 116. An example of a site location map for the protected wreck site at Yarmouth Roads. (12.2.3.a.) (Drawing by K. Watson.)

i. Location maps,
ii. Off-site information,
iii. Site plans showing archaeological, topographic and environmental features,
iv. Sections and profiles.

As a general rule such drawings should be organised according to scale, from large-scale site location maps to close-up plans of specific parts of the site or sections of a deposit. They should be presented and captioned in such a way that cross-reference

W 🡑   E 🡑

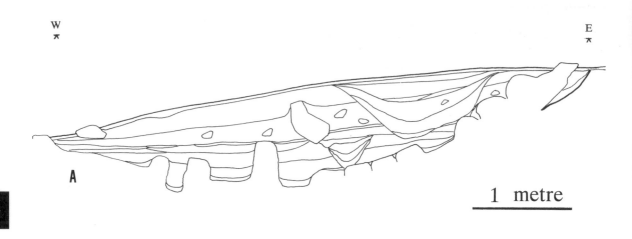

A

1 metre

W 🡑   E 🡑

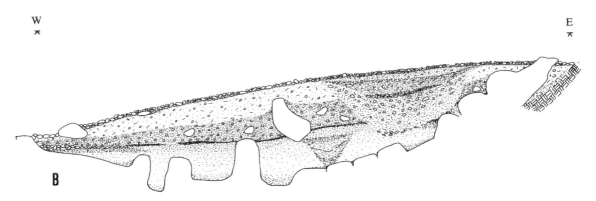

B

Figure 117. Interpreted (A) and 'naturalistic' (B) representations of the same section prepared for publication. (12.2.3.b.) (Drawing by K. Watson.)

between site master plan and details is easy. Off-site information such as the results of survey work around the main site might also be included.

It is advisable to keep all drawings free from unnecessary information. Location maps are more effective when uncluttered with roads, buildings or anything else not directly relevant to the subject (Figure 116). If drawings become cluttered or confused it might be appropriate to create overlays (drawings showing the same main features but providing different details). This can be particularly useful when presenting results, for example, of magnetometer or probing survey or the location and extent of any trenches excavated. Changes in the nature

of sediment across a site can also conveniently be shown in this way. The important point to remember about such overlays is that common datum points linking them to the master plan or section must be clearly marked.

Other maps or drawings can be added. These might include maps showing the nature of the local geology, maps showing the site's location relative to other similar sites in the same country or abroad and distribution maps or plans which aid in any discussion of the site's general significance.

b. Producing finished drawings of field recording

Producing finished illustrations from section drawings and site surveys made in the field is not a process of enhancement or an opportunity for embellishment. However, conventions and styles of presentation may be found which greatly improve the clarity of drawings. This is totally legitimate and should be encouraged if it does not obscure or distort the original information. Decorative borders do little to make up for badly recorded evidence, and detailed renderings of cannon and anchors which bear no resemblance to those actually on the site are probably best avoided.

When inking in section drawings, remember that boundaries between contexts are rarely precise, so solid lines are often best avoided in favour of broken lines or stippling. Conventions can be used to show different sediment types for clarity. It is common practice to offer a record drawing of the section along with an interpretative drawing of the same section where solid boundary lines are shown to aid clarity in discussion (Figure 117).

Each plan, section or overlay should include sufficient information for it to be useable by others, and should include:

i Site name and code, together with the record number of the drawing and the date drawn.

ii. Subject (plan or section of what).

iii. A clearly marked linear scale.

iv. Position – site grid coordinate on plans; reference to plan on which position of section is indicated.

v. Orientation – True or Magnetic North on plans and maps; the direction exposed sections face on section drawings.

vi. Key to symbols used.

Although it has rarely been indicated on archaeological drawings in the past, archaeologists should be more honest about the value of their survey, and so it is recommended the following is included:

vii. Quantified estimate of the survey accuracy. (See Section 9.2.3.).

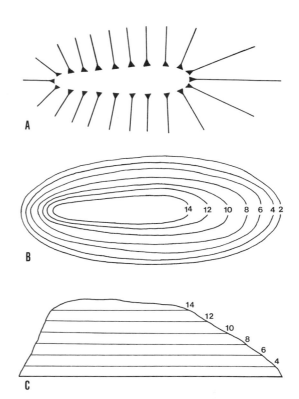

Figure 118. The topographic relief of mound c) can be represented by a) hachures or b) contours. (12.2.3.c.)

c. Presenting topography

Site plans should include an indication of the local topography and environment. Some thought should be given to how such features should be represented. Indicating the direction and degree of slope is very useful and can be done very simply. At the most basic level, direction of slope can be indicated on a plan with arrows or, following more detailed survey work, deduced from contour lines (Figure 118).

Successful representation of the underwater terrain requires effort both in the field and at the post-excavation stage. If the area on and around the surveyed area is relatively flat a more efficient way may be to simply put spot heights at suitable places on the site plan. More complex topography is often shown in contour plans (Section 9.4.6 a.). There are other ways of representing the seabed graphically, including wire diagrams. These are normally only produced by computer printers or plotters following analysis of the data by suitable programs. (See Section 9.4.6.b.)

Changes on the sea, river or lake bed may not be in height, but in texture or material. Differences in sediment, bedrock or vegetation type, size and shape of large stones or boulders, may be indicated, and this can be done effectively in a schematic way with symbols (Figure 92 a and b). An informative topographic site plan may have both contours and symbols to help bring out the detail in a readily understandable way.

12.2.4. The drawn record of archaeological material

a. The aim of illustrating archaeological material

The point of archaeological illustrations is to convey information, not to break up long passages of text. Accuracy and clarity are of the utmost importance. Illustrations should convey technical information about each object – exact dimensions, types of material, method of construction, traces of use and many other features – accurately enough for a researcher to recognise parallels, similarities or differences, with material from elsewhere.

To satisfy these criteria, archaeological illustrations follow set standards and conventions. The subject area is wide, and the reader is referred to the recommended reading list below for details beyond the introductory notes given here. On a large project with much drawing work required it is well worth appointing a supervisor to be in charge of ensuring consistency in terms of conventions used. Artefact photography has been covered in Section 9.5.2. The following section will deal with the basic concepts and techniques involved in recording archaeological material by drawing.

b. Drawing archaeological material

Archaeological drawing can be described as a mechanical process. Artistic flair may be an advantage and expertly executed archaeological record drawings can often be extremely attractive works in their own right. Having said that, the ability to make careful observations and transpose a measurement from an object onto paper are the main skills required to produce acceptable results.

c. Drawing and photography

Drawings have some advantages over photographs. Clarity of, and emphasis on, particular detail can be achieved more readily, and line drawings can often be cheaper and easier to reproduce than photographs. On the other hand photography can be used to record a number of objects relatively quickly. However, photographs cannot be used to present sectional information of complete or near complete objects in the way that drawings can, nor do they tend to offer quite the same opportunities for comparison of form. Illustrations showing hypothetical reconstruction are also much more readily achieved with drawings.

Most people would agree that a photograph alone is not a sufficient illustrative record of an object. Perhaps more importantly, the process of making a measured drawing of archaeological material involves close study of the object over a period of time. Much information often comes to light through this process and helps greatly in refining the resulting record. So, keep notes of observations made while drawing and add them to the written record.

12.2.5. Drawing techniques

No attempt is made here to cover the illustration of every type of archaeological material. Basic advice is offered followed by examples of drawing techniques which are less well covered in the available literature.

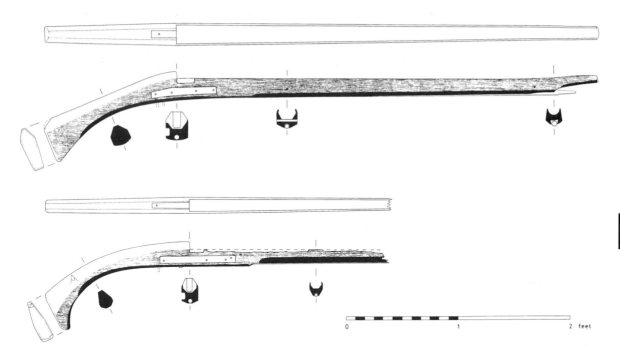

Figure 119. Cross-sections and plan views have been used to describe complex changes in shape along the length of these arquebus stocks (n.b. this was drawn before metric measurements were commonly used in British archaeology). (12.2.5.) (Courtesy of C. Martin.)

Recording by drawing can be divided into a number of areas:

    i. Recording shape and dimensions,

    ii. Recording decorative and surface detail,

    iii. Recording detail related to composition and manufacture,

All the above are essentially objective processes based on careful study and measurement. However, an element of interpretation is involved in many drawings. For example, the orientation of the object on the page, the emphasis given to particular features as opposed to others, the selection of views recorded. This is unavoidable and an illustrator must try to ensure that such decisions do not become the source of distortion and bias. Explicitly interpretive drawings are dealt with in Section 12.2.8 c.

There are a few general conventions which should be noted. As mentioned already, archaeological material is usually drawn as if lit from the top left hand corner of the page. Record drawings do not generally involve perspective, elevations being drawn from as many views as required to convey the available information. More views may be recorded for the archive than are eventually published. Sections through the object are very useful as an adjunct to other views and should always be included when drawing ceramic vessels (Figure 119).

All record drawings should be clearly and permanently marked with the object's record number, the draughtsperson's name and a linear, metric scale which will remain true when the drawing is reduced.

a. Originals and reductions

Most object drawing is done at full size and the results reduced for publication as necessary. Some smaller objects are drawn at more than life-size (often using tracings from carefully scaled and prepared photographs).

It is clear from the outset that reduction for publication must be considered when preparing to start the drawing. This means thinking very carefully about line thicknesses and levels of detail. Lines less than 0.25mm thick will often be lost in a half-sized reduction, and intricate detail will blur if not carefully drawn. It is worth remembering that plans and section drawings will have to be drawn for reduction as well as objects. In these drawings, particular attention must be paid to ensuring that any lettering or labelling remains clearly legible after reduction.

Consideration of the effects of reduction can sometimes leave the full-size drawing looking a little plain but this is preferable to merged and blurred detail when reproduced at published size. In extreme cases it may be necessary to produce a highly detailed record drawing and another, less detailed but still accurate drawing for reduction and publication.

There are advantages to reduction. Reducing a drawing by half can remove many slight blemishes from view, and smooth out slightly rough lines. Drawings for reduction can be checked quickly for suitability by use of a photocopier. Effective illustration for reduction is a skill but like everything else it can be learned and practised.

b.   Recording shape and dimension

An initial step in making a drawn record of an object is to establish its outline and general dimensions. The techniques used will vary from object to object but the example offered here of a technique useful for drawing the outline of a ceramic vessel will serve to introduce methods of working which are applicable in a wide range of situations. Other objects may require to be drawn from a greater number of angles to convey the required information.

Pottery is usually drawn full-size for eventual reduction. This allows the maximum number of measurements to be made. Amphorae form an exception, being drawn at a reduced size (1:2 or 1:4), or being traced from reduced photographs. It has now become a convention to draw pottery with an elevation on the right-hand side and a section in solid black on the left (Figure 120).

There are a number of different ways of drawing pottery and methods will vary with the completeness of the vessel.

Recording the outline and dimensions of a complete or near complete vessel can be achieved using a simple method involving a right angle block and an engineers' square (or any similar device), as follows:

i. Place the vessel on its side on a sheet of drawing paper with its rim or base flat against the right angle block as if it were standing upright on a table. The vessel is likely to have to be suported by plasticine or modelling clay and should not be allowed to move. A line drawn along the base of the block will represent the line of the base or rim of the vessel.

ii. Place the engineers' square against the edge of the vessel. Where the square touches the paper lies directly beneath that point on the vessel and this can be marked with a pencil (Figure 121). By moving the square around the edge of the vessel and marking the points with a pencil on the paper, the outline of the vessel can be plotted out. The more marks that are made, the easier it will be to join them up into an accurate outline. Pay special attention to areas where the outline changes dramatically (such as rims) and to where handles or spouts are attached. The outline of a wide range of objects can be recorded in this way.

iii. An alternative method of drawing the outline of a near complete vessel or large object is to position it firmly on a level surface and then establish a vertical datum either side. Offset measurements can then be taken from the datum to the object to describe the shape as shown in Figure 122. The vertical datums must be positioned exactly opposite each other and the distance between them carefully measured.

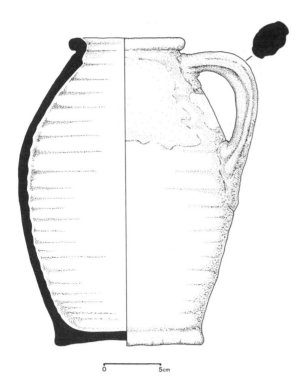

Figure 120. Note how the construction of this pottery vessel is shown in the internal detail. As the vessel was handmade the rim and base lines are not ruled but drawn freehand. Stippling is used to indicate the roughness of the fabric as well as shape. Patches of glaze are shown as simple outlines. It is conventional to show at least one cross-section of any handles that are present on the vessel. (12.2.b.b.)

Figure 121. Once an object has been placed against a right-angled block its outline can be recorded quite quickly and simply by use of an engineers' square or, as in this case, a purpose built tool comprising a ruler set at right-angle to a wooden block (this angle must be very carefully checked). A small notch is removed from the base of the ruler to allow the pencil point to be placed directly under the point being recorded. (12.2.5.b.) (Courtesy of C. Martin.)

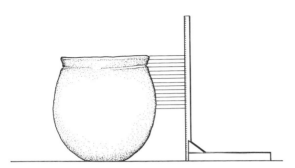

Figure 122. Pottery vessels and a range of other larger objects can be recorded by establishing a vertical datum line and taking offset measurements. Both sides of an object should be recorded independently as it is dangerous to assume that any object (prior to mass production) is symmetrical. (12.2.5.b.)

Drawing the outline of incomplete vessels can be much more complicated. Sometimes only fragments of a vessel will be available, but it is still possible to achieve a useful record of the shape of the object by applying simple techniques carefully.

If less than half of the rim or base of the vessel is available, it may not be possible to use only the techniques mentioned above to draw the outline of both sides of a vessel. Other techniques can be used which make this possible. Clearly it is important to find out how wide the vessel was at the base and at the rim to allow its shape to be reconstructed. This can be done by placing

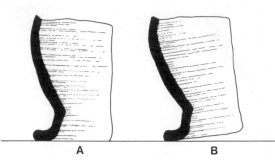

A   B

Figure 124. When attempting to orientate a sherd of pottery correctly on a radius chart, the presence of throwing marks (horizontal lines created during manufacture) can be very useful, especially when rims are rounded or abraded: a) the marks can be seen to be horizontal, indicating that the sherd is in its correct orientation, b) The rim is not correctly aligned and would give a incorrect reading on the chart. (12.2.5.)

Figure 123. A radius chart is simply a sheet of paper onto which semicircles of a known radius have been drawn. Rim or base fragments can be aligned with successive curves until an exact fit is found. (12.2.5.b.) (Courtesy of C. Martin.)

a rim or base fragment on a radius chart (a sheet onto which semicircles of known radius have been drawn – see Figure 123), as follows:

i. Place the rim upside down on the rim scale, in its proper plane. Check its true position by looking along the plane of the paper, and adjusting the angle at which the sherd is held until the arc of the rim or base lies flat on the paper. Rounded or abraded rims can be difficult to orientate correctly as can very small fragments (Figure 124). Move the base or rim across the radius scale maintaining the same orientation until the outer curve coincides exactly with one of the curves of the scale when viewed from above. If the rim fragment fits the curve of 10cm radius, we know that the vessel was 20cm wide at the rim and although we may only

have one piece of that rim, we can now indicate the dimensions of the vessel on the drawing.

ii. Once the dimensions of the rim or base are established, the outline of the sides of the vessel can be drawn. This can be done by using a block as described above but great care must be taken to make sure that the piece of pottery is orientated correctly. Position the pot rim or base against the vertical wooden plane, positioning the rim in its correct plane (as when using the radius chart). Where isolated sherds are being drawn, they should be orientated to provide the maximum complete profile although the angle at which this profile is orientated may have to be estimated to a degree. Use plasticine or modelling dough to stop the pot or sherd from moving. Use an engineers' set square as described previously.

iii. Check, and repeat if possible for the other side. The measurement obtained using the radius chart provides the position of the rim of the opposite side of the vessel. Pots and other objects are very rarely symmetrical and it is not appropriate to make a measured drawing of one side and then use a tracing of this to form the outline of the opposite side.

Figure 125. Callipers are extremely useful in recording the cross-section of a vessel. It can be difficult to obtain measurements from within a deep, complete vessel, or one with a very narrow neck. Fortunately callipers are available in a range of sizes and designs but sometimes considerable ingenuity is required to obtain measurements. (12.2.5.b.i.) (Courtesy of C. Martin.)

However, where only one side of the vessel is available the same piece will have to be used to reconstruct both sides of the outline.

iv. It might be possible to extend the outline by studying the shape of fragments of the body of the vessel; the more pieces that are available the more easily this can be done. Conjectural sections of any outline should be indicated with a dotted line.

If no rim or base fragments are available then it may well not be possible to reconstruct the shape of the vessel being studied. Some indication of shape can be provided by drawing cross sections of the body sherds but there is likely to be an unacceptable amount of guess work involved in reconstructing a complete outline. This does not mean that such pottery fragments are useless; they may have distinctive decoration or construction marks which should be recorded. Therefore, they should not be ignored.

Once an outline has been drawn it is usual to draw a line through the mid point of the pot dividing it in half. The left side is used to show internal detail, the right to show external features (Figure 120):

i. Using callipers, measure the thickness of the wall and draw a cross-section through the vessel (Figure 125). This is shown on the

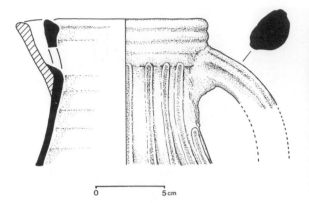

0   5cm

Figure 126. Following convention the spout of this jug has been shown on the left and details of the way in which it was attached to the vessels can be seen in the drawing. Additional views of the spout could be added if required. (12.2.5.b.iii.)

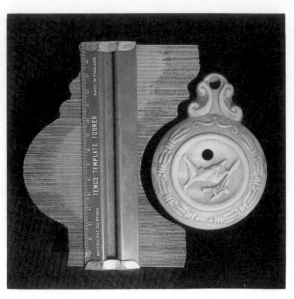

Figure 127. Profile gauges can provide a quick way of checking the shape of a complex object but should always be used in conjunction with careful measurement. Great care must be exercised when using such gauges as it is easy to damage the surface of the object being recorded. (12.2.5.b.) (Courtesy of C. Martin.)

left hand side of the drawing. Careful attention should be paid to the internal details at this stage. In the case of complete pots these may not be easy to observe but the study of broken examples of similar pots may help in assessing what might be there and developing strategies for recording it.

ii. On the right hand side of the pot, indicate external features such as decoration, or technical traits.

iii. Outlines of handles and spouts often cause problems and various conventions exist for showing them in section as well as in profile (Figure 126 and recommended reading). Handles usually appear on the right of the drawing; spouts on the left.

iv. Check the resulting dimensions of the object carefully by direct measurement and with callipers.

Objects can also have their outline recorded 'by eye'. The object is carefully positioned on the paper and supported by modelling clay. It is important that it does not move at all throughout this process. The draughtsperson then positions themselves over the edge of the object and the pencil tip, and then draws round the object keeping directly above the pencil point and object edge. Accurate outlines can be drawn in this way, particularly for fairly flat objects with

well defined edges, but it requires considerable practice and the results should be very carefully checked by measurement. Slight misalignment of pencil, object edge and eye can produce significant errors.

If the illustrator has access to a copy-camera with precise reduction and enlargement facilities, flat objects or materials may be photographed on the copy-camera screen and printed up or down to the desired size. The printed image can then be placed beneath drafting film to be used as a basis for the line drawing. If this method is used, it is essential that a series of individual check measurements are made to ensure that the alteration in scale is accurate.

A variety of pieces of equipment are available to aid in recording outlines: flexi-curves and profile gauges can be used but if used carelessly they do not record the finer details of shape. With practice however, they are useful tools (Figure 127).

Figure 128. When complex decoration is being recorded it can be 'rolled out' as shown here. If the design is repetitive it might not be necessary to show it all in this way. In addition, as this vessel was made of a fine fabric and wheel-turned, no stippling has been used and the rim lines drawn in using a ruler. Compare this with Figure 120 which shows a vessel made of much coarser fabric. (12.2.5.c.)

c. Recording decoration and surface detail

Once the outline and dimensions of an object have been accurately recorded and checked, surface detail can be added. Again this should be done through a process of careful observation and measurement. Tracings from carefully scaled photographs can be used to illustrate complex decoration and the outlines of objects can be recorded in the same way.

Careful attention should be paid to reproducing decoration and deliberately applied surface detail accurately. Other workers will want to use your drawings as a means of comparing the material recorded with objects elsewhere, and the small details of style and shape may be important (Figure 128).

A number of methods of suggesting three-dimensional shape and decoration exist. Stippling (a series of dots) and linear shading are used widely, and conventions exist in terms of the way that various features are represented. Looking at a wide range of published work will help in familiarising yourself with these conventions and the way that they can be both informative and

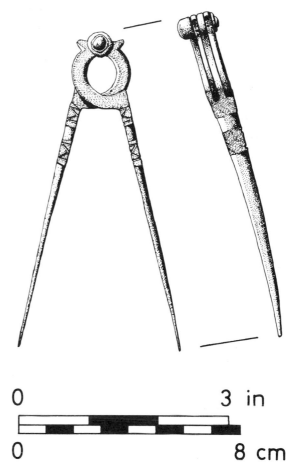

Figure 129. An example of a record drawing of some navigational dividers. Two views have been chosen to convey the maximum amount of information about shape and construction. (12.2.5.d.) (Courtesy of C. Martin.)

attractive. Effectively applied stippling can greatly enhance a drawing, suggesting shape and texture, but it can also be misleading and if carelessly done will obscure as much detail as it shows.

d. Recording constructional and other detail

It is not only decorative surface detail which has to be recorded: other features on the object are important (Figure 129). Is there evidence of the way in which the object was made or repaired? On pottery this might take the form of the internal shape of the vessel or the coil construction indicated by the undulating surface (Figure 120). Iron-work may show evidence of rivets or hammering; stonework might have tool marks on it. These are all relevant in terms of recording the maximum information available.

What about the materials from which the object was made? Care should be taken to distinguish between different materials in composite objects. For example, an iron knife with a wooden handle might be drawn using stippling for the iron and linear shading to convey the grain of the wooden handle (see Figure 130). There is a wide choice of methods but clarity is essential and it is useful to provide a key which explains the conventions you have chosen to use.

Lastly, it is important to avoid misleading additions or omissions. A total absence of stippling on the surface of a pot drawn with beautifully smooth sides might suggest a fine fabric and possibly wheel turned production. If, however, the vessel is in fact made of rough fabric and is asymmetrical then this should be indicated in the drawn record. Similarly, avoid putting hard lines where none exists on the object. The process of drawing involves a certain amount of decision making but if an edge is rounded it should be drawn as such. If a junction or feature is not clear and sharp, dotted and broken lines can be used to describe it in preference to a solid line which suggests a definite boundary.

12.2.6. Drawn records of ordnance

Some additional equipment may be required when drawing ordnance due to the potentially large size of the object being recorded. Larger callipers than are normally employed may be useful, and scale rules, profile gauges and tapes may be more suitable than rulers. For

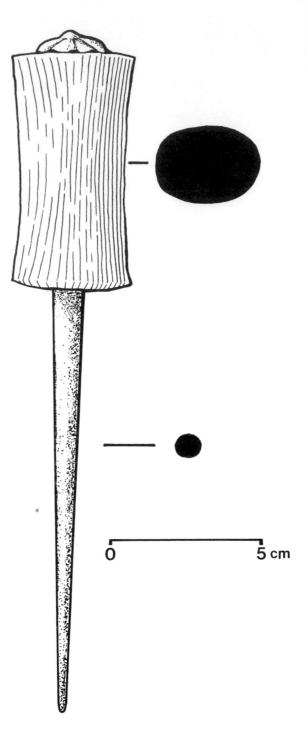

Figure 130. The depiction of a composite object made out of wood and metal. (12.2.5.d.)

tracing and taking rubbings of inscriptions, thin polythene used with fine, permanent marker pens or soft paper (such as thin layout paper) for use with graphite, wax crayons or soft pencils might be considered.

Drafting film is probably preferable to paper in many situations as it is stable in wet environments and will produce clear dyeline copies. Being transparent, it can be taped onto a drawing board covered with graph paper to provide a grid on which to base the drawing.

When drawing reductions of guns, carriages, timbers, etc. it is better for the draughtsperson to use a hand-held board so that they can walk around the object, taking measurements, adding detail and notes to the drawing. These pencil working drawings often get messy, but final ink drawings for record and reproduction can be traced off them.

a. Conventions

Guns should be drawn as a side elevation together with a muzzle end view to show the width of the muzzle and trunnions. If the gun is highly decorated, a plan view may also be necessary. A plan view is often required with a wrought iron gun to record the details of the lifting lugs and hoop configuration.

Large guns can be drawn to a scale of 1:5 or 1:10, with any decoration or inscriptions drawn at 1:1 with the aid of a rubbing or tracing. Care should be taken with inscriptions as spelling can be unusual and even letters reversed. If a letter cannot be deciphered it should not be simply drawn in as a 'best guess'. It is better to leave a space in the drawing and include your interpretation in note form.

b. Method of recording guns on the surface

i. The gun should be placed on a smooth, level floor with the muzzle supported so that the longitudinal axis of the gun is parallel to the floor. The central point of the muzzle should be at the same height as the centre of

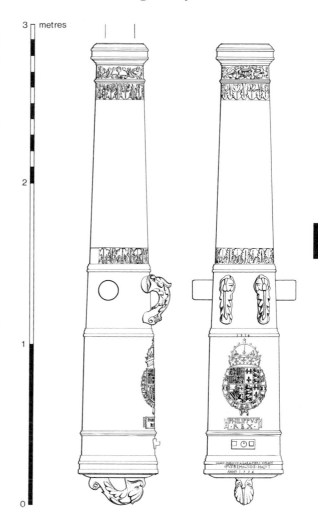

Figure 131. Plan and side elevation of a decorated gun. (12.2.6.) (Courtesy of C. Martin.)

the cascabel. The floor can then be used as a datum line from which to measure the positions of the reinforcing rings, trunnions etc.

ii. If the floor is not level and smooth, or if it is not possible to support the gun so that the floor can be used as a datum line, the gun may be drawn using its longitudinal axis as the datum line. Points on its profile may be plotted with reference to the distance from the muzzle (for example, diameter of gun at 0.5m from muzzle, start of trunnion at 0.73m from muzzle, end of trunnion at 0.85m from muzzle).

253

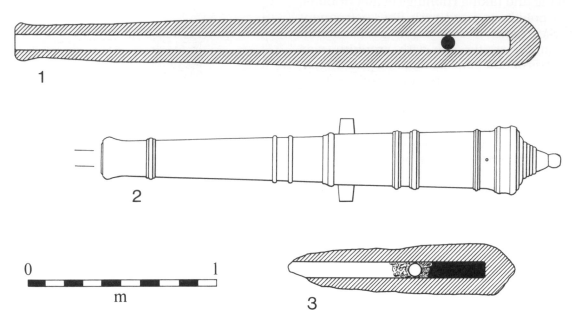

Figure 132. Guns: 1) longitudinal cross-section, 2) plan showing bore diameter, 3) cross-section of eroded fragment showing charge components. (12.2.6.) (Courtesy of C. Martin.)

iii. Two large set squares (marked in centimetres on their vertical edges) supported so that they will stand vertically, can be used to measure the varying diameters of the gun if sufficiently large external callipers are not available. The horizontal distance between the two set squares, when butted up to either side of the gun, gives its diameter at that point.

iv. Diameters should be taken wherever the gun significantly changes in profile, such as at the reinforcing rings, trunnions, dolphins and at a number of positions over the cascabel. The diameters can then be joined up to give the external lines of the gun. Internal callipers can be used to measure the bore. A torch will suggest whether or not the bore is straight-sided, tapered, or chambered.

v. It is preferable to add as much of the detail as possible in the initial drawing phase. However, if time is short, detailed photographs can be helpful when drawing features such as the lifting dolphins. Such details can be outlined and then added at a later stage using information taken from the photographs. Care must be taken to use photographs taken from the correct angle.

vi. It is common to write the following details beneath the gun drawing for publication:
a. Length of basal ring,
b. Overall length,
c. Calibre,
d. Weight.
A marked metric linear scale should be included. The original drawing should also carry the unique number of the artefact.

vii. Although it may be useful to publish length and bore in Imperial (or other) units, those used on archaeological drawings should be metric. If any conversion has taken place this should be clearly stated (quoting the initial figures and the conversion factor used).

c. Drawing gun carriages

If a gun is recovered on its carriage it will probably be convenient to draw the gun first. This should have been fully surveyed underwater to record additional information

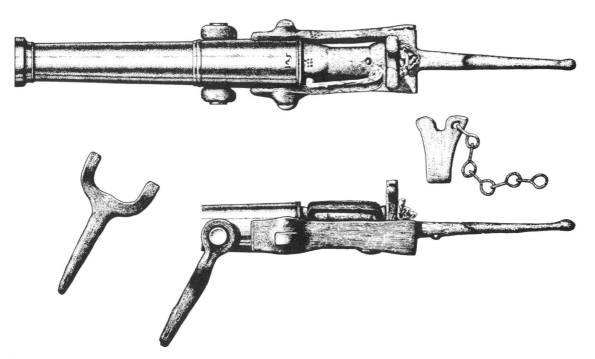

Figure 133. Plan and detail drawings of a complex object: a swivel gun shown using interpretive shading. (12.2.6.) (Courtesy of C. Martin.)

(*e.g.* the angle of the gun in relation to the bed of the carriage, the presence of any wedges or quoins etc.) which will be vital for research and any reconstruction drawings. It is better to do post-excavation drawings at a scale of 1:5 as there may be a lot of detail to record on the carriage as well as the gun.

The surviving components of the carriage may include cheeks, bed, axles and wheels (or trucks). If possible each part should be considered as a separate unit which is recorded by tracing on polythene (Section 12.2.7 b.). The wood should be carefully cleaned to show constructional features (*e.g.* bolt-holes, treenails, rebates, remains of metal straps, hinges or brackets). Different colours may be used to denote features such as iron concretion and nail holes. Each face of the components should be traced so that detail such as variations in thickness can be recorded. Some elements may be inaccessible if the carriage is still partly assembled. In this case comprehensive measurements should be taken before drawing all parts at 1:5 scale.

Tracings are a very useful record to refer to when the carriage parts are under conservation treatment or otherwise inaccessible, and are also the primary source for the 1:5 drawings. Final drawings for reproduction will be inked and in black and white, and a key will be necessary to denote features such as iron fittings, concretion etc. Areas of erosion should also be indicated. The carriage will probably be incomplete so a conjectural reconstruction is useful together with an 'exploded view' to explain the assembly of the components.

d. Wrought iron guns and sledges

It is better initially to record wrought iron guns and sledges found together as single entities. Tracings will not be possible so 1:5 scale drawings should be made. Try to have the sledge placed on a flat, smooth floor which can be used as a datum line. The wheels or trucks will probably have been raised separately. If possible support the sledge so that the barrel of the gun is parallel to the floor. Draw the longitudinal axis of the gun as a horizontal pencil line on the drawing board and, using the graph paper as a guide, mark in the position and dimensions of the hoops on the barrel. It is better to start with a plan view of the gun and sledge, leaving space for an elevation below it. Graph paper backing will make it easy to transfer measurements and the positions of features from the plan view to the elevation.

The draughtsperson should look out for details of the chamber, lifting rings, markings, evidence of a gun-sight and wedges etc.. An X-radiograph (if it can be arranged) is very useful in clarifying construction details.

After the gun drawing is completed the sledge can be drawn around it. Care must be taken to record features such as metal fastenings and rope (particularly the impressions of rope surviving in concretions). Bolt holes on the underside of the sledge may indicate where the axle was attached. An elevation view of both sides may be necessary to show different features. A muzzle-end elevation view is also required.

Any surviving axle, wheels or tiller should be drawn separately before combining with the gun and sledge for a reconstruction drawing. When the gun and sledge are separated for conservation treatment each should be drawn to record any additional information.

If the sledge is found without the gun it is still better to start with a plan view which will also provide information about the shape of the missing gun.

e. Gun furniture and smaller ordnance items

Gun furniture and other smaller ordnance items should be drawn according to the guidelines given for artefact drawing (Section 12.2.5). Handguns and other objects of complex shape should be drawn at a scale of 1:1 if size permits.

Rams, scoops and other gun furniture may be recovered with long handles. In this case a 1:1 view of the head will provide detailed information and an extra view of the complete object at the same scale as the associated gun will also be useful.

12.2.7. Drawn records of timbers

Two main methods of drawing timbers are commonly used. Making scaled drawings, and making full-sized tracings (which are then often scaled down by hand or photographically). Additional materials required may include clear polythene and spirit-based pens (*i.e.* water-resistant) for tracing. Perspex sheet and chinagraph pencils can also be used. A variety of coloured pens are very useful to highlight features such as treenails, iron nails, concretions or repairs on full-sized drawings. However, if the drawing is going to be reduced photographically it may be necessary to use black pens and establish clear conventions to distinguish between the various features.

Supports for timbers are very useful. You will probably work more effectively for longer if the timber is at a comfortable height and excessive bending is not required. If timber is removed from wet storage for drawing it must be kept wet.

a. Scaled drawings

Wood should be drawn at a scale which is most useful for the level of detail required. This is often 1:10, but larger scale drawings are frequently made, in particular to record complex relationships between timbers, and it is not uncommon for 1:1 tracings to be made. At this level of site recording an attempt should be made to show all the major structural features such as holes, notches, joints, fastenings and damage (such as that caused by wood borers or charring by fire). It is important to ensure that all the timbers on the drawing have been individually marked with their unique timber numbers.

There are several methods of drawing timbers in plan. The shape of individual components of a hull can be recorded by means of measurements added to sketches. These enable the main features of construction to be recorded and act as a control on shrinkage and distortion which may subsequently occur. The direct

Figure 134. 1:1 tracing of timber surfaces on polythene. (12.7.b.)

measurements can be used as a basis for the artist's reconstruction in conjunction with 1:10 drawings made from tracings. A drawing frame can also be used, as can photogrammetry (Section 9.3.7), though in both cases some control measurements and additional notes are needed to eliminate possible inaccuracies, and to allow the incorporation of less visible features.

On a scale drawing, many of these details can be shown using a standard set of conventions and symbols. In selecting conventions, care must be taken to ensure that they are consistently used, and that the symbolic representations are not to be confused with realistic representations of actual features on the timber.

b. Tracing timbers

An alternative to scale drawing is to trace the details of the timber onto transparent film at 1:1. This can be done directly onto polythene sheeting, or acetate film which is actually laid onto the timber being drawn, waterproof pens being used to trace the features. Laying the sheet directly onto the timber reduces distortion caused by parallax.

Drawing onto clear PVC rigid sheeting, supported horizontally over the timber, with a chinagraph pencil works well underwater and on land. Once on the surface the drawing can then be photographed and/or transferred onto polythene sheeting, and the PVC sheet wiped clean ready for re-use.

Care is needed to reduce distortion when using any tracing-based method to record more complex three-dimensional shapes, and the drawing should be backed up with linear measurements. For example, a tracing made by laying a polythene sheet directly onto a very curved timber (such as a rib or frame) will not produce an accurate plan view, but an expanded view of the timber surface. To be useful such a tracing must be accompanied by a side tracing of the timber or measurements to describe the curvature.

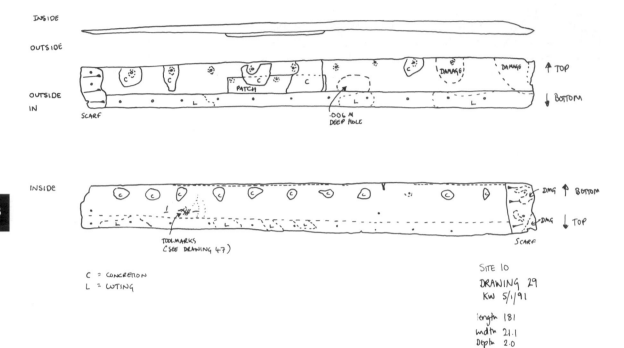

Figure 135. An example of a timber tracing. (Drawing by K. Watson.)

The results can be reduced photographically for redrawing and publication. Before reduction a standard scale should be imposed onto the drawings to allow the accuracy and consistency of the reduction to be checked very carefully. It is very important to remember to label all drawings with identification numbers, and to mark the position of any cross-sections that have been drawn.

c. Some points to remember

i. Care should be taken to ensure that distortion in the drafting film or movement during tracing is minimised. Light pinning or weighting can help but care must be taken not to damage the timber.

ii. Reference points should be marked in all directions and measurements should be made between these points to check for distortion. The marks are also useful for checking the accuracy of subsequent copies.

iii. The tracings are waterproof and useful for checking the originals for shrinkage. However, even waterproof ink on polythene will rub off, and care should be taken in their use and storage.

iv. Tracings may be easily reduced on a large plan photocopier (usual width 58cm, maximum practical length about 3m) or a copy camera. They can be overlapped with reference marks if required. Remember that blue does not photocopy well and so might be worth avoiding as a convention if this method is to be used for reduction. Some photocopiers do not reduce accurately and it may be better to do reductions by hand if there is any doubt.

v. Tracings are useful for working out displays where full-size paper templates are often used, and for checks during conservation.

vi. Tracings must be accompanied by section or profile drawings, preferably on a level datum to record twist. Section lines should mark the position of section profiles.

vii. Tracing can be fast and cheap. Symbolic conventions may be used to designate particular features such as details of fastenings (*e.g.* iron nails may be shown as red circles; wedged treenails as hatched circles etc.). Measurements of fastenings should be marked on the sheet. Once again, care must be taken to distinguish conventions from realistic representation (*e.g.* confusion can occur in the depiction of wedged treenails.)

viii. With the plank-type timbers it may not be necessary to draw edge views – only faces and profiles.

ix. End views of planks showing the orientation of the rays of the grain are an important aid to reconstructing the method of timber utilisation.

x. A photographic record in colour and black/white should accompany the drawings.

12.2.8. Presenting synthesised information

a. Isometric and axonometric representations

A drawing method commonly used in presenting structural information is a projection (possibly isometric or axonometric). These are simply ways of converting the information contained in single plane views derived from the site recording into composite three-sided dimensional views. An isometric drawing is correct along any axis whereas an axonometric representation is correct along one or more (Figure 128).

The representations are usually viewed from a 'common corner', a point at union with the three viewed sides of the object. All principal lines of the projection are parallel to each other within the same plane: the disappearing effect of perspective is not drawn, and there is no foreshortening needed. All isometric projections of timber structures (*e.g.* for details of joints) should always be checked against the originals if they survive.

For standing structures, front, side and back elevations are desirable at 1:10 to provide the necessary information. Plans (for quays, river wharves etc.) should be at superstructural, base-plate and foundation levels, and sections across such structures should show the relationship of the timbers to adjacent deposits.

b. Computer Aided Design (CAD)

Computer drafting has the ability to produce and manipulate two-dimensional and three-dimensional images from survey information.

The use of CAD does not restrict one to working from the keyboard or to inputting data 'from scratch'. A scale drawing made on the site may be entered into the computer by placing the drawing on a digitizing pad (a sensitized electronic drawing surface) and tracing carefully with a pen-like instrument. Highly accurate two-dimensional drawings have been produced in this manner from original drawings. Relative height information can then be added to produce three-dimensional images.

The effects of sag in a building or hogging influences on a ship are readily apparent in three-dimensional perspective views whereas they are difficult to see in two dimensions. The ability to rotate a structure or to change perspective reveals features that would otherwise only be obtainable through tedious redrawing. This feature is equally dramatic in the three-dimensional display of the archaeological stratigraphic sequence. The surface contours, strata, and artefacts can all be displayed in their original spatial relationships. This level of representation allows the archaeologist to analyse the site in ways never available before.

Beyond the potential insights revealed by CAD drawings there is also a significant reduction in the amount of effort required to reproduce graphics. CAD software can replace the task of photographic reproduction, allowing the production of any size drawing at the press of a key.

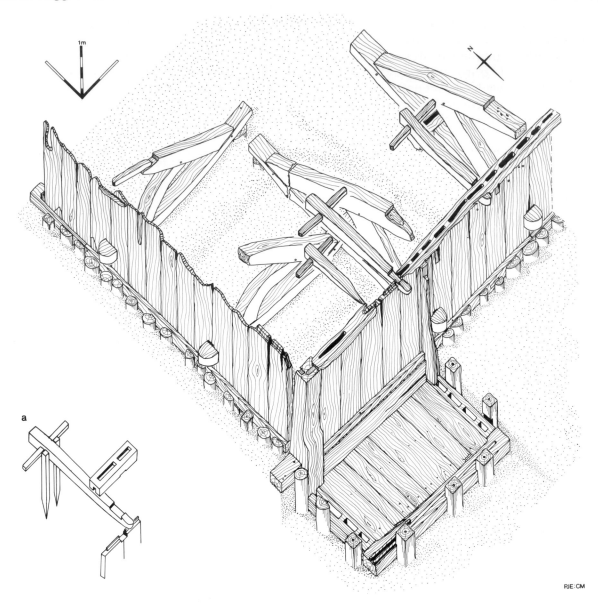

Figure 136. An example of an axonometric projection of a waterfront revetment structure. (12.2.8.a.) (Courtesy of the Museum of London.)

c. Interpretive drawings

Interpretive drawings, reconstructions, views of objects as they might have been used and objects placed together in assumed association, have their place in the depiction of archaeological evidence. However, they should be rigidly separated from record drawings which are representations of the objects as they are, not how it is thought they should be (observations not interpretations). Any element of a record drawing involving hypothetical reconstruction (for example, the shape of missing sections of a pot) should be clearly indicated. Dotted lines are often used.

Of course, some reconstructions can be made with more confidence than others, and such drawings can be fundamental to archaeological work in terms of communicating ideas and exploring interpretations. However, they are not an adequate sole record of an object.

12.3. Specialist Analysis

Almost all projects will benefit from the analytical input of specialists. They will be able to contribute to both the identification and interpretation of the evidence. This is may be because the analytical techniques employed require special training or equipment not available to most projects, or because one person has a great deal of experience of a particular class of material. The level of this input may vary from a major study of material stretching over a considerable time to comments made over the telephone or by letter.

Different specialists will have different requirements in terms of the form in which material should be presented to them, but some general guidance can be offered in terms of maintaining a productive working relationship:

i. Obtain a firm commitment from the specialist that they are willing to do the work and on what terms. Do not assume that they will be willing to look at the material you present at once or that they will do the work for free.

ii. Specialists have skills and knowledge that have often taken a long time to accumulate. They deserve to be treated with consideration and their expertise acknowledged.

iii. Establish the time-scale. How long will the specialist require to study and report on the material? Agree on a timetable. It is easier to hold people to a deadline if they are being paid for their time. Someone working for free may be less inclined to respond positively to unreasonable pressure. So be patient, but make every effort to avoid letting one delayed contribution hold up the whole project.

iv. A specialist will often be able to make extensive and perceptive observations on the material you present for examination, but they may not provide all the answers you were hoping for. They are likely to take a very rigorous approach to what can or cannot be said about the material with certainty. This close attention to detail may seem frustrating but in fact it is a reflection of the problems involved in dealing objectively with archaeological evidence.

v. Information such as the context and association of the material being analysed should be given to the specialist.

vi. Specialists will prefer to do any initial treatment of samples themselves. Therefore your role will probably be limited to delivering the samples in suitable containers.

vii. Additional information may become available from the processing of samples. The need for a continuing dialogue between all specialists, including archaeologists and scientists, throughout this phase is self-evident. Evaluation of archaeological evidence will probably raise new questions to be referred to scientists or modify those originally formulated, whilst scientific studies may also raise problems or provide additional information with a direct and significant bearing on archaeological analysis and later interpretation.

viii. Finds specialists will often be able to make observations on accurate drawings and written records, but on occasion they will want to see the original material. This can raise security problems both in terms of safe transport and in storage at a new location. Keep a very careful record of what has gone where. It may be less trouble to bring the specialist to the material.

ix. It must be borne in mind that specialists may damage, alter or destroy material as part of their analyses. Material that must not be changed should be clearly identified (for example, organic remains for dating purposes should not be treated with biocides and objects for display should not be sectioned).

261

12.4. Recording During the Analysis Stage

The need to establish and maintain an organised recording system which allows easy cross-referencing, for example, between finds, drawings, written records and plans has already been discussed (Section 6.1). Evidence collected in post-fieldwork recording should be entered into the same system. Indeed, it is in the post-fieldwork analysis stage that the flexibility, reliability and efficiency of the system will really be tested.

12.5. Interpretation and Gathering Supporting Evidence from Other Sources

After the evidence has been analysed, conclusions about the site and interpretations of the material and its significance can be offered. Some people argue that interpretation should be avoided until the excavation or investigation is completed, that the objective collection of evidence is the most important part of fieldwork, and that preconceptions should not be allowed to influence what is recorded. However, human nature being what it is, most of us find it impossible not to interpret and formulate ideas as investigations progress, and many would consider it very useful to formulate explanations for the evidence as it appears. Most important is the need to maintain the distinction between observation and interpretation through to final publication.

At this stage it is often useful to cast the net very widely in the search for information that will assist in this phase of the investigation. The evidence from the site itself may well have produced more questions than answers.

12.5.1. Archaeological literature searches

One of the first places to look for supporting or even contradictory information and ideas is the developing corpus of archaeological literature. It is a poor researcher who does not make considerable efforts to become familiarised with the results of similar projects elsewhere. What evidence was recovered? What conclusions were drawn? Do these agree or conflict with the observations from the site you are involved with?

It is not always easy to track down every publication concerning comparable sites and material. A reasonable way to start is to attempt to locate an article which gathers together the available evidence. Following up references within this article may lead to more detailed discussions of particular aspects of the subject concerned. Synthesized works are not generally satisfactory on their own. As a general rule it is important to get as close to the primary source or original publication as possible. Each step away from the original publication may mean that some information has been filtered out by subsequent writers or presented in a way that was not intended by the original researcher.

Open and regular communication with other researchers and frequent attention to journals are good ways of tracking down useful articles. It can take some effort to stay in touch with what other workers are doing and writing, but it is also a fundamental part of archaeological research and essential for effective interpretation and publication.

12.5.2. Historical and background research

Historical search has already been discussed (Section 8.2). Historical research shares many of the same sources but has different objectives. While historical search is aimed at obtaining locational information from historical documents, historical research has much broader goals.

Documentary research can set archaeological material into an historical frame and provide evidence which contributes to a fuller understanding of its significance. For post-medieval wrecks, for example, one might discover details of the vessel's age, nationality, place of construction, its crew and their origins and cause of her loss. For much older sites significant accounts may exist in the work of ancient authors.

Much effort is often concentrated on using documentary research to establish the identity of a vessel that has been located. Securely linking a set of physical remains with a written record can be very helpful. Details of cargo and route may be available, structural details may be elucidated and material which has not survived on the site may be mentioned in the documents.

One of the most interesting aspects of the linking of remains and records, however, is the extent to which they disagree. Constructional drawings may be available for a vessel, but the physical evidence may not conform to the builder's plan. Such drawings cannot be regarded as a substitute for the careful systematic survey of the surviving structure. Differences between the historical records and the physical evidence does not necessarily mean that the site has been wrongly identified. Such differences may be the result of dockyard working practice, later modifications and repairs or changes in function of the vessel. Clearly then, even apparently comprehensive documentary evidence is only another part of the puzzle.

For many archaeological sites there are no relevant written records. Even when documentary evidence is available it should be regarded as an additional source to be evaluated in terms of its potential biases and limitations as well as the information it can offer.

12.5.3. Where to look

Historical sources are commonly available for post-medieval wrecks, but this is not generally so for the medieval period. The evidence for early maritime history in the earlier medieval period in Europe, for example, is almost exclusively confined to chronicles, law codes, and literary or ecclesiastical works. From about the 11th and 12th century AD onwards there exists an increasing volume of everyday records such as financial accounts, inventories, legal cases and administrative records. To this we can add iconographic evidence such as the depictions of craft on seals, coinage, scratched and painted on walls or carved in wood.

Financial accounts and inventories are of special importance in the study of ship construction, rig and equipment. In recording what was paid for labour and materials for the building or repair of a ship, the accounts can tell us much about the process and nature of ship construction. For example, there are numerous surviving accounts and inventories relating to the 200 or so vessels that passed through the hands of the English Crown between the 1290s and 1490s. These ranged from rowing boats to galleys and large sailing ships, and their records tell us a good deal about the late medieval English shipbuilding industry and the types of ships that it produced, as well as providing evidence of vessels from other countries. 'Technical' records of non-royal ships are much rarer, but since the English and most other governments relied on 'civilian' sources for their shipping, the vessels used in royal naval forces are not too different from those owned by commoners (with the exception of some galleys, specialised warships were rare).

Only three medieval shipbuilding treatises are known to exist; all are Italian and date to the 15th century AD. Generally they were sets of traditional solutions regarding ship construction and rig rather than works of design theory.

Most of the wrecks that have been found around British shores are of post-medieval date, and many can be put into the following categories:

    i. Warships,

    ii. East Indiamen,

    iii. Ocean-going ships,

    iv. Local craft of inland or coastal waters.

The documentary evidence for some (*e.g.* classes i. and ii.) will be better than for others (*e.g.* iv.). However, when available, the combination of historical and archaeological evidence provides an extremely powerful approach for attempts at understanding the past through the interpretation of physical remains.

12.5.4. Ethnology

A significant body of information has been collected by scientists studying the organisation and material cultures of other societies. Many useful ideas in terms of interpreting finds and distributions of material from sites can be found in observing the activities of peoples who continue to use similar materials. Of course there are problems involved in, for example, studying a contemporary fishing community in order to aid in the interpretation of potentially similar prehistoric societies. Different peoples may have different ways of using similar objects. Items of great significance in one area and period may be regarded as mundane elsewhere in other times.

The limitations and difficulties of using such evidence must be clearly appreciated. However, in terms of investigating aspects of function and the manufacture of complex artefacts (such as boats and ships), the ethnological record is invaluable when exploited carefully. Ethnological evidence can also be very closely linked to experimental archaeology.

12.5.5. Experimental archaeology

Material on archaeological sites can be studied and understood at a number of levels – as a part of the site, as a part of a functional assemblage within the site, and as an object in its own right which can provide information about the technology available to the society which made it. However, archaeological evidence is rarely complete. Objects can be broken and distorted, and they may be found in association with other objects and material which have no relevance to the way they were actually used. The evidence of the technology used in the object's construction may be hidden by other features, or may simply be too complex to be understood through a visual inspection alone. Therefore we need to find ways of investigating these aspects of the evidence.

The phrase, *experimental archaeology*, is often used in a very loose way to describe a wide variety of activities. Projects on land have ranged from attempts to cut down trees using flint axes, to the creation of earthworks which are surveyed and sectioned at regular intervals to examine erosional and site formation processes. One group investigates the equipment of the Imperial Roman Army by making and wearing armour and weapons based on the available archaeological evidence. With regards to nautical matters, several well publicised projects involving the building of a full-scale vessel and the completion of particular voyages have been undertaken. One example of a small-scale project carried out by NAS members and others is the reconstruction of a medieval dug-out boat (see Figure 137).

This field of study is not without significant problems, not least of which is the fact that it is possible to spend very large amounts of money and actually gain very little useful information. Why is this so? Consider the full-scale reconstruction of a vessel.

If researchers intend to build a full-size vessel and to investigate its construction and performance, they are immediately faced

Figure 137. Experimental archaeology: reconstructing a logboat; a) roughing out, b) shaping, c) hollowing, d) testing. (12.5.5.) (Courtesy of D.Goodburn and Marine Archaeological Surveys.)

with a problem. How complete is the evidence on which they are basing their reconstruction? If the primary source of information is the excavated remains of a vessel, this evidence may be fragmentary and distorted, especially for the upper parts of the craft. If the evidence is mainly iconographic, then other problems arise. Did the artists understand what they were drawing? Is the constructional information and scale distorted by perspective? Clearly it pays to look for information from as many sources as possible.

When a design has been decided upon and construction starts, what tools and materials will be used? It may be that using modern materials and tools will affect the way the vessel performs. Also some constructional features may only make sense when the tools and technology used in the original are applied to resolving the problem in hand.

The vessel is now complete and ready to take to the water. Who will sail or row her? Do the necessary skills exist? Sailors get the most out of their vessels by applying experience built up over many generations; to what extent can that human element be recreated? Once the sailing starts, how will the performance be recorded? By casual observation, or by measured criteria which can be compared with other measurements taken elsewhere? Finally, how reliable are the results in the light of all the problems highlighted above?

This is not to suggest that experimental archaeology is a waste of time. It certainly is not. It is simply very important to be honest about what is being attempted and what has been achieved and particularly, in the light of the enormous expense involved in some larger projects, whether money is being well spent. Some projects are mainly concerned with the appearance of the vessel or object. The main aim is display and communication. Some projects aim to study construction and therefore pay great attention to the tools and materials used. Such studies may involve only partial or scaled reconstructions. The most ambitious aim is to investigate the performance and function of a vessel through a full-scale reconstruction, although tank testing models and computer modelling are also very significant in this area. All are valid aims and have a contribution to make, even if on occasions it is more in terms of evoking the spirit of past endeavours rather than gathering measured data.

Experimentation is enormously valuable in encouraging us to look more closely at the material we use to make inferences about the past. Often it is the only way to study the complex functional relationship between objects and to approach an understanding of the human element involved in their construction and use. Without an honest assessment of the aims and methods of a project and a detailed, objective record of the results, the usefulness of a reconstruction, whether it be a single object or an entire vessel, will be very limited.

12.6. Producing an Archaeological Archive

The site archive, together with the finds, has to be prepared for presentation at a level suitable for consultation. This should aim to make the evidence comprehensible to those who have never seen the site, but wish to reassess the results, prepare programmes of work on adjacent or contemporary sites, or produce synthetic works on topics that include results from your investigation.

Once the written archive has been compiled, a copy may be deposited with a registered museum, local government record office, archaeological organisation, or other publicly accountable body, for curation in a publicly accessible place. If the results cannot be made available within a reasonable period of time, the director has to reconsider whether the excavation or investigation has been justified. Information that has not been disseminated is no more useful than if it had remained uncollected. In such a case the site will have been as effectively lost as if it had been destroyed by dredging or treasure hunting.

The concept of the 'site archive' has been described as containing all the evidence gathered during fieldwork which must be quantified, ordered, indexed and internally consistent (English Heritage 1989). The first objective of the site archive is to maintain the integrity of the primary field record which may contain the following:

i. Original record forms,

ii. Original dive records,

iii. Original on-site photo and plans records,

iv. Site photographs,

v. Site notebooks,

vi. Reports on site surveys: text and illustrations of specialist pre-excavation survey reports (*e.g.* remote sensing, sediment sampling, diver search),

vii. Site drawings: all drawings produced on-site. The drawings will not be inked in or amended in any way after the fieldwork is completed,

viii. All artefacts and ecofacts recovered from the site,

ix. Copies of correspondence relating to fieldwork,

x. Interim report(s): any interim reports whether published or produced for restricted circulation.

To make the final archive readily accessible and usable by other researchers it should also contain:

i. A brief account of the events and personnel of the project with a summary of the results,

ii. A copy of the research design and excavation strategies with an explanation of any changes during the course of the work. This should also include an assessment of the success of the research,

iii. A description of the understanding of the formation of the site, the character of the objects and structure,

iv. An explanation of the archive structure and contents including a breakdown of documents and records present,

v. A copy of the published report.

12.6.1. Storage of the site archive

The nature and value of the site archive is discussed in Section 3.1.5. Since the aim of archaeology is to gather information for the use of future generations it stands to reason that the information has to survive intact. Complete archives can be bulky and contain a wide range of materials from paper to video film, conserved finds and samples. An environment suitable for one may not ensure the survival of another, and if the archive is split between locations for this reason, then very clear records of what is stored where should be kept at each location. Particular attention should be paid to the safety of computerised records stored on disk as part of the archive. Dust, humidity and direct heat will cause severe problems. The requirement of arranging suitable storage space for this corpus of information should be addressed at an early stage. Museums are sometimes willing to store complete site archives but often only when they have had a direct involvement in the project.

Attention should also be paid to the materials used to create and store the archive. Some tissue papers are acidic and will eventually damage artefacts packed in them. Some slide holders can also cause deterioration in transparencies over time although 'archive quality' variants are available. Cine film deteriorates significantly in a short time, but video-tape is currently thought to survive rather better. The problems of ensuring that suitable packing

and mounting media are used should be considered when planning the costs of the project. 'Archive quality' materials are not cheap.

12.7. Writing an Archaeological Report

12.7.1. Purpose

The quality and quantity of scholarly publication, more than anything else, will influence the future direction and value of work in archaeology underwater. The fact that other workers can use your results in their research with confidence will serve to determine the credibility of you, your project and even the sub-discipline of archaeology underwater. Scholarly publication will demonstrate to the relevant authorities that the work was genuinely archaeological.

12.7.2. Popular and scholarly publication

It is important to appreciate the difference between popular and scholarly publication. Glossy 'coffee table' books which tell the story of a project, include a few decorative photographs of artefacts and the odd technical looking diagram for effect are not adequate publications in terms of making archaeological evidence available to other researchers. They certainly do not completely fulfil the fieldworker's obligation to disseminate information. Such volumes have a vital role to play in communicating archaeological discoveries and ideas to the general public and should not be dismissed out of hand. However, they should also be recognised for what they are and no more. Projects which present such books as a final publication rather than a preliminary communication lay themselves open to criticism.

This is not to imply that reports have to be dry and dull. Although glossy full-page photographs of 'the team' are unlikely to feature prominently, good writing style and presentation are very important. This said, the emphasis in a scholarly publication is on presenting objectively recorded evidence fully and clearly.

A scholarly report will rigidly differentiate between analysis and inference. It will state what was found and describe the evidence as objectively as possible, clearly highlighting any subjective elements. Conclusions drawn from the evidence will be presented as a separate section. Clarity and accuracy are more important than a good story and, although details of the way fieldwork was conducted are important, such information should be presented as an additional way of assessing the validity of the results obtained and conclusions drawn. Details of the logistics of a project will usually only merit a brief appendix, unless they have a major and direct bearing on the nature of the results achieved.

A scholarly publication aims to present evidence in a way that allows other researchers to make their own judgements and draw their own conclusions about a site. This means that it is important to try to avoid being over selective about what is included. Evidence presented should not be limited to that which supports the conclusions drawn in the report. Honesty about conflicting evidence is one mark of a good researcher. Evaluating and resolving such conflicts, without distorting the facts or resorting to unsupported speculation, is a fundamental part of archaeological work.

Practical considerations mean that an element of synthesis is inevitable, but the fuller the report, the more useful it will be. Evidence not included can be referenced in the archive and microfiche provides an opportunity for making large amounts of data readily available.

12.7.3. Report preparation

Many people find writing reports, especially for publication, a very difficult experience. The problem is often knowing what to start with, and additional anxiety over grammar

Figure 138. NAS publications provide opportunities to publish archaeological information at various levels. (12.7.2.)

and content often contribute to indefinite postponement of this stage of the investigation. The preparation and correction of manuscripts can be greatly simplified by the formatting flexibility afforded by word processing (Crummy 1987).

a. What sort of report?

Decide what sort of report you are writing: popular account, expedition report, interim statement or full report. Some projects are substantially unpublished except perhaps for brief notices until the appearance of the final report; some issue detailed seasonal interim reports and specialist reports in advance of a final report. An increase in the range of fieldwork has been accompanied by an increase in the size and type of publication. The range extends from leaflets that summarise progress during work, to popular reports aimed at both public and professional, to academic publication either as reports in journals or as complete monographs.

Interim reports, a brief account of the fieldwork and an outline of some of the major results, can serve to inform other workers and gather further information from them. A suitable periodical for an interim report would be the *International Journal of Nautical Archaeology* (*IJNA*) published by Academic Press for the Nautical Archaeology Society. Someone working on a similar project elsewhere may read it and be able to offer assistance or advice. If the final report is likely to take a considerable time to produce, great effort should be made to produce an interim statement.

The key to any report is layout. Draft this before starting to write, paying attention to the need for specialist contributions, and add deadlines to each stage. The layout chosen will not necessarily be the same as used in other reports, but common section topics are related to strategy, methods, results, analysis, and interpretation.

b.   The layout for a site report

The following is an example of the layout for a site report:

i. Summary (about 100 words),

ii. Introduction: the aims of the work, and general description,

iii. The site and its environment: description with plans and maps,

iv. Past work in the area,

v. The research design and the fieldwork strategy including a discussion of their effectiveness,

vi. The structural features: the hull structure (in the case of a wreck) or buildings/ occupational features. Correlations of stratigraphy with features and objects,

vii. The objects, environmental and scientific evidence. This should include description, numerical information, diagrams, tables, plates and scale drawings and discussion of function, parallels, significance and implications,

viii. Discussion of site formation and chronology,

ix. General discussion: assessment of the site in its wider context,

x. Bibliography,

xi. Acknowledgements,

xii. Appendices: supportive specialist reports on specific topics, usually too detailed for inclusion in the main body of text or including numerical data. These must be related to the main text and to each other.

12.7.4.   Guidance for writers

Before you start writing make sure that you are familiar with the publisher's requirements. Papers submitted to academic journals may have to be to a set format or length so check with the editor, or look for the 'notes for contributors' in previous issues. It is often best to write to the editor with a brief summary of the report before it is submitted. In addition to notes for contributors, it is often worthwhile consulting one of the current guidelines to manuscript format such as that published by the Council for British Archaeology (Megaw 1979) or for the American Journal of Archaeology. If you are worried about your grammar and syntax, you can always ask someone more skilled in this field to read or advise. You should not let it put you off producing a report.

Complete the manuscript, and offer it to journals that cover the appropriate region, period or speciality. You will then be in a position to apply for grants, should any be required.

a.   Informative titles

One responsibility an author has is to ensure that the report title accurately reflects the type of site or range of occupation discussed in the article.

A cardinal rule is to assume that the reader has no prior knowledge of the site or project. A title such as 'Port Augusta 1983-5' may mean little to other archaeologists unfamiliar with the country or period, or subject of the project. Geographical references should be explicit: for example, 'off Penzance (Cornwall, UK)' rather than 'off Penzance'. A date for the site, however approximate and tentative, will help readers identify sites relevant to their period interest. Try to indicate the type of investigation being summarised or described, and whether the report is a preliminary account, one of a series, or final report.

b. Appropriate acknowledgements

Many people will have worked very hard to bring the project to completion. A public acknowledgement may be the only reward that they receive. It is a common practice to acknowledge not only individuals and institutions that have provided assistance in fieldwork and report writing, but also those who have allowed the project to take place. All unpublished information such as comparable finds from similar sites should be sourced and due acknowledgement made (either as a footnote, or 'personal communication').

c. Acknowledging specialist contributions

Establish at an early stage the form in which the specialist input is going to be presented and credited. Is a separate written report going to be submitted by the specialist for inclusion in the report and archive, or is information from the specialist report going to be integrated into the main text? The specialist concerned may have strong views on the subject so do not take anything for granted. Certainly, any input of this kind must be clearly and fully acknowledged. If information provided by a specialist is to be integrated into the main text, then the source of the information must be made clear. Equally, great care must be taken in editing major contributions for publication. A slight change in wording may alter the meaning of a sentence dramatically, especially where a complex technical discussion is concerned. Therefore, consult as fully as possible with the author concerned and be as accommodating as possible without allowing unnecessary wordiness.

d. Bibliographies

Restrict a bibliography to material cited in the report. The text should include reference to previous or immediately forthcoming reports of genuine significance arising from the project in question. Inclusion of secondary publications (such as conference notices and news items) may obscure the more important publications.

e. Referencing

Most archaeological journals, including *The International Journal of Nautical Archaeology and Underwater Exploration* (*IJNA*), now use the 'Harvard' system for referencing. The reference will appear in the text as the author's family name followed by the year of publication and where relevant the page number, all in parentheses (brackets). The bibliography may then be laid out as in this publication, although often without the International Standard Book Number (ISBN). We have included it (where known) as this unique number is increasingly used for computerised book searching in libraries and bookshops. The coded information includes the language of the publication, the trading name of the publisher, and the publisher's number for the publication.

f. Illustrations

Some of the factors which must be considered when planning illustrative material in the publication are as follows:

i. What is the illustration going to contribute to the report? Is it to emphasise a point or provide material for comparison with other sites? The illustrations which are most informative and useful in terms of comparisons with other deposits may not be the most attractive.

ii. Just as text can be either descriptive or interpretive, so can line drawings (Section 12.2.8 c.). Descriptive plans depict artefactual and non-artefactual features in their observed archaeological associations without any overlain reconstruction of the structure. An interpretive plan attempts reconstruction by phase, or event.

iii. Include as many interpretive illustrations as are required to communicate your ideas. Do not, however, include them at the expense of record drawings and always identify them as interpretive in the caption and text.

iv. What size must the final drawing be, and what size must it therefore be drawn to allow for reduction? It is useful to keep a common reduction factor in mind for as many drawings as possible (1:4 is common for pottery).

v. If the figure is a composite one involving pasting up onto a board, try and keep it to a transportable size.

vi. Has the appropriate scale been drawn in or accurate dimensions indicated?

vii. When mounted, are all the figures the right way round?

viii. Has the desired degree of reduction and top of the figure been indicated on the back?

12.8. Suggested Reading

a. the drawn record of archaeological material

Addington, L.R.
    1986   *Lithic illustration: Drawing flaked stone artifacts for publication.* Prehistoric Archaeology and Ecology Series, University of Chicago Press.
Adkins, L. and R.A.
    1989   *Archaeological Illustration.* Cambridge, ISBN 0-54-35478-1.
Blake, H. and Davey, P.
    1983   *Guidelines for the Processing and Publication of Medieval Pottery from Excavations.* Department of the Environment Occasional Paper No.5.
Bryant, R.
    n.d.   *Drawing for microfiche publication.* Association of Archaeological Illustrators and Surveyors Technical Paper 7.
Council for British Archaeology
    n.d.   *Manual on the preparation of material for microfiche publication.* London.

Goubitz, O.
    1987   Calceology: a new hobby: the drawing and recording of archaeological footwear. In Friendship-Taylor, D.E. Swann, J.M. and Thomas, S. (eds.), *Recent research in archaeological footwear.* Association of Archaeological Illustrators and Surveyors Technical paper 8, 1-28.
Green, C.
    n.d.   *Drawing ancient pottery for publication.* Association of Archaeological Illustrators and Surveyors Technical Paper 2.
Green, J.
    1989   *Marine Archaeology: A Technical Handbook.* London, ISBN 0-12-298630-X.
Griffiths, N., Jenner, A. and Wilson, C.
    1990   *Drawing Archaeological Finds, A Handbook.* London, ISBN 1-87312-00-X.
Maney, A.S.
    n.d.   *The preparation of archaeological illustration for reproduction.* Association of Archaeological Illustrators and Surveyors Technical Paper 1.

b. drawing guns

Brown, R.R., and Smith, R.D.
    1988   Guns from the sea. *IJNA* 17.1
Roth, R.
    1989   A proposed standard in the reporting of historic artillery. *IJNA* 18.3: 191-202.
Smith, R.D.
    1988   Towards a new typology for wrought iron ordnance. *IJNA* 17.1: 5-16.

c. drawn records of timbers

Coles, J.M.
    1990   *Waterlogged Wood.* English Heritage, London, ISBN 1-85074-335-5.
Marsden, P.
    1991   Recording ancient ships. In Coles, J.M. and D.M. Goodburn (eds.), *Wet Site Excavation and Survey. Conf. Proc., Museum of London, October 1990.* WARP Occasional Paper No.5, ISSN 0950-8244.

271

d. presenting synthesised information

Barto Arnold III, J.
　1982　Archaeological applications of computer graphics. In Schiffer, M.B. (ed), *Advances in archaeological method and theory* 5: 179-216.

Blakely, J.A., and Bennett, W.J. (eds)
　1989　Analysis and Publication of Ceramics. In *The Computer Data-Base in Archaeology*. British Archaeological Reports S551, ISBN 0-86054-698-5.

Teske, M.
　1989　*Processing and Graphic Presentation of the SHARPS data from the 1989 Dokos excavation.* Hellenic Institute of Marine Archaeology, Enalia, 1.

e. interpretation and analysis

Anderson, A.
　1984　*Interpreting Pottery.* London.

Binford, L.R.
　1983　*In Pursuit of the Past.* Thames and Hudson, London. ISBN 0-500-27494-0.

Bradley, R.
　1990　*The Passage of Arms.* Cambridge, ISBN 0-521-38446-X.

Flannery, K. V. (ed)
　1976　*The Early Mesoamerican Village.* Academic Press, New York.

Hodder, I.
　1987　*Reading the Past.* Cambridge, ISBN 0-521-32743-1.

Peacock, D., and Williams, D.
　1986　*Amphorae and the Roman Economy.* London.

Renfrew, C., and Bahn, P.
　1991　*Archaeology: Theories, methods and practice.* Thames and Hudson, London. ISBN 0-500-27605-6.

Schofield, J. (ed)
　1991　*Interpreting Artefact Scatters: Contributions to Ploughzone Archaeology.* Oxford, ISBN 0-946897-25-5.

Steffy, J.R.
　1994　*Wooden Ship Building and Interpretation of Shipwrecks.* Texas A & M University Press, College Station. ISBN 0-890096-552-8.

f. historical and background research

Friel, I.
　1983　Documentary sources and the medieval ship: some aspects of the evidence. *IJNA* 12.1: 41-62.

Lyon, D.J.
　1974　Documentary sources for the archaeological diver. Ship plans at the National Maritime Museum. *IJNA* 3.1: 3-19.

Mathias P., and Pearsall, A.W.H. (eds)
　1971　*Shipping: a survey of historical records.* Newton Abbot.

Platt, C.P.S.
　1969　*Medieval archaeology in England. A guide to the historical sources.* Pinhorns.

g. ethnology

Filgueiras, O.L.
　1988　*Local Boats. Fourth International Symposium on Boat and Ship Archaeology, Parts i-ii.* British Archaeological Reports International Series No 438(i-ii), Oxford, ISBN 0-86054-566-0.

Greenhill, B.
　1976　*Archaeology of the Boat: A new introductory study.* London, ISBN 0-7136-1645-8.

Hornell, J.
　1970　*Water Transport: origins and early evolution.* Newton Abbot, ISBN 0-7153-4860-4.

McGrail, S. (ed)
　1984　*Aspects of Maritime Archaeology and Ethnology.* London, ISBN 0-905555-740.

McKee, E.
　1983　*Working Boats of Britain: their shape and purpose.* London, ISBN 0-85177-277-3.

h. experimental archaeology

Coates, J. F. and Morrison, J. S.
1986 *The Athenian Trireme: The history and reconstruction of an ancient Greek warship.* Cambridge, ISBN-0-521-31100-4.

Coates, J. F., Platis, S.K., and Shaw, J.T.
1990 *The Trireme Trials 1988: report on the Anglo-Hellenic Sea Trials of Olympias.* Oxford, ISBN 0-946897-21-2.

Coles, J.
1979 *Experimental Archaeology.* Cambridge.

McGrail, S. (ed)
1977 *Sources and techniques in boat archaeology.* British Archaeological Reports Supplementary Series 29, ISBN 0-904531-82-1

McGrail, S.
1974 *The building and trials of the replica of an ancient boat: The Gokstad Faering. Part I: Building the replica.* Maritime Monographs and Reports No. 11, National Maritime Museum Greenwich, London.

Vinner, M., and Pederson, O. C. (eds)
1986 *Sailing into the past.* The Viking Ship Museum, Roskilde, ISBN 87-85180-11-4.

i. archive

Tyers, P. and Vince, A.G.
1983 *Pottery archive users' handbook.* Museum of London.

Walker, K.
1990 *Guidelines for the preparation of excavation archives for long-term storage.* UKIC Archaeology Section, London, ISBN 1-871656-06-0.

j. writing an archaeological report

Crummy, P.
1987 *Reducing publication costs.* Institute of Field Archaeologists Technical Paper No 6, Birmingham, ISBN 0-948393-05-2.

English Heritage
1989 *The management of archaeological projects.* English Heritage, London, ISBN 1-85074-246-4.

Megaw, J.V.S. (ed.)
1979 *Signposts for archaeological publication: a guide to good practice in the presentation and printing of archaeological periodicals and monographs.* Council for British Archaeology, London.

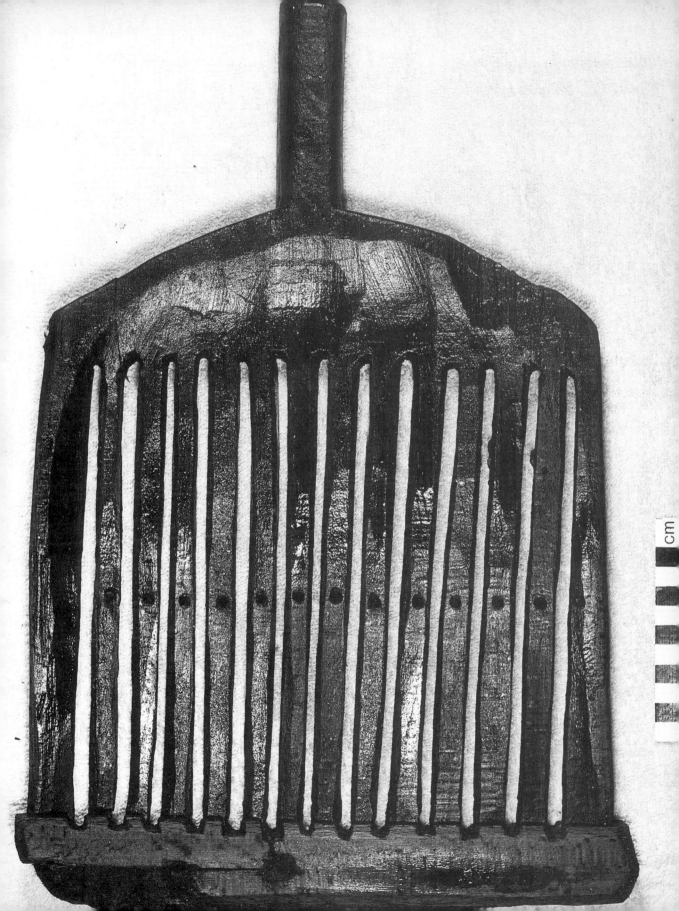

13. Presenting and Publicising Archaeological Work

13.1. Opportunities for Communication

13.2. Suggested Reading

13.1. Opportunities for Communication

a. During a project

Preliminary results of project work can be publicised while research is continuing. This can raise awareness amongst other researchers and may help in attracting sponsors and other forms of support. In Section 12.7.3 interim publications have been mentioned but there are many other ways of communicating results and information which do not oblige researchers to commit themselves to definitive statements before the work is finished.

b. At the end of a project

By the time a project has been seen through to publication a considerable amount of time and effort will have been expended. The archaeological community should be aware and appreciative of your efforts but they are in fact only a small fraction of those potentially interested in the past. Archaeological results and ideas need to be communicated to a wider audience than just fellow researchers.

It is important to have a clear idea of the aim of the presentation. Is it to inform or to enthuse? Ideally, these will be combined but presenting a lot of facts will not always be suitable. Generating support for a project, or archaeology in general, may be better achieved by an entertaining and wide ranging approach rather than an academic lecture.

13.1.1. Conferences

Conferences occur in a wide range of forms, from major international events to local seminars. Speaking at a conference provides researchers with the opportunity to present their work to a group of people with similar interests. Some might have constructive comments to make, others may be able to provide references or examples of which you were not aware. All of them will go away knowing that you are involved in that particular area of research.

The same considerations apply when you are a member of the audience. Not only will you find out who is doing what but you will have a chance to meet the people concerned. Discussions face to face can often achieve much more than written communications. International conferences are particularly valuable in this respect, offering many opportunities to meet fellow researchers who would normally be contactable only by letter or perhaps telephone.

Some conferences publish proceedings. A paper presented at a conference is not expected to be a definitive and final statement about a project. Therefore, not having completed research to final publication standard should not prevent you from offering a paper for publication in this form. Some of the most interesting papers are those which take a discursive approach rather than consisting of a bald listing of facts.

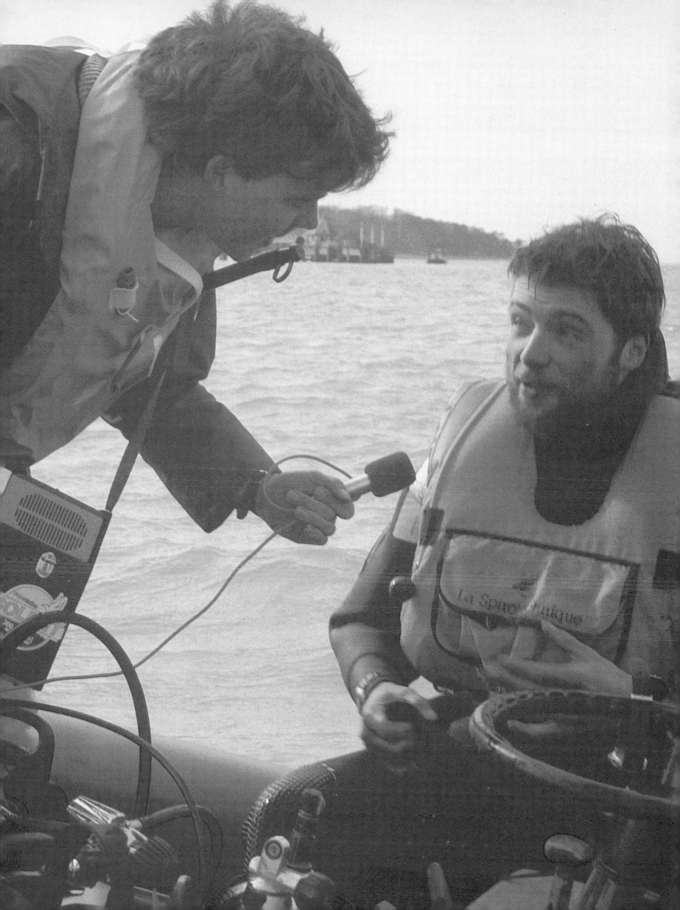

13.1.2. Talks and informal presentations

There are many opportunities for communicating through informal talks and seminars. At a local level, presenting project work to diving clubs can be very productive. They may know of significant sites in the area, and your presentation might convince them to approach these sites in a responsible, archaeological manner. Perhaps some members of the club might want to become involved in archaeology as a result of hearing you talk. Local archaeological societies will also be glad to hear about what you have done and may also provide a source of help for future field work or post-fieldwork processing of information.

Clearly, the form that a presentation to a local society will take will be very different to a paper presented at an academic conference. It might be more appropriate to adopt a more descriptive approach but good visual aids are important for all types of audience.

13.1.3. Displays

Organising a display of project work is another effective way of reaching a wide range of audiences. Such displays can range from large budget exhibitions produced by a professional designer, to presentations prepared entirely by team members. Venues for displays include major museums, the foyer of a sponsor's premises or the local church hall, and the planning timescales will vary from years to weeks. A wide range of material can be used effectively. Static displays can involve photographic and drawn material, text and interpretive illustrations. Video footage can either add interest as part of a display or form an easily distributed and attractive presentation in its own right.

If archaeological material is going to be displayed, careful attention must be paid to questions such as security, the extent to which the environment can be controlled and whether the material concerned is robust enough to be transported and exhibited.

Unconserved material is rarely suitable for display due to its potential instability and the need for a carefully controlled environment. Much conserved material will also require a controlled display environment. This may be available in a museum setting but not always in a mobile exhibition. Some displays involve allowing visitors to handle archaeological material, and there is no doubt that this can be very rewarding, especially for children and those with impaired sight. However, it is clearly important to select the material to be subjected to this treatment very carefully. Most archaeological material may not be appropriate, and certainly no unrecorded or unconserved material should be put at risk in this way.

Displays of information gathered from project work are often very popular with local people in the area of the site. Such displays are not only good in terms of informing local people; they can often encourage them to be concerned with the well-being of the site and watch for any destructive activities. The potential returns for a little effort are considerable.

Displays of project work can be a very useful focal point for fund-raising activities. Current sponsor's names can be prominently displayed and potential sponsors may be attracted by a dynamic and attractive presentation. You will be trying to convince them that they should support you by showing that you are serious about the work. You will also be trying to demonstrate that they will receive good publicity. An attractive, informative display that will be seen in a variety of locations may be very effective in achieving this.

13.1.4. Television, radio and newspapers

The media can provide many opportunities for communication with a very large and varied audience. Even small scale coverage is useful because the regional and national media often pick up stories orignally covered locally. However, although press coverage can be very useful in publicity terms, it can also be very unpredictable. The treatment of a story which a journalist feels will be suitable for publication may differ greatly from your own. The following points are some of those which should be borne in mind:

i. Will involving the press help you?

ii. News is crude – journalists will simplify the story, for example, 'could be' changing to 'is'. Accept journalism or avoid it.

iii. In Britain, news about archaeology is still usually presented in one of a limited number of ways: ritual (*e.g.* druids), King Arthur, human sacrifice/cannibalism, the oldest, the biggest, the best (more important than ...) and, of course, treasure. If you want to avoid these give the journalist another angle.

iv. 'Off the record' is taken to mean the information can be used but is not attributable.

v. Do not be rushed into answering journalists' questions. Call them back when you have considered your response.

vi. Try to get as much control as possible (but remember even the journalist does not have final control over what is printed). Review the journalist's record of the interview. Check quotations. Discuss the journalist's view of the story and how it will be presented. Is it a feature article or a news item? Check who else they are talking to.

a. Drafting a press release

Local television, radio and newspapers are always looking for good stories. They will recognise that archaeological projects underwater can provide interesting news if they are presented to them properly. Journalists are busy chasing other stories so do not wait for them to come to you. A well written press release will remind the media that the project exists, highlight significant events and provide them with sufficient facts to produce a piece easily and quickly. If you help them they are more likely to be supportive and treat your project in a way which is acceptable to you. Bear in mind the following when drafting a press release:

i. Be aware of what makes news. Interesting elements of news include discoveries, pictures (especially with people in them), objects, conflicts or crisis and links with local history. The local media are likely to be supportive of long running stories with the opportunities for updates.

ii. Newspaper articles are written with all the important points in the first paragraph. These are then repeated and enlarged upon in the rest of the article. Reflect this style in your press release.

iii. Keep the press release short and simple. Avoid technical language and overlong supporting detail. Be ruthless about short sentences and paragraphs.

iv. Assume no prior knowledge of the subject. It is a challenge to explain everything while keeping within point iii.

v. The press release can be supported by background notes. Strike a balance between keeping the journalists informed of the background and keeping it short enough so it will actually be read.

vi. Establish contact with the News Editor and follow up your press releases with phone calls.

13.1.5. Education

An obligation to communicate the results of research involves addressing all levels of society, including the archaeologists of the future. School children are unlikely to be able to benefit directly from academic publications and presentations aimed at informing fellow researchers or even interested amateur divers. However, they will benefit from learning about the past.

To present information to a younger audience in an effective manner can often require a lot of additional effort. The whole style and content of your display or talk may have to be modified and yet still convey the essential ideas of archaeology and the results of your work; no mean task when you are already busy. It is obviously of benefit to generate an awareness of the remains of the past in schoolchildren. Discovering about

279

the past can be both fun and educational. It may offer a future career or just an area of interest for them but it will certainly be good for the discipline; an informed public will be more sympathetic to the work of making the most of our heritage.

Research without communication at every level is of very limited use. Similarly, there is little point in complaining about lack of funding if great effort is not put into explaining to the public and Governments why the funding is required.

You have done the work, now get out there and tell them about it.

13.2.   Suggested Reading

Adkins, L., and R.A.
> 1990   *Talking Archaeology: a handbook for lecturers and organizers.* Practical Handbooks in Archaeology No.9, Council for British Archaeology, ISBN 0-906780-87-X.

Corbishley, M. J.
> 1983   *Archaeological Resources Handbook for Teachers.* Council for British Archaeology, ISBN 0-906780-33-0.

14. Bibliography

Where available the ISBN number has been quoted as these are increasingly used by libraries and book stores as unique identifying numbers for books.

Ackroyd, N. and Lorimer, R.
　1990　*Global Navigation: A GPS user's guide.* London. ISBN 1-85044-232-0.

Adams, J.
　1985a　Excavation strategies and techniques. In Gawronski, J. (ed), *Amsterdam Project. Annual report of the VOC-Ship 'Amsterdam' Foundation 1985.* Amsterdam. ISBN 90-71690-01-6.

　1985b　Sea Venture, a second interim report, part 1. *IJNA,* 14.4: 275-299.

　1986　Survey and recording. In Gawronski, J.H.G. (ed), *Annual report of the VOC-Ship Amsterdam Foundation 1985*: 19-21, Amsterdam. ISBN 90-71690-01-6.

Adams, J., van Holk, A.F.L. and Maarleveld, T.J.
　1990　*Dredgers and archaeology: ship finds from the Slufter.* Ministerie van Welzijn, Volksgezondheid En Cultuur, Archaeologie onder water, Rotterdam ISBN 90-800467-1-X.

Addington, L.R.
　1986　*Lithic illustration: Drawing flaked stone artifacts for publication.* Prehistoric Archaeology and Ecology series, University of Chicago Press.

Adkins, L. and R.A.
　1983　*The Handbook of British Archaeology.* London. ISBN 0-333-34843-5.

　1989　*Archaeological Illustration.* Cambridge. ISBN 0-54-35478-1.

Aitken, M.J.
　1990　*Science-Based Dating in Archaeology.* London. ISBN 0-582-05498-2.

Altes, A.K.
　1976　Submarine Antiquities: A Legal Labyrinth. *Syracuse Journal of International Law and Commerce* 4,1.

Anderson, A.
　1984　*Interpreting Pottery.* London.

Anderson, R. K.
    1988   *Guidelines For Recording Historic Ships*. National Park Service, U.S. Department of the Interior, Washington D.C.

Aston, M.
    1985   *Interpreting the Landscape: landscape archaeology in local studies*. London. ISBN 0-7134-3649-2.

Atkinson, K., Duncan, A. and Green,J.
    1988   The Application of a least squares adjustment program to underwater survey. *IJNA*,17.2:119-131.

Baker, P.E. and Green, J.N.
    1976   Recording techniques used during the excavation of the 'Batavia'. *IJNA* 5.2: 143-158.

Baker, P.E. and Henderson, G.
    1979   James Matthews excavation. A second interim report. *IJNA* 8.3: 225-244.

Bannister, A. and Raymond, S.
    1984   *Surveying*. London. ISBN 0-582-98874-8.

Barker, P.
    1977   *The Techniques of Archaeological Excavation*. London. ISBN 0-7134-2739-6.

    1986   *Understanding Archaeological Excavation*. London. ISBN 0-7134-3632-8.

Barto Arnold III, J.
    1981   An Airborne Magnetometer Survey for Shipwrecks and Associated Underwater Test Excavations. In Cockrell, W.A. (ed), *In the Realms of Gold, Proceedings of the 10th Conference on Underwater Archaeology*. San Marino, California, USA.

    1982   Archaeological applications of computer graphics. In Schitter, M.B. (ed), *Advances in archaeological method and theory* 5, 179-216.

    1981   Remote Sensing in Underwater Archaeology. *IJNA*10.1: 51-62.

Bass, G.F.
    1990   After the Diving is Over. In Carrell, T.L. (ed), *Underwater Archaeology Proceedings of the Society for Historical Archaeology Conference*, Tucson, Arizona.

Battarbee, R.W.
    1988   The use of diatom analysis in archaeology: a review. *Journal of Archaeological Science*, 15: 621-644.

Bayliss, M., Short, D. and Bax, M.
    1988   *Underwater Inspection*. Plymouth, UK. ISBN 0-419-13540-5.

Berry, A.Q. and I.W. Brown, (eds.)
1994 *Erosion on Archaeological Earthworks: Its Prevention, Control and Repair.* Clwyd County Council, Mold. ISBN 0-900121-57-2.

Bettess, F.
1984 *Surveying For Archaeologists.* Durham. ISBN 0-900926-50-3.

Blackmore, H. L.
1976 *The Armouries of the Tower of London, vol 1, Ordnance.* Her Majesty's Stationery Office, London.

Blake, H. and Davey, P.
1983 *Guidelines for the Processing and Publication of Medieval Pottery from Excavations.* Department of the Environment Occasional Paper No.5.

Blakely, J.A. and Bennett, W.J. (eds)
1989 Analysis and Publication of Ceramics. In *The Computer Data-Base in Archaeology.* British Archaeological Reports S551. ISBN 0-86054-698-5.

Botma, H.C. and Maarleveld, T.J.
1987 Underwater heightmeter: A new handheld precision instrument for elevation measuring in underwater surveying. *IJNA* 16.2: 87-94.

Bradley, R.
1990 *The Passage of Arms.* Cambridge. ISBN 0-521-38446-X.

Breiner, S.
1975 *Marine Magnetic Search.* Geometrics Technical Report No.7, Sunnyvale, California.

British Sub Aqua Club
1987 *Sport Diving.* London.

1987 *Safety and Rescue for Divers.* London. ISBN 0-09-163831-3.

1986 *Seamanship for Divers.* London. ISBN 0-09-166291-5.

Brothwell, D.
1981 *Digging up Bones.* Oxford. ISBN 0198585101.

Brouwer, N.J.
1993 *International Register of Historic Ships.* New edn. Oswestry. ISBN 0-904614-46-8.

Brown, R.R. and Smith, R.D.
1988 Guns from the sea. *IJNA* 17.1.

Brown, R., Bump, H., and Muncher, A.
1988 An in situ method for determining the decomposition rates of shipwrecks. *IJNA* 17.2: 143-146.

Bryant, R.
  n.d.   *Drawing for microfiche publication.* Association of Archaeological Illustrators and
          Surveyors Technical Paper 7.

Buglass, J. and Rackham, J.
  1991   Environmental Sampling on Wet Sites. In Coles, J.M., and Goodburn, D.M. (eds),
          Wet Site Excavation and Survey. WARP Occasional Paper No. 5, Exeter, ISSN
          0950-8224.

Carpenter, A.C.
  1993   *Cannon: The Conservation, Reconstruction and Preservation of Historic Artillery.*
          Halsgrove Press, Tiverton. ISBN 1-874-44802-7.

Carpenter, J.
  1983   The conservation of shipwreck artefacts in the field. In Jeffrey, W. and Amess,
          J. (ed), *Proc. of the Second Southern Hemisphere Conference on Maritime
          Archaeology.*

Carter, J., Covill, J., Stevens, W. and Grenier, R.
  1987   A Feasibility Study of a Diver Operated Computer and Data Acquisition System
          Designed for Underwater Archaeology. In Albright, A.B. (ed), *Underwater
          Archaeology Proceedings of the Society of Historical Archaeology Conference,*
          Savannah.

Caruna, A.J.
  1994   *The History of English Sea Ordnance Volume 1: The age of evolution, 1523-1715.*
          Jean Boudriot Publications, Rotherfield, ISBN 0-948864-20-6.

Cederlund, C-O.
  1980   Systematic registration of older sinkings and wrecks in Swedish waters. *IJNA*
          9.2: 95-103.

Chaplin, R.E.
  1971   *The Study of Animal Bones from Archaeological Sites.* Seminar Press.

Cipolla, C. M
  1965   *Guns and Sails in the Early Phase of European Expansion 1400-1700.* London.

Clark, A.
  1987   *Scientific Dating Techniques.* Institute of Field Archaeologists, Technical Paper
          No.5, Birmingham. ISBN 0948393041.

Clarke, D. L.
  1978   *Analytical Archaeology.* Bristol. ISBN 0-416-85460-5.

Clarke, R.W. and Blackshaw, S.M. (eds)

1982   *Conservation of iron.* National Maritime Museum Monographs and Reports No 53, Greenwich.

Cleere, H.
1989   *Archaeological Heritage Management In The Modern World.* London. ISBN 0-04-445028-1.

Clydesdale, A.
1990   *Chemicals in Conservation, a guide to possible hazards and safe use.* 2nd Edition, SSCR.

Coates, J. F. and Morrison, J. S.
1986   *The Athenian Trireme: The history and reconstruction of an ancient Greek warship.* Cambridge. ISBN-0-521-31100-4.

Coates, J. F., Platis, S.K. and Shaw, J.T.
1990   *The Trireme Trials 1988: report on the Anglo-Hellenic Sea Trials of Olympias.* Oxford. ISBN 0-946897-21-2.

Coles, J.
1979   *Experimental Archaeology.* Cambridge.

Coles, J.M.
1990   *Waterlogged Wood.* English Heritage, London. ISBN 1-85074-335-5.

Coles, J.M., Coles, B.J. and Dobson, M.J.
1990   *Waterlogged Wood.* WARP Occasional Paper No.3, Exeter, ISSN 0950-8244.

Coles, J.M. and Lawson, A.J. (eds)
1987   *European Wetlands in Prehistory.* Oxford. ISBN 0-19-813406-1.

Conlon, V. M.
1973   *Camera Techniques In Archaeology.* London. ISBN 0-212-98422-5.

Corbishley, M. J.
1983   *Archaeological Resources Handbook for Teachers.* Council for British Archaeology. ISBN 0-906780-33-0.

Council for British Archaeology
        Manual on the preparation of material for microfiche publication. London.

Council of Europe
1978   *The Underwater Cultural Heritage.* Doc. 4200 (Rapporteur J.Roper), Strasbourg.

Cronyn, J.M.
1990   *The Elements of Archaeological Conservation.* London. ISBN 0-415-01206-6

Crummy, P.
1987   *Reducing publication costs.* Institute of Field Archaeologists Technical Paper No 6, Birmingham. ISBN 0-948393-05-2.

Cycon, D.E.
    1985   Legal and Regulatory Issues in Marine Archaeology. *Oceanus* 28, 1: 78-84.

Daley, T.W. and L.D. Murdock
    1992   Excavating and raising artifacts from a marine environment. In Payton, R. (ed.) *Retrieval of Objects from Archaeological Sites*. Archetype Publications, London: 133-146. ISBN 1-873132-30-1.

Daniel, G.
    1975   *A Hundred and Fifty Years of Archaeology*. London. ISBN 0-7156-1069-4.

Dean, M.
    1988   *Guidelines on Acceptable Standards in Underwater Archaeology*. St Andrews, Fife, Scotland. ISBN 1-871170-00-1.

Dimbleby, G.
    1967   *Plants and Archaeology*. London.

Dorrell, P.
    1989   *Photography in Archaeology and Conservation*. Cambridge. ISBN 0521-32797-0.

Dromgoole, S.
    1989   Protection of Historic Wreck: The UK Approach Part I: The Present Legal Framework. *International Journal of Estuarine and Coastal Law*, 4, 1: 26-51.

Dromgoole, S.
    1989   Protection of Historic Wreck: The UK Approach Part II: Towards Reform. *International Journal of Estuarine and Coastal Law*, 4, 2.

Eckstein, D. *et al.*
    1984   *Dendrochronological Dating*. Handbooks for Archaeologists No.2, European Science Foundation, Strasbourg. ISBN 2-903148-39-2.

English Heritage
    1989   *The management of archaeological projects*. English Heritage, London. ISBN 1-85074-246-4.

Evans, J.G.
    1978   *An Introduction to Environmental Archaeology*. St Albans ISBN 0246115955.

Fagan, B.M.
    1978   *In the Beginning: An Introduction to Archaeology*. Boston.

Ferrari, B.J. and Adams, J.
    1990   Biogenic modifications of marine sediments and their influence on archaeological material. *IJNA* 19.2: 139-151.

287

ffoulkes, C.
1937   *The Gunfounders of England.* Cambridge.

Filgueiras, O.L.
1988   *Local Boats. Fourth International Symposium on Boat and Ship Archaeology.* British Archaeological Reports IS 438(i-ii), Oxford. ISBN 0-86054-566-0.

Fisher, D.
1983   *State papers available for research in the South West.* Nautical Archaeology Society, South West Section.

Flannery, K. V. (ed)
1976   *The Early Mesoamerican Village.* Academic Press, New York.

Flemming, N.C.
1971   *Cities in the Sea.* London.

Flemming, N.C. and Max, M.D.
1988   *Code of Practice for Scientific Diving: principles for the safe practice of scientific diving in different environments.* Unesco, Technical Papers in Marine Science No.53, Paris.

Fletcher, J.
1978   *Dendrochronology in Europe. Principles, interpretations and applications to archaeology and history.* British Archaeological Reports IS 51, Oxford.

Friel, I.
1983   Documentary sources and the medieval ship: some aspects of the evidence. *IJNA* 12.1: 41-62.

Fryer, J.G.
1983   A simple system for photogrammetric mapping in shallow water. *Photogrammetric Record,* 11(62): 203-208.

Gamble, J.C., Clark, P.F. and Pagett, R.M. (eds)
1989   *Underwater Association Code of Practice for Scientific Diving.* 4th ed., Underwater Association for Scientific Research Ltd., NERC, London.

Gawronski, J.H.G.
1986   *Amsterdam Project: Annual Report of the VOC-Ship "Amsterdam" Foundation 1985.* Amsterdam. ISBN 90-71690-01-6.

Giangrande, C., Richards, D., Kennet, D., and Adams, J.
1987   Cyprus Underwater Survey, 1983-1984. A Preliminary Report. In *Report of the Department of Antiquitites Cyprus, 1987.* Nicosia, Cyprus.

Gibbins, D.
1990   Analytical approaches in maritime archaeology: a Mediterranean perspective. *Antiquity* 64: 376-89.

Gillespie, R.
  1984   *Radiocarbon User's Handbook.* Oxford University Committee for Archaeology, Monograph no.3. ISBN 0-947816-03-8.

Goodwin, P.
  1987   *The Construction and Fitting of the Sailing Man of War 1650 - 1850.* London. ISBN 0-85177-326-5.

Goodburn, D.M.
  1991   Waterlogged wood and timber as archives of ancient landscapes. In Coles, J.M., and Goodburn, D.M. (eds), *Wet Site Excavation and Survey.* WARP Occasional Paper No. 5, Exeter, ISSN 0950-8224.

Goubitz, O.
  1987   Calceology: a new hobby: the drawing and recording of archaeological footwear. In Friendship-Taylor, D.E. Swann, J.M. and Thomas, S. (eds), *Recent research in archaeological footwear.* Association of Archaeological Illustrators and Surveyors Technical paper 8, 1-28.

Graham, I. and Webb, E. (eds)
  1982   *Computer applications in archaeology 1981* Institute of Archaeology, London.

Green, C.
  n.d.   *Drawing ancient pottery for publication.* Association of Archaeological Illustrators and Surveyors, Technical Paper 2.

Green, J.N.
  1980   The armament from the Batavia. Two composite guns. *IJNA* 9.1: 43-51.

Green, J.
  1990   *Maritime Archaeology: A Technical Handbook.* London. ISBN 0-12-298630-X.

Green, J. and Richards, D.
  1983   Underwater Stereophotogrammetry. In Jeffery, W. and Richards, B. (eds), *Proceedings of the 2nd Southern Hemisphere Conference on Maritime Archaeology.*

Greene, K.
  1995   *Archaeology: An Introduction.* 3rd edn London.

Greener. W.W.
  1881   *The Gun and its Development.* New Orchard Editions Ltd. Reprinted 1988.

Greenhill, B.
  1976   *Archaeology of the Boat: A New Introductory Study.* London ISBN 0819-550027.

Greenhill, B.
  1988   *The Evolution of the Wooden Ship.* London. ISBN 0-7134-3344-2.

Griffiths, N., Jenner, A. and Wilson, C.
1990 *Drawing Archaeological Finds, A Handbook.* Archetype Publications, London. ISBN 1-87312-00-X.

Guilmartin, J.F
1974 *Gunpowder and Galleys.* Cambridge.

Guilmartin, J.F
1982 The cannon of the Batavia and the Sacramento: early modern cannon founding reconsidered. *IJNA* 11.2: 133-144.

Harris, E.C.
1989 *Principles of Archaeological Stratigraphy.* 2nd ed., London. ISBN 012-326651-3.

Health and Safety Executive
1991 *Diving Operations at Work, Guidance on Regulations.* Her Majesty's Stationery Office, London. ISBN 0-11885599-9.

Hinchliffe, J. and Schadla-Hall, R. T. (eds)
1980 *The Past Under the Plough.* Directorate of Ancient Monuments and Historic Buildings, Occasional Paper No. 3, London.

Hodder, I.
1987 *Reading the Past.* Cambridge. ISBN 0-521-32743-1.

Hodges, H.
1971 *Artefacts: an introduction to early materials and technology.* London. ISBN 0-212-35918-5.

Hodgson, J.M. (ed)
1976 *Soil Survey Field Handbook.* Soil Survey Technical Monograph No.5, Harpenden. ISBN 0-904818-40-3.

Hogg, D. F. G.
1970 *Artillery: its Origin, Heyday and Decline.* London.

Hogg A.H.A.
1980 *Surveying for Archaeologists and Other Fieldworkers.* London. 0-85664-767-5.

Hornell, J.
1970 *Water Transport: origins and early evolution.* Newton Abbot. ISBN 0715-348604.

Joint Nautical Archaeology Policy Committee
1989 *Heritage at Sea: Proposals for the better protection of archaeological sites underwater.* National Maritime Museum. ISBN 0-948065-07-9.

Kenchington, T.J. *et al.*
1989 The indispensibility of non-artefactual data in underwater archaeology. In Barto Arnold III, J. (ed),*The Underwater Archaeological Proceedings of the Society for Historical Archaeology Conference*, Baltimore.

290

Kennard, A.N.
1986 *Gunfounding and Gunfounders.* Arms and Armour Press.

Kyriakopoulou, V.
1990 Underwater Surveying with the SHARPS in the 1989 excavation season at Dokos. *Enalia,* 1: 24-26.

Lavery, B.
1987 *The Arming and Fitting of English Ships of War 1600-1815.* London. ISBN 0-85177-451-2.

Leach P.
1994 *The Surveying of Archaeological Sites.* London. 2nd edn ISBN 1873132 35 2.

Lenihan, D.J. (ed)
1987 *Submerged cultural resources study, Isle Royal National Park.* Southwest Cultural Resources Center Professional Paper No.8, New Mexico.

Lenihan, D.J., *et al.*
1981 *The final report of the National Reservoir Inundation Study, Volumes 1 and 2.* United States Department of the Interior, National Park Service, Southwest Cultural Resource Center, Sante Fe, New Mexico.

Lenihan, D.J. (ed)
1989 *Submerged Cultural Resources Study, USS Arizona Memorial and Pearl Harbour National Historic Landmark.* Southwest Cultural Resources Center, Professional Papers No.23, Sante Fe, New Mexico.

Lockery, A.
1985 *Marine archaeology and the diver.* Ontario, Canada. ISBN 0-9692081-0-3.

Lyon, D.J.
1974 Documentary sources for the archaeological diver. Ship plans at the National Maritime Museum. *IJNA* 3.1: 3-19.

MacLeod, I.D.
1982 Formation of Marine Concretions on Copper and its Alloys. *IJNA* 11.4: 267-275.

1987 Conservation of corroded iron artefacts - new methods for on-site preservation and cryogenic deconcreting. *IJNA* 16.1: 49-56.

1989a The application of corrosion science to the management of maritime archaeological sites. *Bulletin of the Australian Institute for Maritime Archaeology* 13 (2): 7-16.

1989b *Conservation of wet wood and metal.* Proceedings of the ICOM Conservation Working group on wet organic archaeological materials and metals. Fremantle, Australia.

291

1989c The electrochemistry and conservation of iron in seawater. *Chemistry in Australia,* July 1989: 227-229.

MacLeod, I.D., *et al.*
1986　The excavation, analysis and conservation of shipwreck sites. In ICCROM, 1986, *Preventive Measures during Excavation and Site Protection.* ICCROM, Rome. ISBN 92-9077-070-8.

Magendans, J.F.C.
1987　The identification of vegetable material: tobacco from the 'Amsterdam'. In J.H.G. Gawronski (ed) *Annual Report of the VOC-Schip "AMSTERDAM" Foundation. 1986* ISBN 90-71690-02-4.

Maloney, E.S.
1978　*Dutton's Navigation and Piloting.* (13th edn). Annapolis. ISBN 0-87021-164-1.

Maney, A.S.
n.d.　*The preparation of archaeological illustration for reproduction.* Association of Archaeological Illustrators and Surveyors Technical Paper 1.

Marsden, P.
1991　Recording ancient ships. In Coles, J.M. and Goodburn, D.M., (eds), *Wet Site Excavation and Survey.* WARP Occasional Paper No.5, ISSN 0950-8244.

Mathias P. and Pearsall, A.W.H. (ed)
1971　*Shipping: a survey of historical records.* Newton Abbot.

McCarthy, M.
1982　A wreck inspection programme as an aid to the co-ordinated management of a large number of wreck sites. *IJNA* 11.1: 47-52.

1986　Protection of Australia's underwater sites. In ICCROM, 1986, *Preventive measures during excavation and site protection.* ICCROM, Rome, 132-145. ISBN-92-9077-070-8.

McGrail, S.
1974　*The building and trials of the replica of an ancient boat: The Gokstad Faering. Part I: Building the replica.* Maritime Monographs and Reports No 11, National Maritime Museum Greenwich, London.

McGrail, S. (ed)
1977　*Sources and techniques in boat archaeology.* British Archaeological Reports, Supplementary Series: 29. ISBN 0-904531-82-1

1984　*Aspects of Maritime Archaeology and Ethnology.* London. ISBN 0-905555-740.

McKee, E.
1983　*Working Boats of Britain: their shape and purpose.* London. ISBN 0-85177-277-3.

Megaw, J.V.S. (ed)
1979   *Signposts for archaeological publication: a guide to good practice in the presentation and printing of archaeological periodicals and monographs.* Council for British Archaeology, London.

Milne, G.
1985   *The Port of Roman London.* London. ISBN 0-7134-4365-0.

Ministry of Defence
1985   *Manual of Map Reading.* HMSO ISBN 0-11-771905-6.

Mook, W.G. and Waterbolk, H.T.
1985   *Radiocarbon Dating.* Handbooks for Archaeologists No.3, European Science Foundation, Strasbourg. ISBN 2-903148-44-9.

293

Morrison, I.
1985   *Landscape with lake dwellings: The crannogs of Scotland.* Edinburgh. ISBN 0-85224-522-X.

Morrison, I.A.
1969   *An inexpensive photogrammetric approach to the reduction of survey time.* Underwater Association Report.

Muckelroy, K.
1977   Historic wreck sites in Britain and their environments. *IJNA* 6.1: 47-57.

Muckelroy, K. (ed)
1980   *Archaeology Underwater: An Atlas of the World's Submerged Sites.* London. ISBN 0-07-043951-6.

Muckelroy, K.
1978   *Maritime Archaeology.* Cambridge. ISBN 0-521-22079-3.

Mueller, J.W. (ed)
1975   *Sampling in Archaeology.* Tucson, Arizona. ISBN 0-8165-0482-2.

Munday, J.
1987   *Naval Cannon.* Shire Album 186, Shire Publications Ltd.

Murdock, L.D. and Daley, T.
1982   Progress report on the use of FMC polysulfide rubber compounds for recording archaeological ships' features in a marine environment. *IJNA* 11.4: 349 -352.

Murphy, L. E.
1990   *8SL 17: Natural site formation processes of a multiple-component underwater site in Florida, Submerged Cultural Resources Special Report.* Southwest Cultural Resources Centre, Sante Fe, New Mexico.

Musées du Chateau des Ducs de Bretagne
  1985   *Archéologie Sous-Marine.* Musees du Chateau des Ducs des Bretagne, Nantes.

Nayling, N.
  1991   Tree-ring dating: sampling, analysis and results. In Coles, J.M., and Goodburn, D.M. (eds), *Wet Site Excavation and Survey.* WARP Occasional Paper No. 5, Exeter, ISSN 0950-8224.

Nayling, N.T.
  1989   *The Archaeological Wood Survey: a review of the potential and problems of waterlogged structural wood.* Ancient Monuments Report 62/89, Ancient Monuments Laboratory, HBMC, London.

O'Keefe, P.J.
  1984   The Law and Nautical Archaeology: An International Survey. In Langley, S.B.M. and Unger, R.W. (eds), *Nautical Archaeology: Progress and Public Responsibility.* British Archaeological Reports, International Series No.220, Oxford. ISBN 0-86054-284-X.

O'Keefe, P.J. and Prott, L.V.
  1984   *Law and the cultural heritage Vol.1: Discovery and Excavation.*

Osborne, P.J.
  1973   Insects in Archaeological Deposits. *Science and Archaeology,* 10, 4-6.

Oxley, I.
  1991   Environmental Sampling Underwater. In Coles, J.M. and Goodburn, D.M. (eds), *Wet Site Excavation and Survey.* WARP Occasional Paper No. 5, Exeter, ISSN 0950-8224.

Padfield, P.
  1973   *Guns At Sea.* London.

Palmer, R.
  1986   *Underwater Expeditions.* Royal Geographical Society, London.

Parker, A. J.
  1981   Stratification and contamination in ancient Mediterranean shipwrecks, *IJNA* 10,4: 309-335.

Parker. G.
  1988   *The Military Revolution.* Cambridge.

Payton, R.
  1987   Conservation of objects from one of the world's oldest shipwrecks: the Ulu Burun, Kas shipwreck, Turkey. In Black, J. (ed), *Recent Advances in the Conservation and Analysis of Artifacts.* Institute of Archaeology, London.

294

Peacock, D. and Williams, D.
1986   *Amphorae and the Roman Economy.* London.

Pearson, C. (ed)
1987   *Conservation of marine archaeological objects.* London. ISBN 0-408-10668-9.

Peterson, H.L.
1969   *Round Shot and Rammers.* New York.

Platt, C.P.S.
1969   *Medieval archaeology in England. a guide to the historical sources.* Pinhorns.

Pugh, J.C.
1975   *Surveying for Field Scientists.* London. ISBN 0-416-075304.

Rebikoff, D.
1972   Precision underwater photo-mosaic techniques for archaeological mapping. *IJNA* 1.: 184-186.

Redknap, M. and Flemming, M.
1985   The Goodwins Archaeological Survey: Towards a Regional Marine Site Register in Britain. *World Archaeology,* 16.3: 312-328.

Renfrew, C., and Bahn, P.
1991   *Archaeology : Theories, methods, and practice.* Thames and Hudson, London. ISBN 0-500-27605-6.

Renfrew, J., Monk, M. and Murphy, P.
1976   *First Aid for Seeds.* Rescue Publication No. 6, Hertford.

Richards, D.G.
1980   Water penetration aerial photography. *IJNA* 9.4 :331-337.

Richards, J.D. and Ryan, N.S.
1985   *Data processing in archaeology.* Cambridge Manuals In Archaeology, Cambridge. ISBN 0-521-25769-7.

Robinson, W.S.
1981   *First Aid for Marine Finds.* Handbooks in Maritime Archaeology No.2, National Maritime Museum, Greenwich. ISBN 0-905555-52-X.

Rodgers, B.A.
1989   The case for biologically induced corrosion at the Yorktown shipwreck archaeological site. *IJNA* 18.4: 335-340.

Rodgers, B.A. and Jensen, J.O.
1990   *Conservation of Water Soaked Material Bibliography.* East Carolina University, North Carolina.

Roth, R.

1989   The Measuring of Cannons. *Journal of Ordnance Society*, Vol. 1 1989.

1989   A proposed standard in the reporting of historic artillery. *IJNA* 18.3:191-202.

Rowlands, P.

1983   *The Underwater Photographers Handbook*. London. ISBN 0-356-09494-4.

Ruggles, C.L.N. and Rahtz, S.P.Q.

1988   *Computer and quantitative methods in archaeology 1987*. British Archaeological Reports IS 393, Oxford.

Rule, N.

1989   Direct Survey Method and its Application Underwater. *IJNA*18.2: 157-162.

Schiffer, M. B.

1987   *Formation processes of the archaeological record*. Albuquerque. ISBN 0-8263-0963-1.

Schofield, J. (ed)

1980   *Site Manual, Part 1: the written record*. London.

Schofield, J. (ed)

1991   *Interpreting Artefact Scatters: Contributions to Ploughzone Archaeology*. Oxford. ISBN 0-946897-25-5.

Schulke, F.

1978   *Underwater Photography for Everybody*. ISBN 0-13-936450-1.

Schurer, P.J. and Linden, R.H.

1984   Results of Sub-bottom Acoustic Survey in a Search for the Tonquin. *IJNA* 13.4: 303-309.

Scollar, J.E.

1975   Transformation of extreme oblique aerial photographs to maps or plans by conventional or means or by computer. In *Aerial Reconnaissance for Archaeology*. CBA Research Report, 12: 52-8.

Shomette, D.G.

1988   New Jersey project: Robots and ultrasonics in underwater archaeological survey. In Delgado, J.P. (ed), *Underwater Archaeology Proceedings of The Society For Historical Archaeology Conference*. Reno, Nevada.

Singley, K.

1988   *The Conservation of Archaeological Artefacts from Freshwater Environments*. Lake Michigan Maritime Museum, South Haven, Michigan.

Smith, R.D.

1988   Towards a new typology for wrought iron ordnance. *IJNA* 17.1: 5-16.

Spence, C. (ed)
    1990   *Archaeological Site Manual.* London. ISBN 0-904818-40-3.

Stewart, J.D.
    1982   Computerising archaeological records – a progress report on the work of the MDA. In *Proceedings Computer Applications in Archaeology Conference*, 4-10, University of Birmingham.

Steffy, J.R.
    1994   *Wooden Ship Building and the Interpretation of Shipwrecks.* Texas A & M University Press, College Station. ISBN 0-89096-552-8.

Stone, D.L.
    1993   *Sailing Ship artifacts of the 19th century.* Underwater Archaeology Society of British Columbia, Vancouver. ISBN 0-9695010-1-3.

Tarlton, K.
    1983   Electronic Navigation and Search Techniques. In Jeffery W. and Amess J. (eds), *Proceedings of the Second Southern Hemisphere Conference on Maritime Archaeology.* ISBN 7234-4668-6.

Teske, M.
    1989   Processing and Graphic Presentation of the SHARPS data from the 1989 Dokos excavation. Hellenic Institute of Marine Archaeology. *Enalia*, 1.

Thomas, C.
    1985   *Explorations of a drowned landscape; archaeology and history of the Isles of Scilly.* London. ISBN 0-7134-4852-0.

Throckmorton, P.
    1990   The World's Worst Investment: The Economics of Treasure Hunting with Real Life Comparisons. In Carrell, T.L. (ed) *Underwater Archaeology Proceedings of the Society for Historical Archaeology Conference.* Tucson, Arizona 1990.

Throckmorton, P. (ed)
    1987   *History From The Sea: Shipwrecks & Archaeology.* London ISBN 085533-614-5.

Throckmorton P. *et al.*
    1969   *Surveying in Underwater Archaeology.* London.

Trigger, B. G.
    1989   *A History of Archaeological Thought.* Cambridge. ISBN 0-521-33818-2.

Tuck, J.A., and Grenier, R.
    1989   *Red Bay, Labrador: World Whaling Capital AD 1550-1600.* St John's, Newfoundland. ISBN 0-929048-00-8.

Tyers, I.
    1989   Dating by tree-ring analysis. In Marsden, P. (ed), A late Saxon logboat from Clapton, London Borough of Hackney. *IJNA* 18.2: 89-111.

297

Tyers, P. and Vince, A.G.
  1983   *Pottery archive users handbook.* Museum of London.

UKIC
  1983   *Packing and Storing of Freshly-Excavated Artifacts from Archaeological Sites.* Conservation Guidelines No.2, United Kingdom Institute for Conservation, Archaeology Section.

UKIC
  1984   *Environmental Standards for the Permanent Storage of Excavated Material from Archaeological Sites.* Conservation Guidelines No.3, United Kingdom Institute for Conservation, Archaeology Section.

UNESCO
  1972   *Underwater Archaeology: a nascent discipline.* UNESCO, Paris.

Upham, N.E.
  1983   *Anchors.* Aylesbury. ISBN 0-85263-636-9.

Vinner, M. and Pederson, O. C. (eds)
  1986   *Sailing into the past.* The Viking Ship Museum, Roskilde. ISBN 87-85180-11-4.

Waddell, P.J.
  1990   Electronic Mapping of Underwater Sites. In Carrell, T.L. (ed), *Underwater Archaeology Proceedings of The Society For Historical Archaeology Conference.* Tucson, Arizona, 57-62.

Walker, K.
  1990   *Guidelines for the preparation of excavation archives for long-term storage.* UKIC Archaeology Section, London. ISBN 1-871656-06-0.

Watkinson, D. (ed)
  1987   *First Aid for Finds.* Rescue/United Kingdom Institute for Conservation, Archaeology Section. ISBN 0-903789-13-2.

Watson, K. and Gale, A.
  1990   Site evaluation for marine sites and monuments records: Yarmouth Roads Wreck investigation. *IJNA.*19.3: 183-192.

Watts, Jnr, G.P.
  1989   The 'sinkentine': a fibreglass shipwreck model to assist in teaching three-dimensional mapping. *IJNA,*18.2: 151-156.

Watts Jnr, G.P.
  1976   Hydraulic Probing: One solution to overburden and environment. *IJNA,*5.4: 76-81.

Westerdhal, C.
  1980   On oral traditions and place names. An introduction to the first stage in the establishment of a register of ancient monuments for the maritime cultural heritage. *IJNA,*9.4: 311-329.

Wheeler, A., and Jones, A. K. G.
    1989   *Fishes*. Cambridge Manual In Archaeology, Cambridge.

Wildesen, L. E.
    1982   The study of impacts on archaeological sites. In, Schiffer, M. B. (ed), *Advances in archaeological method and theory*, Vol 5, 5-96.

Williams, J.C.C.
    1969   *Simple Photogrammetry*. London.

Wilson D.R.
    1982   *Air Photo Interpretation for Archaeologists*. London.

15.   Appendix I

15.1.   Principles of Archaeological Conduct

Archaeological evidence for past human activity is an irreplaceable part of our common heritage. Activities aimed at recovering this information can destroy all traces of the evidence unless it is preserved by adequate recording. Those of us who are involved in archaeology, whether as amateurs or professionals, have a duty to the rest of society to treat this heritage responsibly. Investigations should be conducted in such a way that reliable information is acquired, and the results then made available for others to study.

These objectives should apply to all archaeological work, whether on land or underwater. Adherence to the following principles is a condition of membership of the Nautical Archaeology Society:

i. Nautical Archaeology Society members shall adhere to the highest standards of ethical and responsible behaviour in the conduct of archaeological affairs.

ii. Nautical Archaeology Society members have a responsibility for the conservation of the archaeological heritage.

iii. Nautical Archaeology Society members will conduct their archaeological work in such a way that reliable information about the past may be acquired, and shall ensure that the results are properly recorded.

iv. Nautical Archaeology Society members have a responsibility for making available the results of archaeological work with reasonable dispatch.

16. Appendix II

16.1. The NAS Certification Programme

16.2. Part I: An Introduction to Underwater Archaeology

16.3. Part II: Techniques in Nautical and Underwater Archaeology

16.4. Part III: Underwater Archaeology Field School Modules

16.5. Part IV: Dissertation

16.1. The NAS Certification Programme

16.1.1. Introduction

One of the stated aims of the Nautical Archaeology Society is 'to advance education in nautical archaeology at all levels,' and the NAS has put this into practice by introducing a structured training Programme open to both divers and non-divers. It was designed and developed by archaeologists and sport divers working together, and has proved to be an effective way to learn basic archaeological skills for use underwater.

16.1.2. Administration

The NAS has a full-time Training Officer to organise courses, contribute to the teaching, and develop aspects of the training programme. The training officer is part of the Society's Training Sub committee. This sub-committee, using external assessors where necessary, approves all tutors, lecturers, projects, sites and individual courses before they can be brought into the programme. In this way the standards of all the components of the programme are maintained.

16.1.3. The Programme's Structure

The NAS Certification Programme consists of Parts I – IV which have been designed as a series of components with increasing academic and practical archaeological content. Participants in turn are required to give a gradually increasing commitment as they progress up through the programme. For example, they only have to attend the Part I course but for Part II they have to carry out a small survey and produce a short report.

A brief description and an outline syllabus is given below. The Parts of the programme must be taken sequentially and there is no provision for awarding any Parts in retrospect for previous archaeological experience or qualifications.

A training log book for the entire programme is issued to each participant when they complete Part I (Figure 139). All subsequent certificates, courses, practical experience gained and lecture/conference attendances can then be entered into this log book. Part I courses are often initiated by an individual or group applying to the NAS Training Officer for a course, and a convenient date and venue is then arranged. As the NAS training infrastructure develops, it is hoped to organise courses at set times and locations in advance of individual requests.

16.1.4. The NAS International Programme

The NAS is an international society and a number of Part I courses have been held outside the United Kingdom (*e.g.* India, Ireland, Bermuda, Canada and the USA). The NAS is keen to increase this international dimension to include a greater range of countries running Part I courses and to feature the more advanced levels of the programme. A programme similar to the CMAS system of accrediting diver training is in operation where the Parts I–IV of the NAS Certification Programme are designated as NAS International Stars, 1 – 4.

It would obviously be an advantage for those running training programmes in different countries to have had a common basic standard for their courses. This would enable the value of any certificate or accreditation to be appreciated both by site directors and participants wishing to assist on projects outside of their own country.

16.2. Part I: An Introduction to Underwater Archaeology

Part I is a preliminary course aimed at introducing nautical archaeological and underwater archaeological techniques to divers and non-divers, and to promote their interest in the subject. It provides a broadly-based view of the subject by covering a wide range of topics.

The objectives of the course are that, at the end of Part I, participants should:

i. have been introduced to the basic principles and aims of archaeology;

ii. appreciate the need for the recording, protection and preservation of the underwater heritage;

iii. have been given the necessary knowledge to undertake a basic pre-disturbance survey of a site.

The emphasis during the practical sessions is on surveying and recording. In addition, the theory component stresses the need for the conservation and preservation of our underwater cultural heritage. The format involves a two-day course (often a weekend) which is conducted by approved tutors and instructors. Certain parts of the course can be adapted to suit the special requirements of the individual groups taking part.

The minimum diving qualification for those taking part in the pool exercises is CMAS 1-Star (or equivalent, *e.g.* BSAC Novice Diver). The Part I course is not examined and the Certificate (NAS International 1 star) is awarded for attendance only.

16.2.1. Part I: Outline Syllabus

Part I includes the following elements

i. Definitions, Organisation, Legislation.

Definitions of archaeology, differences between archaeology and salvage, organisation (sport diver involvement, institutions involved in archaeology), legislation relating to archaeology underwater, safety aspects (codes of diving practice, HSE regulations).

ii. Basic Principles, Conservation, Archaeological Science.

Position, association, context, dating, stratigraphy, typology, conservation, archaeological sciences.

iii. Surveying.

Pre-disturbance survey, setting-up, datums, triangulation, datum-offsets, planning frame, drawing up results.

iv. Practical surveying exercises in air and underwater in a controlled environment (*e.g.* a swimming pool); datum fixing; survey methods – triangulation, datum-offset techniques, use of the planning frame, basic recording; plotting and presenting survey data. (Non-divers do not participate in the pool sessions but suitable alternative tasks can be arranged).

v. Search and Survey.

Position fixing, remote-sensing methods, sites and monuments registers, heritage management.

vi. Records, Recording, Publication.

Recording systems, levels of records, publication levels, archives.

16.3. Part II: Techniques in Nautical and Underwater Archaeology

The Part II course is designed to build upon the theory and techniques introduced in Part I with a lecture series of a more advanced nature.   Non-divers can also attend the lecture sessions and undertake above-water projects.

The Part II course is modular and does not necessarily have to be completed in one session.   In addition to the lecture series participants are required to attend at least two full days of conferences related to archaeology, and to undertake and report on a short practical survey.

The NAS Part II "Archaeological Diver Certificate" (NAS International 2 Star) is awarded to participants on completion of the lecture and conference requirements and when a survey report to the required standard has been submitted.

16.3.1. Part II: Lecture Series

The minimum requirement for this component of Part II is attendance at lectures 2/1 and 2/2 and either five of the other ten lectures, or attendance at a survey day school.

a. Lecture Series

2/1 Archaeological standards and principles
2/2 Advanced on-site survey
2/3 Area search and survey methods
2/4 Site and finds recording systems
2/5 Photographic: the uses of photographic recording on site
2/6 Conservation: The implications of uncovering material and first-aid treatment for recovered items
2/7 Archaeological science: Environmental archaeology; on-site sampling; dating techniques
2/8 Historic search methods
2/9 Excavation methods and strategies
2/10 Experimental archaeology
2/11 Management of archaeology
2/12 Open title

b. Survey Day Schools

These will comprise a practical survey of an area or a structure supervised by an approved tutor. To allow non-diving participation these surveys need not be underwater. Day schools will normally include Lectures 2/1 and 2/2

16.3.2. Part II: Conference Requirement

Participants should attend the equivalent of a two-day conference to gain a background knowledge of current work in the field of maritime/nautical/underwater archaeology. Alternative equivalents might be two one-day conferences or ten relevant lectures in addition to the compulsory lecture series of Part II.

16.3.3. Part II: Practical Survey Requirement

To demonstrate that the participant is able to carry out basic archaeological survey and report writing he/she must submit a satisfactory report on a short survey project undertaken by themselves.   It is recommended that all prospective participants in this component of the NAS Programme liaise directly with the Training Sub-Committee in order to agree a suitable topic for the survey and to remain in contact throughout the duration of the project and its writing up. Guidance notes for Part II Project/Survey and report are available from the NAS Training Officer.

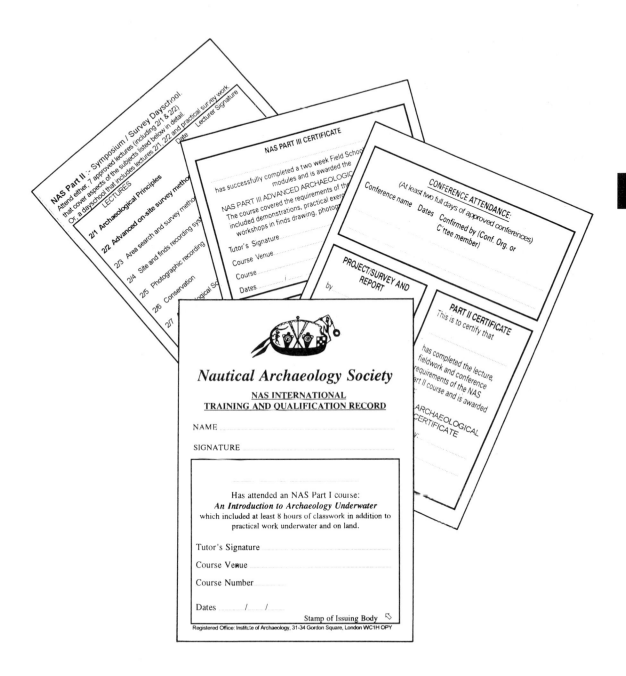

Figure 139. Pages from the NAS Certification Programme log-book.

Figure 140. Survey exercises during an NAS Part I course – Introduction to Underwater Archaeology. (Courtesy of C. Dobbs.)

16.4 Part III: Underwater Archaeology Field School Modules

The main objective of the Part III component of the Certification Programme is to produce a competent underwater fieldworker who has sufficient background knowledge to be an asset to any archaeological project. The minimum diving qualification standard for the open water work within this component is CMAS 2 Star or equivalent (*e.g.* BSAC Sport Diver).

Part III provides the major formal teaching element of the programme in that the participants will attend a number of modular events, either held separately at weekends etc., or run as a field school of one or more weeks. These would normally be held on an actual underwater archaeological site. This part of the programme involves lectures, on-site demonstrations and practical exercises in many of the techniques of archaeology underwater (including section drawing, datum positioning, recording *in situ*, sampling deposits, excavation strategies and methods). Workshops are held where the students obtain practical experience of the handling of archaeological materials, first-aid conservation, finds drawing and photography.

The Part III "Advanced Archaeological Diver Certificate" (NAS International 3 Star) will be awarded to participants after successful attendance of all the components of the field school, either in one session or modular form.

Figure 141. Lecture given during an NAS Part I course – Introduction to Underwater Archaeology. (Courtesy of I. Oxley.)

16.5. Part IV: Dissertation

The final element and the highest grade of the NAS Programme is the Part IV Certificate. The primary objective of this level is to provide a certification appropriate for a fieldworker capable of supervising archaeological work on a site in conjunction with the site director. This component will not involve further formal teaching although guidance and advice will be provided at all stages by the NAS Sub-Committee on Training. To qualify for the final certificate (NAS International 4 Star) the candidate must have fulfilled the following requirements:

i. Have worked on at least three different archaeological sites for a minimum total of twelve full weeks in the time since they completed their Part II certificate.

ii. Have completed a dissertation or extended portfolio of work on an approved project or topic including a full report prepared to publication standard. The Training Sub-Committee will encourage participants who are awarded the Part IV certificate to publish their work in the appropriate manner.

It is expected that participants in the NAS Programme who wish to proceed to higher levels would apply to a university or similar institution offering an appropriate degree or diploma courses.

The NAS welcomes any enquiries concerning the Certification Programme (including from outside the United Kingdom). These should be addressed to the NAS Training Officer, at:

NAS Training Office, c/o 19 College Road, H.M. Naval Base, Portsmouth, PO1 3LJ, UK,
Or telephone 01 705 818419.

17. Appendix III

17.1. Airlift and Dredge Construction

17.1. Airlift and Dredge Construction

17.1.1. Airlift construction

A cheap, versatile design of airlift can be made from lengths of easily obtainable 100mm (4") plastic soil pipe, sold under various brand names.

Basic tools: hand or electric drill with approx. 4mm drill bit, and self-tapping screws to suit; hacksaw (300 mm, 12" blade); small hacksaw; half round file; small round file; small wrench or pipe-grip; pliers ; screwdrivers to suit self-tapping screws and stainless steel worm-drive clips (*e.g.* 'Jubilee' or 'Worm Drive').

a. Materials

The following materials will be required:
  1 x 90 degree galvanised iron 12mm (0.5") bend,
  1 x 12mm brass flanged tank fitting,
  2 x 12mm galvanised barrel nipples,
  1 x valvestock ball valve, same as for dredge (Section 17.1.2) but with 12mm diameter bore/threads,
  As required – *c.*20mm (0.75") internal diameter low-pressure air hose of type used on road repair plant,
  1 x twist action 'Chicago' type coupling, used with above air-hose; spigot to suit bore of hose,
  4 x stainless steel worm-drive clips to suit above hoses,
  1 x 'kidney'-type diving weight, *c.* 2.72kg (6lb), (or smaller for short, 100 mm diameter airlifts),
  3 – 4 metre lengths – 100mm (4") single socketed plastic soil pipe (or separate socket if plain pipe),
  2 x 55 mm stainless steel worm-drive clips,
  P.T.F.E. tape (for sealing threads),
  Solvent weld (glue) suitable for plastic components,
  Solvent cleaner.

b. Construction

To construct the airlift:
i. Cut a length of soil pipe no longer than 1 metre. Clean off burrs from around cut end.

ii. Drill and cut hole to suit threaded end of brass tank fitting approximately 10cm from one end.

iii. Pass tank fitting up through hole from inside tube, ensuring that nylon gasket is in place on flange. Tighten down nut on to outside surface of soil pipe to give firm fixing.

iv. P.T.F.E. tape around threads on both barrel nipples. Screw these into both ends of valvestock tap.

v. Screw one end of assembled valvestock into 90 degree bend.

vi. P.T.F.E. tape around protruding thread of tank fitting. Screw on 90 degree galvanised bend, and valve assembly aligning the centre line of the valve with the centre line of the soil pipe, ensuring that the valve handle, when in the closed position (aligned with the valve body), points along the centre line of the soil pipe (Figure 142).

vii. Fit 'Chicago' coupling to one end of air hose and secure tight with two stainless steel, worm drive clips.

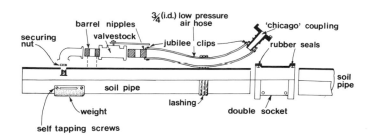

Figure 142. Airlift construction. (17.1.1.) (Drawing by M. Redknap.)

viii. Fit other end of air hose onto barrel nipple in end of valve. As the barrel nipple is threaded, it may be necessary to twist on the air hose. Secure tightly with two stainless steel jubilee clips.

ix. Fit spacer block between tap assembly and soil pipe, as with water dredge, and at either end use extended jubilee clips as clamps, or fix securely with lashing.

x. About half way along its length, lash air hose to soil pipe, leaving 'Chicago' coupling end free.

xi. With four self-tapping screws through the ends of 'kidney weight', secure to the opposite end of the soil pipe from tank fitting. Thus, when holding the air lift by the valve, the weight will be underneath at the forward end (Figure 142).

Alternatively fix weight by passing suitable webbing strap through. Pass end of webbing around soil pipe and secure on circumference using self-tapping screws. Pass opposite end of webbing around soil pipe, overlapping previously fixed end, pull as tight as possible and secure on circumference using self-tapping screws.

xii. Push one end of double socket on to end of this length of soil pipe which is furthest away from tap. Secure socket with four self-tapping screws around circumference.

xiii. Remove rubber sealing ring from other end of coupling. Push in 3 or 4m length of soil pipe. Secure with four self-tapping screws. Should the airlift become blocked, usually around the inlet area, it is easy to remove the self-tapping screws, pull apart the pipes and clear the blockage. This operation can be carried out underwater!

By using additional sockets and soil pipe lengths, the airlift can be extended to suitable lengths so that spoil is carried well clear of the site. The final amount of weight required to counteract excessive buoyancy will depend on the length of airlift in use, and the power (volume of air input) levels required.

By making up several airlift nozzle assemblies as above, it is possible to have instantly available spares so that, in case of an airlift failing whilst in use because of (for example) a faulty valve, a complete new nozzle assembly can be fitted very quickly, thus reducing down-time.

Further fibreglass can then be applied to the finished assembly as before to reinforce and strengthen the previous lay up. The projecting end tabs of the various worm-drive clips can be taped up to prevent them causing injury to personnel and diving suits.

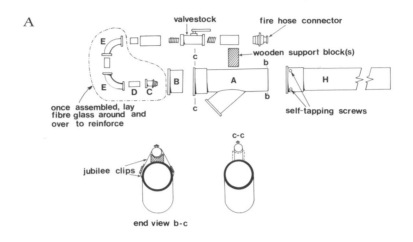

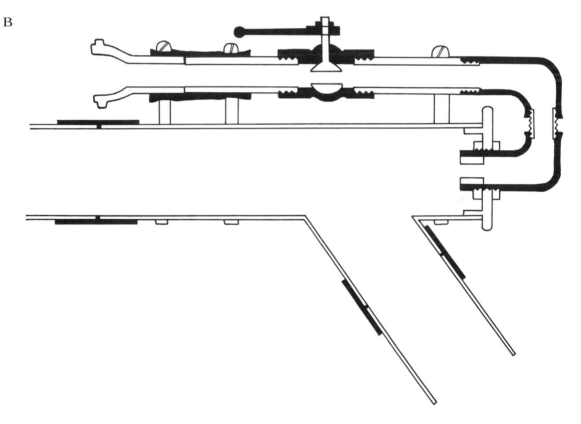

Figure 143. a) Water dredge construction and component parts, b) Detail of a water dredge mouth. (17.1.2.) (Drawing by M. Redknap.)

17.1.2. Dredge construction

a. Materials

The materials are all plastic, except where stated, and available from any good builders' merchant or hardware store, although the terminology may vary between different brands and suppliers:

3–6m length – 100mm (4") single socketed soil pipe. If only plain pipe is available a separate 110mm socket will have to be purchased,

1 x 100mm, 45 degree single branch spigot tail (Figure 143 A – 'A'),

1 x 100mm, socket plug spigot tail (Figure 143 A –'B') to suit above,

1 x 40mm, tank connector (Figure 143 A – 'C'),

3 x 40mm, straight connectors (Figure 143 A – 'D'),

2 x 40mm, 92.5 degree swept bend (Figure 143 A – 'E'),

2 x –100mm (4") length of clear plastic flexible pipe (40mm internal diameter).

1 x valvestock, 250D 500 WOG / 150 WSP ball valve, lever action, with female threads either end (40mm). Metal die cast component (Figure 143 A 'valvestock'),

2 x 40mm, barrel nipples (threaded both ends) to fit valvestock,

1 x 2.5", fire hose connector, spigot to suit 40 mm plastic pipe,

6 x 55 mm, stainless steel worm-drive clips,

P.T.F.E. tape (for sealing threads),

Solvent weld (glue) suitable for plastic components,

Solvent cleaner,

Small fibreglass kit.

b. Construction

Figure 143 a. shows the component parts and their relationships to each other. The small arrows on each component show direction of assembly.

i. Using solvent cleaner, thoroughly clean inside both ends of 'E'. Clean ends of all three 'D'. Apply solvent weld cement to these components and fit together as shown in Figure 143 b. (*i.e.* two swept bends with a straight connector between them). One straight connector in the other end of each swept bend. Make sure that, once assembled, the axis of the two swept bends are aligned before the cement dries. Lay this completed assembly to one side.

ii. Make a hole in the centre of the socket plug ('B') so that the tank connector ('C') is a push-fit. Apply solvent weld cement to the threaded end of the tank connector and around the inside edge of its flange and push into the hole in the socket plug. Clean the outside surface of the socket plug and the inside of the socketed end of the 45 degree single branch ('A') with solvent cleaner. When dry, apply cement to both surfaces and push right home into end of 'A' as shown. Allow assemblies to dry for approximately 15 minutes.

iii. Apply cement to end of straight connector 'D' labelled 'F' in Figure 143a. and insert this into outer end of tank connector, making sure that the centre line of the complete swept bend assembly is in line with the centre line of 'A', the 45 degree single branch. See end view B-C lower cross-section, Figure 143a. At this stage, lay up several good layers of fibreglass all around the socket plug and swept bend assembly so as to reinforce and support it. Allow to dry thoroughly and harden before attempting the next stage.

iv. Wrap P.T.F.E. tape around threads of one end of each nipple, extending about 1" up the thread. Screw this end of each barrel into valvestock using pipe-grips or spanner as required.

v. Warm up ends of 4" lengths of clear plastic hose in hot water.

vi. Push clear plastic pipe onto barrel nipples. Secure with two worm-drive clips.

vii. Push 2.5" fire hose connector into end of clear plastic hose, as shown in Figure 143b. Secure with two worm drive clips.

viii. Push valvestock hose at other end of complete assembly as in vii, (valvestock, fire hose connector) on to end of straight connector 'G' in Figure 143a. Do not put undue strain on swept bend assembly while doing this. Secure with two worm drive clips.

ix. One or two wooden support blocks can be made up and fitted as shown to take the weight of the valvestock tap assembly. The block, or blocks, should be fitted between the tap assembly and the main body as shown. By linking together two large stainless steel worm drive clips and placing these around the assembly to act as clamps, it is possible to bind the components firmly together. (See cross-section 2, Figure 143a, showing clamping method.) This prevents strain on the swept bend assembly.

x. Remove the rubber sealing ring from around the inside of the socket and on the main length of soil pipe, 'H'. Push this length of pipe onto 'A'. Drill four holes equidistant around the circumference of the soil pipe socket, and right through the complete assembly. Screw in four self-tapping screws, making sure that their ends do not project into the bore of the tube. Remove them and cut to length if they do. Should a blockage occur whilst the dredge is in use, the nozzle assembly can easily be detached by removing the self-tapping screws and pulling out the main length of pipe. The blockage can then be easily cleared.

18. Appendix IV

18.1. The Survival of Guns on Archaeological Sites

18.2. The Identification of Guns

18.3. Glossary of Common Terms and Gun Types

18.4. Projectiles, Charges and Tampions

18.5. Suggested Reading

18.1. The Survival of Guns on Archaeological Sites

18.1.1. The implications of recognising guns on the seabed

Many wreck sites are located due to the recognition of guns on the seabed. The increasing use of remote sensing methods (such as magnetometers and metal-detectors), and divers striving to reach greater depths, will probably result in even more gun sites being found in the future.

The durability of the raw materials used to manufacture guns and their (often considerable) size contributes to the relatively good preservation of guns on the seabed. The usually distinctive shape of guns increases their chance of being recognised and they may be the only visible indication that a wreck site is there. These factors mean that not only are guns an enormously informative and important category of our surviving cultural heritage, but that they are also at considerably greater risk than other types of evidence.

Guns are often raised indiscriminately, their protective concretion smashed off and their contents extracted without adequate recording and analysis. They are also often left (partially or inadequately conserved) to disintegrate as ornaments in such places as gardens, public house car parks or dive clubs, irreparably separated from their original context on the site.

This section of the NAS Guide is included to illustrate the information that can be gained from ordnance and ways in which all types of ordnance can be studied and recorded.

18.1.2. Guns found with their carriages and associated gun furniture

As with any other artefact type it is essential to realise that the position and relationship of other objects in association with the gun will yield important information. If the guns were present on the ship to carry out their primary function (*i.e.* not as ballast) then each one may have an associated carriage and collection of gun furniture (rammers, spongers etc.) depending upon the period of the site.

The presence of the carriage may be recognised first if the process of wrecking and the greater weight of the gun has deposited them upside-down. Understanding the development of the gun-carriage is as important as studying the gun, so any carriages or fragments should be carefully recorded and not indiscriminately discarded to clear the way to the gun. Fixing bolts may be fragile and degraded, but their positions and associations will be important in understanding the structure of the carriage.

The relative positions of the various guns on the site may be important in understanding the formation of the site, as guns (particularly the more easily accessible upper and main deck ordnance) were often jettisoned to lessen the draught of a vessel in distress. In addition, guns securely attached to their carriages may have had sufficient buoyancy to be transported considerable distances from the site of the wrecking.

18.1.3. Isolated fragments of guns

Ordnance-related information can be recovered from isolated, individual fragments of guns, such as lifting dolphins, trunnions and cascabel buttons. These objects may be found on sites where guns have been indiscriminately salvaged but they can still provide important evidence if they are recorded in a systematic way.

18.2. The Identification of Guns

If all the information listed in Gun Recording (Section 6.2.7.) is recorded from a gun, it may be possible to make an identification and age determination. The following sections suggest various methods of categorising or classifying ordnance.

18.2.1. Identification by Material Type

The majority of guns are made of iron or an alloy of copper with tin, lead and zinc in varying amounts. In antiquity the latter were referred to as 'guns of brass' although the current definition of brass is copper alloyed with zinc alone. The main constituents, however, are copper and tin and as such they are referred to as 'bronze' guns. Composite guns do exist, principally of copper and iron. Guns of copper and other metals wrapped around with cord, plaster, leather or wood have also been found. Many questions surround the place of such guns in the evolution of the technology of gun founding.

A general trend from wrought iron, to cast bronze and finally to cast iron can be suggested and this sequence is useful for attributing a broad date to a gun. In the UK, there is little evidence for the casting of iron guns before the beginning of the 16th century and these tend not to feature ornate decoration. Such embellishments are more likely to appear on bronze ordnance as they are difficult to cast successfully in iron.

Iron is easily distinguishable from bronze due to the formation over the surface of the object of a massive layer of concretion resulting from the corrosion of the parent metal (Section 11.2.11). Subsequent damage to the concretion layer reveals a black layer which will rapidly oxidise to produce the characteristically red-brown colour of rusty iron.

Bronze guns are seldom covered with very thick concretion, but they can support a surface layer of marine growth. These guns can also be stained or covered with thin corrosion products. If the latter are promptly treated by conservation specialists, a well-preserved, relatively easily identifiable object can be recovered.

The nature of the concretion will be influenced by the composition of the object and its local environment. A study of the concretion, how it was formed and how it isolated the object from the burial environment, can give valuable information both to the conservator and the archaeologist. The indiscriminate removal of concretion will re-activate corrosion processes, so such treatment should not be undertaken without specialist consultation.

315

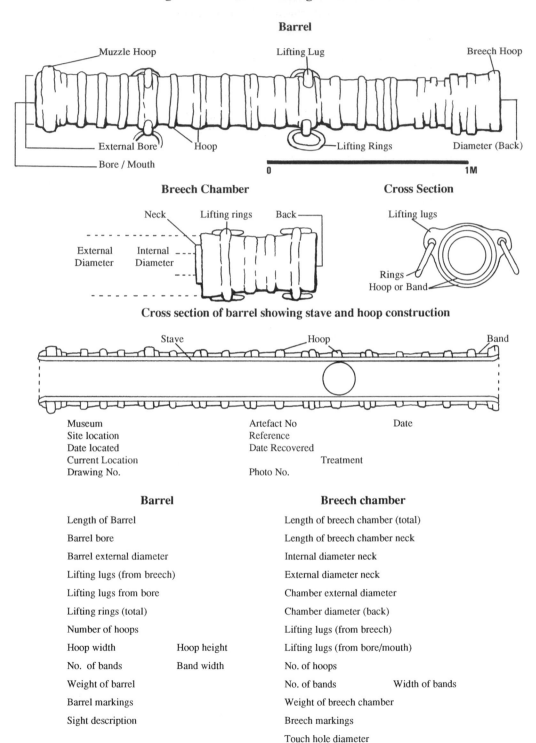

Wrought Iron Breech Loading Tube Gun Record Sheet

Barrel

Muzzle Hoop   Lifting Lug   Breech Hoop

External Bore   Hoop   Lifting Rings   Diameter (Back)

Bore / Mouth

0   1M

Breech Chamber

Neck   Lifting rings   Back

External Diameter   Internal Diameter

Cross Section

Lifting lugs

Rings

Hoop or Band

Cross section of barrel showing stave and hoop construction

Stave   Hoop   Band

Museum   Artefact No   Date
Site location   Reference
Date located   Date Recovered
Current Location   Treatment
Drawing No.   Photo No.

Barrel		**Breech chamber**	
Length of Barrel		Length of breech chamber (total)	
Barrel bore		Length of breech chamber neck	
Barrel external diameter		Internal diameter neck	
Lifting lugs (from breech)		External diameter neck	
Lifting lugs from bore		Chamber external diameter	
Lifting rings (total)		Chamber diameter (back)	
Number of hoops		Lifting lugs (from breech)	
Hoop width	Hoop height	Lifting lugs (from bore/mouth)	
No. of bands	Band width	No. of hoops	
Weight of barrel		No. of bands	Width of bands
Barrel markings		Weight of breech chamber	
Sight description		Breech markings	
		Touch hole diameter	

Figure 144. Wrought iron breech-loading tube gun record form. (18.2.)

Cast Ordnance Record Sheet

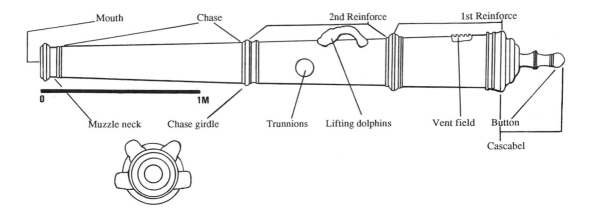

Mouth   Chase   2nd Reinforce   1st Reinforce

0   1M

Muzzle neck   Chase girdle   Trunnions   Lifting dolphins   Vent field   Button

Cascabel

Museum   Artefact No.   Date
Site location   Reference
Date Located   Date Raised
Current Location   Treatment
Drawing No.   Photo No.
Bronze   Iron   Composite   Weight
Lifting Dolphins   Description
Trunnions   Length R.   Length L.   Diam R.   Diam. L

Overall Length   Length to base ring

Base ring to end of first reinforce   First reinforce to second

Chase length   Muzzle length

Length of vent field   Length of chase girdle

length of muzzle neck   Cascabel button to trunnion centre

Trunnion centre to muzzle   Diameter of base ring

Diameter at chase girdle   Diameter at muzzle neck

Diameter at muzzle swell   Diameter at muzzle face

Width across trunnions face to face   Trunnion position   High   Low

Type of gun   Number of calibers

Rifled bore   Smooth bore

Straight bore   Chambered   Length of chamber   Diameter

Date   Gunfounder   Nationality

Monogram   Heraldic devices

Inscriptions   Markings

Crown holes   Total number   Location

Tampion in situ   Date removed   Number

Projectile in situ   Date removed   Number

Type   Diameter   Weight   Markings

Wad in situ   Date removed   Number

Powder   Date removed   Number

Figure 145. Cast gun record form. (18.2.)

Breech Loading Swivel Gun Record Sheet

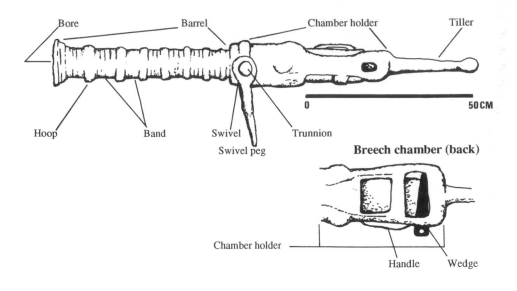

Museum   Artefact No.   Date
Site Location   Reference
Date Located   Date raised
Current Location   Treatment
Drawing No.   Photo No.

Length (mouth to end of tiller)
Tiller length   Tiller shape   Knob   Raised
Chamber holder length
Description of chamber holder   Open   Closed   Wrapped
Wedge description   Length   Hole diameter   Other
Trunnion position   From tiller   From mouth
Trunnion diameter   Integral   Added on trunnion band
Swivel peg (method of manufacture)   Length
Number of hoops   Width   Height
Number of bands   Width
Staves visible at mouth
Weight
Chamber length
Chamber description   Forged   Stave built   Coiled   Cast
Description of chamber back
External diameter at mouth   Parallel sided   Angled
Internal diameter of chamber
If banded, No. of bands   Butting   Separated
Lifting rings   Position (from mouth)   Position (from back)
Chamber handle   Two point contact   Single point contact
Diameter of touch hole
Chamber weight
Tampion in situ   Description
Shot type   Diameter   Weight
Wad   Description
Powder   Sampled   Location   No.
Metal used in construction of   Barrel   Tiller
Metal used in construction of   Chamber holder   Chamber

Figure 146. Breech-loading swivel gun record form. (18.2.)

The concretion covering wrought iron guns is often very irregular, completely obscuring the object within it. The radiography of all concreted objects is advisable before any attempt is made to remove the concretion, especially if mechanical methods are to be adopted (Section 11.2.8).

It is often difficult to differentiate between wrought iron and cast iron, especially underwater (diagnostic features such as the size and shape of the gun are frequently obscured by concretion). The presence of the remains of a wrought iron object may be indicated by laminated or layered corrosion products, perhaps visible in a break in the overlying concretion. The final phases of the corrosion of cast iron, however, are typified by the production of a graphitized object, steel-grey in colour with a greatly reduced weight. Cast iron objects in this condition are easily damaged, even by touching. The last stage of corrosion may be the reduction of the object to a steel-grey fluid.

18.2.2. Classification by Method of Loading

Guns can be classified into two types depending on the method adopted for loading the gun:

a. Breech-loading guns

These guns are either cast bronze, cast iron, or wrought iron and they have a separate chamber to contain the powder. The chamber may be of a different material to the barrel and may be inserted into an integral holder within the gun itself, or it may form the rear part of the gun by slotting onto the rear end of the barrel. The projectile is usually placed into the gun, and not into the chamber. This type of gun could be rapidly re-loaded without the necessity of moving the gun back.

b. Muzzle-loading guns

These guns are sealed at one end. All the loading materials (*e.g.* powder, projectile, wadding etc.) are placed into the gun at the muzzle and rammed down. This group also includes some of the earliest guns made (of cast and forged bronze). Early bronze hand guns (termed hand cannons) were loaded in this way.

On a ship, this type of gun must be brought inboard to re-load, or must be re-loaded outboard. Muzzle-loaders range in size, and include mortars which are very short and have a large internal bore (usually the length of the gun is less than twice the diameter of the bore).

Muzzle-loaders which have a defined area (smaller in diameter than the bore) into which the powder is placed are termed 'chambered muzzle-loaders'. The chamber is either manufactured of staves and hoops or made in one piece and attached to the gun, or cast with the gun.

18.2.3. Classification by Shape or Morphology

The shape of the gun is determined largely by the characteristics of the raw material and the technology available to work it. A natural progression through heating and hammering, to melting large volumes of metal and casting guns is often proposed. This is only applicable to iron ordnance, due to the difficulties of casting iron, and its inherent brittleness. Cast bronze ordnance was used in the 14th century AD. The use of wrought iron was more widespread as it necessitated simply the skill and facilities of the local blacksmith. Although more time consuming, the cost of iron was considerably less than bronze, and the technology was more widely available.

a. Tube guns

This technique of manufacture consisted of placing staves of iron longitudinally over a "former" to create an open ended tube, which was then overlain and strengthened with thick hoops and wide bands. A separate unit, called a chamber, had to be made to contain the explosive charge. Chambers may be constructed of one piece, heated and beaten into shape. Alternatively, they may be made of staves reinforced with a thick plug at one end and a projecting neck, which fits tightly into the open tube of the gun, at the other end. Chambers usually have some form of handle or lifting ring (often in pairs) to allow rapid removal for reloading.

b. Swivel guns

This term is used to describe any gun which was located on a pivoting rest (or swivel), allowing it to be moved, or 'swivelled' horizontally. There would also have been a certain amount of vertical freedom of movement. These guns can be mounted on carriages, although the majority seem to rest on the swivel (or "*miche*") itself. Swivel guns were easily transportable (except those on carriages) and they were designed for rapid fire at close range. They could be deployed by one person and therefore did not require a gun-crew.

Swivel guns were usually made of wrought iron, cast in bronze or iron, or a combination of cast iron and cast bronze. They usually have separate breech chambers, forged or cast with carrying handles, and the internal bore is usually less than 10cm.

c. Cast guns

The early inventories of arms, housed in the Privy Wardrobe of the Tower of London, relating to the 14th and 15th centuries (Blackmore 1976), list "guns of copper" and "pellets of iron or lead". By the late 14th century names which relate to types of guns appear, and by the end of the 15th century names such as 'curtows', 'hakebuss', 'serpentynes', 'ffacons' and 'bumbardelles' are listed, grouped into those of 'brass' and those of 'iron', chambered and non-chambered. By this time the inventories had become the responsibility of the Board of Ordnance. In a number of instances guns were given individual names.

The earliest method used to cast bronze ordnance (Ffoulkes 1937; Kennard 1986) necessitated the making of individual moulds which were broken to remove the finished gun, thus each early cast gun is essentially unique. Although attempts were made at standardization (using length, calibre and weight of gun and of projectile), it is hard to find many guns which comply. The term 'Bastard', which appears on inscriptions on many early guns, is used to describe any gun which did not conform and the proliferation of these 'bastard guns' illustrates this problem of maintaining a standard. An additional problem is that the names of the gun types varied between different countries, as did their main characteristics (*e.g.* length, calibre, weight, projectile type).

By the 16th century, English cast bronze ordnance was generally termed, and ranked (in descending order of calibre) as follows: Cannon royal, Cannon, Demi cannon, Culverin, Demi culverin, Bastard culverin, Saker, Minion, Falcon (Blackmore 1976; Hogg 1970). In a large number of cases the name, gun founder, date and weight are inscribed on the gun itself, often in addition to the Royal monogram. Later monograms include those of the Master General of the Ordnance, and when the Board of Ordnance was abolished in 1855 by the insignia of the Secretary of State for War.

The latter half of the 17th century saw the use of the poundage of the shot to describe the gun, so many guns are described as 68, 48, 42, 32, 24, 18, 12, 9, 6, 3 pdrs. (The increased use of the shell during the nineteenth century complicated this system as guns primarily firing shells were described by their bore size in inches).

The gradual increase in the number of iron guns over bronze which began in the 17th century continued, and England became an exporter of iron guns. Surface decoration is restricted on iron guns, and lifting dolphins are rare. By AD 1800 a breeching loop situated by the cascabel button, or a loop in place of the cascabel button, was common on both bronze and iron ordnance.

18.2.4. Inscriptions and Decoration

A great deal of information can be found on the gun itself. For bronze guns this may mean the entire surface being decorated. The early gunfounders in particular considered themselves craftsmen, and the guns were an advertisement of both their technological skills and their artistry. This is especially true of the larger sizes of guns, which commanded attention both as powerful weapons and as art objects.

The information can either be incised into the gun, cut into the metal, or be raised – termed 'in relief'. There appears to be no absolute rule regarding the positioning of inscriptions and decoration. Much of this information will only become available after conservation treatment and it is not justifiable to remove concretion underwater to locate such markings. Listed below are the most common features with their usual location (conventionally, guns are described from the cascabel towards the muzzle):

a. Monograms

Monograms comprise initials, often surrounded by a garter. There can be an inscription within the garter, and the initials may be surmounted by a crown. Usually the monogram is either the reigning monarch at the time the gun was cast (occasionally the Prince of Wales), or the current Master General of the Board of Ordnance (pre 1855), or the Secretary of State for War (post 1855). Both can be found together. Monograms are usually restricted to the upper surface of the gun, either on the first reinforce, the second reinforce or the chase. Where both occur the Royal Arms are usually in relief on the first reinforce.

b. Heraldic, and other devices

A pictorial representation, often a coat of arms which may also be surrounded by a garter and surmounted with a crown. These can either be the Royal Arms or those of the Master General of the Board of Ordnance or the Secretary of State for War. It is possible to have both an heraldic device and a monogram on the same gun. Restricted to the upper surface of the gun, either on the reinforce or the chase. Usually in relief.

c. Inscriptions

These include any other letters or numbers which appear on the gun including:

i. Weight:

The weight of the gun is usually incised and can be in pounds, or in hundredweight, quarters and pounds. Some 19th century French guns have their weight in kilogrammes following the introduction of metrication by Napoleon. Sometimes this is preceded by a 'P' or a 'K', but often the interpretation has to be based on the most likely explanation for the size and origin of the gun. It is possible to have the weight in two or more places on the gun, and in different units. Other possible units include: A.Lb (Amsterdam pounds), Libre, Libra (French, Spanish)(Roth 1989).

The exact weight of pounds from different countries varies, so the gun should be studied to assess country of origin before quoting exact weight. Ideally the gun should be taken over a weigh-bridge with known margins of error. The historical study of metrology is very complex, and care must be taken. A note should appear with the gun stating whether the weight quoted is as it appears on the gun, or is deduced by some other means.

The weights can be written in the following ways:

1. 'P5668',
2. simply '5668',
3. '4 – 1 – 14' (relating to hundredweights, quarters and pounds),
4. '4 cwt, 1 qtr, 4lb'.

The location of this information varies. Common locations include topside or underside of the cascabel, on the base ring, by the vent, on either the first or second reinforce, on either trunnion.

ii. Name of foundry or founder:

These can appear either as initials, full names, maker's 'marks' or as part of a general extended description. Principal locations (usually on the uppermost surface of the gun) include the base ring, by the vent, on the first or second reinforce and chase, or on the end of one or both trunnions.

iii. Foundry number, gun number (serial number):

The foundry number is often preceded by a letter (*i.e.* G 12 96), relating to the group number (immediately following the letter, the letter is not constant) and the individual gun number. The gun number can also be inscribed alone, often following the prefix 'No'. Principal locations include: underneath the cascabel or breech area, on the breech ring, on or under the first reinforce, on or under either or both trunnions. Occasionally these are found on the muzzle face. Guns do not always have either batch or individual numbers and can have one without the other. If one appears by itself, it is often the gun number.

iv. Date:

Many guns carry the date of casting incised on the gun. The date can appear in either Roman or Arabic numerals and can refer to the calendar date, or to the year of the reign of the monarch, or even date in years following a significant event (*e.g.* a revolution).

The date can be incised on the base ring, the first or second reinforce, the face of either or both trunnions, or the chase.

d. Other markings

In addition to general inscriptions, often describing either the monarch or the founders, other marks occur. These include the BROAD ARROW indicating Government ownership and often chiselled into the upper surface of the gun on the chase or the reinforce. Although most wrought iron guns are plain, a number have marks which are easy to chisel into the surface such as chevrons and often the broad arrow can be found with careful cleaning. Simple numbers in Roman numerals also exist on these guns. Cast iron guns occasionally carry information relating to the iron itself, such as 'Brinsdale Iron', which often occurs on the muzzle face or just inside the bore.

Large vertical lines, possibly located on the trunnions or the base ring, are often sighting aids. Quarter sight scales may be inscribed into the base ring.

Other more commonly found marks include the bore diameter and the shot weight. These are often found incised into the bore of the gun at the muzzle. Breech chambers can carry marks which match them with their particular guns, or denote government issue.

e. Abbreviations

Abbreviations and initials relating to gunfounder or foundry must be learned, or suggested by deductive techniques using the other information available. Common abbreviations include: RGF (denoting the Royal Gun Foundry at Woolwich which was in operation early in the 18th century), AN (denoting 'Arme National').

18.3. Glossary of Common Terms and Gun Types

The following list includes a number of common orndance terms and gun types:

Bastard – General term used to describe any gun which did not conform to set standards for a gun of a particular type; bastard cannon; culverin bastard. (Principally 15–17th centuries).

Bombard – Term commonly used to describe ordnance which is short in comparison with its bore. Traditionally firing a stone shot of up to 300lbs. Thought of as early guns, they date from the 15th century. Many English examples are of iron, though bronze examples do exist. The iron examples can be a mixture of both wrought and cast iron. They are usually chambered pieces, but their chambers were not always removable and so they were muzzle-loading. They have no trunnions. Notable examples include Mons Meg and the Dardanelles gun (Brown and Smith 1989).

Bore – Internal diameter of gun at mouth.

Rifled bore – (first recorded c. AD 1520). The inside of the barrel has been relieved forming grooves, often spiralled. The spiral grooving forces the projectiles to turn, creating a spin. The spin reduces the tendency for the projectile to depart from a straight line, therefore increasing accuracy. The grooves can be straight, and the shape varied; the distance apart of the grooves can also vary. Straight grooves were also made on cannons to aid despatching a tight fitting projectile.

Smooth bore – A gun with a bore which has not been rifled.

Breech-Loader – A gun which has a separate chamber into which the powder is loaded.

Calibre – Internal diameter of the bore; can also be used to describe the diameter of the bullet.

Calibres – The length of the gun expressed in the number of times the bore can be divided into the length of the gun.

Cannon – Used generally to describe any gun large enough to be carriage mounted. Specifically used from the 16th century to describe the largest group of ordnance, with a bore size ranging from 8.5 inches to 6 inches, firing predominantly cast iron shot weighing between 60lbs and 24lbs. Subdivided by size into further groups (Blackmore 1976). Examples exist both in iron of some, but not all, of the subdivisions. Smaller hand held guns were termed 'hand cannons' during the 14th and 15th centuries.

Carronade – Initially a cast iron gun, firing large projectiles, shells and grape shot at low velocity. The carronade was short and light and used for short range naval warfare. First produced in the late 18th century by the Carron Company in Scotland, it remained in service until the late 19th century. It was retained in its mount by means of a bolt secured through loops on the side of its mount and through a large loop beneath the gun. It was elevated by a screw.

Mortar – 16th century onwards. Muzzle loading (of cast bronze, cast iron, or wrought iron) and chambered. A mortar has a very large bore and is very short. Primarily used for firing stones, bullets or grenades and shells at an elevated angle. Bed mounted, initially without trunnions, whereas later examples include them.

Swivel gun – Any gun which is manoeuvred by means of a swivel. These have a separate powder chamber. In use from the 15th to the 18th centuries, possibly later. Can be of brass or iron with chambers of either brass or iron. Small bore.

18.4. Projectiles, Charges and Tampions

Projectiles are many and varied, as almost anything can be fired from a gun. A gun containing coffee beans has been recovered from the sea, and the heads of Turkish prisoners were fired from the guns of St. Angelo during the Great Siege of Malta in 1565.

18.4.1. Implications of removing the contents of guns

Obviously, as with any other source of archaeological information the contents of guns (including projectiles, wadding and explosive materials) should be recorded and investigated to an acceptable standard if any attempt is made to remove them. The relative positions of all components and their condition should be recorded. Contact should be made with analysts interested in the composition of gunpowder in order to determine optimum sampling techniques for the powder remains.

It should be stressed that this removal exercise is best left to an experienced conservator as the various components of the charge and shot can suffer significant damage during the operation. In addition, attempts made without the advantage of conservation expertise and facilities may leave deposits in the bore which can compromise subsequent stabilisation treatments.

18.4.2. Traditional projectiles

Spherical shot are traditional projectiles of stone, cast iron, cast bronze, cast lead, lead covering cast iron or stone, lead cast over iron dice. With regard to stone shot, the type of stone is important; limestone is durable and easily worked, so is an obvious choice. Granite is very heavy, and often used where it is abundant. Naturally the type of stone used will depend on availability, either local or through trade. The nature of the working, whether finished or unfinished and whether or not tool marks are distinguishable as well as the weight, diameter (measured with calipers), and circumference should be recorded.

18.4.3. Projectile types

a. Cast iron shot

Many cast iron shot carry the stamp of the reigning monarch or possibly the maker and shot weight. These should be recorded as well as the diameter, circumference and condition of the iron. The weight of the shot should be recorded but care must be taken in the use of this data as corrosion processes in the sea can change the parent metal into lighter compounds. On-site location and association information (together with the condition of the shot) is important in assessing the effect of the burial environment. Individual shot from one assemblage can also show differential corrosion effects, so if possible all shot should be recorded *in situ* and numbered before lifting, if this detailed information is required.

Spherical shot was also attached together either with a bar, or a chain, or formed of segments which when together form a sphere but separate upon leaving the gun.

Detailed drawings of different types of shot can be found in published texts (Munday 1987; Petersen 1969; Blackmore 1976).

b. Encased shot

This includes anything which is grouped together within a container, such as grape shot. Anything can be placed within a canister or bag and fired from a gun. Particularly favoured items include pebbles, nails, iron dice, flint fragments.

c. Incendiary shot

A shot which has been wrapped in a cloth or rope which has been impregnated with an inflammable mixture, usually around spikes projecting from the shot.

d. Shells, exploding shot

These are cases into which either explosive powder, or a mixture of powder and a further projectile, were placed. They have a fuse hole, and often surface features such as lifting lugs. They can be spherical, cylindrical and cylindro-conoidal in form.

18.4.4. Tampion, tompion

Tampions are shaped blocks of wood placed into the bore of guns to protect them from damp. A tampion may have also been placed in the mouth of a breech chamber to seal in the powder. In muzzle-loaders tampions were also placed in the muzzle after the powder (*i.e.* separating the powder from the projectile). In some instances these are wooden tampions but wads of hair, or hay were also used. From muzzle to breech the sequence can be: tampion, projectile, wad/tampion, powder. Tampions, often made of softwood, are larger in diameter than the bore of the gun but with a suitable chamfer to make them a tight fit.

18.5. Suggested Reading

Blackmore, H. L.
1976 *The Armouries of the Tower of London, vol 1.* Ordnance, Her Majesty's Stationery Office, London.

Brown, R.R. and Smith, R.D.
1988 Guns from the sea. *IJNA*, 17.1.

Carpenter, A.C.
1993 *Cannon: The Conservation, Recontruction and Preservation of HIstoric Artillery.* Halsgrove Press, Tiverton. ISBN 1-874-448-02-7.

Caruna, A.J.
1994 The History of English Sea Ordnance Volume 1: The age of evolution, 1523-1715. Jean Boudriot Publications, Rotherfield, ISBN 0-948864-20-6.

Cipolla, C.M.
1965 *Guns and Sails in the Early Phase of European Expansion 1400–1700.* London.

ffoulkes, C.
1937 *The Gunfounders of England.* Cambridge.

Green, J.N.
1980 The armament from the Batavia. Two composite guns. *IJNA* 9.1: 43-51.

Greener, W.W.
1881 *The Gun and its Development.* New Orchard Editions Ltd. New edition 1988.

Guilmartin, J.F.
1074 *Gunpowder and Galleys.* Cambridge.

Guilmartin, J.F.
1982 The cannon of the Batavia and the Sacramento: early modern cannon founding reconsidered. *IJNA* 11.2: 133-144.

Hogg, D.F.G.
1970 *Artillery: its Origin, Heyday and Decline.* London.

Kennard, A.N.
1986 *Gunfounding and Gunfounders.* Arms and Armour Press.

Lavery, B.
1987 *The Arming and Fitting of English Ships of War 1600-1815.* London, ISBN 0-85177-451-2.

MacLeod, I.D.
1982 Formation of Marine Concretions on Copper and its Alloys. *IJNA* 11.4: 267-275.

Munday, J.
1987 *Naval Cannon.* Shire Album 186. Shire Publications Ltd.

Padfield, P.
1973 *Guns At Sea.* London.

Parker. G.
1988 *The Military Revolution.* Cambridge.

Peterson, H.L.
1969 *Round Shot and Rammers.* New York.

Roth, R.
1989 A proposed standard in the reporting of historic artillery. *IJNA* 18.3: 191-202.

Roth, R.
1989 The Measuring of Cannons. *Journal of Ordnance Society*, Vol. 1 1989.

Smith, R.D.
1988 Towards a new typology for wrought iron ordnance. *IJNA* 17.1: 5-16.

Index